Practicing Medicine in a Black Regiment

Practicing Medicine in a Black Regiment

The Civil War Diary of Burt G. Wilder, 55th Massachusetts

EDITED BY RICHARD M. REID

UNIVERSITY OF MASSACHUSETTS PRESS

Amherst and Boston

Printed in the United States of America
LC 2009045171
ISBN 978-1-55849-739-9

Designed by Richard Hendel
Composition by Westchester Book, Inc.
Printed and bound by Thomson-Shore, Inc.

Library of Congress Cataloging-in-Publication Data
Wilder, Burt G. (Burt Green), 1841–1925.
Practicing medicine in a black regiment : the Civil War diary
of Burt G. Wilder, 55th Massachusetts /
edited by Richard M. Reid.
p. cm.
Includes bibliographical references and index.
ISBN 978-1-55849-739-9 (pbk. : alk. paper)
1. Wilder, Burt G. (Burt Green), 1841–1925—Diaries.
2. United States. Army. Massachusetts Infantry Regiment,
55th (1863–1865) 3. United States—History—Civil War,
1861–1865—Medical Care. 4. United States—History—
Civil War, 1861–1865—Personal narratives. 5. Massachusetts—
History—Civil War, 1861–1865—Personal narratives.
6. United States—History—Civil War, 1861–1865—Participation,
African American. 7. Massachusetts—History—Civil War,
1861–1865—Participation, African American. 8. United States.
Army. Surgeons—Diaries. 9. Surgeons—Massachusetts—Diaries.
I. Reid, Richard M., 1943– II. Title.
E513.555th .W55 2010
913.7'415—dc22
2009045171

British Library Cataloguing in Publication
data are available.

To Jamie, Chris, and Andrew —

the best sons that I have ever had.

CONTENTS

PREFACE

Some years ago, while working on North Carolina's black Civil War soldiers, I made use of the extensive Burt Green Wilder Papers at Cornell University, including Wilder's Civil War "diary." The author's account of life in the 55th Massachusetts during the early summer of 1863 certainly allowed me to better understand life in General Edward A. Wild's African Brigade, but it also offered much more that was valuable to anyone interested in the Civil War. At the time I was struck not just by the historical value of Wilder's comments but also by the literary quality of his writings. I understood, as a Civil War historian, that his writings provided important additions to the literature left by the war's participants, but, in all honesty, I was as captivated by his stories of Miff and Billy as I was by his accounts of the regiment's military activities. He was clearly an uncommon man in many ways, and his entries concerning the black soldiers in the 55th Massachusetts reflected an uncommon perception by a white American of African Americans through the Civil War era.

Further research on Wilder and his career after he had left the 55th Massachusetts reinforced my conviction that he was an extremely important nineteenth-century figure whose life could serve as a prism to focus light on a range of critical topics relating to both the war and its aftermath. Long after the war, as he successfully established his scientific credentials, he used his experiences and his research while surgeon in the 55th Massachusetts to counter the scientific racism that was increasingly pervasive in much of American life. His life among the soldiers of the Massachusetts regiment had left him with the obligation, he strongly felt, to do justice to his black comrades, and this attitude reinforced and underpinned his professional training.

By the time that Wilder retired from Cornell University in 1920, he was convinced that the story of the men of the 55th Massachusetts provided a crucially valuable lesson that Americans, in an era of Jim Crow, needed to learn. He then started to prepare an account of his experiences with the 55th Massachusetts. While he published widely, including a very small history of the regiment, he never finished his planned work on his service in Massachusetts black regiment. I would like to think that he would be pleased by this work

While much of the actual historical research for any book can be a lonely and isolating activity, the conceptualizing, drafting, and redrafting of a manuscript requires extensive feedback and advice from many colleagues and friends. This book reflects that collaborative aspect of the historical profession. Along the way I have received help and support from a large number of scholars and archivists. Elizabeth Ewan read the preliminary draft of the diary and gave me important feedback and reinforced my belief in the value of the project in its initial stages. Tara Abrams, a historian of science here at the University of Guelph, helped me position the postwar Wilder in the context of growing professionalism of American scientists. Diane Purdy, who helped me prepare the diary for publication, was as captured by the personality of Miff as I was. Other colleagues here and elsewhere put up good-naturedly with my constant discussion of Wilder and his activities. To all of them I owe a dept of gratitude. Their help has enabled me clean up numerous errors while forcing me to clarify many of my ideas. I am sure that any flaws still in the book are the result of my not being an "active listener."

During my various research trips to Cornell University, the staff at the Carl A. Koch Library was always helpful, courteous, and professional in all their dealings. I particularly wish to thank the University Archivist, Elaine D. Engst, for all her assistance in helping me trace what had happened to the Wilder material, from his death in 1925 until the University Library received possession of the documents after 1953. We share the same belief that the importance of Burt Wilder as a scientist and an educator has for too long been overlooked. My final thanks go to the staff at the University of Massachusetts Press, to Clark Dougan and his faith in the value of Wilder's writings and to Carol Betsch for all her help in getting the manuscript into the shape that it is. As always, I draw inspiration from my wife Susan.

Practicing Medicine in a Black Regiment

INTRODUCTION

In the months immediately following the outbreak of the American Civil War, young black men across the Northern states attempted to volunteer to fight against the Confederacy. Given widespread white racism, however, the government was unwilling in 1861 to use black troops. Just two weeks after Fort Sumter surrendered, Secretary of War Simon Cameron announced that "this Department has no intention to call into the service of the Government any colored soldiers."[1] Although President Abraham Lincoln personally opposed slavery and its extension, he believed that, as president, he was bound by the Constitution and was therefore compelled to defend the existing right of loyal Southerners to hold slaves. In the early months of the war, as Lincoln came under increasing pressure from abolitionists to use the exigency of the war to abolish slavery and enlist African Americans in the struggle, he feared that linking the war to emancipation would alienate many whites, slaveholders and non-slaveholders alike, in the loyal Border States.[2] With a keen appreciation of the strategic and political importance of these states, Lincoln was convinced that their loss could cost him the war, and so on racial issues he was resolved to move cautiously, especially in the first year of the conflict.[3] As a result, Lincoln's response to the conflicting pressures from abolitionists and conservatives was equivocal and fluid. His unwillingness to adopt a doctrinaire position only increased the widespread confusion about the government's actual policy.[4]

Nevertheless, throughout much of 1862, abolitionist politicians, such as John A. Andrew, the governor of Massachusetts, repeatedly requested

1. Noah Andre Trudeau, *Like Men of War: Black Troops in the Civil War, 1862–1865* (Boston: Little, Brown, 1998), 8.

2. John David Smith, "Let Us All Be Grateful That We Have Colored Troops That Will Fight," in *Black Soldiers in Blue: African American Troops in the Civil War Era*, ed. John David Smith (Chapel Hill: University of North Carolina Press, 2002), 10.

3. Roy P. Basler, *Collected Works of Abraham Lincoln* (New Brunswick, N.J.: Rutgers University Press, 1953), 4:533.

4. Historians have long debated whether Lincoln was a "reluctant Emancipator" or an adept leader who understood the social and political constraints that he faced while moving aggressively toward emancipation. For a recent thoughtful discussion of this question, see Phillip Shaw Paludan, "Lincoln and the Greeley Letter: An Exposition," in *Lincoln Reshapes the Presidency*, ed. Charles M. Hubbard (Macon, Ga.: Mercer University Press, 2003), 79–98.

the authority to raise black regiments. Black enlistment, the governor believed, would give the men "a *chance* to vindicate their manhood, and to strike a telling blow for their own race, and the freedom of all their posterity."[5] Although the potential for black involvement in the war increased with the passage of the Second Confiscation Act and the Militia Act in July 1862, the administration did not officially reverse itself on the question of enlisting black soldiers until after the final Emancipation Proclamation.[6] Once the president had issued the proclamation, Andrew, Wendell Phillips, Francis W. Bird, and other Massachusetts radicals traveled to Washington in early January to get permission from Lincoln and Stanton to raise black regiments in their state.[7] At the end of January, Secretary of War Edwin Stanton, as part of a larger effort, authorized the governors of three northern states, Connecticut, Massachusetts, and Rhode Island, to raise regiments of black soldiers staffed with white officers. Andrew immediately established an advisory committee selected from influential Northern families to help organize the first black regiment, the 54th Massachusetts Volunteers, put out a call for African American recruits from across the Northern states, and began issuing commissions to promising officers.[8] Because of the opposition of many white Northerners to the use of black soldiers, Stanton stipulated that Andrew handpick his white officers. Andrew knew the officers he wanted. The new regiments, he announced, "shall be commanded by officers who are eminently and techni-

5. Richard H. Abbott, *Cotton and Capital: Boston Businessmen and Antislavery Reform, 1854–1868* (Amherst: University of Massachusetts Press, 1991), 119.

6. The Confiscation Act allowed the president to free slaves of persons "engaged in rebellion" and to employ them "in such manner as he may judge best." The Militia Act allowed the government to employ blacks "for any military or naval service for which they are found competent." Historians have debated the motives behind and the importance of these acts. See Mark E. Neely Jr., "Confiscation Act of July 17, 1862," in *The Abraham Lincoln Encyclopedia* (New York: McGraw-Hill, 1982), 67–68; Benjamin P. Thomas and Harold M. Hyman, *Stanton: The Life and Times of Lincoln's Secretary of War* (New York: Knopf, 1962), 233, 237, 238; Mary Frances Berry, *Military Necessity and Civil Rights Policy: Black Citizenship and the Constitution, 1861–1868* (Port Washington, N.Y.: Kennikat Press, 1977), 42; Smith, *Black Soldiers in Blue*, 13–15.

7. Ira Berlin, Joseph Reidy, and Leslie S. Rowland, eds., *The Black Military Experience*, ser. 2 of *Freedom: A Documentary History of Emancipation, 1861–1867* (Cambridge: Cambridge University Press, 1982), 75.

8. Some of the key members were George Luther Stearns, Amos A. Lawrence, William I. Bowditch, John Murray Forbes, Francis G. Shaw, and Morris L. Hallowell. Donald Yacovone, *A Voice of Thunder: The Civil War Letters of George E. Stephens* (Urbana: University of Illinois Press, 1997), 28–30.

cally gentlemen."[9] A few days later, he wrote another abolitionist, Francis G. Shaw, outlining in more detail the qualities he sought. The officers should be "young men of military experience, of firm Anti-Slavery principles, ambitious, superior to a vulgar contempt of color, and having faith in the capacity of Colored men for military service." He expected that they would be "gentlemen of the highest tone and honor," and he saw Harvard as a natural source for many of the officers.[10] To help him find the right officers, he enlisted the assistance of an experienced but disabled officer, Colonel Edward A. Wild.[11]

A major problem facing Andrew was the small pool of black men of military age in Massachusetts. Because his state had an enlistment potential of only four hundred black soldiers, Andrew obtained permission from other Northern governors less convinced of the values of black soldiers to recruit in their states.[12] He appointed the white abolitionist George L. Stearns to head the effort to get black volunteers, and Stearns quickly established a network of influential African Americans across the northern states who did much of the actual recruiting—men such as Frederick Douglass, Henry Highland Garnet, John Mercer Langston, Martin R. Delany, and T. Morris Chester.[13] Andrew's assurance that the black recruits would receive pay, equipment, and protection equal to white soldiers was critical in obtaining the involvement of these men and persuading young black

9. Richard F. Miller, "Brahmin Janissaries: John A. Andrew Mobilizes Massachusetts' Upper Class for the Civil War," *New England Quarterly* 75, no. 2 (2002): 224.

10. At least thirty-five Harvard graduates were among the officers of the two black infantry regiments and the one cavalry regiment set up by Andrew. See ibid., 225–26.

11. Because Wild had served as captain in the 1st Massachusetts Volunteers and then as colonel of the 34th Massachusetts Volunteers, he could personally assess the ability and character of many of the potential officers. Richard Reid, *Freedom for Themselves: North Carolina's Black Soldiers in the Civil War Era* (Chapel Hill: University of North Carolina Press, 2008), 13, 22–23.

12. There were only 1,973 black men of military age in the state. If they enlisted at the same rate as white volunteers, Andrew would get 394 black soldiers. Richard F. Miller, "For His Wife, His Widow, and His Orphan: Massachusetts and Family Aid during the Civil War," *Massachusetts Historical Review* 6 (2004): 100. The commander of the 55th would later recount that many Ohioans initially considered it "a good joke to get the 'darkies on to Massachusetts.'" William F. Cheek and Aimee Lee Cheek, *John Mercer Langston and the Fight for Black Freedom, 1829–65* (Urbana: University of Illinois Press, 1989), 390–91, 395–96.

13. Edwin S. Redkey, "Brave Black Volunteers: A Profile of the Fifty-fourth Massachusetts Regiment," in *Hope & Glory: Essays of the Legacy of the 54th Massachusetts Regiment*, ed. Martin H. Blatt, Thomas J. Brown, and Donald Yacovone (Amherst: University of Massachusetts Press, 2000), 22.

men to join. Enthusiasm was so high, and the agents were so successful, that in May 1863, after the 54th Massachusetts Volunteers was full, efforts were begun to raise a second regiment, the 55th Massachusetts Volunteers. Only after reaching Readville, their camp of instruction, did men find out that the promises of large bounties made by some recruiters were false; they were eligible for only a fifty-dollar state bounty.[14] It was just the start of some men's disillusionment at their treatment by the government.

Andrew was able to draw on experienced and capable officers to organize the second black regiment. Norwood P. Hallowell, the new lieutenant-colonel of the 54th Massachusetts and the son of a wealthy Philadelphia Quaker, was promoted to colonel of the 55th Massachusetts to provide continuity and to oversee its establishment.[15] Two other officers, Captain Alfred Stedman Hartwell and Lieutenant William Nutt, also moved over to the 55th Massachusetts, accepting commissions as lieutenant-colonel and captain, respectively.[16] All of the field and staff officers, and most of the company officers, had previous military experience. In the ranks of both black regiments, a majority of the enlisted men were drawn from outside the state. In the case of the 55th Massachusetts, the largest block of these men, 375 recruits, were from Ohio, Indiana, and Illinois, while more than a hundred came from Pennsylvania.[17] Although all recruits could receive bounties offered by the state, out-of-state dependents were ineligible for the various forms of Massachusetts family aid.[18] During the next year, while the men waited to be paid what they believed was owed them, this lack of funding increased the hardships faced by many families of the 219 men in the regiment who were married.[19] However, one

14. Charles B. Fox, *Record of the Service of the 55th Regiment of Massachusetts Volunteer Infantry* (Cambridge, Mass.: John Wilson and Son, 1868), 17.

15. Russell Duncan, ed., *Blue-Eyed Child of Fortune: The Civil War Letters of Colonel Robert Gould Shaw* (Athens: University of Georgia Press, 1992), 329.

16. Hartwell was a Harvard graduate and had taught at Washington University in St Louis before joining the 3rd Missouri Reserves as corporal and then the 44th Missouri Volunteers as a lieutenant. He joined the 54th Massachusetts as captain in March 1863. Following the war, he obtained a law degree and ultimately became chief justice of the Hawaii Supreme Court. Nutt served as sergeant in the 2nd Massachusetts before becoming a lieutenant in the 55th Massachusetts. At the end of the war, he served in the Freedmen's Bureau in Virginia. Fox, *Record*, 98, 99; Yacovone, *A Voice of Thunder*, 319.

17. Cheek and Cheek, *John Mercer Langston*, 395.

18. Miller, "For His Wife, His Widow, and His Orphan," 74, 76, 83, 99.

19. Decades after the war, in a paper delivered to the National Negro Conference, Burt Green Wilder outlined the demographics of the regiment. Out of a total of 980 enlisted men, 430 were of "mixed blood," while 247 had at some time in their lives been slaves. Among the men, 319 could both read and write, while 477 could only read. Interestingly,

highly symbolic measure of Andrew's commitment to these regiments was the fact that the black Massachusetts regiments, unlike all but one other black regiment, kept their state designation when the Bureau of Colored Troops decided to renumber all the black regiments in the Union Army.[20] It was a badge of distinction, and they wore it proudly.[21]

Given the personnel and preparation of the two regiments, where they served, and how they fought, the contrasting ways that Americans have remembered the two Massachusetts regiments is instructive. Because both drew heavily from free blacks across the Northern states, their ranks were filled with the same type of men. Most had been farmers or laborers, with significant numbers of waiters, barbers, seamen, cooks, and teamsters and a leavening of craftsmen and artisans.[22] The officers in both regiments were selected largely from the "Brahmin caste."[23] The efforts of Andrew and others ensured that the regiments were, by Civil War standards, well equipped and armed and had received adequate training before they were transferred south. Moreover, both regiments spent most of their service in the long-drawn-out campaign to take Charleston that wore down officers and men. Each regiment was praised for its action at Honey Hill and elsewhere, and by the end of the war, the casualties suffered by the 55th Massachusetts were not much less than that of the 54th.

Nevertheless, the 54th Massachusetts was destined to become the best-remembered Civil War black regiment. Its attack on Battery Wagner on July 18, 1863, and the death of Colonel Robert G. Shaw and many of his men in a courageous but futile assault on the Confederate earthworks captured the public imagination and ensured that these men would always

---

he credited only 52 with being "church-members." Burt G. Wilder, "The Brain of the American Negro," *Proceedings of the National Negro Conference, 1909* (New York: Arno Press, 1969), 49.

20. The three black Massachusetts regiments, the 54th and 55th Massachusetts Volunteers and the 5th Massachusetts Cavalry, plus the 29th Connecticut kept their original names while all other black regiments, in early 1864, were redesignated United States Colored Troops. James G. Hollandsworth Jr., *The Louisiana Native Guard: The Black Military Experience during the Civil War* (Baton Rouge: Louisiana State University Press, 1995), 96. Well into 1864, however, many of these regiments were still referred to by their original state designations.

21. Duncan, *Where Death and Glory Meet*, 79.

22. There were some differences. More men in the 55th Massachusetts were farmers (60%) than laborers (10%), while in the 54th Massachusetts only about a quarter were farmers and a third identified themselves as laborers. In the 55th Massachusetts, 247 enlisted men had been slaves, while in the 54th the numbers has been estimated at least 160. Redkey, "Brave Black Volunteers," 24, 26; Fox, *Record*, 110, 112.

23. Miller, "Brahmin Janissaries," 205–6.

have a special place in the public memory. For a series of reasons, Shaw and his men became enduring national symbols of the sacrifice and dedication of the black soldiers and their white officers.[24] Other black regiments that had fought equally bravely, including the 55th Massachusetts, would never receive the same recognition or fame. Monuments, such as Augustus Saint-Gaudens's relief in Boston, are always about both remembrance and forgetting.[25] Soldiers of the 55th Massachusetts, unfortunately, were destined to fall into the less remembered category, but as they arrived in Readville to join the regiment, all that lay in the future.

In the first week of May 1863, Burt Green Wilder, a young medical cadet working at the Judiciary Square Hospital in Washington, D.C., accepted a commission as an assistant surgeon in the 55th Massachusetts Volunteer Infantry.[26] He joined his regiment at Readville, Massachusetts, in time to help with its organization in the weeks before the unit was transferred to North Carolina, where it was expected to act as a "nest egg" for a black brigade.[27] After less than a week, however, the regiment moved to South Carolina to assist in the siege of Charleston. For the next twenty-seven months, as he looked after the health of the black soldiers, Wilder kept a detailed

24. The attack on Battery Wagner was not the first time that black regiments had been tested in battle. African American soldiers had fought fiercely at Port Hudson and Milliken Bend weeks earlier, but their action had been largely ignored by the eastern press. The 54th Massachusetts, on the other hand, was always newsworthy, and Battery Wagner protected Fort Sumter and Charleston, the city that Northerners perceived to be the birthplace of secession. Moreover, Shaw, with prominent family connections and a recent bride, provided the ideal martyr. Significantly, Augustus Saint-Gaudens's relief on the Boston Commons is titled the Robert Gould Shaw Memorial but is now remembered more for the sacrifice of the black soldiers.

25. David W. Blight, "The Meaning or the Fight: Frederick Douglass and the Memory of the Fifty Fourth Massachusetts," *Massachusetts Review* 36, no. 1 (Spring 1995): 148.

26. Established by Congress in August 1861, the U.S. Army corps of medical cadets was composed of medical students between the ages of eighteen and twenty-three who had studied medicine for two years and completed one course of lectures at a medical college. The serious shortage of trained medical personnel was the reason for its creation. For more information on the cadets, see Guy R. Hasegawa, "The Civil War Medical Cadets: Medical Students Serving the Union," *Journal of the American College of Surgeons* 193, no.1 (2001): 81–89.

27. While Andrew was willing to have the 55th Massachusetts transferred to North Carolina, he wanted the 54th to be used in an active theater where it could demonstrate the value of black soldiers. Gov. Andrew to Maj.-Gen. Foster, 14 May 1863, Edward A. Wild Papers, United States Army Military History Institute; *War of the Rebellion: A Compilation of the Official Records of the Union and Confederate Armies* (Washington, D.C.: Government Printing Office, 1880–1901), ser. 3, vol. 3, 110.

account of his life in the regiment. Before going to sleep most evenings, after he had finished his medical rounds, filled out reports, requisitioned and organized supplies, and completed his other military duties, he would write a summary of the day's events in letters that were sent to and kept by the woman whom he would later marry.[28] In rich detail, he described the many tasks of an army surgeon, the range of personalities and ambitions within his regiment, and the growing frustration of the black soldiers as the equitable treatment they had been promised was slow to be realized.

Rather than a record that emphasizes combat and battles, Wilder's writing captures both the mundane and the exceptional social aspects of life in a black regiment. During this period, the regiment served first in the siege of Charleston and then in Florida before returning once again to the South Carolina campaign. Although the regiment was not involved in the fighting at Olustee, Florida, it did, once back in South Carolina, fight on James Island and then at Honey Hill, where half of the officers and a third of the enlisted men engaged became casualties.[29] In February 1865 the 55th Massachusetts was the first black Union regiment to march into Charleston. During the summer, the regiment saw Reconstruction service in areas around Orangeburg, South Carolina, where its officers supervised the contracts between the planters and the newly freed black laborers. If the initial concerns of the many white farmers about the behavior of the officers diminished, the disillusionment among some freed people grew.[30] Perhaps because the regiment was scattered in different locations at the time, Wilder is silent on this issue. In September 1865 the regiment returned to Boston, where the men, including Wilder, were paid off and formally discharged from the army.

At the start of the war, Wilder was already a remarkable young man with impressive intellectual credentials; in the decades ahead, he would become an important scientist and educator. Born in Boston in 1841 into a family that had arrived in America in 1638 as part of the Puritan exodus,

28. Starting in November 1862, Wilder "wrote almost daily letters, which were all preserved." The process by which Wilder transformed the letters into the manuscript described as "Burt Green Wilder's Diary, 1863–65" and held in the Division of Rare and Manuscript Collections, Cornell University Library, is more fully described in the Editorial Note.

29. Fox, *Record*, 44; *Official Records*, ser. 1, vol. 44, 430–33.

30. A number of the regiment's officers oversaw the contracts, but Capt. Charles C. Soule, acting as chairman for the "Commission on Labor," who toured the neighborhood advising the ex-slaves to work hard, to expect little, and to abide strictly by their contracts, created the greatest unease among blacks. The black audience labeled such officers "rebels in disguise." Julie Saville, *The Work of Reconstruction: From Slave to Wage Laborer in South Carolina, 1860–1870* (Cambridge: Cambridge University Press, 1994), 26–28; Fox, *Record*, 80–82.

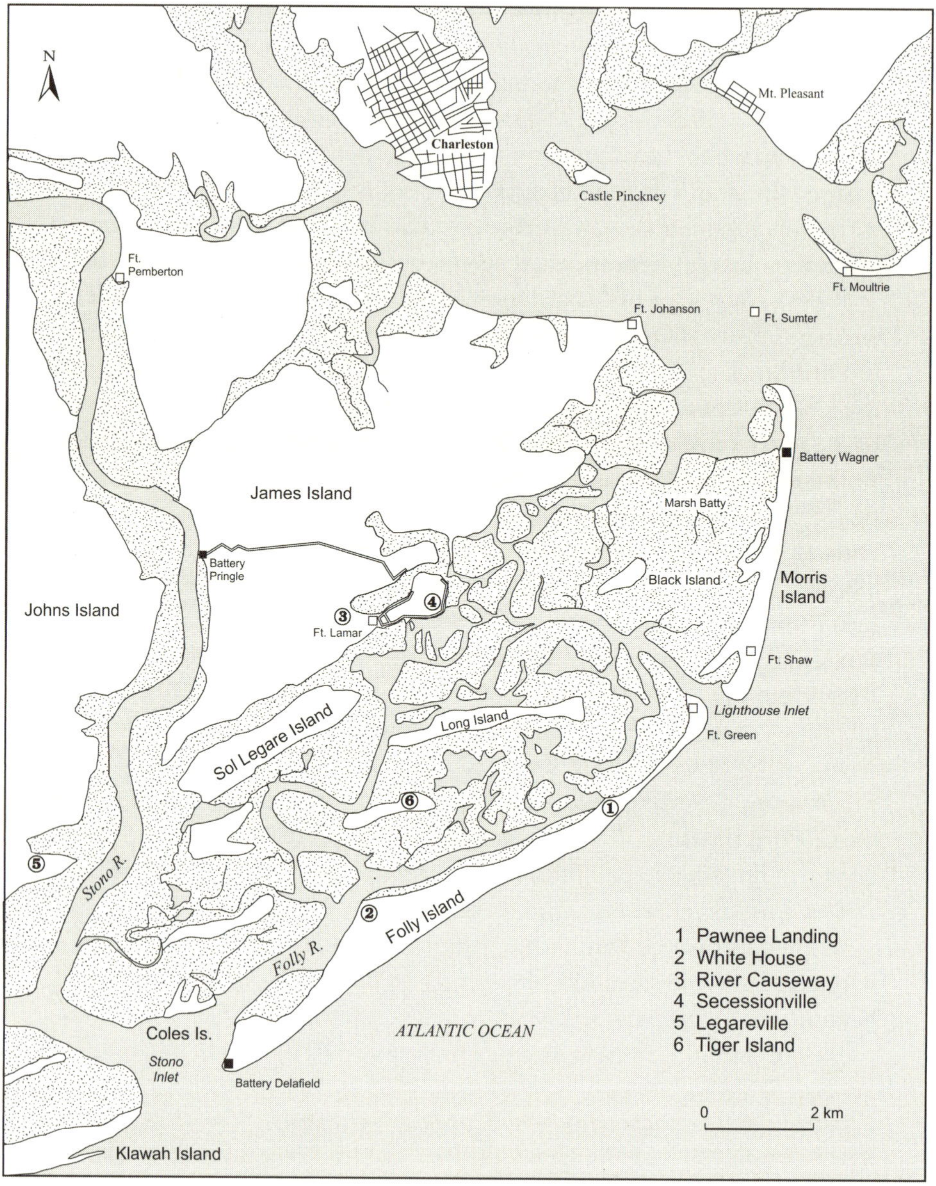

Charleston Harbor and the surrounding islands where the 55th Massachusetts was primarily engaged. The exact topography of the islands is in constant change.

he grew up within a distinct New England reform community.[31] Both his grandfather and his father had served in the state legislature, and the latter had been state auditor.[32] Even before graduating from high school, Wilder began a study of spiders and other insects that ultimately drew him to the attention of Louis Agassiz, a Harvard professor of zoology and geology who was one of the country's first world-class scientists.[33] At eighteen, he entered the Lawrence Scientific School of Harvard. His years there brought Wilder into close contact with Agassiz, Asa Gray, and Jeffries Wyman, with whom he studied comparative anatomy—leading scientists of the day who made Harvard "the center for the theoretical study of natural history in America."[34] By the time he received his degree in *anatomia summa cum laude* in 1862, he had already given public lectures on a variety of natural-history topics, two of which were published.[35] At Harvard he also formed lasting friendships with Charles Pickering Bowditch and Oliver Wendell Holmes Jr.

Wilder's comparative anatomy studies with Wyman allowed him to be appointed an acting medical cadet without the mandatory attendance at a medical school, and when he entered the war, he seemed headed for a medical career.[36] Although he had early reservations about becoming a

31. Wilder described his parents as "Swedenborgians, homeopaths, haters of oppression and vegetarians." His father was, among many things, a "natural musician." "A Biographical Sketch of B. G. Wilder," Burt Green Wilder Papers, Cornell University Library (hereafter cited as Wilder Papers, CU).

32. John H. Selkreg, *Landmarks of Tompkins County, New York* (Syracuse, N.Y.: D. Macon, 1894), 178.

33. Wilder soon became identified as one of Agassiz's better-known students. Mary P. Winsor, *Reading the Shape of Nature: Comparative Zoology at the Agassiz Museum* (Chicago: University of Chicago Press, 1991), 35.

34. Wilder's love of natural history was reinforced by these scientists. Toby A. Appel, "Jeffries Wyman, Philosophical Anatomy and the Scientific Reception of Darwin in America," *Journal of the History of Biology* 21, no. 1 (1988): 70. At the time when Wilder was associating with them, Wyman's status and influence was equal to that of Agassiz. Toby A. Appel, "A Scientific Career in the Age of Character: Jeffries Wyman and Natural History at Harvard," in *Science at Harvard: Historical Perspectives*, ed. Clark A. Elliott and Margaret W. Rossiter (Bethlehem, Pa.: Lehigh University Press, 1992), 96–120.

35. The two papers were "Contributions to the Comparative Myology of the Chimpanzee," *Boston Journal of Natural History* 7 (1859–63): 352–84, and "Notes on the Muscles of a Hog's Snout," *Society of Natural History Proceedings* 9 (1862): 1.

36. In July 1862 Wilder was appointed an acting medical cadet and assigned to Dr. J. H. Brown. Three months later, he passed a series of medical exams, and on 27 October he became a medical cadet. Most of his service was in the Judiciary Square Hospital, but in March 1863 he was ordered by Dr. John B. Brinton in the Surgeon General's office to "proceed to the St. Elizabeth Hospital. You will examine every case of amputation in the institution and

doctor, he wrote in September 1863 that his "natural repugnance to medicine as a profession is lessening as I realize what an opportunity it offers for usefulness, for helping others not only physically but morally, and for cheering the despondent."[37] However, his deep fascination with the natural world soon pushed him in a different direction. By June 1864, while still planning to complete his medical degree, he was questioning whether he would ever actually practice.[38] His life-long interest in spiders, vertebrate brains, and comparative anatomy were stimulated by his many experiences while serving as a surgeon in the Southern states. Indeed, the spider that would be named after him, *Nephila wilderi*, and about which he would write several scientific articles, was one that he discovered during his time in South Carolina. A month later, he had decided that medicine was not "my chosen line of science."[39] In making this decision, Wilder was following a common path for mid-nineteenth-century biological scientists, many of whom, including his mentor, Jeffries Wyman, used their "medical training as a means of preparation for a scientific career."[40] The creation of new positions for scientists at American universities established after the war facilitated this trend, and Wilder was quick to take advantage of the new opportunities.

For two years Wilder worked at Harvard's Museum of Comparative Zoology under the direction of Louis Agassiz before being appointed professor of zoology at Cornell in September 1867.[41] As a founding member of

---

make full notes of the history and present condition. You will then make a written report to this office." "By order of the S.G., J.H.B." Wilder Papers, CU.

37. Diary entry for 27 September 1863.

38. Diary entry for 19 June 1864. Wilder may have been influenced by the comparatively poor professional standing of physicians in mid-nineteenth-century America. He was probably aware of Dr. Oliver Wendell Holmes's statement before the Massachusetts Medical Society in 1860 that he "firmly believed that if the whole materia medica, *as now used*, could be sunk to the bottom of the sea, it would be all the better for mankind, —and the worse for the fishes." Michael A. Flannery, *Civil War Pharmacy* (New York: Pharmaceutical Products Press, 2004), 15–16.

39. Diary entry for 21 July 1864. Wilder received his medical degree from Harvard in 1866, but, in fact, he did not practice medicine.

40. Clark A. Elliott, "Models of the American Scientist: A Look at Collective Biography," *Isis* 73, no. 1 (1982): 90–91.

41. "Biographical Sketch of Burt Green Wilder," Wilder Papers, CU; Comstock, *Science*, 531. Cornell University was established in 1865 as New York's land grant institution. It was named after Ezra Cornell, who donated his farm in Ithaca as a site for the university along with a $500,000 grant from his personal fortune. The new president, Andrew Dickson White, guided the building of the university over the next two years. Cornell received its first students in September 1868. Wilder remained there for the next forty-two years. Agassiz's influence at Cornell and Wilder's being seen as one of "Agassiz's best students" cer-

the Cornell faculty, Wilder had a significant impact on both the school and the students. He was widely known as an inspiring teacher and a brilliant lecturer; thousands of students came through his classes and were influenced by his emphasis on a hands-on practical experience.[42] He introduced practical laboratory work, or "practicums," into his large zoology and physiology classes, where students spent a third of their time in actual personal investigation.[43] He was also credited, in 1867, with devising the " 'slip-system of notes,' the use of which has become universal."[44] His former students described him as "an older brother inspiring his pupils to the most enthusiastic and earnest effort," and in 1893, to recognize his twenty-five years at Cornell, sixteen of them, men and women who had become noted scholars, contributed original papers to what was one of the first American Festschriften.[45]

An article on Wilder's retirement published in the *Anatomical Record* listed the four main priorities that had guided his actions at Cornell. He wanted to give the best possible elementary education to beginning students. He sought to encourage the interested and gifted students to do advanced work and investigate special problems. He saw the need to combine the study of human and comparative anatomy to better prepare and encourage future physicians. Finally, and the goal of which he was especially proud, was to establish independent departments for the science

---

tainly had played a part in the appointment. Edward Lurie, *Louis Agassiz: A Life in Science* (Chicago: University of Chicago Press, 1960), 360

42. J. M. Comstock, "Burt Green Wilder," *Science* 61, no. 1586 (22 May 1925): 531–33.

43. American higher education was undergoing a radical transformation from the didactic pre-war system, established to serve an elite clientele and based on rote learning, to a more open, experimental, and socially encompassing system.

44. In 1867 Wilder described the system that was based on brief statements of fact, ideas, or references to books written lengthwise on slips of paper equal to one-sixth of a sheet. Comstock, "Burt Green Wilder," 533.

45. *The Wilder Quarter Century Book: A Collection of Original Papers Dedicated to Professor Burt Green Wilder* (Ithaca, N.Y.: Comstock Publishing, 1893), 9–11. Seventeen years before he would retire, Wilder had already taught 3,261 students in the required physiology course alone. While many of his students were devoted to him and praised his high standards, others in the Cornell community knew him better for his long opposition to intercollegiate sports, secret societies, and foot stamping in class. He had students hoping to attend his lectures fill out a form indicating their position on foot stamping in class and return it to him. When one critic in the Ithaca paper attacked him for his opposition to intercollegiate football and speculated that he was a "crippled crank," Wilder quickly sought testimonials on his active life from his former principle, J. Emory Hoar, Colonel Fox, and a close neighbor. While he clearly did not mind being thought a crank, he did not want anyone to think that he was disabled. Wilder Papers, CU.

disciplines at Cornell and to train the new heads: by the time he retired, there were seven departments with full professors as heads.[46]

Wilder was more than just an influential teacher, though, and published extensively, not only in scholarly but also in popular magazines.[47] Throughout his career, he saw the importance of communicating his research and ideas to a broader and more diverse audience than his academic peers. Starting in August 1866, when he published "How My Acquaintances Spin" in the *Atlantic Monthly*, Wilder wrote more than a dozen articles on natural history for such periodicals, including *Scribner's Monthly*, *Harper's New Monthly Magazine*, and *The Galaxy* as well as the *Atlantic*. In September 1866 he even published "Memoirs of a Cripple," a children's version of the *Atlantic Monthly* article on the new spider he had discovered while serving with his regiment on Folly Island, off the coast of Charleston. At one level, the piece served to introduce young readers to an aspect of natural science. At another, however, the article can be seen as a metaphor to introduce young children to the evils of slavery. In the story, the narrator (a spider) provides "a lengthy tale of the captivity of a multitude of her race from one particular region; details of the voyage in cramped quarters without food or water; and a emphasis on the theft of her labor in the form of the raw material she produces (in this case, silk)." Although Wilder adds a cautionary note in the story to avoid greed or too great a haste "to be rid of [one's] old cloths; for in this [the spider's] misfortune began," he clearly empathizes with the female spider and is scornful of the unproductive "gentlemen spiders." Brandy Parris, a scholar of children's literature, interprets "Memoirs of a Cripple" as a new hybridized genre of children's animal stories in which Wilder "uses science to define the inherent worth of blacks as sympathetic and Southerners as unsympathetic."[48]

Although Wilder believed in the need to write for a broad audience, he realized that science now required a rigorously analytical approach. He had taken to heart the advice passed on to him by Jeffries Wyman: "The days of the mere descriptive naturalist have gone by, when he can get much glory from his labours; the *thinking* naturalist alone is the one

46. "Retirement of Professor Burt Green Wilder," *Anatomical Record* 5, no. 7 (1911).

47. See Selected Bibliography.

48. Brandy Parris, "Difficult Sympathy in the Reconstruction-era Animal Stories of *Our Young Folks*," *Children's Literature* 31 (2003): 32–35. Of course, by stressing that the spider's problems and difficulties increase when she casts off her old skin and becomes hungrier, Wilder is also addressing the dangers of rapid social and racial transformation.

who will command much respect."[49] Moreover, Wilder, and the other naturalists with whom he worked, believed in studying natural history not only "in its true sense, earnestly and scientifically" but also collegially.[50] Despite his heavy teaching load at Cornell and frequent lecturing at other universities, he published extensively and gave papers most years at the annual meeting of the American Association for the Advancement of Science. In 1885 he became president of the American Neurological Association and a vice president of the American Association for the Advancement of Science (biological section).[51] A decade later he served as the vice president of the Association of American Anatomists.[52] His achievements are the more impressive for his having, for much of his time at Cornell, no assistant, little lab space, and virtually no necessary apparatus.[53]

Wilder's long tenure at Cornell and his involvement in national associations occurred at a transitional time for American scientists. When he moved to Ithaca, he was representative of his peers—New England–born, medically trained, and focused on the natural sciences. By the end of his career, however, more American scientists came from the middle Atlantic and north-central states and worked in fields such as physics and chemistry, and a majority held doctorates.[54]

By 1880 Wilder's major research interest was the study of the morphology of the brain, and by the end of the decade he had begun to amass his celebrated collection of the organ.[55] In 1893 he helped establish the Cornell Brain Association, which, along with the Mutual Autopsy Society of Paris

49. Wyman to Burt Green Wilder, 25 July 1864, Wilder Papers, CU.

50. Winsor, *Reading the Shape of Nature*, 34–35. Wilder's association with Agassiz brought him into a circle of scientists that included Joel Asaph Allen, Albert Bickmore, Addison Emory Verrill, and Frederick Ward Putnam. Collegiality involved the exchange of new research in papers, presentations, and debates and Wilder was always active.

51. By the mid-1880s there were nine sections—Mathematics and Astronomy, Physics, Chemistry, Mechanical Science, Geology and Geography, Biology, Microscopy and Histology, Anthropology, and Economic Science and Statistics. The chair of each section gave an annual address of general interest and served as a vice president of the overall association. Sally Gregory Kohlstedt, Michael M. Sokal, and Bruce V. Lewenstein, *The Establishment of Science in America: 150 Years of the American Association for the Advancement of Science* (New Brunswick, N.J.: Rutgers University Press, 1999), 43–44.

52. "Biographical Sketch of B. G. Wilder," Wilder Papers, CU.

53. For a long time there was not even a microscope in his lab. Comstock, "Burt Green Wilder," 533.

54. Elliott, "Models of the American Scientist," 90–91.

55. By the time that Wilder retired from Cornell University in 1910, he had collected approximtely two thousand human and animal brains.

and the American Anthropometric Society, worked for the preservation of brains after death for the benefit of scientific research.[56] Wilder challenged the argument that gender, race, and antisocial behavior could be linked to detectable differences in the size, shape, weight, and amount of convolutions of the brain.[57] His belief that such differences could not be detected, at least not by the naked eye or by any nineteenth-century instruments, brought him into conflict with many of his fellow scientists who increasingly argued that race was rooted in human physiology.[58] Despite voices such as Wilder and Franz Boas, racial stereotyping became a deeply entrenched part of the scientific and popular imagination by the end of the nineteenth century.[59] Wilder's diary persuasively establishes that his commitment, as a scientist and a social activist, to racial justice for African Americans had been fostered by his time spent with the 55th Massachusetts.

During the nineteenth and early twentieth centuries, increasing numbers of American scientists and social scientists focused their research around the concept of race and sought to measure, quantify, and categorize perceived physiological differences between groups.[60] A majority accepted the various forms of "scientific racism" that were being advanced by men such as Louis Agassiz, Samuel George Morton, and Robert B. Bean.[61] These scientists presented "evidence" from their studies in anthropometrics, craniometry, and the morphology of the human brain that posited a

56. John S. Haller Jr., *Outcasts from Evolution: Scientific Attitudes of Racial Inferiority, 1859–1900* (Carbondale: Southern Illinois University Press, 1971), 37; *New York Times*, 4 March 1907.

57. The arguments he opposed were illustrated by J. Barnard Davis, who stated in 1869 that the "weight of the brain, like all the other peculiarities of human races, is a *race character*, appertaining to each race specifically." J. Barnard Davis, "On the Weight of the Brain in the Negro," *Anthropological Review* 7, no. 25 (1869): 190–92.

58. Edward H. Beardsley, "The American Scientist as Social Activist: Franz Boas, Burt G. Wilder, and the Cause of Racial Justice, 1900–1915," *Isis* 64, no. 1 (1973): 50–66.

59. For a detailed discussion of the ways that scientists used various measurements of cranial capacity to support a racial hierarchy, see Stephen Jay Gould, *The Mismeasure of Man*, rev. ed. (New York: Norton, 1996), 63–141.

60. In the United States, scientific racism helped to create and justify institutional racism. Martin Fichman, *Evolutionary Theory and Victorian Culture* (Amherst, N.Y.: Humanity Books, 2002), 86.

61. As Matthew Jacobson points out, what was "new" was the range of sciences and social sciences, from biology and genetics to psychology and anthropology, focusing on the concept of race as a real and measurable entity with implications for national public policy. Matthew Frye Jacobson, *Whiteness of a Different Color: European Immigration and the Alchemy of Race* (Cambridge: Harvard University Press, 1998).

hierarchy of human groups.[62] Wilder stood out among his peers for his public opposition to arguments that suggested an innate physiological inferiority of African Americans and for his willingness to criticize scientists such as Bean and Robert W. Shufeldt and writers such as Owen Wister and Margaret Deland.[63]

In 1909 Wilder addressed the National Negro Conference, precursor to the National Association for the Advancement of Colored People. He believed that it was critical to refute any argument for a physiological justification for discrimination because it was a time when the "American Negro is on trial, not for his life but for the recognition of his status, his rights and his opportunity."[64] This conviction had its roots in the war. According to the historian of science and medicine Edward H. Beardsley, the key to understanding Wilder's intellectual development and his opposition to contemporary prejudice was his time in the 55th Massachusetts.[65] Certainly Wilder's Civil War experiences and the close social contacts he had with black soldiers reinforced and provided a practical validation of his scientific belief in the essential equality of African Americans.[66] At a reunion of the black Massachusetts regiments at Faneuil Hall in Boston in July 1913, Wilder expressed his fundamental belief: "This country will never be wholly great," he told the black veterans, "until it is possible for a Negro to enjoy all the opportunities accorded to any other citizen of equal character."[67]

62. Significantly, Jeffries Wyman demonstrated the methodological sloppiness of these studies when he measured a single skull with eight of the different materials generally used, such as sand, white mustard seeds, shot, and water, and produced eight very different measurements. Haller, *Outcast from Evolution*, 17–18.

63. John David Smith describes Shufeldt as one of "early twentieth century's most venomous 'scientific' white racists." He was a U.S. Army surgeon and an ethnologist who published extensively. In characteristic fashion, Wilder wrote a cutting review in the *Nation* of Shufeldt's *America's Greatest Problem: The Negro* shortly after it appeared in 1915. He attacked the medically trained veteran for venturing beyond his strictly scientific work. "That might, at least, have been free from the needlessly frequent references to topics connected with *psychopathia sexualis* which characterize this and some of his other publications." John David Smith, *Black Judas: William Hannibal Thomas and the American Negro* (Athens: University of Georgia Press, 2000), 192–94; typescript copy, 26 November 1915, Wilder Papers, CU.

64. Wilder, "The Brain of the American Negro," 22.

65. According to Beardsley, "The pivotal influence on Wilder was his war experience" ("The American Scientist as Social Activist," 52, 55–58).

66. One example of the formative impact of his regimental experiences on his commitment to equality was an article he wrote in 1906 to counter the biases he saw around him, "Two Examples of the Negro's Courage, Physical and Moral," *Alexander's Magazine* 1 (January 1906): 22–25.

67. "Reunion," *(Brookline) Chronicle*, 19 July 1913.

In 1910, as Wilder, a man who flourished on activity, faced his retirement years, his attention turned back to the letters he wrote during his Civil War service. He envisioned writing what he called a "Record and Recollection of the Civil War," and the letters were to be the core of the work. He was motivated to begin by several reasons, not the least of which was that, by the first decade of the twentieth century, many of the participants on both sides who might supplement or correct his impressions were passing away. Wilder was, of course, only one of many veterans who, through public talks and published accounts, wished to recount or recreate their experience in the war and to influence the struggle for the contested meaning and memory of the conflict. But Wilder had a more fundamental concern too. By the time that he returned to his letters, it was evident to those who chose to look that the growing spirit of reconciliation in the United States had come at the cost of ignoring slavery as a root cause of the war and of minimizing the role of African Americans in it.[68] Many of the achievements of black Americans had been rolled back and their civil rights eroded. This, Wilder believed, was another critical reason to publish his diary; his account would address the "urgent need of impartial evidence that the American negro not only requires but merits justice, sympathy and encouragement."[69] It was a theme he had stressed the previous year at the National Negro Conference, citing his professional credentials (his time in the army and his training as a scientist) to counter growing white prejudice.[70] W. E. B. Du Bois, who was in attendance, wrote that Wilder's presentation "left no doubt in the minds of listeners that the whole argument by which Negroes were pronounced absolutely and inevitably inferior to whites was utterly without scientific basis."[71]

In the spring of 1910, as a way of confirming many of the details he had recorded during the war, Wilder toured those parts of the South associated with his service, and he began an extensive correspondence with both Union and Confederate veterans. Over the next few years he would

68. The ways in which the national pursuit of reunification and reconciliation undermined the emancipationist legacy of the war is examined in David W. Blight's masterful *Race and Reunion: The Civil War in American Memory* (Cambridge: Harvard University Press, 2001).

69. Transcribed note, n.d. [1910?], Wilder Papers, CU.

70. He told the audience that at numerous times "there have been occasions when I was tempted to exclaim, 'Yes, a white man is as worthy as a colored man—provided he behaves himself as well.'" Wilder, "The Brain of the American Negro," 22.

71. Elliott M. Rudwick, "The National Negro Committee Conference of 1909," *Phylon Quarterly* 18, no 4 (1957): 413.

receive numerous letters from former enlisted men of the 55th, and their common salutation, "Dear Comrade," speaks to both their feelings for Wilder and his involvement with the Grand Army of the Republic.[72] On his return to Cornell, between 30 July and 29 October, he "copied on the typewriter the historic portions of the letters."[73] Sometime after completing the transcription, Wilder added notations, questions, and alterations in pencil. In some instances, most frequently in his discussions of the 55th's combat experience, he crossed out part of the original text and added a new line or phrase.[74] Such changes, however, compose a very small part of his manuscript.

The result, the document now held at the Cornell University Library, is a personal narrative in diary form, not yet developed into a true memoir. The transcription reveals a good deal about Wilder's personality and values. Four years after finishing his draft, he outlined his thoughts on the value of recollections: "Reminiscences of the events of a half century ago are very unreliable unless formed upon records made *at the time* and *on the spot*. It may also be assumed that my previous training as a naturalist rendered my observation more than unusually trustworthy."[75]

A number of diaries of surgeons serving in white regiments have been recently published or republished, but little exists on black regiments.[76]

72. Samples of these letters include Jordan M. Bobson to "Hon. Sir, M.D., Comrade and friend," 17 April 1906; W. H. Dupree to "Dr. Wilder, Comrade," 23 February 1910; William Scott to "Dr. Burt G. Wilder, Dear Comrade," 2 December 1914, 18 December 1914; David Lee to "Dear Comrade," 11 March 1918; George S. Walker to "Dear Comrade," 13 July 1914. Wilder Papers, CU. Earlier historians such as Stuart McConnell have painted a bleak picture of the treatment of African Americans in the GAR, but several recent works argue that the GAR was far more inclusive than previously portrayed. Two excellent examples are Barbara Gannon, "The Won Cause: Black and White Comradeship in the Grand Army of the Republic," Ph.D. diss., Pennsylvania State University, 2005, and Andre Fleche, "'Shoulder to Shoulder as Comrades Tried': Black and White Veterans and Civil War Memory," *Civil War History* 51, no. 2 (June 2005: 175–201.

73. By this Wilder meant that he removed all personal comments that he may have made to or about Sarah Cowell Nichols, the woman with whom he had gone through school and whom he would marry in 1868. B. G. Wilder to A. Lawrence Lowell, 27 June 1914, Wilder Papers, CU.

74. These changes may have resulted from letters he received after 1910. Occasionally, his correspondence with the ex-soldiers included a list of questions. It is important to note that these related almost entirely to the military engagements of the regiments or, in letters to some of the black soldiers, to the issue of unequal pay that they faced at the start of their service.

75. Ibid.

76. These accounts include James M. Greiner, Janet L. Coryell, and James R. Smither, eds., *A Surgeon's Civil War: The Letters and Diary of Daniel M. Holt, M.D.* (Kent, Ohio: Kent

Wilder's account as a young surgeon is useful both for what it reveals about life and service in an important Northern black regiment and for its insights into the formative years in his becoming an influential scientist, educator, and social activist. He entered the war as a medical student with a career as a physician ahead of him; he left the army as a man with expanding scientific interests, an increased commitment to social justice for disadvantaged groups, and a long academic career before him. His entry for 1 March 1864 reflects the tension between his commitment to duty and his love of natural science. In a foreshadowing of his future career direction, he wrote, "I studied Guthrie's 'Surgery' as well as I could, but was interrupted by a huge brown spider that crawled up my sleeve."

Wilder's record is particularly valuable because he wrote well and extensively about the medical service and quotidian life in a black regiment in addition to depicting the natural history he observed through the South. He was very conscious that his life as an army surgeon was, in many ways, easier than that of the line officers in command of the black soldiers. At the same time, his entries demonstrate that, even for a surgeon, life was difficult, hours of work long, and personal illness never very far away.

The 55th Massachusetts was a regiment with an unusually competent and complete medical staff while it served in the South. The Army Medical Department increased the numbers of its medical officers from the 78 available at the start of the war to more than 12,000 in 1865, including 5,532 acting assistant surgeons. But, by the time most black regiments began to commission officers, the number of qualified medical personnel available was desperately low.[77] A majority of the black regiments in 1863 were unable to fill their official complement of a surgeon and two assistant surgeons, and frequently the men appointed as acting surgeons were unqualified or incompetent.[78] In this connection, the historian Margaret Humphreys argues that "African American regiments received de-

State University Press, 1994); Thomas P. Lowry, *Swamp Doctor: The Diary of a Union Surgeon in the Virginia and North Carolina Marshes* (Mechanicsburg, Pa.: Stackpole Books, 2001); Cynthia Dehaven Pitcock and Bill Gurley, eds., *I Acted from Principle: The Civil War Diary of Dr. William M. McPeeters, Confederate Surgeon in the Trans-Mississippi* (Fayetteville: University of Arkansas Press, 2002); John Herbert Roper, ed., *Repairing the "March of Mars": The Civil War Diaries of John Samuel Apperson, Hospital Steward in the Stonewall Brigade, 1861–1865* (Macon, Ga.: Mercer University Press, 2002); John H. Brinton, *Personal Memoirs of John H. Brinton, Civil War Surgeon, 1861–1865* (Carbondale: Southern Illinois University Press, 1996).

77. When the war started, twenty-four of the medical staff resigned to join the Confederate army and three more quit or were fired. Flannery, *Civil War Pharmacy*, 17, 20.

78. Margaret Humphreys, *Intensely Human: The Health of the Black Soldier in the Civil War* (Baltimore: Johns Hopkins University Press, 2008), 57–62; Joseph T. Glatthaar, *Forged*

cidedly second-class medical care" and that few units had their quota of physicians.[79] Yet, here again, the 55th Massachusetts was the exception. Both the surgeon, Dr. William S. Brown, and the second assistant surgeon, Dr. Warren M. Babbitt, were practicing physicians when the war began, and Brown had previous military service.[80]

Even in the 55th, however, detached service or leave furloughs frequently left the medical officers understaffed and doubling up on responsibilities. Despite the fact that the regiment carried three qualified surgeons on its rolls, there were periods of time when Wilder was the only medical officer with it. Babbitt did not join until September 1864, and he was subsequently detailed away from the regiment much of the next two months.[81] Even Brown was periodically away, leaving Wilder the regiment's only medical officer. He was the medical officer with the least experience, although his service at the Judiciary Square Hospital had given him a crash course in "practical surgery." Of course, the greatest demand on all Civil War surgeons was in combating diseases, not repairing injuries, and here Wilder felt inadequate.[82]

Although there were guidelines for the duties of assistant surgeons, situational needs and personal expertise frequently dictated who would do what. The assistant surgeon was responsible for establishing and maintaining the hospital tent, providing the necessary water, fuel, straw, and blankets, and setting up and overseeing the kitchen with the help of the hospital steward, cooks, and such nurses drawn from the regiment as necessary. Multiple entries in Wilder's diary indicate that he performed these tasks constantly. The assistant surgeon was also responsible for maintaining a complete record of all cases of illness and wounds. This task could be sometimes shared, but frequently the entire burden fell on Wilder. In addition, the assistant surgeon normally took the early "sick call" of the enlisted men, deciding which soldiers were ill enough to go to hospital, who should be excused from duty but assigned to quarters or

---

in Battle: The Civil War Alliance of Black Soldiers and White Officers (New York: Free Press, 1990), 187–89.

79. Humphreys, *Intensely Human*, 57–58.

80. Fox, *Record*, 99–100.

81. Indeed, for part of the time the surgeon did not know where he was. Fox, *Record*, 99–100.

82. Diary entry for 27 September 1863; Fox, *Record*, 99–100. Even in white regiments, soldiers were twice as likely to die from disease as from a wound. Federal doctors treated about 425,000 traumatic cases during the war and approximately 6 million non-traumatic cases. Fortunately, black troops on the Carolina coast were among the healthiest regiments. Flannery, *Civil War Pharmacy*, 22–23; Humphreys, *Intensely Human*, 81–83.

light duties, and who was faking illness.[83] This duty was particularly onerous when more than a hundred enlisted men were reporting as ill.[84]

When the regiment went into combat, the regimental surgeon established a field hospital well to the rear of the conflict while an assistant surgeon, with a detail of stretcher-bearers composed of hospital nurses and band members plus an orderly who carried a hospital knapsack with medical supplies, set up a post several hundred yards behind the firing lines. Stretcher-bearers would bring the wounded there for triage before carrying them farther back to the field hospital. Experienced regiments often wanted both assistant surgeons in the medical post, but few black regiments operated with a full allotment of surgeons.[85]

Wilder's life in the regiment was all the more demanding because his superior, Dr. W. S. Brown, was always willing to offload chores to the assistant surgeons.[86] In addition, Wilder's willingness to extend medical help to civilians, both at Folly Island and on the mainland, contributed to his workload. Moreover, because of Wilder's expertise and training, he was involved in some activities outside the realm of combat officers', or even other assistant surgeons', experiences. The United States Sanitary Commission, initially under the direction of Frederick Law Olmsted, undertook anthropological surveys of white and black soldiers in the volunteer army, and by the last year of the war Wilder was drawn into that effort.[87]

In early 1863 Benjamin Apthrop Gould, an astronomer and mathematician and the president of the American Association for the Advancement of Science, took over the statistical investigation and assigned special examiners to specific locations across the country to collect a spectrum of information on Union soldiers.[88] The examiners had been trained, provided with instructions and forms, and supplied with an array of instruments such as andrometers, spirometers, dynamometers, calipers, and measuring tape. They collected data on the body measurement and

83. George Worthington Adams, *Doctors in Blue: The Medical History of the Union Army in the Civil War* (Baton Rouge: Louisiana State University Press, 1952), 63–67.

84. Diary entries for 14, 22 August, 13 September, 4 October 1863.

85. Glatthaar, *Forged in Battle*, 161–62; Humphreys, *Intensely Human*, 57.

86. William Symington Brown was a Scottish physician living in South Reading, Massachusetts, at the start of the war. He had previously served as assistant surgeon in the 34th Massachusetts Volunteers. Fox, *Record*, 99.

87. Lundy Braun, "Spirometry, Measurement, and Race in the Nineteenth Century," *Journal of the History of Medicine and Allied Sciences* 60, no. 2 (2005): 145–46.

88. Haller, *Outcasts from Evolution*, 22.

weight of the soldiers as well as their lifting strength, measured by a dynamometer, and their "vital capacity," defined as the difference between a soldier's total lung capacity and the residual volume recorded using a spirometer.[89]

Although there is no evidence that Wilder received the training described, in July 1864 he received a large shipment of material from the Sanitary Commission "for sociological and physiological reports of our men when a more convenient time arrives."[90] It was not until well into April 1865, and after the fighting was over, that the time was convenient. During the next four months, when the regiment was not on the move and when his duties allowed, Wilder took the measurements requested by the commission. Once Wilder set up the instruments and began measuring soldiers in his regiment, however, he found some of the instructions ambiguous.[91] Gould wanted subjects to be categorized as "Full Blacks," "Mulattoes," and "Indians" so they could be compared to the data being compiled for "White" soldiers. The commission inspectors, and Wilder, were told to estimate the proportion of "black blood although they were not told how."[92] Indeed, Wilder was forced to write directly to Gould to get further information on the exact method for taking measurements. In later years Wilder may have seen the bitter irony that he provided some of the information Gould used to construct a simple narrative emphasizing the inherent

89. The investigation focused on seven anthropometric indicators—height, body-mass index, waist-hip ratio, the ratio of shoulder width to chest circumference, and the ratio of chest circumference to height, lifting strength, and vital capacity. Dora L. Costa, "The Measure of Man and Older Age Mortality: Evidence from the Gould Sample," *Journal of Economic History* 64, no. 1 (2004): 5–6, 19–21. That the term "lung capacity" was replaced by the more vague but evocative "vital capacity" suggests that cultural determinants played as great a role as scientific methodology in the research.

90. Diary entry for 9 July 1864. It is not clear whether Wilder had been specifically selected because of his studies in comparative anatomy or because Gould was trying to increase the data on black soldiers by using surgeons in the USCT to record information. The key link was that Gould relied on the advice of his friend Louis Agassiz, who knew Wilder well. Wilder took part in the survey even though Surg.Gen. Joseph K. Barnes was hostile to Gould's efforts. William Q. Maxwell, *Lincoln's Fifth Wheel: The Political History of the United States Sanitary Commission* (New York: Longmans, Green, 1956), 313. Barnes's bureau was conducting its own anthropometric survey using military doctors. Since the Sanitary Commission reportedly used its own examiners, and Gould did not cite him when listing the people working on the survey, new questions are raised about Wilder's participation. Haller, *Outcasts from Evolution*, 19–31; Benjamin Apthorp Gould, *Investigations in the Military and Anthropological Statistics of American Soldiers* (Cambridge: Riverside Press, 1869; repr., New York: Arno Press, 1979), x.

91. Diary entries for 21, 25, 28 April, 3, 24 May, 28 June, 2 August 1865.

92. Braun, "Spirometry," 150–52.

physical differences between blacks and whites. It may also explain Wilder's determination to counter scientific racism at the end of the century with his own research on the human brain.[93]

Wilder, while serving with the 55th Massachusetts, was also an active supporter of the newly created United States Army Military Museum. Surgeon General William A. Hammond envisioned a medical museum as one way to expand the practical training and increase the competency of army doctors, and in 1862 the museum was established in Washington with John H. Brinton as its first curator.[94] Brinton, formerly one of Grant's medical directors in the Army of the Tennessee, had just returned to Washington to serve as chairman of the federal medical examining board convened in that city. Wilder had done work for Brinton while he was a medical cadet in Washington and he strongly supported the idea of collecting medical specimens to assist in the research and teaching of military medicine and surgery. While in the field and despite his heavy workload, Wilder diligently prepared a number of specimens that he forwarded to Washington.[95]

Historians and researchers who have used Charles Fox's *Record of the Service of the Fifty-fifth Regiment of Massachusetts Volunteer Infantry* will find Wilder's manuscript an excellent companion piece. Although Fox's publication was based on his own diary, the manuscript was revised by and for a group of officers acting on behalf of the Association of Officers of the Fifty-Fifth Massachusetts Volunteers.[96] The result was a semi-

93. Wilder used his research to take on both scientists and popular writers who depicted the brains or skulls of African Americans as physiologically different—a difference that reflected diminished capacity. He tried to get Owen Wister, best known for his first novel, *The Virginian*, to recant publicly a passage from his *Lady Baltimore* being published in installments in the *Saturday Evening Post*. In that work, Wister described the skull of a black South Carolinian as being quite similar to the skull of a gorilla. When he did not get the retraction that he wanted, Wilder gave a paper to the American Anthropological Society in December 1905 outlining his concerns. Wilder, "The Brain of the American Negro," 26–30.

94. Hammond had an ambitious plan to improve army medicine which brought him into conflict with various interests. His decision to remove calomel and antimony from the standard supply table led to a politically motivated court-martial and Hammond's leaving the army. Ira M. Rutkow, *Bleeding Blue and Gray: Civil War Surgery and the Evolution of American Medicine* (New York: Random House, 2005), 245–51; Flannery, *Civil War Pharmacy*, 150–55; Frank R. Freemon, *Gangrene and Glory: Medical Care during the American Civil War* (Madison, N.J.: Fairleigh Dickinson University Press, 1998), 86.

95. Diary entries for 24 March, 30 July 1864.

96. Given that the committee helping Fox included Colonel Alfred Hartwell and Dr. William Brown, men with whom he had repeatedly clashed, it is not surprising that little of the regimental dissent or rivalry described by Wilder appears in the book. Fox, *Record*, i.

official history of the regiment which covers the military campaigns of the 55th in extensive detail but lacks any of the discussions of the various officers' character strengths and weaknesses, personal rivalries, and ruthless ambition which Wilder provides. Because Wilder wrote less about military events and far more about the social dynamics within the 55th Massachusetts, his writings give readers a better understanding of the tensions and antagonisms within the regiment.

Readers who are familiar with the growing literature on black soldiers will find both familiar themes and fresh information in Wilder's account of life in the 55th. The army that Wilder joined was full of contradictory forces, and his record captures some of this dynamic. On the one hand, the military was an institution composed overwhelmingly of civilians who brought to it the values, attitudes, and prejudices concerning African Americans that were held by the wider white society. Overt racism was manifested in many ways.[97] Even in the 55th Massachusetts, some of the white officers threatened to resign if black sergeants were mustered in as commissioned officers.[98] On the other hand, if the army was to function as an efficient and effective organization, then logic and necessity dictated that it operate as a color-blind institution.

To encourage black recruitment, volunteers had been promised status equal to that of all other Union soldiers along with equal protection in the face of the enemy. The chain of command would be undermined if men of equal rank were not recognized as having equal authority. The demands and vagaries of the war meant that all regiments had to be combat-ready and, wherever possible, equipped and trained accordingly. To do otherwise might imperil an entire army. Of course, all this occurred in an environment of fierce competition for limited resources.

From the time that black regiments were first established, and especially in their early months of service, these units were frequently called on to do more than their share of fatigue duty, or manual labor.[99] The idea

97. Virtually all studies of black soldiers include examples of the discrimination they faced. Berlin, Reidy, and Rowland, *The Black Military Experience*, 303–31. Some historians, however, including Barbara Gannon, Andre Fleche, and Christian Samito, have recently argued that blacks found more equitable treatment in the Union army.

98. Noah Andre Trudeau, *Voices of the 55th: Letters from the 55th Massachusetts Volunteers, 1861–1865* (Dayton, Ohio: Morningside, 1996), 181.

99. Many of the studies of black regiments have highlighted this issue. Hollandsworth, *The Louisiana Native Guard*, 96–97; Glatthaar, *Forged in Battle*, 182–85; Reid, *Freedom for Themselves*, 48, 56–57, 68–72, 148, 207–8, 300; James M. Paradis, *Strike the Blow for Freedom: The 6th United States Colored Infantry in the Civil War* (Shippensburg, Pa.: White Mane

that such activity was blacks' "natural" function was held by many white officers, just as it was by a majority of Northern civilians. In one typical example, the engineering officers in charge of the siege work on Morris Island in Charleston harbor testified that the black soldiers were capable of a greater amount of work than white soldiers, although they were less skilled and "more timorous."[100]

The perception of just how black soldiers should be employed and whether or not they should serve primarily as auxiliary troops did change dramatically in the months after the black regiments entered the Union army, and especially after they had demonstrated their courage under fire. Certainly, however, when the 55th Massachusetts first arrived at Folly Island, the regiment was immediately assigned disproportionately heavy fatigue duties. James Henry Gooding, a corporal in the 54th, reported that the day after arriving "the [55th] regiment was introduced to Messrs. Shovel and Spade, a firm largely interested in building rifle pits, breastworks and batteries."[101] On 2 August 1863 General Quincy A. Gillmore notified General Alfred H. Terry, commander on Morris Island, that Wild's "colored brigade, 2,000 strong will be encamped on the north end of Folly Island, for fatigue duty at the landing and on this island, on your requisition." This was at the same time that General Israel Vogdes, in command of Folly Island, promised to "furnish 1,000 men for grand guard duty in the trenches every other day."[102]

Moreover, it was not just the amount of work they were being told to do that angered the black enlisted men; they were frequently required to perform services that would not have been demanded of or accepted from men in a white regiment. When Wild's regiments first arrived on Folly Island, the 1st North Carolina Colored Volunteers were charged to dig wells and put up tents for white New York regiments. Nevertheless, many senior officers understood the unfairness and ineffectiveness of such a policy. [103] On Folly Island, General Vogdes initially drew the fatigue

Books, 2000), 35–36, 61; Berlin, Reidy, and Rowland, *The Black Military Experience*, 484–87, 490–95, 515–16.

100. *Official Records*, ser. 1, vol. 28, part 1, 329.

101. Henry James Gooding and Virginia Matzke Adams, eds., *On the Altar of Freedom: A Black Soldier's Civil War Letters from the Front* (Amherst: University of Massachusetts Press, 1991), 47.

102. *Official Records*, ser. 1, vol. 28, part 2, 35.

103. Colonel Beecher complained that, when "they are set to menial work doing for white regiments what those Regiments are entitled to do for themselves, it . . . reduces them to the position of slaves again." Berlin, Reidy, and Rowland, *The Black Military Experience*, 493.

parties almost entirely from the black units, but he was forced to change his policy by General Gillmore, who prohibited "the employment of colored troops to perform menial or unmilitary service for white troops."[104] Decades after the war was over, a fellow officer, Walter Wild, suggested an explanation of Vogdes's motives to Wilder: "I do not know of any reason for the ill treatment that Vogdes served out to your regiment except the general disgust of all the old West Pointers against the use of Colored Troops. That became plain to me in many ways when later on I was Brigaded with Regular Officers in the 25th Corps in Texas."[105] Wild may have exaggerated the hostility of regular army officers; perceptions of what the black soldiers could do, how they should be used, and the quality of their military service were always dynamic and fluid during the war years.

The extra fatigue duties imposed on the black troops around Charleston were especially onerous because of the poor health and the heavy burden of disease that were all too common in black regiments. Part of the problem, certainly for a regiment such as the 55th Massachusetts, lay in the Northern soldiers' period of adjustment to the southern climate and pathogens. Shortly after the 55th arrived on Folly Island, a soldier from the 54th warned that the "sickly season has now about commenced" and that men were dying daily.[106] The hot, humid weather, a poor water supply, new pathogens, and the severe physical demands placed on the regiments all took their toll.

Since far more members of black regiments died of disease than were killed in battle throughout the war, Wilder's day-to-day activities as a regimental surgeon deepens our understanding of the life of black soldiers. In the summer of 1863, while the regiment was on Folly Island, Wilder sometimes saw several hundred men a day at the morning sick calls. The tension caused by the demands for black labor and the burden of illness came to a head when General Vogdes personally told Wilder that his sick list was too large and that he should not allow the men "to impose" on him. Wilder was indignant that, at a time when the general "was taking our men, 400 or 500 at a time, and many of them have been out four or five nights in succession at hard work," Vogdes would try to pressure him into allowing men who were physically unfit for labor to be sent on fatigue duty.[107]

104. Diary entry for 20 September 1863.
105. Walter H Wild to Burt Green Wilder, 31 March 1914, Wilder Papers, CU.
106. Gooding, *On the Altar of Freedom*, 47–48.
107. Diary entry for 17 August 1863.

Given the conditions under which the 55th Massachusetts served, and in comparison with other regiments, the numbers of black soldiers in the 55th who died of disease, perhaps 128 men, was below the norm.[108] By contrast, the 54th Massachusetts lost 160 soldiers to illnesses; the 1st North Carolina Colored Volunteers, with which the 55th Massachusetts was first brigaded, had 151 men die from disease; and the 39th United States Colored Troops (USCT), a Southern-raised unit that also served in the East, had 239 men succumb to diseases. Regiments that served along the Mississippi or in Texas had even higher mortality rates. In the 5th United States Colored Heavy Artillery, based in Vicksburg, 697 men died of illness.[109] The majority of deaths among the black soldiers resulted from diarrhea and dysentery; malaria, typhoid, and assorted camp fevers were other common causes. Fewer men died of respiratory and digestive disorders. The germ theory of disease would emerge only in the 1870s and 1880s, so surgeons like Wilder were limited in what they could do to help the men—although experience was an effective, if sometimes slow, teacher.[110]

Of course, it was not just enlisted men who suffered from hard work, little rest, and virulent pathogens. Indeed, in August 1863, when the 55th Massachusetts had been in South Carolina for just a month, Wilder reported that he was the only officer in the regiment who had not been ill.[111] A significant number of the officers of the 55th were forced to resign their commissions during the war because of ill health and disabilities, although few were as unfortunate as Lieut. Leonard C. Alden. In October 1864, after several weeks of declining health resulting from the conditions on Folly Island, Alden started north on a sick furlough. He never

108. Although Frederick Dyer claimed, decades later, that 128 men died of disease, Wilder cited a smaller number, 112 (and 54 in battle). Frederick H. Dyer, *A Compendium of the War of the Rebellion* (1908; repr., Dayton, Ohio: National History Society / Press of Morningside Bookshop, 1979), 798; Wilder, "The Brain of the American Negro," 49.

109. Humphreys, *Intensely Human*, 82–86. Dyer, *A Compendium*, 1721, 1723, 1729, 1728.

110. The suppression of hospital gangrene offers one example of what could be accomplished through trial and error. Rare at the start of the war, it increased dramatically in the second and third years of the conflict. Repeated amputation of parts of the affected limbs or the use of hydrochloric or nitric acid on the wounds did little to control the spread of decaying flesh. Over time, doctors found effective ways to limit the disease—bromine baths of the wound, isolating the patients, clean dressings, separate sponges, and hand washing by caregivers in chlorinated soda. Rutkow, *Bleeding Blue and Gray*, 134–36; Flannery, *Civil War Pharmacy*, 14, 22–23.

111. Diary entry for 20 August 1863.

made it home. He got only as far as Beaufort Hospital at Hilton Head before he died of chronic diarrhea.[112]

Wilder's manuscript also provides new insights into the bitter controversy of the unequal pay initially paid to the black soldiers.[113] As early as the summer of 1862, in the case of the 1st South Carolina Volunteers, Secretary of War Stanton had promised that all black recruits would "receive the same pay and rations as are allowed by law to volunteers in the service."[114] At the time of their enlistment, the men of the Massachusetts regiments, like other early black recruits, had also been promised that they would receive pay and equipment equal to that of white soldiers. But, although the men of the 55th Massachusetts left their state well equipped, they soon found out that they were to be paid at a different rate from white soldiers. In September 1863 Colonel Hallowell informed the men that they would receive only ten dollars a month, minus three dollars for a clothing allowance. According to a ruling made by William Whiting, the solicitor to the War Department, the proper rate of pay for black troops was established by the Militia Act of 1862. Framers of the Militia Act had assumed that blacks who joined the army would be laborers and not combat soldiers. By contrast, white privates received thirteen dollars a month plus three dollars for a clothing allowance.[115]

Stanton, despite his earlier promise, confirmed the lower rate of pay on 4 June 1863. The men were bitter, not just because they were being denied critical funds, but because it symbolized a range of discriminatory measures against them. One soldier in the 55th Massachusetts voiced the anger of many: "No chance for promotion, no money for our families, and we are little better than an armed band of laborers with rusty muskets and bright spades."[116] Governor Andrew and supporters of the black troops in Massachusetts were also outraged. The two black regiments had been raised under the same regulations and authority as other state volunteers and the distinction made by Whiting was "contrary to the law

112. Fox, *Record*, 14, 95–96.

113. For a sample of the extensive literature dealing with this issue, see Herman Belz, "Law, Politics, and Race in the Struggle for Equal Pay during the Civil War," *Civil War History* 22 (September 1976): 197–213; Berlin, Reidy, and Rowland, *Black Military Experience*, 362–405; Howard Westwood, "The Causes and Consequences of a Black Soldier's Mutiny and Execution," *Civil War History* 31 (1985): 222–36; Glatthaar, *Forged in Battle*, 169–75; Smith, *Black Soldiers in Blue*, 49–52.

114. *Official Records*, ser. 1, vol. 14, 377–78.

115. Smith, *Black Soldiers in Blue*, 49.

116. Miller, "His Wife, His Widow, and His Orphan," 101.

and to justice."[117] Despite appeals by the soldiers and their supporters, it would not be until June 1864 that Congress would establish equal wages for all soldiers, and even then the issue was not settled.[118] At almost the same time that Congress acted, one company in the 55th Massachusetts wrote President Lincoln demanding to be discharged and warning of "more stringent measures" if nothing were done to address their concerns.[119]

The various entries that Wilder made on this topic not only attest to the deep anxiety within his own regiment about the matter of pay but also expose how close the soldiers in both the black Massachusetts regiments came to an actual mutiny over the issue.[120] During late October and early November, the enlisted men gathered privately to discuss their options.[121] When the paymaster first visited the regiment in November 1863, only a few men accepted payment at the reduced level.[122] A letter to the *Christian Recorder* written in April 1864 by an enlisted man in the 55th Massachusetts captured the sentiment of most. Why would Congress not pay black soldiers equal wages? The writer explained: "I rather think that it is the color and quality and citizenship of the United States that is the reason they want us to take ten dollars per month, and three deducted for clothing. No, never will I take it. You may sever my head from

117. Fox, *Record*, 86.

118. Congress's passage of the appropriations bill that authorized equal pay for black soldiers, retroactive to 1 January 1864 for all black soldiers and to their time of enlistment for all who were free in April 1861, did not immediately solve the issue. Not until July did Attorney General Edward Bates rule that the restrictive Militia Act did not dictate wages to black soldiers, and only in August did the War Department authorize regimental commanders to issue the equal wages, once they had ascertained who had been free at the start of the war. Berlin, Reidy, and Rowland, *The Black Military Experience*, 366–68.

119. Trudeau, *Voices*, 116–17.

120. That Wilder made only limited comments on the pay issue corroborates his claim that he would not "undertake to set forth more than I personally saw and heard." He had extensive correspondence with former enlisted men in the years after he transcribed his letters, but information that was new to him was never added to the manuscript; he did, however, use it in other papers and talks. B. G. Wilder to F. T. Miller, 29 April 1913, Wilder Papers, CU.

121. Charles Mitchell, one of the black sergeants who was later commissioned, explained to Wilder in 1909 that there "were several meetings held quietly by some of the non-commissioned officers and enlisted men in the tents of the first sergeants, and in groups in the company streets" to decide what to do. Although Mitchell was responding to Wilder's questions and the exchange occurred before the surgeon began to transcribe his letters, the material was not included in the 1910 transcription. Charles S. Mitchell to B. G. Wilder, 26 May 1909, Wilder Papers, CU.

122. Some of the married men hesitated because of the plight of their families but then decided to refuse the pay. Diary entry for 22 November 1864.

my body first."[123] By February 1864, Wilder's fellow officers had heard rumors that the 54th Massachusetts had stacked their arms and refused orders, and they believed that the 55th Massachusetts might follow the 54th's example.[124] The rumors proved false but, by May 1864, matters seemed to be reaching a critical stage. During the 55th's return from Florida, an enlisted man "snapped a pistol at an officer" and was almost stabbed in response.[125] Fox wrote that the issue of unequal pay was "becoming more serious every day, and constant watchfulness and care was required to prevent trouble."[126]

When Colonel Hartwell suggested that officers receive their next pay at the camp of the 103rd New York, the enlisted men soon found out and were bitter at his proposal.[127] The following day, a picket detail refused to fall in for duty, although most of the men were eventually persuaded by Captain Charles E. Grant to do their job.[128] Just a few days later, after a confrontation between Private Wallace Baker and Lieutenant Thomas Ellsworth, the private struck Ellsworth. The black soldier was tried and convicted of mutiny and executed by firing squad.[129] On 14 July, Wilder

123. Trudeau, *Voices*, 93–94.

124. Diary entry for 2 February 1864.

125. Diary entry for 22 April 1864. When Lt. Josiah A. Bean, the officer of the guard, tried to stop loud talking below decks after taps, Sampson Goliah, one of the enlisted men involved, announced that he would not stop "for any damn white officer" and claimed that "you Massachusetts men have bene [*sic*] humbugging us long enough." After Goliah had been tied to the ship's rigging for ninety minutes, more than a dozen men came to his aid. Serious injury was only narrowly averted. In Goliah's subsequent trial on seven specifications of mutiny, he raised as exculpatory evidence the broken promise of equal pay. Although the soldier faced punishment for a capital offense, he was sentenced to hard labor, forfeiture of pay, and a dishonorable discharge. Christian G. Samito, "The Intersection between Military Justice and Equal Rights: Mutinies, Courts-martial, and Black Civil War Soldiers," *Civil War History* 53, no. 2 (2007): 187–90; Yacovone, *A Voice of Thunder*, 274–75.

126. Fox, *Record*, 26. Gen. Schimmelfennig also believed that the suffering of the men and their families had created the "greatest discontent" and that "in several instances a spirit of mutiny has been developed." *Official Records*, ser. 1. vol. 35, 69.

127. Hartwell found it difficult to balance conflicting demands. While some soldiers felt he was not supportive, Gen. Foster warned Hartwell that his correspondence showed "an inclination to make trouble, or it at least appears that your course is not calculated to allay existing difficulties." *Official Records*, ser. 1, vol. 35, pt. II.

128. Diary entry for 15 June 1864.

129. Diary entry for 18 June 1864. The incident was triggered after Baker, who had been sent to quarters for arriving at inspection unprepared, returned and ultimately told the lieutenant, that "I won't stand to attention for you or any other damned white officer." A brawl ensued. Yacovone and Samito both cover the case in some detail. Yacovone, *A Voice of Thunder*, 74–75, 317–18; Samito, "The Intersection between Military Justice and Equal Rights," 170–72.

wrote that "this morning we feared the long dreaded explosion among the men was at hand." The sergeant-major of the regiment informed Lieutenant-Colonel Fox that the men had decided not to do any duty that day, and it was only Fox's quiet negotiations that avoided a major crisis.

Fortunately, by August, Fox could tell the men that Congress had authorized equal pay for black soldiers and that the War Department was implementing the new law. Nevertheless, he had the unpleasant task of explaining that only men who testified that they were free in April 1861 would receive the retroactive portion.[130] The reaction varied within the companies, but some men felt deeply insulted that such an oath would be required, and a few soldiers refused to take it.[131] In fact, it was not until October that the paymaster arrived at the regiment and all the men who took the oath were paid. Several days later, the enlisted men organized a celebration to which the officers were invited to celebrate "the victory of the colored race as represented by the payment of our men."[132]

In any case, unequal pay remained for long periods of time only an abstract, if highly charged, issue in the 55th, for the regiment had been sent to South Carolina without much of their regimental baggage, including the pay books. As a result, paying even the handful of those willing to accept the reduced wages was impossible for many months, and for many soldiers and their families, the delay caused severe financial hardships.[133] One black sergeant wrote Governor Andrew in early 1864 that the "horrible sufferings of dear sufferin familys" were "more than manhood can beare."[134] Given the hardships at home, Wilder was impressed that most of the black soldiers, when they had the opportunity to be paid, declined to accept the unequal pay offered by the army as a matter of principle.

130. When Congress equalized pay for white and black soldiers, soldiers enslaved at the start of the war received retroactive pay only to 1 January 1864, the argument being that their emancipation made up the difference. Smith, *Black Soldiers in Blue*, 51–52: diary entry for 21 August 1864.

131. Fox, *Record*, 35–36.

132. Diary entry for 10 October 1864. An extended description of the celebration was sent to both the *Christian Recorder* and the *Weekly Anglo-African*. Trudeau, *Voices*, 149–54.

133. The dependents of soldiers who were residents of Massachusetts were eligible for direct cash assistance from the state as well as aid from private organizations such as the Committee of One Hundred. This limited assistance was desperately needed by many families. The dependents in the black regiments who did not live in the Bay State (and a majority of the volunteers came from outside Massachusetts) could not receive these benefits. Miller, "For His Wife, His Widow, and His Orphan," 74–76.

134. Keith P. Wilson, *Campfires of Freedom: The Camp Life of Black Soldiers during the Civil War* (Kent, Ohio: Kent State University Press, 2002), 178.

They also refused an offer from Governor Andrew and Massachusetts officials to pay them the wage difference between white and black soldiers. Wilder was deeply moved by their integrity and moral courage and found it especially remarkable that they performed so bravely at the battle of Rivers Causeway at a time when they felt betrayed by their government. The dignified and principled conduct of the black enlisted men had a major influence on Wilder's later writings and public presentations.[135]

Wilder's entries on the impact of the pay controversy touch on other themes. The black soldiers believed that, because the government had broken its contract with them, they should be allowed to withdraw their services, and many officers in the 55th Massachusetts accepted the logic of their position. Indeed, President Lincoln received a letter signed by seventy-four enlisted men in the regiment's Company D that demanded their back pay and "our imediate [*sic*] Discharge Having Been enlisted under False Pretence as the Past History of the Company will Prove."[136] The men would have known that, a month earlier, their colonel had asked the secretary of war to muster the regiment out of service "for the reason that the men have not been paid according to the contract made with Government."[137] Wilder, a sophisticated New Englander with important contacts in the North, believed that if Congress adjourned without resolving the issue, it would be impossible for the regiment to continue in service, and he worried about the likely loss of a valuable unit.[138] He was sufficiently convinced that the regiment might be mustered out that he began considering alternative employment if the regiment was disbanded. Wilder's diary also substantiates that the abilities or clumsiness of particular officers were key factors in how this issue unfolded. If Colonel Hartwell's insensitivity, as Wilder believed, fed the soldiers' sense of bitterness, then the diplomacy, tact, and firmness of men such as Fox and Grant prevented what might have been a full-blown mutiny in the 55th Massachusetts.[139]

The army's reluctance to commission any of the regiment's black non-commissioned officers also fueled the soldiers' sense of grievance. Although Wilder said relatively little in his diary about the struggle to

135. "Fifty-Fifth Massachusetts Volunteer Infantry, Colored" (a paper presented before the Massachusetts Historical Society, Brookline, 28 May 1914, Wilder Papers, CU); "Two Examples of the Negro's Courage"; "The Brain of the American Negro."

136. Berlin, Reidy, and Rowland, *The Black Military Experience*, 401–2.

137. Ibid., 398.

138. Diary entry for 23 April, 12 July 1864.

139. It should be noted that Wilder had developed a close friendship with Fox and felt little respect for Hartwell. Diary entries for 22 April, 15 June, 14 July 1864.

promote these men, he did describe the mixed reaction among the white officers when promotions did occur. The War Department had long been opposed to commissioning black line officers.[140] At the start of 1864, however, enlisted men in the 55th were publicly advocating the justice and benefits of offering commissions to qualified black sergeants. Wilder believed that several of the sergeants were "superior in all respects to many white officers that I have seen," and he hoped that they would be promoted.[141]

Within a few months, Governor Andrew, after appealing to Stanton and soliciting help from Senator Charles Sumner, exercised his gubernatorial authority to commission officers for state volunteer regiments, offering commissions to a few highly qualified freeborn blacks in the 54th and 55th Massachusetts.[142] Three qualified black sergeants in Wilder's regiment, John F. Shorter, James M. Trotter, and William Dupree, could not take up their commissions as second lieutenants until they had been mustered out as enlisted men. The War Department, however, ordered General John G. Foster, commanding the Department of the South, not to discharge the sergeants, thus leaving them in limbo.[143] Despite Wilder's hopes and expectations, the three sergeants were not discharged as enlisted men so that they could accept their commissions until 1 July 1865.[144] The long delay caused Trotter to "doubt our getting justice," while another

140. When Stanton authorized Massachusetts to raise black regiments, he reiterated that the regiments must have white officers, and the Bureau of Colored Troops followed that principle. There were two exceptions to this policy. The three Louisiana Native Guard regiments originally accepted by Gen. Benjamin Butler in 1862 all had black captains and lieutenants before Gen. Banks purged the regiments of their black officers in early 1863. The other category of black officers included a handful of chaplains and surgeons, the latter often contract surgeons, who were not in command positions. Hollandsworth, *The Louisiana Native Guard*, 15–16, 38, 43–44, 72–74; Glatthaar, *Forged in Battle*, 8–9, 36,124, 279–80; Berlin, Reidy, and Rowland, *The Black Military Experience*, 18–26; Smith, *Black Soldiers in Blue*, 260–61.

141. Trudeau, *Voices*, 62; diary entry for 19 January 1864.

142. Berlin, Reidy, and Rowland, *The Black Military Experience*, 307–8, 336–37; Glatthaar, *Forged in Battle*, 176.

143. In July, Trotter wrote to Edward Kinsley that "this *acting* Lieutenant is not at all pleasant when you reflect that no other thing stands in the way but our *color*. We, of course, have bought no uniforms yet as we do not know how it will end." Trudeau, *Voices*, 123; Berlin, Reidy, and Rowland, *The Black Military Experience*, 343–44; Glatthaar, *Forged in Battle*, 179.

144. Five other enlisted men, Charles L. Mitchell, Abram Shadd, Richard White, Martin Becker, and Armstead Jones, received commissions but were never mustered, because of the discharge of the regiment or because of their disabilities. Fox, *Record*, 28, 33, 108–9; Trudeau, *Voices*, 241.

enlisted man complained to the *Weekly Anglo-African* that, despite the regiment's heavy losses at places such as Rivers Causeway, "our noble government will still deny us just treatment." The writer believed that the black sergeants were denied their commissions "because *God did not make them White.* No other objection is, or can be offered. *Three cheers for 'our country.'*"[145] In a letter to "Franky" Garrison, son of William Lloyd, Trotter vented his frustration over being told by a white officer in the regiment that it was "too soon" and that "time should be granted the white officers to "*get rid of their* prejudices."[146]

More bitterness was generated in November 1864 when Charles L. Roberts, a white private in the 35th Massachusetts, was commissioned lieutenant instead of Dupree, especially because the black sergeants believed that Colonel Fox had played a role in Roberts's appointment.[147] Even when Shorter, Trotter, and Dupree finally received their commissions in early 1865 after being mustered out as sergeants, the black lieutenants faced hostility from white regimental officers. Wilder was particularly angered by Colonel Hartwell's apparent reversal of support for the new black officers and chagrined that his friend Fox "seems to be giving way to prejudice in the matter."[148] Yet, despite any prejudice that may have been displayed in early 1865, no officer resigned, and the black officers, including two who had never been mustered in as officers, were regular members of the Association of Officers of the 55th Massachusetts for many years after the war ended.[149]

Given the soldiers' belief that they had been treated badly by their government, the combat performance of the 55th Massachusetts which so impressed Wilder was all the more remarkable. In early July 1864, the regiment took part in a well conceived but complex and badly implemented offensive against Charleston. The 55th was part of a column attacking Battery Lamar and the Confederate fortifications on James Island. Although

145. Trudeau, *Voices*, 127.

146. Trotter not only shared a friendship with William Lloyd Garrison's son Francis but was also on good terms with Lt. George T. Garrison. Trudeau, *Voices*, 141.

147. Ibid., 157.

148. Diary entry for 30 June 1865.

149. Shorter died shortly after the regiment was mustered out, but Trotter and Dupree regularly attended all meetings of the association, as did Charles Mitchell, who had been discharged for disability after Andrew had commissioned him but before he was mustered in as an officer. Abram W. Shadd, who was practicing law in Mississippi, was also recognized, on his death, as a member of the association by the other officers although he had never been officially mustered in as second lieutenant. Record Book of the Association of Officers of the 55th Massachusetts, Wilder Papers, CU; Fox, *Record*, 108–9.

the black soldiers showed conspicuous courage and initiative in capturing two guns at Rivers Causeway, the separate attacks on James Island and elsewhere were too uncoordinated to succeed. The regiment lost more than two dozen men and several officers before the attack was finally called off.[150]

Four months later the 55th Massachusetts took part in a Union attack on Honey Hill, eighty-four miles southwest of Charleston. General John P. Hatch planned to cut the Charleston and Savannah Railroad in the vicinity of Grahamville, but he was blocked at Honey Hill by hastily organized South Carolina and Georgia troops.[151] Once again, poor planning and critical mistakes by Union commanders allowed Confederate reinforcements to occupy strong defensive positions before the Union attack.[152] The black soldiers were forced to attack the enemy's fortifications on a narrow front across a swampy creek bordered by thick undergrowth that impeded movement. The "terrible fire" of the Confederate artillery and muskets shattered repeated attacks by the 55th Massachusetts despite the courage of the officers and men.[153] At dusk the Federal troops broke off the action and retreated to Boyd's Neck, where they could be supported by the navy's gunboats. The attack had cost the regiment 137 officers and men, about half of the officers and a third of the enlisted men engaged in the attack.[154]

Much of Wilder's diary has less to do with regimental politics or military actions than with his day-to-day life in the regiment and his fascination with things around him. Notwithstanding the exigencies of wartime service, Wilder was very conscious that his time serving on the southern Atlantic coast provided him with an exceptional chance to expand his scientific knowledge of the region's fauna. He devoted much of his free time to collecting samples, preparing specimens, and dissecting whatever new species he could collect, from sea turtles to shovel-nosed sharks.

150. Fox, *Record*, 29–31; Trudeau, *Voices of the 55th*, 119–22, 125–27.

151. Gen. Henry W. Halleck ordered Foster to cut the railroad after he had received confirmation from Gen. William T. Sherman that he would be at the coast by the first of December and a request to break the Charleston and Savannah Railroad to cut off the Confederate forces in Savannah. Leonne M. Hudson, "A Confederate Victory at Grahamville: Fighting at Honey Hill," *South Carolina Historical Magazine* 94, no. 1 (June 1993): 19–20.

152. Honey Hill was one of the locations along the rail line that Gen. Robert E. Lee had fortified in 1862. Hudson, "A Confederate Victory at Grahamville," 22.

153. *Official Records*, ser. 1, vol. 56, 428.

154. Fox, *Record*, 44.

Some of his discoveries he sent back to Wyman to add to Harvard's collection.[155] As his scientific interests became known, officers and soldiers from different regiments began to arrive at his tent with exotic flora and fauna. He could boast that few other collectors had brigadier-generals providing them with specimens. Given Wilder's training and early interests, it was natural that he would be excited by the new spiders that he encountered. However, he also involved other officers in the regiment in collecting spiders and winding hundreds of yards of silk from them for handmade jewelry. One of them, Major Sigourney Wales, even designed a small crank-powered machine by which hundreds of yards of silk could be drawn out of the spiders.[156]

Some of the officers may have been intrigued by the novelty of the activity or seen it as a diversion, but they were also motivated by something else. The commercial possibilities offered by the region's resources encouraged many Northern officers who served in the South to think of business ventures there. While little became of the commercial venture of drawing silk from spiders, for a time officers such as Fox, Wales, and John Mowry devoted their time and energy to, and even envisioned investing sizable capital into, Wilder's research with the spiders–they were serious enough that they patented Wales's machine.[157]

Wilder's diary also reveals the important role that music played in the lives of both the enlisted men and the officers.[158] Many of the fellow officers with whom he shared a strong bond played instruments or were accomplished singers. During the war, music served as an important recreation and release from stress not just for the officers but also for the men. Fox noted that on the evening of the arrival of the first squad of recruits at Readville, and after roll-call and a spontaneous prayer by one of the men, "the whole squad joined in singing one of their peculiar hymns." It was a practice followed by other companies when they were formed in Massachusetts and it led to the formation of a number of glee clubs. The best of these groups, Fox claimed, came from Company F, and

155. Wyman set up the Museum of Comparative Anatomy housed in Boylston Hall in 1858, based initially on his own extensive collection of specimens. Wilder was happy to supply the museum with specimens. Appel, "A Scientific Career in the Age of Character," 104–7.

156. Diary entries for 29, 31 October, 13, 19 November 1864.

157. Diary entry for 19 April 1865.

158. Wilder found his release from the hardships, suffering, and tensions of the war in studying, playing his flute, and riding. His passion for music was shared by many men in the regiment.

Wilder frequently mentions them. Even before the regiment left Boston, the musical abilities of the men were attracting visitors, including the governor.[159] A fund was quickly established to buy instruments, and, before the regiment sailed south, a band of seventeen of the youngest recruits had been established and they "played with effect" as the men marched through Boston.[160] Symbolic of the role of music in the regiment was that in October 1864 it was a hymn composed by an enlisted man, "All Hail," that was sung by all the soldiers to celebrate the granting of equal pay.[161]

Wilder's involvement with music continued long after he left the army. Near the end of his career at Cornell, he began to compose regularly. He set two well-known American poems to music—Oliver Wendell Holmes's "Old Ironsides," and Joyce Kilmer's "The Peacemaker"—and composed the "Founder's Hymn" in honor of Ezra Cornell.[162] For Wilder, music was intertwined with his sense of social activism. He was able to combine his musical creativity with his advocacy of racial justice by writing the words and music for "Fiat Justitia," an international hymn that was used for the first Universal Races Congress in London in 1911 and that was picked up by a number of black schools and colleges.[163]

The pages of Wilder's diary capture much of his complex personality—strongly self-disciplined, with an intellectual muscularity and a reformist mindset. In many ways, Burt Green Wilder represented exactly the type of officer that Governor Andrew had wanted, a "gentleman of the highest tone and honor" with a commitment to duty and a faith in the African American soldier. He was also a fairly representative example of what historians of nineteenth-century American society have called the "culture of character." Certainly at Harvard "the slow and arduous process of achieving excellence of character" was of central importance.[164] Wilder was also a product of the reform tradition so prevalent in mid-nineteenth-

159. Fox, *Record*, 2.

160. Ibid., 3–4.

161. Wilson, *Campfires of Freedom*, 166. Wilson's book has an excellent chapter on the importance of music in the lives of the enlisted men.

162. He also composed the music for "Slumber Song" and "Last Night." "Biographical Sketch of B. G. Wilder," Wilder Papers, CU.

163. *New York Times*, 14 September 1925. His title was from the first words in the Latin legal phrase "fiat justitia ruat caelum," which translates as "let justice be done, though the heavens fall."

164. Appel, "A Scientific Career in the Age of Character," 96.

century New England. An abolitionist and a temperance advocate, he would also champion women's suffrage, serve in the Non-Smokers' Protective League, and sit on the Simplified Spelling Board. Yet he was also a man of contradictions. His "tenderness towards animals" prevented him from hunting or fishing for sport, but he annually collected hundreds of animals, primarily cats, for his dissection labs at Cornell.[165] He emerged as a trained scientist and evolutionist from the Unitarian-dominated Harvard, yet he belonged to the "New Church (Swedenborgian denomination)." He was proud of his physical abilities, especially his horse riding, but for years he strongly and publicly opposed interuniversity athletics, especially football.[166]

Wilder had had little contact with African Americans before he joined the 55th Massachusetts, but his accounts of his interactions with the black soldiers reveal a remarkably open mind for a mid-nineteenth-century American. His first impressions of the black soldiers upon arriving at Readville were positive. "These negroes are very nice folk," he wrote shortly after joining the regiment. "They don't drink, swear or quarrel as much as the white soldiers that I have seen so far."[167] After a month of service on Folly Island, he recorded, "I prefer them to the white soldiers in many respects," and he found them more stoical than the white officers whom he treated.[168] Given the growing respect that he felt for the black soldiers, it is not surprising that he welcomed the new black officers into the regiment, even if other white officers did not. "There are no finer men or better soldiers in the regiment," he wrote of Trotter, Dupree, and Shorter, "but they are looked down upon because of a little colored blood. Even Col. Fox seems to be giving way to prejudice in the matter. With all his faults Major Nutt is sound on that point."[169]

Wilder, however, was a man of his times and there were limits to his social progressivism. While he was angry when one of the sergeants of the 55th Massachusetts was denied access to a South Carolina train, he accepted limits to social change. "Of course it would be foolish and do harm to insist upon the southerners going further than we do in the north," he wrote, "and they may still exclude a civilian because he is colored: but

165. His advocacy of the painless but lethal use of chloroform was his solution to this particular contradiction.

166. Selkreg, *Landmarks*, 178; Comstock, "Burt Green Wilder," 532–33; Appel, "Scientific Career in the Age of Character," 96, 97.

167. Diary entry for 19 June 1863.

168. Diary entries for 7, 24 September 1863.

169. Diary entry for 30 June 1865.

all United States soldiers are alike, white or black, and if a colored soldier is decent and well-behaved he must be allowed the same privileges as a white one."[170]

Although Wilder displayed greater compassion to the black soldiers than many officers in the regiment, his rigid sense of discipline, and perhaps an element of paternalism that even he embodied, meant that he was willing to accept the sacrifice of an individual for the common good if necessary. In part, this may have stemmed from his belief that many of the black soldiers lacked the education or previous experience to understand fully what a dereliction of duty meant.[171] A number of times he felt that capital punishment was the least of two evils. The incident in June 1864, at the height of the men's anger over the pay issue, involving two soldiers' refusal to fall in for picket duty led Wilder to fear that it was a sign of what was to come. "In my judgment," Wilder wrote, "the two who refused should be tried by drum head court martial and shot: better two than risk artillery on the entire regiment if their pernicious examples spread."[172] He felt the same way when Corporal Andrew Smith shot Private Alfred Pelette, who was trying to desert and who had ignored the sergeant's order or the threat that he would shoot.[173] Wilder believed that the sergeant's "prompt action might be the means of saving the lives of others who might be tempted to follow Pelette's example & be shot for disobedience."[174]

Wilder's long-held belief in the need for discipline helps explains his terse account of his shooting of Private William Morris of Company G, who was outside the camp without a pass and who may have been deserting. When Morris escaped into thick bushes, Wilder gave two warnings to come back and then he and Major Wales fired into the bushes, killing the private. "Of course I am sorry," wrote the surgeon, "but the lesson was sadly needed; there were twenty men in the guard house for 'running

170. Diary entry for 29 June 1865. Decades later at the National Negro Conference, Wilder reversed the sentiment, saying that there were time that he was tempted to say, "Yes, a white man is as worthy as a colored man—provided he behaves himself as well." Wilder, "The Brain of the American Negro," 22.

171. Diary entry for 30 May 1864.

172. Diary entry for 15 June 1864.

173. Pelette would recover and desert again. Andrew Smith in Company B would end the war as color sergeant. At the battle of Honey Hill, he was the enlisted man credited with saving the regiment's flag. After the war, Wilder assisted Smith in an attempt to receive a Medal of Honor, but because there had been no "official recognition at the time," it was unsuccessful. Andrew Smith to B. G. Wilder, 3 March 1913, Wilder Papers, CU; Fox, *Record*, 119, 122; Trudeau, *Voices*, 169–70.

174. Diary entry for 30 March 1865.

guard.'"[175] A regimental examining board exonerated him, but, because many of the enlisted men wanted a more objective review, Wilder requested a board of inquiry formed outside the regiment; in the end, however, that board merely accepted the first report. Perhaps Wilder's conscience, or his sense of fairness, caused him to seek out the entry in George Garrison's diary to provide a third-party account of the incident.[176]

Certainly it was Wilder's sense of personal duty and obligation that led him to add the following footnote to his paper to the National Negro Conference: "Should the writer be spared until other conditions permit, he will regard it as a sacred duty to put in a form accessible to others his observations and impressions of the military and personal conduct of the Fifty-fifth Massachusetts as recorded in daily letters, all of which have been preserved."[177] Wilder was working on his Civil War material the day before he died.

EDITORIAL NOTE

The document now held as part of the Burt Green Wilder Papers at Cornell University Library under the title "Burt Green Wilder Diary (typescript in 1910), 1863–65" has a more complex provenance than first appears. It is in the format of a diary with almost daily entries, but it was never a true diary. Starting in November 1862, Wilder wrote almost daily letters to Sarah Cowell Nichols, a former schoolmate and his future wife, and these letters were all kept, at least until sometime after 1910.[178] In that year, facing retirement from Cornell University, Wilder envisioned writing a "Record and Recollection" of his Civil War experiences that would deal with his service as a medical officer in the 55th Massachusetts. Over a two-month period, starting on 30 August and finishing on 29 October, he "copied on the typewriter the historic portions of the letters."[179] As the finished document revealed, Wilder was only an adequate typist. As he transcribed the

175. Diary entry for 5 June 1865. Wilder believed, perhaps not accurately, that the men were angered by Wales's action but that they "have nothing to say against me."

176. Wilder would have also been aware of the Garrison family's close friendship with James Trotter, who was a conduit for the attitudes of the enlisted men.

177. Wilder, "The Brain of the American Negro," 54.

178. Wilder had attended Brookline High School with Sarah, and they were married on 9 June 1868. She died 17 November 1904. There is remarkably little personal information on her in the Wilder Papers. On 11 June 1906 Wilder married Mary Field, a pupil of his at the Anderson Summer School of Natural History. Mary died of Bright's disease in February 1922 after an extended illness.

179. By this he meant that all personal references to Sarah were removed. B. G. Wilder to A. Lawrence Lowell, 27 June 1914, Wilder Papers, CU.

letters into the new "diary" format, he indicated the date of the transcription at the top of each page that he completed. As he went through the Civil War letters, he occasionally added questions to himself in parenthesis in the text, questions that he presumably planned to answer in the final draft.

Starting at this time, and continuing for the next four or five years, Wilder began extensive communications with former soldiers, both black and white, Union and Confederate, who had served alongside or fought against the 55th Massachusetts at James Island or Honey Hill. Frequently he sent the veterans a list of questions about the deployment of troops, lines of advance, and the exact order of engagement in the fighting at the two places. He also contacted R. E. Mellichamp, an Episcopal minister in Charleston who had published a history of James Island with maps, to get better information on the topographical nature of Folly, Morris, and James islands and to ensure that he had the correct place names.[180] Wilder's letters reveal that even a trained naturalist was not always exact in his observations. "I never cease to regret," he told Mellichamp, "paying so little attention to certain features while on the island in 1865."[181] Wilder also sought to refresh his mind by revisiting the parts of the South where he had served and by examining official documents in Washington.

Despite all of Wilder's communications and personal research, he made very few alterations to the transcription that he finished in 1910, although he did incorporate much of the new information into talks he gave on the black troops and into an extended pamphlet on the 55th Massachusetts that he wrote in 1914.[182] The limited changes that Wilder made were scattered through the 1910 transcripts but concentrated more heavily around the regiment's combat experiences. There Wilder frequently scratched out words or whole phrases and penciled in new additions. True to his pledge not to include events that he did not personally see or hear, the alterations were all, at least in his mind, made for the sake

180. Although he provided Wilder with information, Mellichamp's letters indicate that the spirit of reconciliation had not overwhelmed all South Carolinians. "You talk of writing a book," Mellichamp wrote, "by no means mention me at all—as giving any information or otherwise." R. E. Mellichamp to B. G. Wilder, 23 August 1913, Wilder Papers, CU.

181. B. G. Wilder to R. E. Mellichamp, 6 May 1914, Wilder Papers, CU.

182. The pamphlet on the history of the 55th Massachusetts was first printed in 1914 and then reprinted in 1917 and 1919. The popularity of this publication (in addition to frequent requests for one, two, or five copies, P. A. Jenkins requested one hundred and Orville T. Chamberlain, commander of the army and member of the Navy Medal of Honor Legion, ordered fifty pamphlets, for example) may have diminished Wilder's belief that he had to finish the project.

of accuracy and only augmented what he had originally written.[183] In 1914 he claimed to be "about ready to put into shape for publication material which I believe to be not only valuable to the historian but interesting to the public."[184] About this time, however, he admitted that the project had "taken more time than anticipated."[185]

Whatever his intentions, there is no record that Wilder did anything more with the 1910 manuscript, although both the Gorham Press and G. P. Putnam and Sons expressed interest in his project.[186] By 1915, he was giving talks on his experience as a medical cadet in Washington, and in 1919 he began work on a small volume on Dr. Oliver Wendell Holmes, although it also was never completed. Ill health, first of his wife and then of himself, marked the end of his active writing.

Wilder died on 25 January 1925. On his death, his papers and numerous personal effects were kept by his former nurse, Frances Sharf, who stored them in an unheated cottage in New Hampshire for the next twenty-eight years.[187] At some time during this period, the cottage was rented to loggers, following which Mrs. Sharf and her husband found "many of their possessions, including, she thinks, some of the Wilder material, damaged or missing."[188] In 1953 negotiations were begun that led to the current collection of Wilder papers being donated to Cornell University. By this time, the original letters written to Wilder's first wife had disappeared, although it is not clear if they had been lost while the papers were stored in New Hampshire or had been destroyed at some point after 1910 by Wilder himself. Certainly his daughter, Bertha Wilder Reed, believed the latter: "While he was a surgeon in the Civil War, he wrote almost daily to my mother—really a diary . . . But, for some reason—unknown to me—he destroyed all these documents. Anyway, that is my guess."[189] All that now

183. B. G. Wilder to F. T. Miller, 29 April 1913, Wilder Papers, CU.

184. Ibid.

185. B. G. Wilder to Richard G. Badger, 14 February 1913, Wilder Papers, CU.

186. Richard G. Badger to B. G. Wilder, 12 February 1913; B. G. Wilder to Richard G. Badger, 14 February 1913; Richard G. Badger to B. G. Wilder, 28 May 1917; P. G. Putnam to B. G. Wilder, 26 May 1914, Wilder Papers, CU.

187. Information in the acquisition file for the Wilder Papers suggests that there had been a series of disputes before and after Wilder's death between Sharf and Bertha Wilder Reid, one of Wilder's daughters.

188. Among the things that Sharf detailed but that do not exist now in the collection was a "manuscript, incomplete, of a novel about a drummer boy in the Civil War, on which Wilder was working at the time of his death." Bradford Reed to Edith Fox, 9 February 1953, acquisition file, Wilder Papers, CU.

189. Bertha Wilder Reed to Edith Fox, 3 February 1960, acquisition file, Wilder Papers, CU.

remains of Wilder's accounts of his service with the 55th Massachusetts is the 1910 manuscript.

As editor, I followed a number of protocols in preparing Burt Green Wilder's 1910 manuscript for publication so that readers could identify changes made by Wilder both in the initial transcription and then in the following years. Spelling errors made in the document that were clearly the result of sloppy typing or missing letters (for instance, "hte" for "the" or "c mment" for "comment") have been corrected without indication. Consistently misspelled words or older conventions (Wilder spells General Gillmore's name as "Gilmore," refers to General Schimmelfennig as "Schimmelpfennig," and uses "honour" for honor) are noted and left in place. Words misspelled once but spelled correctly at other times (except proper nouns) have been corrected. The grammar and punctuation original to the manuscript have not been changed.

While typing the original transcription of his daily letters, Wilder clearly deleted personal material about his wife, the exact nature of which will never be recovered. However, the new additions and alterations, made in 1910 and in later years, are identified wherever possible for the reader. The additions made to the 1910 draft in that year take two forms. At various points in his original transcription, Wilder inserted questions to himself, placed in parentheses, which he clearly planned to answer at some point in the future. He also added one new passage, written on 3 October 1864, as he transcribed his Civil War letters. The new material was drawn from one of Wilder's letters written home to someone other than Sarah Nichols, and it discussed the alleged cowardice of Lieutenant-Colonel Fox at Honey Hill.[190] *Italics* are used throughout the manuscript to identify material that Wilder included in the 1910 draft but that clearly was not original to the letters written to Sarah.

Then there is the matter of post-1910 textual changes. In the years after Wilder completed the transcription, he occasionally returned to his manuscript and made various revisions, all of which I have identified. Two new entries, written by other soldiers but addressing issues being discussed by Wilder, were inserted into the pages of his manuscript well after 1910. The fact that he would include material not written by himself and that contradicted his stated principle of putting down only what he personally heard and saw is an indication of how important he felt the ad-

190. Wilder does not indicate to whom the letter was originally addressed. One can speculate that the topic was not one that he wished to convey to Sarah. Diary entry for 25 December 1864.

ditions were.[191] The first insert is an account, written by a corporal in the 103rd New York, describing the execution of Private Wallace Baker for mutiny in June 1864, which augmented Wilder's original but short entry.[192] The second insert, added only in 1919, was taken from the diary of Captain George T. Garrison, an officer in the regiment and the son of William Lloyd Garrison, and reflected on the shooting of Private William Morris by Wilder in June 1865.[193] The contents make clear that Wilder had tried unsuccessfully to find additional material on this issue. Because these two inserts were not part of Wilder's 1910 transcription, I have placed them in **bold** type to indicate a later addition.

Another variety of post-1910 textual emendation consists of limited changes made either for stylistic reasons or because Wilder believed that the alterations, based on new material that he had obtained, improved his manuscript's historical accuracy. These changes, while few, fall into several categories, and in each case I have employed either ~~strikeout~~ or **bold** type or a combination of the two. Scattered throughout the transcription are a small number of changes, often simply the replacement of one word for another, that Wilder presumably made for stylistic reasons. One example of this type of alteration involves changing a verb from "~~started~~" to "**moved**."[194] At other times Wilder made minor adjustments to his language, as when he replaced "~~Before breakfast this morning~~" with "**This A.M.**"[195] For the most part, such alterations do not fundamentally alter the reading or intent of the original transcription.

Other changes in the text, however, are more important and may reflect the writer's different perspective in his later years. Especially in the later parts of the manuscript involving the regiment's combat, Wilder frequently crossed out the word "rebels" where it occurred and replaced it with either "confederates" or "enemy" (or he occasionally left the deleted

191. An important factor that limited any mention of black dissent in his letters to Sarah was Wilder's sense of discretion. In June 1864, for example, at the height of the enlisted men's anger over the issue of unequal pay and when some men were sullenly avoiding their duties, Wilder wrote, "Of course, these things must not be made public until they can no longer be concealed." Decades later, he may have wanted to capture more of the emotions of the time. Diary entry for 15 June 1864.

192. Wilder inserted this account into the pages of his manuscript on a separate page but indicated in pencil in the margin of the manuscript where it should be entered. Diary entry for 18 June 1864.

193. Wilder inserted the entry from Garrison's diary on a separate page. His intent appears to have been to add it to his diary entry for 5 June 1865.

194. Diary entry for 29 November 1864.

195. Diary entry for 17 August 1863.

word without a replacement). It raises the possibility that after 1910 Wilder, like many other Americans swept up in the spirit of reconciliation, had modified his attitude toward his opponents. In addition, the language that Wilder used in the entries where he returned to the site of one of the regiment's engagements and found unburied skeletons was significantly altered after 1910, perhaps for the same reason.[196]

In other places, the alteration of a single word may be an important indicator of a significant change of meaning as the scientist looked back on his writing. In an entry for September 1864, Wilder crossed out the word "public" and inserted "soldiers" from the following sentence: "This past year has done wonders towards convincing the ~~public~~ **soldiers** that the negro is entitled to be treated as a man."[197] Civil War historians will find such changes important.

Occasionally there are entries that have been rephrased or deleted entirely because of Wilder's concern for preserving his public image or propriety. Thus, in one case where he had voluntarily treated a young girl in Charleston who was ill with cold and fever, he altered his original diary entry to read: "She has a small white curly dog ~~which perhaps I can get~~ **with whom I made friends**."[198] Sometime after 1910 Wilder had second thoughts about an entry that described his response when he and a comrade were left on foot miles from their camp after their horses ran off.[199] He returned to the manuscript and penciled a line through the sentence "I fear we both ejaculated [a] short but expressive word, but it did no good." These changes are infrequent, but, because they speak to Wilder's core values, readers may find them interesting.

The few parts of the diary where Wilder made numerous changes all relate to the fighting done by the 55th Massachusetts. Accounts of the attacks at Rivers Causeway and at Boyd's Landing have been significantly modified from their original form. The explanation for these changes lies in the extensive communication after 1910 that Wilder had with Confederate and Union veterans who helped him re-create, to his own satisfaction, what really had occurred when the 55th went into action.

On one specific topic, the capture of two small cannons on the causeway, Wilder wrote numerous letters to veterans to establish exactly how the fighting progressed. At a time when veterans on both sides were dis-

196. Diary entry for 18 March 1865.
197. Diary entry for 29 August 1864.
198. Diary entry for 16 March 1865.
199. Diary entry for 29 March 1865.

puting whose regiment deserved more credit, Wilder clearly wanted to present a fair and balanced account of what had occurred. He also realized that, as a surgeon, he was always located several hundred yards behind the actual fighting and with a very limited view of what was happening. At the same time, he was keenly aware that black troops had not received the credit they deserved in many of the accounts of the Civil War, and he wanted to ensure that their contribution was properly recognized.

Wherever possible, I have identified in footnotes all persons mentioned for the first time in Wilder's manuscript. The footnotes have also been used to provide explanatory information where I thought appropriate.

The Civil War Diary of
BURT GREEN WILDER
1863–1865

J[udiciary] S[quare] H[ospital],[1] 1863

Sunday, May 3rd, I made quite a call upon Lt. Oakley and his wife whom I found in considerable anxiety as to whether her brother, a captain of the 7th (1st?) Wisconsin was not killed or mortally wounded; his name was in yesterday's paper, but now the news is suppressed and nothing can be known with certainty. . . . Perhaps wounded will arrive tomorrow, for if rumours be credited a great fight is in progress. Adams[2] and Rothrock[3] have been to call on the Baileys. Mrs. Bailey was very cordial and said she hoped we all would come as often as we had time and inclination.

¶ **Monday, May 4th, 7:20 P.M.** I have been at work upon a Report for Dr. Marsh[4] which he and Adams made out wrong and sent to Dr. Brinton,[5]

1. In June 1862, Wilder had entered the U.S. Army Hospital at Judiciary Square in Washington as an acting cadet. After three months of studying with Dr. Brown, he passed the required examinations to become a medical cadet. He was later detailed for special duty under surgeon John H. Brinton, "then engaged upon the *Surgical History of the War.* The Judiciary Square Hospital was one of the new pavilion-style hospitals built in 1862 at the urging of the Sanitary Commission. It consisted of ten separate pavilions with twenty beds each. The pavilions were raised three feet off the ground as part of a ventilation system. "Biographical Sketch of B. G. Wilder," Wilder Papers, CU; Ira M. Rutkow, *Bleeding Blue and Gray: Civil War Surgery and the Evolution of American Medicine* (New York: Random House, 2005), 150, 155, 166.

2. James Foster Alleyne Adams, Wilder's "most intimate friend" and a schoolmate, also worked as a medical cadet in Washington. He later practiced medicine in Pittsfield and wrote *Malaria in New England* (1882) and *The Health of the Farmers of Massachusetts* (1874). Wilder Papers, CU.

3. Joseph Trimble Rothrock, a Pennsylvanian and fellow student of Wilder's at Harvard, graduated with a B.S. in botany in 1862. Enlisting in the Union Army, he reached the rank of captain in the 20th Pennsylvania Cavalry before being seriously wounded at Fredericksburg. Wilder Papers, CU.

4. Asst. Surg. E. J. Marsh was in charge of Judiciary Square Hospital. He recommended Wilder for the position of assistant surgeon. Wilder Papers, CU.

5. Dr. John H. Brinton of Philadelphia, one of the top doctors to pass the Regular Army Medical Corps examination, graduated from Jefferson Medical College in Philadelphia and studies in Paris and Vienna before teaching at his alma mater. After serving in the field in the West, he was recalled to the surgeon general's office in Washington in June 1862. He then became the first curator of the new United States Army Medical Museum and was influential in creating the six-volume *Medical and Surgical History of the War of the Rebellion* (1870–88). His memoir, first published in 1914, has been reprinted. *Personal Memoirs of John H. Brinton, Civil War Surgeon, 1861–1865*, foreword by John Y. Simon, preface by John S. Haller (Carbondale: Southern Illinois University Press, 1996); Rutkow, *Bleeding Blue and Gray*, 245–49.

who returned it; putting it in shape takes as much time as at first and is more perplexing. I walked near the Surgeon General's[6] office this afternoon, but did not feel like speaking to him. Indeed, if it were not for the idea of going to the field I might defer saying anything till after the arrival of the wounded who should soon arrive. Or course you have the glorious news of our victory; we have almost despaired of any real success upon the Rappahannock, and this is all the more inspiriting.[7] It is strange in this city; no one is excited; there are no crowds in the streets near the newspaper offices; no public demonstrations of joy. In Boston it must be very different. . . . Adams seemed to be quite charmed with Annie Bailey; their relations amuse me; they are a good deal alike, bright, lively and rather sarcastic; by some chance they always sit together when he is there, generally all the evening, and carry on a rattling conversation; they certainly seem to enjoy each other immensely.[8] Before breakfast this morning I wrote an abstract of my communication (to the Potomac Side Naturalists Club?) so as to condense nearly fifteen pages into two; this evening I must preside in regular turn; the entertained of one evening being the president at the next; so I shall not feel called upon to make any communication this evening. The negro (soldier?) whose leg was cut off died at 3:30 P.M. yesterday, I suppose because he had lost so much blood in the first place, for neither the accident nor the operation would, in themselves, be sufficient to cause death.

11:30 P.M. The meeting was quite interesting and we stayed till it seemed as if no one ever would leave, so we came away.

¶ **Tuesday, May 5th, 7:30 P.M.** It gives me much pleasure to find that you are willing I should go to the field as surgeon. The position is certainly not perfectly safe, and we cannot count upon coming out unhurt or even

6. William Alexander Hammond, a native of Maryland who received his medical degree from the University of the City of New York in 1848, was appointed surgeon general in April 1862 and revitalized the Medical Department. His opposition to the use of calomel and antimony and his advocacy of advancement based on merit rather than seniority led to a politically motivated court-martial and his removal from office. He later founded the American Neurological Association, an organization in which Wilder became prominent. Michael A. Flannery, *Civil War Pharmacy* (New York: Pharmaceutical Products Press, 2004), 19, 150–55.

7. In fact, by May 4, Lee had defeated the Union forces under Gen. Hooker at Chancellorsville and driven them back across the Rappahannock. Presumably, Wilder was responding to earlier reports of success.

8. They were married on 20 October 1870. "Reflections on Life as a Civil War Medical Cadet," Wilder Papers, CU.

alive; but some one must go and why not I? This morning, being at the Surgeon General's on business, I met him at the door and spoke to my desire to learn whether I could be discharged at any time; he said I would and that he had told Dr. Brinton to so inform me. On returning I found a letter (from Brinton?); this leaves me perfectly free to seek another position. I shall send a letter to General Wild[9] with certificates from Wyman,[10] Page,[11] Marsh and Brown[12]. (Was Wild organizing a colored brigade then?) Of course, even if sure of another position, I shall not leave here at once, for the 150 men were transferred elsewhere or returned to their regiments today in anticipation of the arrival of wounded. Recitation came today; perhaps we shall now take up a Surgery in addition to this book on Medicine. . . . Florence Bailey says Topsy is very well, and Eva is now making great sport among my boots and shoes.

¶ **Thursday, May 7th, 7:45 P.M.** As was anticipated the wounded, about fifty, came at 9:00 a.m. and everyone has been full of work all day. Many are bad cases; two or three shot through the lungs, one through the head, and many in the body or legs; one, shot through the knee, had his limb amputated at the thigh this afternoon; in this case, what has been done

9. Edward Augustus Wild, a doctor in Brookline, Massachusetts, before the war, served as captain in the 1st Massachusetts and colonel of the 35th before losing his right arm at the Battle of South Mountain. While recuperating, Gov. Andrews asked him to help in the selection of officers for the black Massachusetts regiments. Wild was made brigadier general and ordered to raise a black brigade in North Carolina. In order to encourage Southern volunteering, the 55th Massachusetts was to be the "nest egg" of the brigade. Wilder frequently spelled his name "Wilde." Reid, *Freedom for Themselves*, 13–14, 23.

10. Jeffries Wyman, born near Boston, earned his medical degree from Harvard by age 23. He taught at Hampden-Sydney College in Virginia before returning to Harvard. By then his interests had shifted from medicine to comparative anatomy and anthropology. Wilder worked with Wyman at Harvard first as a student and then as an assistant after receiving his M.D. degree in 1866. For more on Wyman, see Toby A. Appel, "Jeffries Wyman, Philosophical Anatomy, and the Scientific Reception of Darwin in America," *Journal of the History of Biology* 21, no. 1 (1988): 69–94; *Dictionary of Scientific Biography, vol. 14* (New York: Scribners, 1970), 533.

11. Jesse Williams Page, born in Maine and trained as a doctor at the University of Maryland, was an inspector for the Sanitary Commission for the Department of North Carolina (Foster General Hospital, New Bern).

12. Dr. Francis H. Brown, born in Boston in 1835, received his medical degree in 1861 from Harvard, where he had studied with Wyman. He worked at the Judiciary Square Hospital while Wilder was a medical cadet. By 1864, he was the assistant surgeon at the United States General Hospital at Readville, Massachusetts. He was one of the founders of the Children's Hospital in Boston and wrote *Harvard University in the War of 1861–1865*. "Francis W. Brown," Wilder Papers, CU.

but once before in this hospital, I held the large artery with my fingers instead of using a tourniquet. Among the wounded are several rebels; one, from Virginia, is a perfect gentleman; all of them say they are tired of war. My work is as before. I take notes of special cases, and also act as Dr. Marsh's cadet for a dozen of the more severe cases.

¶ **Friday, May 8th, 10:20 P.M.** We all have been very hard at work today, for a hundred bad cases came this morning and we may have more tomorrow. There were two amputations of the thigh this afternoon, and lots of dressing of wounds, so we did not get supper till nearly 8:30.

¶ **Saturday, May 9th, 9:45 P.M.** This evening I have been working on my report and making the evening visit with Dr. Marsh. One of our men, shot through the chest and with some ribs broken, died this evening, and two died in other wards. Before breakfast my nurse called me to a man bleeding fast from a large artery at the shoulder where the arm had been amputated on the field; I opened the wound at once by cutting the stitches while the nurse controlled the artery as well as he could by pressure behind the collar bone; but we could not take up the end in the wound and tie it until Dr. Marsh and Dr. Badger came; then I controlled the artery, Dr. Marsh took up the artery and Dr. Badger put a ligature about it and the man was safe; had it not been discovered in season he would have bled to death.

¶ **Sunday, May 10th, 7:30 P.M.** This morning came three letters from Surgeon General Dale,[13] from Prof. Wyman, and from my father. The first offers me a position in the 55th Mass.; Wyman is rather non-committal, but evidently does not advise my remaining here with no special chance for promotion; father is very desirous that I should accept. My chief reason for hesitating now is the needs of our wounded. Dr. Marsh does not like negroes and therefore does not advise me to go but he also says I ought not consider anything but my own advantage. I shall write Dr. Dale that I incline to accept. I do not understand why I should be needed by the 55th now and would much rather wait till the pressure here is reduced; still my

13. William Johnson Dale, born in Gloucester in 1815, graduated from the Harvard medical school in 1840 and practiced in Boston. Commissioned surgeon general of Massachusetts in 1861, he had general supervision of all matters connected with the state's medical staff. He became a brigadier general in 1863. *Appleton's Cyclopedia of American Biography*, vol. 2 (New York: Appleton, 1887), 57.

previous experience leads me to be cautious about refusing offers.[14] Adams and Rothrock strongly urge my acceptance, and the latter says he would accept a captain's commission in the same regiment; that would be splendid. I have been very busy today, not completing the dressing of the wounds of the bad cases till 2:00 o'clock, and having more to do in the afternoon. One of the sick in our ward was taken with spasm of the glottis this morning and could not breathe; in a few minutes he would have died had not Dr. Marsh cut a slit in the trachea just below the larynx and put in a tube through which he could breathe; some years ago I was present when the same operation was done upon one of Mrs. Edgerly's children by Dr. (now Brigadier General) Edward Wild.

¶ **Monday, May 11th, 10:10 P.M.** From a Boston paper received this morning I infer that the 55th is as yet very small, and Dr. Dales' desire for me as the "Acting Surgeon" may mean that I am expected to examine recruits; so this evening I have been studying the rules laid down (in the Army Regulations?) for that duty. This afternoon I went to the office of the Surgeon General hoping to see Dr. Brinton, but he was out. I asked Dr. Smith[15] (Assistant S.G. or Med. Director?) how long it would take to obtain my discharge and he said it could be done in a day; if there were not so much to be done at the hospital I cold probably get a leave of absence for seven days to go to Boston for the examination; but Dr. Marsh thinks it could not be granted. If I resigned and should not pass the examination I should be out of the service, and the opportunity of re-entering would be less than at first; also it might be less easy to leave when I wished.

¶ **Tuesday, May 12th, 7:30 P.M.** This morning I telegraphed General Dale that I should leave tomorrow night. I do not feel very certain as to what is best for me to do; Rothrock is sure it is best for me to try for the regimental position. One of my men who had been shot through the lungs died today; also the youth whom Major Ben Perley Poor[16] came for.

14. As Wilder would find out when he reached Readville, a regimental medical officer was necessary to ensure that the recruits were physically fit enough for the hardships that they would face.

15. Joseph R. Smith had replaced Col. R. C. Wood as the assistant surgeon general after friction developed between Wood and Surg. Gen. Hammond. Freemon, *Gangrene and Glory*, 178; Rutkow, *Bleeding Blue and Gray*, 244–45.

16. Benjamin Perley Poore, from an old Massachusetts family, became a widely popular newspaper correspondent, editor, and writer. He organized a company in the 8th Massachusetts and served, for a limited time, as major in that regiment. Donald A. Ritchie, *Press*

Camp Meigs,[17] Readville, Mass., 1863

Monday, May 18th, 8:30 P.M. I found Mr. Gooding's horse a splendid one and, so far as I can judge, worth the price, but he had arranged to sell him at auction next Saturday; so I took the refusal of him at $175.00. On the train were Gov. Andrew[18] and staff, General Dale, Professors Agassiz[19] and Rogers[20] and others. The flags were presented to the 54th and the surgeon of the cavalry regiment had a horse provided for me. This afternoon I examined a lot of men who had been passed by a surgeon in Buffalo; I rejected five of them; one had a sore leg, another weak lungs, and most of them were under size.

¶ **May 23rd, -** I have been at the camp all the week & very hard at work, for recruits have been coming in fast. I have to examine them & am gaining quite a reputation for strictness, rejecting half a dozen that had been accepted by the surgeon specially sent to Buffalo. We have nearly 400 men now. Yesterday I organized the hospital. The hospital steward is a German who has had five years experience in that capacity in the French army & seems well qualified. Whether he drinks or not remains to be seen. We have a good cook, nurse, wardmaster, & nine patients, some pretty sick. I have engaged a horse six years old from Mr. Gooding of Brookline; price $162:00.

¶ **June 12th, -** The surgeon, Mr. Brown,[21] arrived Tuesday afternoon. He took hold at once & examined fifty recruits Wednesday & seventy today.

Gallery: Congress and the Washington Press Gallery (Cambridge: Harvard University Press, 1991), 5, 73–79 Benjamin Perley Poore, *Perley's Reminiscences of Sixty Years in the National Metropolis* (Philadelphia: Hubbard, 1886), vol. 2.

17. Camp Meigs, a training camp located about ten miles southwest of Boston in Readville, had been established in 1862. Both white and black regiments were formed here. Yacovone, *A Voice of Thunder*, 23, 235–36.

18. John Albion Andrew, the governor of Massachusetts from 1861 to 1866, was a driving force behind the enlistment of black regiments in the state. Sifakis, *Who Was Who in the Civil War*, 12.

19. Born in Switzerland in 1807, Jean Louis Rodolfe Agassiz came to the United States in 1846 and two years later accepted a position at Harvard in zoology. Edward Lurie, *A Life in Science* (Chicago: University of Chicago Press. 1960).

20. William Barton Rogers, a respected geologist and educator, moved to Boston in 1853. An important force in the establishment of the Massachusetts Institute of Technology, he was its first president. Elliott and Rossiter, *Science at Harvard University*, 79, 82, 110–11.

21. William Symington Brown was a Scottish physician living in South Reading at the start of the war. He had previously served as assistant surgeon in the 34th Massachusetts Volunteers. Fox, *Record*, 99.

There are twenty sick in the hospital & forty in quarters; we now have 850 men & will soon be full. At the Boston Society of Natural History last Wednesday I read part of my graduation thesis; it will be published after it is put in shape this summer. I like my horse greatly.

¶ **June 19th,** - These negroes are very nice folk. They don't drink, swear or quarrel as much as the white soldiers that I have seen thus far.

¶ **June 28th,** - So far I like our officers very much. Last evening I called on Dr. Bowditch whose summer place is at the foot of Blue Hill near by. Both he & Mrs. Bowditch are very helpful to our soldiers. James Freeman Clarke[22] is to preach to us this afternoon. The guns have come & our men look quite [like] soldiers.

On board the steamer, "Cahawba," 1863
Tuesday, July 21, noon. If my boy[23] does not arrive in time let him return to camp and come on with the sick.

¶ **Thursday, 23rd, 9:00 P.M.** We had quite bad weather Tuesday afternoon but it has been bright since yesterday morning. Like most of the others I was seasick and could keep nothing on my stomach till one of the captains offered me a glass of claret which gave me great relief. Last night I got a bottle for the quartermaster,[24] who was much worse off (He and I are room-mates), and gave part to the chaplain[25] and Dr. Brown who room together. Today I have been able to eat a little; the band played this evening and then some of the officers sang. The quartermaster told me last night that his wife could not bring herself to admit that it was

22. James Freeman Clarke was an influential Unitarian minister, a social reformer and opponent of slavery, and a prolific author who wrote *Anti-Slavery Days: A Sketch of the Struggle Which Ended in the Abolition of Slavery* (Boston, 1883). Richard S. Newman, *The Transformation of American Abolitionism: Fighting Slavery in the Early Republic* (Chapel Hill: University of North Carolina Press, 2002), 4, 193.

23. Frank E. Thayer, age 10 from Dedham, became Wilder's orderly. He was later a merchant in Springfield. Wilder Papers, CU.

24. Lt. George B. Mussey, a teacher and resident of Edgartown before serving as quartermaster sergeant in the 1st Massachusetts Cavalry, was commissioned as quartermaster in the 55th in May 1865. Fox, *Record*, 100.

25. William Jackson was born a free black in Norfolk, Virginia, before his father moved the family to Philadelphia following the Nat Turner insurrection. A Baptist pastor, he was living in New Bedford when he was appointed chaplain of the 55th Massachusetts. Fox, *Record*, 101.

his duty to go to the war again; how hard for them both (better if he had not).

¶ **Friday, 24th, 1:00 P.M.** The water is smooth and the weather is fine; already we feel the change of latitude, and less need as to clothing. The voyage has done much to make the officers acquainted with each other; I have been interested in observing them; some are very fine fellows, especially Captains Soule,[26] Goodwin,[27] Bowditch[28] and Pratt,[29] and Lt. Thurber.[30] Land is now just visible and Lt. Col. Hartwell[31] is kneeling be . . . **[Last part of sentence runs off the page and is unreadable.]** . . . of porpoises at which there was much ineffective firing of pistols and guns by both officers and men till I protested (Why?) against the men being allowed to use their guns. Billy is quite well although, like other horses, he is tired with standing so long; the stalls are too narrow for lying down. I am not sure that they were seasick but they eat little the first day. Yesterday Billy eat the fodder of the horse next to him first and then his own, so he evidently was not seriously ill then. They were hoisted on board separately in a box, and most of them were scared. Frank's mother came to the steamer Tuesday in a carriage and said she had been much troubled about him; for although she had told him he might go in a good position

26. Capt. Charles Carroll Soule, born in Boston, graduated from Harvard College in 1862. He served first as a private and then as a lieutenant in the 44th Massachusetts before being commissioned in the 55th, where he commanded Company K. Fox, *Record*, 102.

27. Frank Goodwin, of Boston, served in the 44th Massachusetts before accepting a captain's commission in the 55th. He was breveted major in March 1865. Fox, *Record*, 102.

28. Capt. Charles Pickering Bowditch, of Boston, graduated from Harvard College in 1863. He commanded Company A, 55th Massachusetts, before transferring to the 5th Massachusetts Cavalry. After the war he would achieve fame as an archaeologist. Fox, *Record*, 102.

29. Capt. Wheelock Pratt, born into two generations of Massachusetts soldiers, lived in New York and Georgia before joining Company C, U.S. Engineering Battalion, in 1861. After accepting a commission in the 55th Massachusetts and while directing engineering work in front of Fort Wagner, he received a shell wound that led to his death three years later. Fox, *Record*, 90–91.

30. James Danforth Thurber, a native of Plymouth, had graduated from Harvard in 1858 and had previously served as a private in the 13th Massachusetts.

He was promoted first to captain and then brevetted to major by March 1865. Fox, Record, 103.

31. Alfred Stedman Hartwell, of West Dedham, graduated from Harvard in 1858 and taught at Washington University in St Louis before enlisting as first a corporal in the 3rd Regiment Missouri Reserve and then an officer in the 44th Massachusetts Volunteer Militia. He became colonel of the 55th Massachusetts and was brevetted brigadier general in November 1864. Fox, *Record*, 98.

he had gone off early one morning without telling her; however, since he had gone so far he might continue. I had a long talk with him and like him better and better; he has been very good on the steamer and has become a general favorite with offers and men. I had to take Jerry because Frank is not strong enough to care for the horse. 10 P.M. This evening I have been lying on the hatch way looking at the moon and listening to the singing of the officers.

¶ **Saturday, 25th, 10 A.M.** We are at anchor about three miles from Morehead City[32] waiting for the tide to turn and enable us to land. This is the most tedious part of the trip for we reached here at 6 and all expected to land at once. The Colonel[33] went ashore in a sailboat at eight. Assistant Surgeon Pease[34] of the 54th is on board.

3 P.M. All safely ashore. That night Q.M. and I had a fine supper of hardtack and sardines, with a precious lemon.

¶ **Sunday 26th.** We are encamped at Fort Spinola near (opposite?) Newberne.

¶ **Monday, 27th, 5 P.M.** We reached the wharf at Morehead City at noon and the horses were taken off first. The deck of the steamer was fifteen feet above the floor of the wharf. There was no box as in Boston, so a broad piece of canvas was put under the horse. Under each horse, in turn was passed a broad piece of strong canvas the ends of which, provide with iron rings, met over his back. Into the rings was put a hook at the end of a rope, and by means of a pulley the animal was hoisted from the deck and then lowered to the wharf; none was hurt but they were all astonished. Then the regiment was marched off the boat and up the railroad to some

32. Morehead City, Beaufort, and Fort Macon had all been captured by Union forces during March and April 1862. From Morehead City, a railroad line ran up to New Bern on the Neuse River. Robert M. Browning, Jr., *From Cape Charles to Cape Fear: The North Atlantic Blockading Squadron during the Civil War* (Tuscaloosa: University of Alabama Press, 1993), 35.

33. Norwood Penrose Hallowell, a Philadelphian, graduated from Harvard College in 1861. He served as lieutenant in the 20th Massachusetts before becoming lieutenant colonel of the 54th in April 1863. Two months later, he was promoted to colonel of the 55th Massachusetts. Fox, *Record*, 98.

34. Giles Moseley Pease, a native of Boston who attended Harvard College, served as acting assistant surgeon in the U.S. Navy beginning in late 1861 before joining the 54th Massachusetts.

woods where they waited while the stores were unloaded. Then a long train of open cars took us. A short halt was made at the scene of the first battle of Newbern[35] at which several of our line officers were present. The long breastwork is unchanged upon which our troops charged up the railroad. From Morehead City to Newbern is forty miles; at eight we reached this place, two miles from the city. It looked cheerless enough at first for nothing could be seen but a great plain. But at the other side of the plain is the camp of the 1st N.C. (colored)[36] and presently there came a colored surgeon[37] with an officer to take our sick into their hospital; this gave us time to provide for ourselves. Dr. Brown and Dr. Pease were met by friends who invited them to their camps. I was asked also but thought best to decline; the Q.M. says he thinks the colonel does not like it very well that Dr. Brown should leave the regiment. The Q.M. and I made a bed of boxes and blankets and slept soundly till morning.

8 P.M. The regiment has just marched in from the late brigade drill[38] and I went to speak to Gen. Wild who came along with our colonel. He greeted me cordially and asked about the conditions here. I knew he was very busy here and sent him the parcel from this wife. I was actuated also by dislike of the attitude of Dr. Pease who said he should call on him at once, remarking, "There is nothing like a little brass." Dr. Pease, not being on any special duty, contrived to go to General Wild's Headquarters and to be invited to join this regiment; he affected to regard the remark of

35. On 14 March 1862, Union forces under Gen. Burnside attacked Confederate fortifications below New Bern. After a short but fierce engagement, Confederate troops led by Gen. Lawrence O. Branch retreated to Kinston and Burnside's men occupied New Bern. Glenn Tucker, *Zeb Vance: Champion of Personal Freedom* (Indianapolis: Bobbs-Merrill, 1965), 122–25.

36. The 1st North Carolina Colored Volunteers was the first of the regiment raised in North Carolina that was to form, along with the 55th Massachusetts, Gen. Wild's African Brigade. Richard Reid, "Raising the African Brigade: Early Black Recruitment in Civil War North Carolina," *North Carolina Historical Review* 70 (1993): 266–301.

37. John V. De Grasse, who earned his medical degree from Bowdoin Medical School in 1849, was one of the very few black surgeons commissioned during the Civil War. Rayford W. Logan and Michael R. Winston, *Dictionary of American Negro Biography* (New York: Norton, 1982) 69; Robert G. Slawson, *Prologue to Change: African Americans in Medicine in the Civil War Era* (Frederick, Md.: National Museum of Civil War Medicine, 2006), 10, 11, 31, 33.

38. Wild was determined to have the black soldiers ready as soon as possible, so "much to the astonishment of all" in the 55th Massachusetts, the general had ordered a brigade drill the day after the Northerners had arrived. An enlisted man in the 55th was equally surprised that "the First North Carolina done better firing than the 55th, and as for drilling, I never saw a regiment, white or black, drill better." Fox, *Record*, 9; Trudeau, *Voices*, 37.

General Dale to Dr. Babbitt[39] as of little consequence, and to so impress Gen. Wild. When he spoke to me I said that I regarded what Dr. Dale said as conclusive, especially since he had told me that Pease was to join the 54th. Pease then interviewed Dr. Brown and Col. Hallowell, but came back to me reporting that while the former assented the latter felt it would not do, of which I was glad. Now Pease talks of joining one of the North Caroline negro regiments at Gen. Wild's suggestion. This incident has made me more unwilling to go to Wild's headquarters excepting on business. I am content to work myself into a higher position if I deserve it, and of that I am by no means sure; for a full surgeon ought to know much more than I, and even if the place is offered I shall accept it only in case no one can be had whom I think better qualified. . . . Frank is very smart and does a great deal for others as well as taking excellent care of me. He has just set up a small tent for himself. At Morehead City he bought a watermelon for 25 cents and then sold each half for as much.

Camp Newberne, N.C., 1863

Tuesday, July 28, 8:30 P.M. This evening I rode to Newberne but did not try to find Alice Ropes[40]. A gentleman connected with the contraband camp[41] brought me an invitation to take tea with them all on Sunday but I have not yet been able to go. She will be glad to see any one from the North. Newberne is a queer old town, not so dirty as might be expected, and with some very pleasant residences; it is finely shaded with trees. Most of the inhabitants are colored, but I met several whites, nice looking of both sexes. The camp is full of singing, all sorts and strangely

39. Warren Mason Babbitt, an assistant surgeon, graduated from the New York Medical College in 1858 and joined the 55th Massachusetts in September 1863. He was later appointed surgeon in the 103rd USCT. Fox, *Record*, 99–100.

40. Alice Shephard Ropes was the daughter of Hannah Ropes, feminist reformer and matron of the Union Hospital, Georgetown, D.C. After Hannah's death from pneumonia in January 1863, Alice moved to New Bern to teach the emancipated black students there. For more on the Ropes, see Hannah Anderson Ropes, *Civil War Nurse: The Diary and Letters of Hannah Ropes* (Knoxville: University of Tennessee Press, 1980).

41. Prior to 1864, there were three freedmen or contraband camps just outside of the New Bern fortifications. In January 1864, Confederate general George Pickett launched an unsuccessful attack on the Union enclave, during which a number of ex-slaves were captured or killed. As a result, a new camp, the Trent River Settlement, was established in a more secure position. Rev. Horace James, *Annual Report of the Superintendent of Negro Affairs in North Carolina, 1864–1865* (Boston: W. F. Brown, 1866), 7–8; Joe A. Mobley, *James City: A Black Community in North Carolina, 1863–1900* (Raleigh: North Carolina Department of Natural Resources, 1981), 24–25.

mingled, but the combination is not unpleasant. I pulled a tooth yesterday and another today.

¶ **Wednesday, July 29th, 9:10 P.M.** At five o'clock I started for Newbern, saw Gen. Wild; had quite a chat with his brother[42]; he directed me to the Rev. Mr. James,[43] where Alice Rogers lives. He was not at home. I took tea with Alice and three lady fellow teachers and a gentleman named Doolittle who brought the invitation. Alice and one other have three hundred pupils; they say they are docile, polite, and eager to learn and not at all unpleasant. There is great need of more teachers.[44]

¶ **Thursday, July 30, morning.** We are off on an expedition. I hope to do my duty.

On board the schooner "Recruit"

Sunday, Aug. 2, I have not yet recovered from the seasickness that afflicted many of us since leaving Hatteras Inlet Friday afternoon, so this letter will not be very lively. Thursday we were aroused at three o'clock by orders from General Wild to be ready as soon as possible after daybreak to leave for Charleston, S.C., where we learned our forces had been repulsed.[45] Our

42. Capt. Walter H. Wild acted as an aid to the general in the organization of the 1st North Carolina Colored Volunteers before commanding Company E, 36th United States Colored Troops (USCT). *Massachusetts Soldiers, Sailors, and Marines in the Civil War, vol. 7* (Norwood, Mass.: Norwood Press, 1933) 314.

43. Rev. Horace James, an evangelical Congregationalist from Worcester, was serving as chaplain in the 25th Massachusetts in North Carolina when he was appointed to be "Superintendent of all the Blacks" in the Department of North Carolina. After the war, he helped establish the Freedmen Bureau in North Carolina and tried unsuccessfully to run two plantations. Stephen Edward Reilly, "Reconstruction through Regeneration: Horace James' Work for the Blacks in North Carolina, 1862–67," Ph.D. diss., Duke University, 1983.

44. Almost as soon as Union forces occupied parts of the Confederacy, Northern aid societies began to send people and supplies south. Despite the initial opposition of the military governor of North Carolina, Edward Stanley, the superintendent of Negro affairs, Rev. Horace James, was able to organize schools for the freedmen and recruit Northern teachers, supported by Northern societies. By the start of 1865, the New England Freedmen's Aid Society had sent twenty teachers to the state, the American Missionary Society supported twenty-two, and the National Freedmen's Relief Society provided twenty-four teachers, of whom four were African Americans. James, *Annual Report,* 17, 20–23, 29–30, 40–44.

45. The 55th Massachusetts had been sent to North Carolina to serve as the core of a black infantry brigade to be raised in that state, but the failure of Gen. Quincy A. Gillmore to capture Fort Wagner led to his request for more troops. The 55th Massachusetts and the 1st North Carolina Colored Volunteers were part of the reinforcements sent to Gillmore.

horses and all baggage except the most necessary were to be left in the camp; Jerry remained to care for my horse.[46] Before seven the left wing of our regiment, consisting of companies D, H, I and K, under Major Fox,[47] marched up the railroad to Newbern where we were expected to embark on the schooner "Recruit"; but she was not on hand; showers came up and wet us some, but partial protection was afforded by some hay sheds on the wharf. At about ten a small tug took us to the schooner, and then, carrying some of the 1st N.C. regiment, tugged us down the river. As we passed the wharf at our camp we saw a steamer, the "Maple Leaf," just ready to start with the rest of our regiment on board, and a schooner in tow with more of the 1st N.C. Gen Wild was on a small tug. At the mouth of Hatteras Inlet we were met by the two mail steamers, one of which, the "Albany," probably carried our mail; so exasperating. Since leaving the Inlet we have been becalmed and have made only 60 of the 260 miles between Newbern and Charleston. There is nothing for us to do and there are only two books on board; so we lie around; most of us sleep on deck.

¶ **Monday, Aug, 3, 4:15 P.M.** I feel much better today, but share the general discontent over our inactivity when there is so much to be done at Charleston. At midnight a breeze sprang up, but in the morning it turned against us, and we have had to tack, making slow progress. Last evening it was so warm that I lay on my overcoat instead of putting it on, and when the cool breeze came up at midnight I awoke from a dream that I was in our house in Brookline and that a storm was rattling the doors and windows and I was running about to close them. This forenoon the major and I alternated in reading aloud Scott's "Life of Napoleon," the only large book on the vessel. Our officers are evidently reflecting seriously upon the great losses of the 54th at Charleston and speculating as to their own fate.[48] Some of them like this irregular kind of life but I do not, and I shall

---

Stephen R. Wise, *Gate of Hell: Campaign for Charleston Harbor, 1863* (Columbia: University of South Carolina Press, 1994), 119, 137–38; Reid, *Freedom for Themselves*, 40–42.

46. Wild expected that the move would be temporary and that the fledgling brigade would soon be back in North Carolina. He was wrong. Reid, *Freedom for Themselves*, 41, 67–68.

47. Charles Bernard Fox, a civil engineer in Newburyport, served in both the 13th Massachusetts Infantry and the 2nd Massachusetts Cavalry before joining the 55th as major. He was promoted lieutenant colonel in December 1863. Fox, *Record*, 98–99.

48. On 18 July 1863, Col. Robert G. Shaw and some 600 men of the 54th Massachusetts led the Union attack on Battery Wagner (more frequently referred to as Fort Wagner). The black soldiers forced their way into the fort and held parts of the wall for almost an hour before being pushed back. The attack cost the regiment its commanding officer and

be glad to get out of it when I can with a clear conscience. I mean to remain in the service during the war, but would prefer something more like what I was doing with Dr. Brinton. This afternoon we were for a time in the gulf stream; the water was of a lighter green with a peculiarly soft look. Several flying fish were seen by me for the first time. ~~I am so glad that I called on Alice Ropes.~~ There is not much sickness on board; we get decent meals for 25 cents.

¶ **Tuesday, Aug. 4, 1863, 6:15 P.M.** All day we have had adverse winds and are still 80 or 90 miles from Charleston; sending troops by sailing vessels seems a poor plan. While we were at supper there came up a shower with a gust so fierce as to tip the vessel and spill our tea into our laps; the wind has now ceased but the vessel is rolling and pitching uncomfortably.

¶ **Wednesday, Aug. 5, 6:30 P.M.** This afternoon a great sea turtle floated by; I have seen also sharks, flying fish and a dolphin (not the porpoise but a brilliantly colored fish). There is a cat on board with which I have made friends; but she lies most of the time in the cabin where I can stay only long enough to eat my meals; it is fortunate that the weather permits us to stay on deck; I pity the soldiers below.

¶ **Thursday, 6th, 7 P.M.** Last night there was a regular gale and now the waves are very high; we have had a glimpse of the land twenty miles to the south but Charleston harbour is still to see.

¶ **Friday, 7th, 6 P.M.** (comp. Fox[49]) Some ten miles out we were met by a small steamer with Gen. Wild and Lt. Col. Hartwell on board; it towed us in by the blockading fleet to our present position about 2 miles from Morris Island; this is covered with tents and at its city end is Battery Wagner upon which our unsuccessful attach was lately made. Sumter and Moultrie are in plain view, the former large, square, and apparently very strong. We have been anchored here about an hour, and have witnessed the shelling of a point near Moultrie by one of our gunboats; two of the shells burst in air but the other struck well, raising a cloud of smoke and dust. Sunset. The shelling has ceased and some of the vessels have steamed

---

another 272 killed, wounded or captured, 42 percent of its men, but it had a powerful symbolic impact in the North. Russell Duncan, *Blue-Eyed Child of Fortune: The Civil War Letters of Colonel Robert Gould Shaw* (Athens: University of Georgia Press, 1992), 50–55; Wise, *Gate of Hell*, 92–118.

49. Fox gives the date for this arrival as August 9. Fox, *Record,* 11.

farther from the forts. Sumter just fired a shell that exploded in the air near the gunboat that had been firing; this is my first glimpse of the actual war, and although distant and safe I seem to feel the dreadful spirit of destruction embodied in the shells. The "Crocker," that had the Lt. Col. and two companies on her arrived at about the same time and is at anchor near us; Major Fox has gone on board the "Mary Benton" to see the General and Colonel. Of the blockading squadron I can count more than twenty vessels, mostly large steam gunboats, and it seems almost impossible that a vessel should elude them.[50]

¶ **Sunday, Aug. 9, 11:30 A.M.** Last evening a sutler's schooner anchored near and we obtained some luxuries, condensed milk, butter, preserves and two huge watermelons.[51] The shelling continued at intervals last night but ceased at 9 this morning. Last night I had an example of the readiness with which negroes resign themselves to death when ill. A man who has been long subject to epileptic fits and who never should have been accepted, had four the other day and has been ill since; he had four fits last evening and insisted that he should die and that nothing need be done for him; his comrades and even the nurse had the same feeling; but I insisted on doing what I could for him; he passed a very comfortable night and this morning thanked me heartily. (Fox, p. 14–15, evening, sacred songs sung by men)

Folly Island

8 P.M. This afternoon we were towed over the bar, several hard bumps indicating the slight depth of water. The deck was considerably higher than the wharf so that the landing plank was quite inclined; in crossing several men fell, but even when their head struck the plank they made no complaint. We are on the best part of Folly Island, and close to the hard beach so that the breeze reaches us and bathing is convenient. I have a

50. Through 1862 and early 1863, Charleston was the South's main blockade running port. The Union campaign against Charleston ended this role and by October 1863 Confederate general Josiah Gorgas admitted that "the only port now left to us is Wilmington." The South Atlantic Blockading Squadron employed most of the Navy's monitors against the port and by the late summer, Adm. John A. Dahlgren had more than sixty warships under his command. Robert M. Browning Jr., *From Cape Charles to Cape Fear: The North Atlantic Blockading Squadron during the Civil War* (Tuscaloosa: University of Alabama Press, 1993), 266; Wise, *Gate of Hell*, 23–24, 212–14, 251–52.

51. A sutler was a civilian merchant licensed to sell provisions to the soldiers at a reasonable price, although the commanders of some black regiments were opposed to their presence. Wilson, *Campfires of Freedom*, 63–64, 70.

nice tent adjoining that of the Quartermaster. Frank has gathered a lot of dry palmetto leaves and they make a much more comfortable bed than the planks of the boat.

¶ **Monday, Aug. 10, 8:00 P.M.** I am very well but keep pretty quiet during the middle of the day. This morning I drew two teeth for a lieutenant.

¶ **Tuesday, 11, 8:45 P.M.** This is a curious sort of life and rather uncivilized; it would be more enjoyable were it not so hot. Also, leaving so suddenly as we did, and with expecting to return soon our hospital accommodations and medical supplies are limited. Soon after midnight one of the lengthwise poles of my primitive bed came out and let me down. At that time the cannonading was quite rapid and an alarm had been given in our camp by firing of the sentinels. The colonel and some other officers were about. I found two sick men needing attention. Frank worked like a hero this afternoon; got some more bed poles and fresh leaves for the bed and the floor; to the admiration and envy of the other officers he has planted some tree tops at the sides of the entrance to the tent. Men and officers bathe a good deal, but the beach slopes so gradually that the surf is pretty far out and there is some fear of sharks.

¶ **Wednesday, [August] 12th, 7:30 P.M.** On Morris Island they are mounting a great gun; it weights 27000 pounds and throws a ball of 300 pounds that is expected to make deep impressions upon Sumter.[52] Five hundred of our men were at work over there last night and the same number will go tonight. The Q.M. and I have just enjoyed a hearty laugh at the expense of Frank; the latter was telling me that when he went to the former to borrow the hatchet, the edge of which we had turned yesterday, he said "Aren't you a cheeky fellow?" And the Q.M. entered my tent just in time to hear his remark repeated and my comment that it was well merited. Frank had quite a tumble today from a plank set between the branch of a tree and the ridge of my tent; his ankle was sprained, but it is better now.

52. Wilder appears to refer to the famous "Swamp Angel," an eight-inch Parrott rifled gun established in a marsh battery to fire on Charleston, rather than to the ten-inch Parrott that fired on Fort Wagner. Work on the Swamp Angel battery was begun on the night of 10 August. The gun fired thirty-six times on Charleston before its breach burst on the night of 23 August. Sgt. Isaiah Welch of Company C wrote that he "stood on the parapets surrounding the 'Swamp Angel,' and saw men fall around me like hail-stones." Wise, *Gate of Hell*, 148–50, 169–72; Trudeau, *Voices*, 40.

¶ **Thursday, Aug 13th, 8:00 P.M.** Day before yesterday was my birthday but there was so much going on that I never remembered it till after going to bed last night.

¶ **Friday, 14th, 7:00 P.M.** Just before supper the Q.M., Major, Captains Crane[53] and Goodwin and myself had a magnificent surf bath; the waves were very high, higher than our heads, and I was overwhelmed several times.

This is the finest beach I ever saw, and were other conditions in keeping our stay here might be regarded as a delightful summer outing. The bathing is good for us all and will enable us to endure better what is in store for us. My own hardest work is done before breakfast. I rise at 5, take a cup of coffee, and am ready for "Sick-call" at 5:30. Many are ailing more or less, and I have to attend to 60, 70, 80 or even 90; but as the men become used to the climate and the poor water the numbers will be reduced. The hottest part of the day is between ten and twelve, when I lie down or read. Today I took five men and tried to go to Morris Island for Sanitary Commission[54] stores; but we failed because I had not secured a pass from the Brig. General in command. The Q.M. and Adjutant[55] have just been in here talking over things and from what they say it seems that our regiment is being called upon for an excessive amount of work. The colonel is evidently concerned about it. For the first time last night I was not roused by the bustle of making out a new detail for duty. I have just been to give the colonel something for an attack of nausea; I urged him to keep well covered to call upon me at once if necessary. His is a hard position, having to bear all the troubles of the regiment. Among other things he said he felt that the sick in the hospital were not adequately cared for; three

53. Capt. William Dwight Crane, of a prominent Boston family, left Harvard College to join the 44th Massachusetts before receiving a commission in the 55th. He was killed leading a charge at the Battle of Honey Hill. Fox, *Record*, 91–92.

54. The U.S. Sanitary Commission was established in June 1861 to coordinate (and appropriate) the volunteer activities of women wanting to contribute to the war effort. Jeffries Wyman was one of the original commissioners. It provided nurses and hospital and ambulance services for the wounded, raised money and donations for the soldiers, and more. It provided critical supplies for men like Wilder. For a detailed discussion of the work of the commission, see Maxwell, *Lincoln's Fifth Wheel*; Jeanie Attie, *Patriotic Toil: Northern Women and the American Civil War* (Ithaca: Cornell University Press, 1998); and Judith Ann Giesberg, *Civil War Sisterhood: The U.S. Sanitary Commission and Women's Politics in Transition* (Boston: Northeastern University Press, 2000).

55. William Penrose Hallowell, the colonel's older brother, was also a Philadelphia resident. He resigned owing to illness in February 1864. Fox, *Record*, 14, 100.

have died there since we arrived. He evidently did not blame me for they are under the immediate care of Dr. Brown. I told him that I had thought of asking the Sanitary Commission for supplies, but supposed Dr. Brown had got all he needed or could. But the Q.M. took my list of desiderata and got them this afternoon, so now we are pretty well supplied. We (Dr. Brown, the Chaplain and myself) eat at the hospital, where fair soup is made, supplemented by what can be had from the sutler; I live mainly on rice, peas, mush and molasses, with the inevitable hard tack and coffee; I have a good appetite.

¶ **Saturday, 15th, 7:15 P.M.** The colonel is up and better today. Lt. Garrison[56] sent for me today for a slight illness; most of the officers were on the boat with Dr. Brown and naturally consult him when ill.[57] I am somewhat lame from striking my foot against a root. Before breakfast I had 140 men to attend to, mostly for diarrhea, caused by the water. Yesterday I caught a pretty little snake, red and black, hence called the "calico"; it is harmless.

¶ **Sunday, 16th, A.M.** It is a lovely morning and not very warm. There has been no firing so far; it seems as if they might omit it on one day so as to let it be more like Sunday. Two nights ago I dreamed that we were attacking a small fort and that several officers were wounded and in need of attention; but I awoke before there was any time for operations upon them.

12:45 P.M. Dr. Brown has been in for half an hour and we have chatted more sociably than usual; but I fear shall never have much in common. It may not be right for me to say or even think so, but he seems to me to lack energy and industry; I might not do half so well in his place but I would try harder than he seems to. This is a barbarous way to live; my only means of cleanliness an undershirt and toothbrush; fresh water is too scarce to bathing purposes, but there is plenty in the ocean. We have no soap. My table is a rough box; my floor sand covered by palmetto leaves,

56. George Thompson Garrison, the eldest son of William Lloyd Garrison, was a printer in Boston before accepting a commission in the 55th Massachusetts. He was promoted to captain in 1865 and maintained correspondence with Wilder after the war. Fox, *Record*, 104; Wilder Papers, CU.

57. Wilder's observations may be accurate, but it was a common practice in Civil War regiments for the officers to be served by the surgeon while the assistant surgeons focused on the enlisted men. Of course, the officers, unlike the men, were able to seek aid from the medical officer in whom they had greatest confidence. Adams, *Doctors in Blue*, 65.

which also soften the irregularities of the poles constituting my couch; the foot of the latter is my seat. I am thankful for a tent to myself; the line officers are three in a tent. Another man died last night. The chaplain officiates at funerals and has charge of the mail. I do not fancy him; he is indolent; in spite of my predisposition to like him it chokes me to talk with him.[58]

¶ **Monday, 17th, 7:00 P.M.** It is raining quite hard. But the tent is impervious so far. Our meals today, as supervised by Dr. Brown, were beef steak **and potatoes** for breakfast, beef soup for dinner, and for supper a sort of plain pudding made of bits of hard bread soaked in water, tea and apple sauce; into the pudding Dr. Brown put a bit of salt pork in place of butter; I suppose it did no harm and that it may be difficult to escape the "abomination" altogether in the army, but I would rather go without. The Sick Call now comes ~~after~~ **before** breakfast the change pleases me. ~~Before breakfast~~ **This** ~~morning~~ **A.M.** I accomplished more on my thesis than on any day since leaving Readville; it must be completed soon for Mr. Scudder[59] will be asking for it. Brig. Gen. Vogdes,[60] in command of the island, called while I was studying our sick list this morning and said it was too large; and hoped I did not allow men to impose upon me and when not really ill; it makes me somewhat indignant for he has been taking our men, 400 or 500 at a time, and many of them have been out four or five nights in succession at hard work; I am determined that none shall go who are unfit. Dr. Squires, the chief medical officer on the island, also called and said he wished a "Morning Report" daily at 9 A.M. Dr. Brown was away at the time and when I told him he "waxed exceeding wroth" and said it was impossible; I think so too, but

58. Wilder's dislike of the black chaplain William Jackson was not unique. One of the enlisted men outlined some of Jackson's problems in a letter to the *Liberator.* He had heard that, as mail officer, Jackson had some disputes with the men; he had threatened to shoot one of the sergeants and had actually drawn his revolver. Jackson, the soldier wrote, "was never popular with the men, and for some time past they have been murmuring against him, as he never held service." Jackson resigned 14 January 1864. Trudeau, *Voices*, 60; Fox, *Record*, 101.

59. Samuel Hubbard Scudder, born in Boston, graduated in 1862 from Harvard College's Lawrence Scientific School, where he studied under Louis Agassiz. He became a leading American entomologist. Mary P. Winsor, *Reading the Shape of Nature: Comparative Zoology at the Agassiz Museum* (Chicago: University of Chicago Press, 1991), 35–37, 133, 164.

60. Israel Vogdes, a Pennsylvanian, graduated from West Point in 1837. In November 1862, he was a brigadier general commanding U.S. forces on Folly Island. Sifakis, *Who Was Who in the Civil War*, 677–78.

the responsibility rests with him. Frank always talks in the evening as long as I will let him; his remarks are never foolish and often entertaining for example, just now he said, I have caught a beetle that talks with his head; after I had shown how it was done he guessed he would learn a lot about bugs and things. I think it is good for me also to talk about common things and in a simple way.

¶ **Tuesday, [August] 18th, 7:30 P.M.** The wind is a gale and the air is full of sand, fine and penetrating; at supper the hominy gritted between our teeth (I believe there is such a cereal as "grits"). The whizzing of the projectiles is quite distinct even at this distance. This afternoon a colored regiment, said to be the 1st Phila., marched along the beach.[61]

8:30 P.M. The major came for me to ascend with him a sort of lookout near the camp so as to watch the firing; but we saw only one shell and two solid shot.

¶ **Wednesday, 19th, 10:40 P.M.** This afternoon I went to Morris Island for the first time, and have desire to go again; while there I did an hours work but six more hours were consumed in the passage owing to damage by the gale last night. Although the inlet is not one-fourth of a mile we were on three different steamers on the way. The Q.M. went with me, and on the return were several officers with their men coming back after the days work in the trenches; I got a cold supper at 10 o'clock, and have been making out some official papers.

First Account of the Silk Spider[62]

Thursday, 20th, 9:00 P.M. This has been an unusually busy day, yet I am conscious of accomplishing less than I should in a cooler and more invigorating climate. I arose at five and had my customary bath in the ocean. Then I conferred with Dr. Brown as to the drawing of ~~the~~ rations for the hospital, and till 6:30 worked on my thesis. After breakfast I prepared the report of the sick for the adjutant, with a duplicate for Dr.

61. Officially designated the 3rd USCT, this regiment under the command of Col. Benjamin C. Tilghman, was formed in Camp Penn in early August 1863. Unlike the 55th Massachusetts, however, it was not allowed to parade through the city when it left for war. *Christian Recorder*, 8 August 1863; Dyer, *Compendium of the War of the Rebellion*, 1726.

62. The spider from which Wilder would draw yards of silk proved to be a new species and was subsequently named *Nephila wilderi*. Wilder published a number of papers on it during his career, including one in the *Atlantic Monthly* in August 1866. Wilder Papers, CU.

Squires, the chief medical officer of the island, who very inconsiderately requires us to send him, three miles off, a report by nine o'clock. Sick call occupied me till eleven; then I drew a tooth and felt so weary that I laid down and slept till one. We had pea-soup for dinner. Then I talked with Dr. Bown about our affairs, and very seriously with the steward for not doing as well as I thought he should. Then I directed the work of four men putting up an extra hospital tent for use ~~as a dispensary~~ at the morning sick call. Since supper I have been attending to the Major, Lt. Colonel and Q.M., all of whom are more or less ailing. Three of the line officers are also under my care. Thus far I am the only officer who has not been ill; but most have been exposed at night and have had to work harder than I. Yesterday noon I caught a large and very handsome spider from which, as it remained quite near the top of my tent, I wound off silk at the rate of 6 feet a minute for an hour and a quarter; that made 450 feet or 150 yards; I sent the Quill on which it is wound, and hope the lovely color will remain.

¶ **Friday, 21st, 5:30 P.M.** At last I have letters from home.

¶ **Saturday, 22, 9 P.M.** Dr. Brown came in to borrow my artery forceps. Frank remarked, no one suits Dr. Brown, referring to a terrific scolding of the hospital cook for putting too much salt in the pea soup. Of course it was too salty for me, but such things seldom happened I said nothing. Dr. Brown is really quite undignified sometimes in his language and I fear the men do not respect him as they should the surgeon of the regiment. Frank says he has heard them call him "that old crabbed," and make uncomplimentary comparisons between him and that "black whiskered young doctor."[63] Their preference for me, however, gives me more to do, since they seldom apply to him for aid. Sometimes I lose my patience with them either for their stupidity or because I think some are deceiving me as to the extent of their illness.[64] Yesterday 200 reported themselves sick but this morning fewer and I cut down the excused ones to 140. It was a

63. In contrast to the descriptions of Brown left by Wilder (and Frank), Esther Hill Hawks described her former teacher as "genial" and recounted how enjoyable some of the women found his company. Schwartz, *A Woman Doctor's Civil War*, 90, 160, 162.

64. Surgeons had the ultimate authority to decide if enlisted men were fit for duty. In September 1864, a captain in the 6th USCT tried to intercede on behalf of one of his men whom he believed was seriously ill, even though the regiment was about to go into combat. The surgeon refused to be influenced and set the soldier back to his company. Paradis, *Strike a Blow for Freedom*, 69–70.

good occasion for a short but severe address to them on the folly and wickedness of such deception, wronging their comrades and me and their country; the good effect of my words was apparent in the demeanor and language of those who came to me afterward for advice and medicine. I began at 5:30 and with half an hour for breakfast was through at 10. Then there were various things to do, and afterward I read "Orly Farm" till dinner. After dinner I read aloud to Lt. Messenger[65] who is ill and unable to read himself; he was grateful and hopes I would again; he seems a good deal alone and I like him very well.

¶ **Monday, 24th 7:30 P.M.** On Saturday the Q.M. and I disagreed on a matter connected with the hospital supplies; he thought I was unreasonable and I thought him unaccommodating. Yesterday I was disposed to go to him on the old terms, but felt that I had not been in the wrong and so delayed. Also I had a presentiment that he would be ill and need my care. So it proved. After dinner he had an attack that I feared might end in common malarial fever; he sent for me and I remained all night in his tent, keeping cold water on his head till ten and then lying on the floor to rise frequently to do for him. At time he was slightly delirious. During today he improved and was about more or less. I was occupied and saw little of him. About five he sent me a nice lot of writing paper, and when I thanked him we gradually returned to our former cordial relations, and discussed many things together in the old fashion.

8:40 P.M. The wind has been rising all day and is now quite high; for the second time I have had to tie the flaps of my tent. Frank and I have made a floor and a more secure bed. From an ammunition box 18 inches long, 12 wide and 6 deep I have made a sort of pigeon-hole case for my table and shall find it very convenient. The big 300 pounder on which our men worked so hard was disabled Saturday by the premature explosion of a shell.[66] Fort Sumter can be seen with the naked eye in a clear day; it looks badly used; the two sides this way are full of holes and the intervening angle is broken down. I commonly rise soon after 4:30.

65. William Dorance Messenger lived in Peterboro, New York, before enlisting in the regiment. He resigned his commission in December 1863. Fox, *Record*, 15, 107.

66. On 22 August, after warning Confederate authorities that Charleston would be fired on if Morris Island and Fort Sumter were not evacuated, the marsh battery opened fire on the city, 7,900 yards away. Some sixteen shells were fired with some incendiary shells containing "Greek fire." The shelling continued on the evening of 23 August, before the thirty-sixth firing of the Swamp Angel exploded the gun's breech. The huge gun was not replaced. Wise, *Gate of Hell*, 169–72.

Tuesday, [August] 25th, 8:15 P.M. The regiment is drawn up on the beach under arms. It seems that half an hour ago there was heard a volley of musketry from the direction of Stone [sic], the southern end of the island, followed by a few scattering of shots; at the same time was seen much signalling among our gunboats by means of rockets and colored lights. All I can learn is that orders came for the regiment to "fall in," but now they are returning to their tents. The grateful Q.M. has now given me a rubber cushion that serves as a pillow by night and a softener of my hard seat by day. From 11 to 1 I worked on my thesis and with great delight; it represents the three years observation of facts and reflection upon their significance.

Thursday, 27th, 7:15 P.M. The colonel has just been in with his brother, the adjutant; the former says we shall leave for Newbern in three weeks[67]; he brought me three crash towels[68] and some thread of two colors; a supply was sent him from home and he has been sharing them with the officers. He thinks of buying some lumber off our own sutler, who has just arrived, and making a floor for the hospital tent. We examined some cicadas; they are twice the size of ours at the north and make a tremendous dreadful shrilling. I caught them on a tree that had been felled at my request for some hospital purposes that occupied me all the afternoon. The adjutant had a bag of ginger snaps and poured some on my table; I do not care for them but they are the first sweet thing of any kind I have tasted since leaving home and were quite acceptable. Frank has been near the front on Morris Island today; he saw one man struck by a shell and others that had been mangled in the same way shortly before. He is a venturesome little fellow but very shrewd and knows how to take care of himself. Some of our men are singing, and it sounds very well. Last night the wind was fiercer than I ever knew, here or elsewhere; suddenly it ceased and was followed by a heavy rainfall. The expected great assault has not been made, perhaps because the winds would have hindered the ships, but last night the 24th Mass. carried the enemy's advance line of pickets, capturing 80 men, most of whom surrendered willingly.[69] Our foremost parallel

67. Gen. Wild desperately wanted to return his command to North Carolina and was lobbying, unsuccessfully, for the move. Fox, *Record*, 18.

68. Crash towels were made from a coarse kind of linen cloth.

69. The 24th Massachusetts, with the 3rd New Hampshire in reserve, attacked the line of Confederate rifle pits that harassed the Union sappers advancing toward Wagner. The Northern soldiers quickly overwhelmed the Southern troops and established a new front line just a few hundred yards from Battery Wagner. Wise, *Gate of Hell*, 173–75.

is now less than 150 yards from Wagner; indeed the hostile entrenchments are so near that today the men are reported to have amused themselves by throwing bits of brick at one another.

¶ **Saturday, 29th, 7:15 P.M.** I have said nothing of my liking for natural history but it has gradually become known and not a day passes without some specimen being brought to me; today, for example, Frank brought a cicada, another boy a starfish, the steward a pretty little bird that is either ill or injured, the major a fish vertebra, the colonel a tiger beetle new to me; even General Wild sent an insect by a mounted officer. After dinner I called on Gen. Wild who sent word by Col. Hallowell and Major Fox that he had something interesting to show me. It was a sea-anemone. It was quite odd that I, a doctor, should be conversing with him who had been my doctor when I was a child. I told him that I regretted writing to him to use his influence with Dr. Dale because I passed the examination successfully. But he said that on getting it he saw Dale and the latter said you cannot have Wilder for the N.C. regiments; I want him for the 55th. Yesterday a man suddenly dropped something that he was carrying and Lt. Thurber took it on a stick to the Q.M.'s tent and he called me. It was a "Portuguese Man-of-War," about 4 inches long, with purple in color and with tentacles attached to one side. I put it in a basin of water without touching its tentacles. After examining it about ten minutes I felt a stinging over the back of my hand, especially the middle joints of the fingers. This steadily increased, extending up the arm, and finally reached my chest so that on that side I could scarcely breathe; this lasted for about an hour; and the pain in the arm gradually ceased but did not quite disappear from the place where it began till after I arose this morning. Just as the most intense pain was passing off from those joints a sort of dew came out in large drops; yet at no time was there redness or other sign of irritation.

¶ **Monday, [September] 1st, 7:45 P.M.** Capt. Soule was on duty at Morris Island today and tells me that he looked round the end of our last parallel at Wagner, not 50 yards away. Yesterday the Ironsides and Monitors went in and for a time the firing was terrific.[70] For three days I have been fully occupied with our Monthly Report, and should have completed my share

70. The Union squadron, led by the USS *New Ironsides*, a wood-framed iron-cased steam frigate carrying 18 guns, plus the squadron of six monitors, approached to within 500 yards of Fort Sumter and fired 245 shots before retiring. Sumter was largely demolished. Ivan Musicant, *Divided Waters: The Naval History of the Civil War* (New York: HarperCollins, 1995), 158, 400–401; Wise, *Gate of Hell*, 188, 252.

of it this afternoon but for the following incident. Two brothers named Peterson[71] were wrestling and one was thrown so heavily that his left arm was dislocated at the elbow, forcing the two bones of the forearm beyond the humerus. Dr. Brown was out of the camp and I was called. The man was in great pain and seemed likely to faint. I had him taken to the hospital and given chloroform, which not only averted pain but relaxed the muscles so that the bones could be pulled into place. Dislocations are comparatively rare in army practice and I had never seen a case in Washington or even studied the subject; but my anatomy enabled me to recognize the conditions and to apply the force in the right direction; of course to have failed would have been very mortifying. Another time I think if necessary, I could reduce the dislocation without the anaesthetic. Yesterday afternoon Gen. Wild inspected the regiment and we were mustered for pay, but no one knows when we shall get anything. I have but two dollars but our immediate expenses are slight, mainly for small sutler's supplies.

¶ **Wed., Sept. 2, 8:30 P.M.** Shortly after midnight I was wakened by a very heavy and continuous firing from the gunboats; it literally shook the earth; I never heard such before; yet today I have learned nothing of its meaning. I rejoice to say that the Report is finished; it has tasked mine eyes severely; this evening I have helped Dr. B. consolidate it. This afternoon I met an old Cambridge acquaintance, Mr. Higginson,[72] who is visiting the colonel and adjutant. Dr. Brown has twice remarked that he was sick of this life and that he should resign if he thought it would be accepted. At the time he was irritated by something connected with the mess arrangements. We get along very well together, but his irritability is trying. The "A" tent so far occupied by me has been replaced by a wall tent on the same spot the former has been turned over to Frank and the Chaplain's boy, Amos. The greater space in this tent, and especially the vertical sides up to 3 or 4 feet will enable me to make some improvements when I have time and materials; we all have to depend upon boxes and barrels for lumber. All the field and staff officers now have each a wall tent excepting the chaplain. I should have had mine a week ago but gave it up to Dr. Brown. At first the colonel said, "Draw only five wall tents, one for the

71. There were four Petersons from Barnesville, Ohio, in Company F, David S. (23), Marcus (29), Joseph H. (24), and Ferdinand (22). It is not clear which ones were wrestling. Fox, *Record*, 131.

72. Clearly a member of Thomas Wentworth Higginson's family from Cambridge, but his identity is unknown.

adjutant, one for the Q.M. and three for store houses" but when they came the colonel said he would like one, and the Lt. Col. and Major said the same. The Q.M. included one for me, but when it arrived I felt that it would not do for the assistant surgeon to have a larger tent than the surgeon and offered it to him.

¶ **Thursday, 3rd, 8:00 P.M.** The days are perceptibly shorter and the mornings and evenings cooler. Gen. Wild sent for me today to show and give me some interesting specimens, a wasp that was catching spiders to store in a mud cell for its young when hatched, and a piece of wood perforated by some marine worm.

¶ **Sunday, 6th, 4:30 P.M.** Altho it was very hot yesterday and my head ached a little I took four men and went to Morris Island for Sanitary Commission stores for our sick in hospital. That is under Dr. Brown's care ~~and it is not my duty~~ but I had heard several officers express the belief that delicacies were needed, so I asked Dr. Brown if he wished anything; at first he objected to making the request; indeed he commonly objects to whatever I propose; but when I said if he had no positive objection I should go. The result should convince him that the Commission is glad to supply us; indeed the agent added some things not on my list. So far as I can judge Dr. Brown has not eaten a meal with satisfaction; indeed I doubt if he is satisfied with anything in the world but himself. He buys sardines and preserved fruit and as they are paid for from our common fund I eat some of them, but I should be content without them.

¶ **Monday, 7th, 4 P.M.** Glorious news. Wagner and Gregg were evacuated by the enemy last night.[73] I cannot say that I really enjoy this life at all; nothing reconciles me to it except the consciousness of duty and the hope that I may be able to make some useful observations upon the negroes. I prefer them to the white soldiers in many respects . . . On one account I wish my service were elsewhere. D.B. is daily becoming more odious to me. He is civil and seems to have no personal animosity; but socially and officially our ideas and ways are so antagonistic that I cannot bear to be

73. By 6 September, Union sappers had reached the edge of Wagner's moat, and the constant shelling had destroyed much of the interior and killed or wounded many of the defenders. Confederate engineers agreed that the battery was indefensible, and during the night of 7 September, the Confederate garrison withdrew. The planned Union attack entered the fort shortly after, capturing a handful of Confederate soldiers. Burton, *Siege of Charleston*, 178–82; Wise, *Gate of Hell*, 199–203.

with him; when the other assistant arrives perhaps we shall see less of each other.[74]

7:15 P.M. After supper from the look out we could see the flashes of what is evidently a great cannonade in the harbour; the monitors seem to be attacking Moultrie.

This noon I was surprised and pleased to see Sam'l H. Scudder. He had come down as one of a Committee in charge of Sanitary Commission supplies on a schooner; ice and fresh vegetables for this and other regiments.

Yesterday a strange scene was enacted in the broad regimental street. A fellow named Ditcher,[75] young in years but old in wickedness, always a terror at sick call because he pretended to be ill when I was quite sure he was not, and who was sent to Morris Island for hard labor on account of misconduct, was there detected after stealing a hundred dollars from a wounded friend over there. He was sent back here for punishment. His head was shaved close; his uniform was stripped from him; about his neck was hung a placard stating his offence; his hands were tied and, with sharp bayonets close to his back, he was marched twice through the camp; since then he has been standing upon a barrel at the guard house. Why should not so depraved a rascal be shot? We feel already the more cheerful attitude of all by reason of the evacuation of the forts; probably, too, it saved many lives; our miners had already reached the ditch of Wagner and an assault was to have been made this morning. Our men report that torpedoes[76] were planted in the fort marked by small sticks for the rebels but some of our soldiers have been killed by them. Deserters or captives say it was intended to destroy Wagner by firing the magazines, but this was prevented by the early approach of our troops.

¶ **Tuesday, [September] 8th, 8:00 P.M.** Mr. Scudder arrived this evening and his bed is made up in my tent; he brought with him a mattress, pillow, soft blanket and "mirabile dictu" a pair of linen sheets, not seen by me

74. The second assistant surgeon, Dr. Warren M. Babbitt, did not join the regiment until 14 September 1863. Fox, *Record*, 100.

75. There were two Ditchers in the 55th Massachusetts, both in Company F and from Pennsylvania. Pvt. Henry Ditcher, who enlisted at age 21, died on Folly Island in February 1865, of "anasarca." Benjamin F. B. Ditcher, age 18, deserted his regiment in July 1865. Fox, *Record*, 130.

76. In late July 1863, Confederate soldiers began laying out "torpedoes" in front of Wagner. They were usually artillery shells covered in the sand with a board over the contact fuse. Pressure on the board caused an explosion. Wise, *Gate of Hell*, 75, 134–35.

since leaving the "Cahawba." I am glad to accommodate him if only for the sight of such comforts and refinements. This afternoon the Q.M. had another feverish and nervous attack and I have been caring for him. I have just made for him a small bag for keeping ice on his head; I had to thread the needle and was quite proud of the achievement; encouraged I actually darned my socks with some of the thread given by the colonel. It is reported that a heavy explosion at 8 this morning was caused by the blowing up of the magazine at Fort Moultrie[77]; the adjoining village of Moultrieville was fired by our shells.

¶ **Wednesday, Sept. 9th, 8:30 P.M.** I met Mr. Scudder at Gen. Wild's where I had gone for a large spider; but as it was of the same kind as that from which I wound the silk the other day I gave it to Mr. S.

¶ **Friday, Sept. 11, 4:30 P.M.** I have just lanced a sort of boil in the roof of a man's mouth, which he said nearly sent him crazy. I have to draw so many teeth now that they make no impression on me; the 1st NC regiment, near us, has no dental instruments at all so the men come to me; I am becoming hardened to the necessary pain inflicted and am willing to do it for the sake of the teeth, of which quite a collection is forming. Gen. Wild seems to be in excellent health; also his brother, Walter. The former is very considerate and, in view of the heavy details upon ~~our regiment~~, the brigade, has no guard near his tent which stands somewhat apart from the two camps.

¶ **Sunday, 13th, 3:30 P.M.** The early Sick Call is very objectionable in one respect; one would like to begin the day pleasantly, but among the 150 to 175 men who report for treatment or excuse from duty are always a few whom I have reason to suspect of malingering; the effort to detect their frauds irritates me and sometimes, probably, renders me unjust to the really ill. When Dr. Babbitt arrives I hope he will perform this duty. The flies are greedy and undiscriminating; they will remain on a morsel till it actually enters the mouth, and they plunge headlong into ink and other unsuitable liquids; they can bite severely too.

¶ **Monday, 14th, 8:00 P.M.** Dr. Babbitt arrived today and when I found that he was as little familiar with camp life as I was at first I superintended the

77. A shell from the monitor *Weehawken* set off ammunition for an eight-inch Columbiad stored within the fort. Sixteen men in the fort were killed and twelve more were wounded. Burton, *Siege of Charleston*, 191–92.

pitching of his tent. Referring to Frank's remarks ~~about Dr. Brown~~ the other day, of course it is undesirable for him to speak so of an officer or for me to listen, and I ordered him to refrain in the future, whatever he heard; but it began in a very natural complaint at what he regarded as an imposition upon himself and indirectly upon me; Dr. B. had no boy and sometimes orders mine about in an unwarrantable way. I worked on my thesis for an hour before dinner and hope to every day after this; this morning Dr. Babbitt was present at Sick Call and I hope that he will attend to it here after. He is a pleasant and handsome man, and married. Mr. Scudder went to Hilton Head last evening but will return soon. He brought me a box of ale in small stone battles; I have never cared for any thing of the kind but this enervating climate and rather trying life seems to suggest its use and very likely it will do me good. I am so thankful to keep well.

¶ **Tuesday, Sept. 15, 7:15 P.M.** Mr. Scudder told us that a small vessel in Lighthouse Inlet[78] had some sweet potatoes, so today Dr. Babbitt and I undertook to get some. We took two men and two bags and walked to the inlet; of the several vessels there, no one knew which had the desired vegetables; not even the Post Q.M. could tell us. After waiting an hour for information and a boat we were able to borrow the boat of our sutler and at last were directed to the vessel we sought, some distance up a creek. About thirty feet from the shore the boat grounded. Our men waded to dry land, and the burly boatman carried Dr. B. and me, separately, on his back. We got half a bushel of potatoes and a squash. After reaching Folly Island we called at a bakery and obtained some warm biscuits from the wife of the baker; she was the only woman I saw on either island. One of my patients to whom I gave a little whiskey last night is now out of his head and threatened to attack me because I would give him no more.

¶ **Wednesday, 16th, 8:00 P.M.** I accompanied Mr. Scudder to Morris Island this afternoon; on the way we stopped at Gen. Wild's to look at some insects that he had sent me word about and remained so long that we had to run to the steamer and climb up the side by a rope. On board was a Major Bardwell[79] of a colored Pa. regiment, whom Mr. S. had met at Cambridge; he had been a professor of mathematics at Antioch. I went to the Sanitary

78. Lighthouse Inlet was the dangerous sweep of water separating Folly from Morris Island. Hagy, *To Take Charleston*, v.

79. Frederick W. Bardwell, a major in the 3rd USCT, was promoted to command the regiment in May 1865.

Commission, bade Mr. S. goodbye, and obtained a box of dried codfish, a bottle of ginger extract, two boxes of condensed milk, and two bottles of cherry brandy, the latter especially for Captain Bowditch. I was able to work on my thesis both before breakfast and for two hours in the forenoon.

❡ **Thursday, [September] 17th, 7:30 P.M.** About midnight [of the 16th] began a terrific storm of wind and rain that has only recently abated, and the sky is still threatening. Shortly after it began I had waked and was listening to distant carronading when a volley of musketry sounded near by, and the report was circulated that our pickets had been driven in and an attack was expected. While hastily dressing I heard the order for the regiment to "fall in" and it was soon drawn up on the beach. Dr. Brown and Dr. Babbitt and I ~~walked~~ went to the hospital to make sure that the instruments and supplies were in order. The furious rain soon soaked through the single "fly" under which we stood, and we pitied the soldiers fully exposed on the beach. All remained so for nearly two hours. Returning to our quarters we heard that the alarm was premature, but that an attack was expected at four; at that hour we all went out again, but the rain was a deluge and we were soon allowed to return. General Wild and his brother had ridden up at the first alarm on his way to Gen. Vogdes, the Post Commander; he said there were anticipations of attacks from both sides of us, from the Lighthouse Inlet and from Pawnee Landing further south, near the middle of the island.[80] Naturally there was little sleep or comfort for us for the rest of the night. Such false alarms are bad because the real attack is liable to be disregarded. We are under orders for four o'clock tomorrow morning so I shall retire early. The hospital tent blew down soon after dawn but was put up again; that is certainly a comfort in any emergency there are plenty of men to help. This forenoon I went to the bakery where we got the biscuits the other day and drew a tooth for the woman; her husband supported her head while I gave her chloroform and drew the tooth. Then I worked on my thesis and after dinner read Huxley's "Man's Place in Nature" which Mr. Scudder had left with me.

❡ **Friday, 18th, 7:00 P.M.** The regiment was under arms on the beach for two hours after four, but I did not get up and nothing happened. This afternoon I superintended men fixing our mess tent.

80. This false alarm may have been the result of information reaching Gen. Gillmore that two Confederate brigades, Anderson's Georgians and Wise's Virginians, had been sent to the city. Burton, *The Siege of Charleston*, 197–99; Wise, *Gate of Hell*, 212.

¶ **Saturday, 19th, 7:30 P.M.** Today I asked Col. Hallowell about the pay of the men and he said he had been in great trouble concerning it; he had told them their pay would be the same as that as white soldiers, and now there were reports that it would be only $10.00 month; even for that it was necessary to have pay-muster-rolls, and they could not be made out without the company books which are all with our baggage in Newbern. He had sent a request to have them forwarded here, but had reason to believe Gen. Wild did not favour it because it would seem to lessen the chance of his entire brigade returning to Newbern. The colonel asked me to use any personal influence that I might have with Gen. Wild, so today while at his quarters to get some specimens he had sent word about I referred to the subject and he assured me that he had lately endorsed and forwarded the request to Gen. Gilmore.[81] The general also said that something must be done to relieve Dr. DeGrasse of the 1st N.C. He is the only surgeon and is ill, while we have three in good health. So he will order Dr. Brown to take charge of the medical affairs of the brigade, with the understanding that he will detail Dr. Babbitt to assist Dr. DeGrasse. Of course that will compel me to reassume charge of the early Sick Call, but it cannot be helped. This morning I borrowed the horse of the Q.M., who had obtained one somehow although those of the regiments are still in Newbern and rode to Pawnee Landing,[82] about three miles to the south, where the attack was expected; there are six pieces of light artillery there and it would be no easy matter to cross the marsh in front of them

¶ **Sunday, Sept. 20th, 4:45 P.M.** I have just returned from Morris Island where I got some needed supplies from the Sanitary Commission. While there I read two of Gen. Gilmore's General Orders.[83] One prohibits the employment of colored troops to perform menial or unmilitary service for

81. John Quincy Gillmore, from Ohio, graduated at the head of his class at West Point. He was a major general and commander of the X Corps and the Department of the South in July 1863. Wilder consistently misspells Gillmore's name. Sifakis, *Who Was Who in the Civil War*, 249.

82. The fortifications at Pawnee Landing guarded the storehouse and commanded Folly River. It had two batteries with two guns in each. Hagy, *To Take Charleston*, 57.

83. On 17 September, Gillmore issued General Orders Number 77, prohibiting the use of black soldiers "to prepare camps and perform menial duties for the white troops." The problem was not erased, however, and in November he issued General Orders Number 105 to remind officers that "Colored troops will not be required to perform any labor which is not shared by the white troops, but will receive in all respects the same treatment, and be allowed the same opportunities for drill and instruction." Berlin, *The Black Military Experience*, 494.

white troops. In one case they had been employed to form a camp and pitch tents for whites. This has been a glorious day, clear and cool. Sometimes my work is hard or trying, but I get some opportunity for study and writing. With the exception of my immediate superior (who treats no one with much courtesy) all the officers and men are friendly and helpful. After dinner I crossed the river (to Long Island?). There is a rebel battery in full sight in the edge of the woods on James Island; it has fired all day at intervals, sometimes at Morris Island, but occasionally in this direction; but the shells do not reach us. A new battery is being erected at the north end of the island beyond the wharf.

¶ **Monday, [September] 21st, 5:00 P.M.** The other evening I had quite a zoological symposium. Several big red ants ran up and down the 1 table; a green tree toad perched on the corner of a box; a large toad hopped about my feet; a spider hung over my head; to cap the climax a cat walked in, looked about and departed without waiting to be patted. The nights are becoming quite cool, and I have really suffered; I brought no blankets; my overcoat does not cover my feet and besides I want it to lie upon; the Sanitary Commission have no blankets; so I have borrowed from the hospital stores that one that has not been used and is not needed just now and expect to sleep comfortably tonight unless aroused by the rebels.

¶ **Tuesday, 22nd, 7:30 P.M.** Another glorious day, a day for work, and I have improved it. Dr. Brown was taken ill last night so today I performed his duties as well as my own; in addition I superintended putting up beds in the new hospital tent. In the afternoon I went to the San. Com. for bedsacks, towels and tin cups.

¶ **Wed. Sept. 23rd, 10:30 P.M.** Talked with Col Hallowell, as to Dr. Brown. The colonel asked if I would take the place of chief surgeon of the regiment. I replied that I would now, if a vacancy occurred, although I might not have felt like it when I first joined. He said he was sure I had skill enough but had doubted whether I had sufficient acquaintance with the forms and methods of making our returns, etc. I admitted unfamiliarity but said I could learn them. I was not surprised at what he intimated for from various quarters I cannot avoid hearing complaints of Dr. Brown. Dr. Brown is better today but unable to so anything; while he is off duty Comparative Anatomy must wait. Yesterday blank cartridges were fired and flags displayed in honor of the recent promotion of Gilmore to be Major General. Hearing heavy firing alarmingly near I went to the rear of the camp and found that one of our gunboats that has hitherto lain in the inlet between this and Morris Island was shelling a structure that was going up on James Island. I have never been so near large guns before. . . . My tent could hardly be mistaken for any other; a great box is nearly covered with coral and branching sponges; there are some interesting shells and wood perforated by worms; insects are pinned on the walls and beneath the table are bottles of snakes and other insects.

¶ **Thursday, 24th, P.M.** The colonel is about to leave for the north on a thirty days furlough. The major is left in command but of course the Lt. Colonel will when he returns. Dr. Brown was able to attend to the hospital today. The morning I lanced an abscess in the finger of Capt. Wales[84]; there are several minor surgical cases under my care just now; a toe nearly crushed off, a finger crushed yesterday, a foot that had to be lanced this morning, and a hand accidentally shot a few days ago; the man whose arm was dislocated some time ago has been on duty for several days. The Q.M. and I have had one of the official controversies which occur about once in three days. We need hay for the hospital beds and it is his business to get it; his teams have been busy, but he says tomorrow I can have one and get it myself; from the "Regulations" I proved that it was his duty. Fortunately we are on excellent terms personally. Today he brought me a loaf of soft bread on the condition that I eat it myself; if I give any of it away he says I must pay 25 cents for it; and now Dr. Brown is far from well and would relish it, but the Q.M. well knows that I have not 25 cents, so I am in his power. I fear we shall not be paid in time for Mr. Rogers to be repaid what he loaned me for getting my horse; it is due in November. . . . Since writing the above I have had a conversation with the colonel; he says the furlough was wholly unexpected, and was probably obtained from Washington by his father or some friend; that he will have some pieces of dead bone removed from his arm. The major has just called to say that our pickets were "driven in"; but as no special concern was apparent in his voice or manner I was prepared for the further statement that the cause was not fire but water; the tide is very high and the marsh is flooded; the pickets always have to wade more or less in going to their posts, but now they were in danger of drowning. I drew a most dreadful tooth this afternoon; it was in the upper jaw and had three diverging roots, but the

84. Sigourney Wales was a clerk in Chelsea before joining the 13th Massachusetts as a sergeant. He joined the 55th as captain and was promoted to major in late 1863. Fox, *Record*, 99.

man never made a sound; yet our valiant captain declares he must have chloroform if his finger is lanced again.

¶ **Friday, Sept. 25, 7:00 P.M.** The Q.M. got a bale of hay with which to fill the hospital sacks. Under the immediate charge of a Lieutenant thirty men worked at and about the hospital this morning; and by the replacement of a small tent by a larger one in which Dr. B. has fixed up a nice table and seats; before the tent was so small that we really could not sit up right. There were two extra bed sacks and they will be used by Dr. B. and me till needed by the sick at the San. Com. I learned that Mr. Scudder has been ill ever since reaching Hilton Head; I am glad that he got there in season for he will be far more comfortable than he could be here. There was a cat at the San. Com. And another in the camp of the 1st N.C. near us; perhaps I can get the latter.

¶ **Saturday, 26th, 8:00 P.M.** The Adjutant suffers greatly from rheumatism and last night I had to assist his servant to remove his clothes and then rub his neck and shoulders with liniment; I fear he also will have to leave us.

¶ **Sunday, 27th, 3:00 P.M.** It is a great comfort to have a tent to myself; I hope it will never be necessary for me to share a tent with any one, however well I may like him. My natural repugnance to medicine as a profession is lessening as I realize what an opportunity it offers for usefulness, for helping others not only physically but morally, and for cheering the despondent. I may have to practise for some years until there offers a position in my chosen line; at present I am often and painfully conscious of my lack of regular medical training. Of practical surgery I saw so much in Washington that I feel fairly competent to deal with ordinary emergencies; but on the medical side I feel comparatively ignorant and I must study hard in order to justify my position and be equal to my probable responsibilities; among the articles included in our recent Requisition for supplies are some books on practise which I hope they will send. . . . The arrival of the hospital mess chest improves the culinary department greatly. Last evening Dr. Brown entertained a correspondent of the N.Y. Tribune who, during supper, enlarged our minds by as much as he could conveniently say in that time. At one today we were reviewed by Gen. Wild; it is important, no doubt, but I would rather be excused.

¶ **Monday, Sept. 28th, 7:15 P.M.** The grand review took place at 12:30 and both Dr. Brown and I honoured Gen. Gilmore by our presence. There were two batteries of artillery and eight or ten regiments of infantry; probably ten thousand in all; there are said to be twice as many on Morris Island.[85] We had to march 8 or 10 miles but the beach was hard and the breeze cool; if our horses were here it would have been more enjoyable. A cat came in a little while ago and lay quietly for a time but has now departed.

¶ **Tuesday, 29th, P.M.** One of the hospital nurses has made me a chair from a barrel by cutting out about a third of the upper and open half; with a cushion it is quite comfortable. I append a rough diagram of the arrangement of the "furniture," if boxes and barrels may be so termed. (Not found, delete?)

Imitation "What is It?" A few days ago I heard that the boy of Col. Beecher[86] of the 1st N.C., was the "What is it" of Barnum[87] and went to see him. Col. B. had got him from Col. H. (it looks like Howe) in New York. We called him in and examined him closely. He is an extraordinary negro boy, not at all idiotic or monkeyish like the real "What is it.[88]" He says that he sometimes took the place of the other, and was instructed by Barnum how to behave; he said the other boy never talked. He told a straight and consistent story.

The cat, a pretty black and white, has returned and is quite sociable; it has had a bit of meat. This afternoon the Medical Inspector of the department made an official visit. Dr. Brown was away so I went to the hospital to meet him. To my surprise and delight he proved to be Asst. Surgeon Schell of the regular army, a friend of Dr. Marsh and for some weeks stationed at Judiciary Square hospital. I gave him the desired information

85. In fact, the number of men on Folly Island in August, and through to October, was 9,846, while on Morris Island the troop strength was 13,067. In October, there were 13,259 soldiers on Folly and only 7,910 on Morris. Hagy, *To Take Charleston*, 47.

86. James Chaplin Beecher, son of Lyman Beecher, was an ardent abolitionist and had been chaplain of the 67th New York Regiment and then lieutenant colonel in the 141st New York Regiment before assuming the duties of raising the 1st North Carolina Colored Volunteers (later the 35th USCT). Glatthaar, *Forged in Battle*, 13, 240–41; Reid, *Freedom for Themselves*, 25, 32–39.

87. P. T. Barnum, a well-known American entrepreneur famous for his elaborate hoaxes, helped found the Ringling Brothers and Barnum and Bailey Circus after the war. Benjamin Reiss, "P. T. Barnum, Joice Heth, and Antebellum Spectacle of Race," *American Quarterly* 51, no. 1 (1999): 78–107.

88. William Henry Johnson, who most commonly played the role, was from Bound Brook, New Jersey, and may have suffered from microcephaly. Johnson, who cooperated with the hoax, looked relatively normal, but Barnum used context, costume, innate prejudice, and Johnson's acting skills to create the appearance of a mixture of ape and man.

concerning the regiment and he invited me to visit him at Hilton Head. Frank caught some crabs today and they were excellent eating.

¶ **Wed. [September] 30th, 8:30 P.M.** Our baggage and horses have come at last.[89] Billy was so frisky that Frank, whom I sent to Pawnee Landing for him, dared not ride him and so he was brought me by the soldier who has been caring for him since Jerry was taken ill at Newbern. At once I mounted and took a short ride on the beach; he is fat and saucy. Although my trunk is only partly unpacked the tent is already transformed; we all hope that the rebels will not come at once and interfere with our comfort.

¶ **Thursday, Oct 1, 8:00 P.M.** Slowly and luxuriously did I dress this morning in garments that I hardly expected ever to see again.[90] Lt. Col. Hartwell has just looked in to ask me to go with him to Gen. Gilmore's headquarters at about the middle of the island on business connected with getting Lt. Alden,[91] who is very ill, off on the next steamer.

11:30 P.M. The tide was so high that after a mile or two we had to leave the beach for an inside road through the dark woods where it was muddy and often water.[92] It was so late that the necessary papers could not be made out tonight and I shall go for them and make my medical certificate at 6 in the morning.

¶ **Friday, 2nd, 7:30 P.M.** I am really tired tonight for, besides the ten mile ride this morning to and from Gen. Gilmore's, I had to go to Pawnee Land-

89. When Gen. Wild had been ordered to move his partially organized brigade to South Carolina, he believed it temporary. In addition, he was given short notice and told to depart in light marching order. As a result, the regiments left behind most of their baggage, personal belongings, and even company books. It was not until 28 September that the gear left behind was forwarded to South Carolina. Reid, *Freedom for Themselves*, 41.

90. Wilder was more fortunate than many of the enlisted men. Fox reported that both public and private property had been stolen from the baggage held at New Bern. "A number of knapsacks are missing, and from many of those remaining, overcoats, dress-coats, and trousers had been stolen. No allowances could be obtained for these losses, – a manifest injustice." Fox, *Record*, 13–14.

91. Leonard Case Alden, born in Boston in 1839 and a descendent of John Alden of the *Mayflower*, also graduated from Harvard. He was given a medical furlough because of his health but died in the army hospital at Hilton Head of malaria in October 1863 on his way home. His commission had been the first issued in the regiment, and he was the first officer to die. Fox, *Record*, 95–96; Trudeau, *Voices*, 9.

92. Vogdes had some of the roads build through the trees so that they could not be seen from the Confederate fortifications. Hagy, *To Take Charleston*, 18.

ing and to be on my feet all the rest of the day. Yesterday Lt. Alden was put on board a steamer to go to Hilton Head. Today, he is too ill to climb up the side of the mail steamer, the "Fulton," so he will be cared for at the hospital in Hilton Head till the next steamer goes north. He has been under Dr. Brown's care, Capt. Bowditch under mine; the former has Typho-malarial fever, the latter Diarrhea following Dysentry. Col. Hartwell has issued orders that commissioned officers must have written certificate of illness in order to be excused from duty, and as, just now, the most trying duty is the drill that begins at 4 A.M. we are liable to be roused early.

¶ **Sunday, Oct. 4th, 7 P.M.** The following statement of one days work may illustrate the fact that an army officer really has no time when he is sure to be undisturbed. I woke at 3:30. At 4 Lt. Woodward[93] came in for a certificate of illness; so I lighted my candle and filled out the blank for him. Then I heard the regiment filing out to the beach and the first orders given. Then I dozed till 5:45 when Sick Call was sounded; I dressed hastily and on the way stopped at the major's tent to ask him to set the call hereafter at 6:15, which is as much after the men's breakfast as the present hour is before, and it is then hardly light. I also looked in at the Q.M.'s tent; he said he was very tired, not having gone to bed till after midnight. At the hospital awaited me more than 200 men; fully 200 had to be excused from duty today. This long drill before breakfast is very hard on the officers and must be even harder for the men; some time ago the order was issued to be under arms at 4 A.M., and very likely is it better to move about than to stand still, but as soon as I am satisfied that it is the cause of our large checklist I shall report it officially; perhaps the necessity for the early start may cease. At 7:30 I had a good breakfast of bread, sardines and coffee. Then I planned to ride on the beach but a poor fellow begged me to relieve him of two aching teeth, one upper and the other lower. I am getting quite a collection, but sometimes have to use argument or persuasion because there is a prevalent superstition that unless a tooth is burned it is liable to ache again. Returning to my tent the Q.M. tried to torment me by saying that I would have to purchase forage for my horse this month because I had neglected to hand him the requisition that I made out last night and the general requisition had been sent off early this morning; but presently he admitted that in my absence

93. George Moore Woodward was an attorney in Worcester before serving as a private in the 44th Massachusetts Infantry. He joined the 55th in June 1863 and was promoted captain in September 1864, two months before being seriously wounded at Honey Hill. Fox, *Record*, 103.

he got them from my tent and all was well. At 8, the second Sick Call, I went to the hospital again and prescribed for the ailing who had been excused earlier; in the interval the names had been copied by a clerk so all I had to do was to enter opposite the names the complaint and the treatment. The remedies were administered by the steward who stood at my right hand.[94] Then Frank brought me some hot water and I had a real bath and change of raiment in honor of the Sabbath. After dinner, when I had anticipated putting my newly acquired properties into better order, Dr. Brown said a toothache would prevent his going to the Sanitary Commission for ice and wished I would go. So Frank went ahead to be ready to hold my horse while I was absent. I secured 200 pounds of ice and on the way back called upon Gen. Wilde, at his request of the previous day, to examine some peculiar marine animals. On reaching camp I learned that the steward was too ill to give out the afternoon medicine at 4 o'clock and performed the duty for him. Then the Adjutant called, and after him the Lt. Col., now in command, to repeat to me his criticisms of the condition of the hospital as made to Dr. Brown this morning. The latter passed just then and was called in for a conference the result of which was that I have an oversight of food and sanitary conditions for the men in quarters; it will involve considerable extra time and labor but is very important, and may enable Dr. B. to do more for the hospital patients. I forgot to say that before dinner a lieutenant came to see me as to his leg which is affected with boils; I advised opening some of them but he naturally shrank and concluded to wait awhile. I do not wonder. After supper I visited Lt. Woodward and had to listen to a lament by another officer as to the scarcity of honest men; I suspect he was threatened with a bilious attack. Since then I have been interrupted three times by Dr. Brown and once by the Q.M.

¶ **Monday, Oct. 5th, 7:00 P.M.** Doubtless my good health is largely due to frequent rides upon Billy. Our food has much improved; we now get soft bread, baked on the island, and always have it toasted. But it is fifty cents a pound and not very good; I am thinking of having some sent from home. I am pleased to say that Dr. B. has improved recently in both the perfor-

94. Richard Hecker, a "chemist" from New York City, was the first hospital steward of the regiment. Despite the fact that he was subsequently discharged by court-martial, his occupation fitted him for the position. The hospital steward was a combination of pharmacist, administrator, and clerk who maintained the hospital and the pharmacy under the surgeon's direction and compounded the preparations. Fully qualified stewards were in desperately short supply. Humphreys, *Intensely Human*, 59, 60–62; Flannery, *Civil War Pharmacy*, 80–90.

mance of his duties and in his demeanor to me, but he can never be an acceptable companion for me.

¶ **Tuesday, 6th, 7:30 P.M.** In one respect the medical officer of a regiment is better off than any other because his official duties are commonly performed at the hospital and I have often congratulated myself on the undisturbed tranquility of my canvas house. Just now, however, Capt. Goodwin looked in to ask for certificates to enable four of his men to draw new clothing to replace what had to be destroyed when they had smallpox at Readville. The completion of my thesis is sadly interfered with by the new duty of inspecting the dinners of the twelve companies daily in company with Major Fox, but it is very important and perhaps I can write sometimes in the afternoon, although that is a less favourable time for me. Frank popped his head in a moment ago to ask if anything more was wanted tonight; he is doing very well and seems happy and contented. He gets along very well with the other boys who are all colored and, with one exception, older than himself. His tent is just back of mine and at 6:15, the hour of Sick Call, I wake him. While I am gone he opens the tent, airs the blanket on a line and puts things in order; after breakfast he makes up the bed again and does whatever is to be done. Adjutant Hallowell has received a leave of twenty days from the medical board which now awaits only the approval of Gen. Gilmore. Last night I had been asleep only an hour when the Q.M. woke me to say that an attack was made on Morris Island; I rose and dressed but we were not called upon to participate.

¶ **Thursday, 8th, 8:30 P.M.** Capt. Soule has just been in to say that his mother and sister are coming to Port Royal the last of the month to spend the winter on the estate where Mr. Soule now is. They are sent free by Dr. Russel of the educational commission and are to do a certain amount of teaching. Soule will be able to visit them.

¶ **Friday, [October] 9th, 8:10 P.M.** The major has just told me that hereafter, for the present, the regiment will not be called out till 5:30, a great comfort for all.

¶ **Sunday, 11th, 8:00 P.M.** Companies F and G left today for an island called Botany Bay near Edisto, about thirty miles off.[95]

95. Throughout the war, companies in the 55th Massachusetts, and in many other regiments, served on detached duty away from their regiment, sometimes only for days

¶ **Monday, 12th, 7:30 P.M.** Capt. Soule was officer of the day today so I made with him a thorough sanitary inspection of the camp, opening every tent; among other suggestions was one that they should be left open as much as possible for ventilation.

¶ **Tuesday, 13th, 7:15 P.M.** While riding on the beach this evening I saw a plank floating in the water; rode out as far as it was safe for the horse and was able to stop it from being carried off; got it on shore and then hired two men for two apples each to bring it to my tent; lumber is scarce and for the most part we have to put up with empty boxes. The tent boxes are the most serviceable. This will enable me to improve my floor considerably. Today I have a new tent mate, a very pretty tortoise shell cat, playful and affectionate; she is asleep on the bed and bids fair to stay with me longer than the other. Last night the Colonel came to say that an attack was expected at Pawnee Landing and that the band would be at my disposal for carrying the wounded; so I slept in my clothes and the regiment was under arms twice during the night, but nothing happened; the alarm was general on both islands.

¶ **Wednesday, 14th, 7:45 P.M.** The fine plank saved from the waves has been exchanged with the Q.M. for a tent box with which a smooth floor has been made; Frank is ecstatic over it, and says it is better than any other excepting the Q.M.'s. An inspector from the Sanitary Commission came today and in Dr. Brown's absence I took him about and gave the desired information.

¶ **Thursday, Oct. 15th, 8:00 P.M.** I have been working all the afternoon in connection with a shelter for our horses made of a tent fly supported on posts.

¶ **Friday, 16th, 7:30 P.M.** I had a call today from Assistant Surgeon Mann[96] of the 1st N.C. regiment; he was left in Newbern with the sick and has recently arrived; he is older than most of our officers and somewhat gray; he is peculiar in some respects; has published a novel, "Wolfsend."

---

but often for extended periods. While detached, they often had no medical personnel with them.

96. Dr. Daniel Mann, a white surgeon appointed by Wild, came in repeated conflict with de Grasse, whom he accused of undermining his authority and of being an alcoholic. The charges seem to have been racially motivated. Reid, *Freedom for Themselves*, 69, 73–74.

¶ **Sunday, 18th, 7:30 P.M.** Today I explained to the Orderly Sergeants of the several companies some new regulations as to Sick Call that will facilitate performance of that duty for both the men and myself; Canterbury,[97] who takes care of the horses of Dr. Brown and myself, came for advice as to sending money to his wife and showed me a letter from her; it was well written; indeed, in the hospital in Washington I never saw a letter from a white soldier's wife better expressed or indicating truer affection; he is thirty years old and she twenty-one, and they have three children; he begged me to answer it for him which I did to his great satisfaction. Yesterday Dr. Brown and I examined fifteen men for various kinds of disability; one will be recommended for discharge, six for admission to the Invalid Corps, and the others for the Post Hospital or General Hospital; it took considerable time to make out the necessary papers. It is a perfect moonlight night; all seems so peaceful that it is hard to realize that we are living, as it were, on a volcano.

¶ **Wednesday, Oct. 21st, 8:00 P.M.** A short time ago I went to the street of Co. A., where a larger prayer meeting was in progress; there were visitors from the 1st N.C. and one of them was very eloquent and emphatic. He uttered prayers for every body everywhere and under all circumstances. It seemed very genuine although certain features of the performance were somewhat grotesque. The chaplain, I hear, is not asked to attend these meetings; he is a very inferior sort of man, and the men have little respect for him; it is a pity for a really competent chaplain would be of much use among us. This morning firing began, mostly from our batteries against Sumter where it is said that mortars have been mounted by the garrison; even at this distance the shock is perceptible through the earth. I do not pretend to be a judge of military matters but it seems to me that progress here is pretty slow.[98] This afternoon the Q.M. and I, while riding on the beach, met Gen. Gilmore in a carriage with a lady, presumably his wife; she is the first we have seen on the island. Gen. Wild has returned to Newbern and the brigade is in command of Col. James Beecher of the 1st N.C.,

97. Pvt. James Canterbury of Company E, a farmer in Chillicothe, Maine, before volunteering in the 55th Massachusetts, was discharged for disability in August 1864. Fox, *Record*, 127.

98. Wilder was perceptive. The capture of Battery Wagner and a subsequent failed attack on Fort Sumter marked the effective end of the army's campaign against Charleston, although the city remained a highly symbolic target until it fell in March 1865. The stalemate after September 1864 allowed troops to be shifted temporarily from Charleston to Florida in early 1864. Wise, *Gate of Hell*, 205–18.

he is a brother of Henry Ward[99]. There was quite a blanket exchange today. I bought two nice ones off the Q.M. One I shall use myself, giving Frank my old one which was not quite long enough for me. The other I have given to Canterbury in exchange for his old one, which I shall use for Billy till the arrival of the one I have sent north for.

¶ **Thursday, 22nd, 9:15 P.M.** This afternoon was spent upon the Discharge papers of five men; also, partly, in exhorting the company commanders to do their part of them carefully so that there may be no delay. Strict as I meant my examination of the recruits to be at Readville the disabilities of some escaped our scrutiny. Dr. Mann called to ask my advice upon a peculiar question, viz., as to whether, in the absence of the Surgeon of a regiment, the Colonel has the power to assign the respective duties of the 1st and 2nd Assistant surgeons. I expressed the negative opinion, but took him to Dr. Brown, who said the same and advised him to consult the chief medical officer of the island.[100]

¶ **Monday, 26th 8:30 P.M.** This afternoon it was quite cool and I rode rapidly down the beach. Meeting Dr. Schell, the Medical Inspector, we galloped together; he complimented Billy highly. In one respect the horse is peculiar. As soon as he feels me on his back he is ready to start; needs neither work nor spur, but is off as soon as the reins are lifted from his neck. But if anyone else mounts him he refuses to budge; the steward tried it today and Billy plunged and reared.

¶ **Tuesday, 27th, 8:15 P.M.** Through the chaplain we learned that the daily inspection of the meals of the several companies has already effected an improvement upon which the men comment favourably. This afternoon I was on horseback five hours; the first four accompanying the Q.M. to Pawnee Landing and then to Gen. Gilmore's Headquarters on business; afterward I had to superintend the work of one who had cut down and split trees for use about the hospital. This morning the tide was so high as to threaten to inundate the camp; it reached within three yards

99. Henry Ward Beecher, the eighth son of Rev. Lyman Beecher and brother of Harriet Beecher Stowe, was born in Litchfield, Connecticut, and educated at the Lane Theological Seminary. He became an influential reformer opposing slavery and endorsing temperance and women's suffrage. Sifakis, *Who Was Who in the Civil War*, 46.

100. The real issue in dispute was whether Asst. Surg. DeGrasse, who was black, had seniority over Asst. Surg. Mann, who was white. Reid, *Freedom for Themselves*, 74.

of the hospital; so now an embankment of trees and earth has been thrown up in front of it and it looks quite like a fort.

¶ **Wednesday, [October] 28th, 8:30 P.M.** Today we have enlarged and improved the shelter for our horses and done more upon the hospital. Frank has mounted on his cap my metal letters, U.S., and is occasionally taken for a Major General, to his great satisfaction.

¶ **Thursday, 29th, 8:20 P.M.** Dr. Schell dined with us today. Directly after dinner we (two men under my direction) effected some needed improvements at the hospital. The cook tent was mounted upon the top of the log stockade, the stove was moved in, and used in the preparation of supper. The grounds have been cleared and the store tent repitched just back of the cook tent. The arrangements are now as on the accompanying diagram. The evening I have been copying my thesis, having "locked the door," i.e. tied the strings of the tent flaps; but they have been untied for a sentinel from the guard house with a man who is too ill to remain there; by Capt. Crane, by Capt. Goodwin, for the Sergeant Major[101] with a Circular from regimental headquarters, for the Q.M. twice, and by Frank three times; so that my attention was often distracted. During the last two days several regiments have come over from Morris Island, and tonight they will probably move farther south. Major Fox says the near walls of Sumter have been demolished to half their height, and that he saw a shell pass completely through the fort.

¶ **Friday, 30th, 9:15 P.M.** This afternoon I reduced a hernia, the condition of which frightened me at first; so I feel quite proud; of course a man liable to such a condition should not have been accepted.

¶ **Saturday, 31st, 8:15 P.M.** This afternoon I wrote out four rules to insure the better ventilation of the tents of the men; the Colonel said he would endorse them and transmit copies to the company commanders. The latter, by the way, have plenty to occupy and worry them; many of the men are ignorant, and some ill-disposed, and the reports and returns are quite a burden. This morning we were mustered for pay, but no one seems to know when pay will reach us. After Billy's saddle was taken off he rolled

101. Samuel J. Robinson of Pennsylvania was the first sergeant major of the regiment. He felt bitter that because of the discrimination in the army, black non-commissioned officers could not be promoted. Fox, *Record*, 114; Trudeau, *Voices*, 62.

in the sand opposite my tent in such a way as to entangle his legs about a post; with the advice of the colonel, the major and another officer, and the assistance of four stout soldiers he was disentangled and turned back so that he could rise himself.

¶ **Monday, Nov. 2, 8:00 P.M.** Word was brought that mail had reached Gilmore's headquarters, but the chaplain was unable to get a team for bringing it; he has no horse, so I rode down for it at 5. It was a large bag full, weighing at least fifty pounds; so about half way back I dismounted and walked beside my horse.

¶ **Tuesday, Nov. 3, 10:00 P.M.** This evening I have been copying my thesis which Mr. Scudder wishes by the 15th. At dinner there called on me Dr. Peter Pineo,[102] Medical Inspector, whom I knew in Washington; he is from Boston and went out with a Massachusetts regiment, but has been promoted. He expressed his satisfaction with the sanitary condition of our camp. This morning, while returning from Gen. Gilmore's quarters where I rode to mail some letters, I had been walking alongside Billy and mounted him while he was moving. Just then rode up Col. Serrell[103] of the N.Y. Engineers saying "That is the way they do in Mexico." He also complimented Billy warmly. In the course of conversation it appeared that he regarded the capture of Sumter as advantageous in sentiment rather than for any material advantage.[104] He has been in charge of the works against it, and said it was occupied last night by our forces for a time, but that they withdrew later.[105] Some fragments of the wall were brought away and Major Fox gave me a bit. (Where is it?)

102. Dr. Peter Pineo (1825–1891), a native of Nova Scotia, had graduated from Bowdoin Medical School and was married in Boston in 1850. In 1861 he was commissioned as surgeon in the 9th Massachusetts and served briefly as brigade surgeon before that office was abolished. In early 1863 he was appointed medical inspector of the army with the rank of lieutenant colonel. "Obituary of Peter Pineo, M.D.," *New York Times*, 11 September 1891.

103. English-born Col. Edward W. Serrell commanded the 1st New York Volunteer Engineer Regiment, a three-year unit that served around Charleston and with the Army of the James. He acted as Gen. Gillmore's chief engineer and supervised the "Swamp Angel" battery. Serrell was brevetted brigadier general in March 1865. Wise, *Gate of Hell*, 79, 148–50.

104. Serrell may have been voicing Gillmore's new view that while the fort could be carried by assault, he had "never seen any necessity for doing so." Two months earlier a combined amphibious attack on the fort had been defeated, with heavy losses. Burton, *The Siege of Charleston*, 194–97, 203.

105. Confederate forces did not actually evacuate the fort until the night of 17–18 February 1865. Burton, *The Siege of Charleston*, 318.

¶ **Thursday, 5th, 9:00 P.M.** During the last month we have been annoyed by flies and mosquitoes less than by a very small gnat which come in clouds morning and evening; it makes no noise but stings severely; fortunately it does not enter the tents. Capt. Soule tells me that his mother cannot come down; too bad for him and still worse for his father, alone on the plantation.

¶ **Friday, 6th, 9:00 P.M.** The Q.M. has been made Brigade Q.M. with the rank of captain; he deserved it and his predecessor was inefficient.[106] My thesis is ready to send and I shall be particularly glad to have it off my hands because we are to move our camp in a day or two.

New Camp, Folly Island

Tuesday, Nov. 10, 8:30 P.M. Our new camp is about five miles south of the old one, in the pine woods not far from Gilmore's headquarters. I packed up this afternoon and all my property came safely on a four horse team. My tent is temporarily pitched near where the floor will be laid tomorrow and Frank's is just behind. All the sick are here excepting those in the hospital, so there will be the usual work for me. This has been a cold day, and we are thankful for the shelter of the great trees.

¶ **Wednesday, 11th, 8:00 P.M.** It took four men all day to make a floor for my tent; pine and palmetto logs set a foot from the ground; the tent was pitched upon it just before dark and now things are arranged such as at the other camp. This afternoon a large squad of men have prepared a fine foundation for the hospital tents. We learned today that Col. Hallowell had been honourably discharged, and it is generally regretted. The water is better at this camp. So many regiments are camped near us that the several bugle calls sound very pleasantly; there is a fine brigade band not far off which we enjoy.

¶ **Thursday, 12th, 9:00 P.M.** This has been another busy day. Most of the hospital staff came, and a tent has been put up, so the sick are comfortable. The light frame bunks were mostly broken in transportation so that we were relieved when the Post Surgeon called to say we might have ten from the post hospital which is about to be discontinued. Dr. Brown was

106. Capt. Mussey would serve as brigade quartermaster through the winter of 1863–64 before resigning his commission on 19 August 1864. The new regimental quartermaster was Lt. Ezekiel Fowler and then Lt. George Garrison. Fox, *Record*, 17, 100.

here this noon for a short time. One of the cooks has arrived with his utensils. The chaplain declares that he wished to buy a horse but when one is offered he fails to purchase. Dr. Brown would like to sell him his.

¶ **Friday, 13th, 9:30 P.M.** Today has been even more fully occupied than yesterday for, to my great regret, there was not time for my usual ride. Of course I might have left at any time, but not with a clear conscience; for it is my duty to supervise the work upon the hospital and see that it is done in the best way. I had a sergeant and ten men all day, and they have made good progress, but I will defer description till all is done. Dr. Brown was here at noon. The major has superintended the erection of a shelter for the horses; it is twenty feet square, with room for ten. It is understood that the resignation of Col. Hallowell will be followed by promotions in regular order; that is, Hartwell will be Colonel, Fox, Lt. Col., and Wales, Major. I understand that Wales was not the ranking captain at first but was made so at the special request of Hartwell, while Pratt, the oldest and best of all was put tenth because he allowed himself to be detailed on engineer duty while the batteries were being erected on Morris Island. It is generally thought among the subordinates that Soule and Nutt[107] deserve the majority better than Wales. A few days ago, through Capt. George Pope[108] of the 54th, I received from Mr. Rogers a note to the effect that he had made arrangements to pay Mr. Gooding for my horse in anticipation of our delayed payment here.

¶ **Saturday, Nov. 14th, 9:30 P.M.** It rained a couple of hours just after noon and has been really warm, a great change from three days ago. Again I have had a sergeant and ten men constructing the foundation for the third hospital tent.

¶ **Sunday, 15th, 7:00 P.M.** Notwithstanding the day I had to continue the work on the hospital for we need the three tents. I have also done something on the latter part of my thesis.

¶ **Monday, 16th, 9:00 P.M.** A very sad piece of news. Last night, after a visit from officers of another regiment some of our own became grossly

107. William Nutt, a native of Vermont who moved to Natick, had served in the 2nd Massachusetts and, briefly, in the 54th before joining the 55th Massachusetts as captain. Appointed lieutenant colonel and brevetted colonel by 1865, he served in the Freedmen's Bureau after the war ended. Fox, *Record*, 99.

108. George Pope had been one of several men in the 44th Massachusetts offered commissions when Shaw organized his regiment. Duncan, *Blue-Eyed Child of Fortune*, 29.

intoxicated and the major put four of them under arrest; today two of them have resigned to avoid dismissal. So far as they are known to me they will be no loss.

¶ **Wednesday, 18th, 10:15 P.M.** Dr. Brown has gone to Hilton Head. I have had to visit the hospital several times, and it is considerably farther from my tent than in the old camp; also I drew a tooth for the officer, prescribed for a second, and bandaged the leg of a third; I have consulted the colonel on hospital matters and now must go to the hospital again for medicine for the sentry near my tent who is coughing badly. Then I must write to Prof. Dana[109] in reply to a letter from him received today together with two of his papers. In the absence of Dr. Brown of course I have to make out all the reports, a kind of work that is very uncongenial besides occupying.

¶ **Saturday, 21st.** The long expected box came today; the other officers pronounce my new cap very handsome, and the strap for Billy is just the thing; Frank is delighted with his bag. Lt. Fowler,[110] the new regimental quartermaster, was grossly intoxicated today and fell off his horse while at the Pawnee Landing and again near the quarters of Col. Littlefield. He has resigned to avoid court martial. The barrel of whiskey is kept in my tent; one of the soldiers contrived to slit the tent and steal some by boring a hole; but I tracked him and he will be punished.

¶ **Sunday, 22nd, 9:00 P.M.** There is complaint of fleas in the camp, but as yet I have seen only one and at a safe distance.[111] This evening after dressing the leg of an officer I went to hear him state to his company the situation in regard to the pay. All in that company and I hear nearly all in the regiment decline to accept less than $13.00 per month. Some of the married men hesitate a little on account of their families, but decided with

109. James Dwight Dana was a geologist and zoologist. In 1850 he was appointed to a position in natural history and geology at Yale College, a position he held until 1892. He continued to correspond with Wilder after the war. Wilder Papers, CU.

110. Ezekiel Fowler, a painter in Amesbury, was sergeant major of the 14th Massachusetts, a heavy artillery regiment, prior to joining the 55th. In contrast to what Wilder wrote, he resigned his commission in June 1864. Fox, *Record*, 56.

111. Wilder was fortunate. Many soldiers believed that they were the worst that they had encountered and were a "dreaded pest, almost a scourge" that rendered sleep impossible. Regiments relocated periodically to get away from the fleas and the rats that built up in an established camp. Hagy, *To Take Charleston*, 69–72.

the rest to wait till full justice is done. At the inspection today the colonel and major complimented me warmly on the condition of the hospital.

¶ **Monday, [November] 23rd, 9:00 P.M.** This has been a rainy, dark and dismal day. In the afternoon I warmed up myself and Billy by a canter to the camp of the 112th New York to return the Surgeon some pills borrowed when we first moved down. The brigade commander is now Col. Littlefield[112]; he admires Billy greatly.

¶ **Tuesday, 24th, 9:00 P.M.** For the first time in nearly a week I have been able to work on my thesis; unfortunately new questions arise which cannot be determined without facts of which I am not sure, and so I feel seriously the lack of books on anatomy. Just heard a queer sound in Frank's tent and a laugh from the sutler[113] who occupies it with him; I infer that the former had rolled out of bed, but that it did not hurt him.

¶ **Thursday, 26th, 9:00 P.M.** This has been a fine Thanksgiving day and I wish our men might have had more reason to feel thankful; the next regiment has been paid in full all that was promised when they enlisted, but ours must wait because of a defective law that has permitted gross misinterpretation and injustice. A letter from Mr. Scudder says that the printing of the previous papers has been delayed so that mine will not be started before Dec. 1st; that will enable me to complete it. I am studying the nature and uses of drugs daily from my new book, Still's "Materia Medica"[114] and hope to learn a good deal that will be useful.

¶ **Friday, 27th, 9:45 P.M.** It has been cloudy all day and is now raining gently with a pleasant patter on the roof. I cannot help reflecting how comfortable I am here in the face of the enemy and in a sort of wilderness, yet well housed and fed; so many of our soldiers are on the march in all

112. Col. Milton S. Littlefield was the politically appointed commander of the 21st USCT (formerly the 4th South Carolina Volunteers). Advisers to Andrew distrusted him, senior officers did not respect him, and he was later court-martialed for defrauding black soldiers of part of their enlistment bounties. The charge was not proven, and he was mustered out of the army in 1866. William L. Richter, *Historical Dictionary of the Civil War and Reconstruction*, 362; Fox, *Record*, 19; Trudeau, *Voices*,59.

113. The regiment's sutler was D. W. Johnson. Fox, *Record*, 16.

114. Wilder was reading Alfred Stille's authoritative *Therapeutics and Materia Medica*. Stille was a professor of medicine at the University of Pennsylvania and the author of the first American textbook on general pathology. Flannery, *Civil War Pharmacy*, 35, 182.

sorts of weathers. I am almost ashamed of the luxury of the circular cushion that came in the box; it just fits my barrel chair. This afternoon I made a post mortem, the second since leaving Washington, where they were so frequent. The man had been ailing for some time and excused from all duty, but his face was full and I expected to find a dropsical condition of the internal conditions; so it proved, but the immediate cause of death was an organic defect of the heart that no remedies could have cured; he had not complained of pain in that region. Col. Hartwell has a letter from Col. Hallowell which he read to the major and me; it says that he will recommend Hartwell as his successor, and advises him to refrain from the "gruffness" (something like hauteur, too) to which he is prone; he sent promises to look after the interests of the regiment as far as he was able, and directed that the contents of his trunk be divided among various officers; my share was three pair of white cotton gloves and a box of paper collars, for which I am really grateful.

Nov. 29th, as to pay. (Sheets 1 and 2 are probably with other documents on that subject among Negro Brain papers in my office on a shelf at the west side; the following begins sheet 3.)

The paymaster came and first paid the line officers and the few enlisted men who had decided to accept it.[115] Then the field and staff officers. The payment is up to the last bi-monthly muster, Oct. 31. My pay began May 25th, when I was mustered into service, and was at the rate of $103.20 per month, amounting to $546.35. Of this I exchanged $425.00 for a Treasury note which I shall send to Mr. Rogers; he will pay mother $87.00, Dr. Nichols $20.00; the balance will cover the cost of the horse and his own loan of $125.00. I have also asked him to ascertain from Wm. Philbrick whether the latter wishes to be repaid this loan of $100.00 now or at my next pay day. I shall pay Frank $30.00 for his 4 ½ months service, and the sutler and the hospital fund about $50.00; I have already paid the former Q.M., Mussey, $20.00 for shoes, blankets, candles and rations at different times. Soon after midnight a sergeant roused me in behalf of one of his men who had the colic; I sent him to the steward for the usual remedy, but that did not relieve him; so an hour or two later I had to get into my overcoat and high boots and spend an hour or more with a foolish fellow who (having perhaps taken his pay or borrowed from another who had) had so gorged himself that he was in convulsions; at times his face positively

115. Fox claims that many of the officers planned to decline their pay in sympathy with their men but were persuaded by the enlisted men to accept the pay. Fox, *Record*, 17.

scared me; he could not speak or swallow, but at last I forced a powerful emetic down his throat and relieve was obtained.[116]

¶ **Tuesday, Dec. 1st, 9:30 P.M.** All last evening was spent with Dr. Brown and the Chaplain settling our mess account with the hospital; hereafter we will eat independently of it and of each other. Each has repaid the hospital fund $24.00 for the actual rations since Aug. 210; the share of each for the extras brought from the sutler was $17.00, making my meals for 3 and two thirds months $41.00, which seems to me very reasonable. Yesterday it was very cold and in the evening my fingers were too stiff to write other than figures. The ice has stood in my water pail all day.

¶ **Thursday, 3rd, 11 P.M.** Frank is to leave tomorrow; very naturally his mother wishes to see him. He will take some letters and some messages. By mail I shall send up to the 93rd page of my thesis, completed this evening, but there must still be written ten or twenty more.

¶ **Friday, 4th, 7:15 P.M.** A month's leave is to be granted to one of the Field and Staff officers, to two of the line officers, and to two enlisted men of each company. I shall not urge my claims as against the major and Dr. Brown, both of whom are married; the former's wife needs him at this time. Indeed I cannot approve of the disposition to ask furloughs so soon after commencing service unless one has done something meriting special consideration; so far I hope I have done my duty, but it has involved no unusual deeds. A few days ago we entertained extraordinary visitors, Major Fay of Chelsea and a Miss Gilson; they have been spending two or three weeks with the 40th Mass. They brought various things for the Chelsea men in that regiment. Major Fay was one of the Allotment Commissioners and had told father that he would see me; they gave our regiment a lot of underclothing which the colonel placed in my charge; I gave them to the most needy ones at this morning's Sick Call. To replace Frank I have detailed one of Capt. Soule's younger men, his name is Wiley Abbott,[117] and he is 18 years old; he seems faithful and is used to horses; he is also a good cook; so far he has cooked my meals on the hospital stove, but hereafter most things can be cooked on it; he made an excellent bread pud-

116. The Standard Supply Table used by the army after May 1863 included the extract of ipecac to be used as a "powerful emetic." Flannery, *Civil War Pharmacy*, 118, 120.

117. Wiley Abbott was 18 when he joined Company K, leaving behind a farmer's life in New Richmond, Ohio. He deserted in South Carolina in July 1865. Fox, *Record*, 142.

ding for dinner; I buy bread off the quarter master, and coffee and tea; from the sutler canned meats and vegetables.

¶ **Sunday, Dec. 6, 9 P.M.** ~~This~~ **Yester**day I ~~have~~ experienced the delays resulting from military red tape. It is so cool that some of the men are greatly in need of socks, their own being worn out; for some reason none are to be had from the Q.M. Major Fay left a few pair but more are needed and I decided to apply to the Sanitary Commission on Morris Island. For some reason the authorities are very strict now. A pass was signed by Col. Hartwell; it was approved by Col Littlefield, the brigade commander; then I had to take it part way up the island to Gen.Vogdes, the post commander; then back to the adjutant of Gen. Gilmore; these goings to and fro consumed the afternoon. I was ready to start at I today, but on asking Q.M. Mussey if he would accompany me he consented, provided I would wait and dine with their brigade mess; I assented provided he would take supper with me. After a six mile ride we reached the Inlet just in time to see the steamer leaving, and so lost an hour. On Morris Island we first interviewed Col. E.N. Hallowell[118] of the 54th on regimental business; then I got a dozen pair of old fashioned knit socks, but again missed the return boat, having to wait an hour in the cold wind.

¶ **Tuesday, Dec. 8, 8 P.M.** Today we were reviewed by a captain from the office of the Inspector General in Washington together with Gen. Vogdes, Col. Littlefield and their staffs. To me it was rather less of a nuisance than such ceremonies generally are because I was on horseback; in the course of the evolutions a ditch had to be crossed; some of the horses hesitated at it and one ignominiously waded through, but Billy leaped it in fine style. I regret to say that his activity is not always commendable; some days ago I was carrying three bottles of wine to Col. E.N. Hallowell (probably sent in the box from our former colonel); they were in the large saddlebags that are strapped to the saddle and hang one at either side; while I was in the tent of Gen. Vogdes Billy took the opportunity to roll over; fortunately the sand was deep and soft and to my great relief the bottles were not broken. The other day, however, I astonished him. We were riding in a thick wood, and I dropped the rein on his neck and let him choose his own course; after dodging sever low limbs we came to one that crossed just above his

118. Edward Needles Hallowell, a firm abolitionist, was promoted to colonel of the 54th Massachusetts after the death of Robert Shaw at Fort Wagner. Emilio, *A Brave Black Regiment*, 328–29; Yacovone, *A Voice of Thunder*, 250.

head; I raised it but did not observe a strong vine that took off my hat and nearly carried me after it over Billy's tail. I always ride in the woods after breakfast and usually again in the afternoon. Col. Hartwell has directed that the Inspection Board report to him at Reveille, 5 A.M., so Major Fox and I have to be quite early.

¶ **Wednesday, 9th, 7:30 P.M.** I am glad to say that the order mentioned above was due to orders from higher authorities and has been modified somewhat. When Major Fox and I reported to the Colonel at five this morning we were told that we only had to make sure that the men had their breakfast at 6; the surgeon's call is set for 6:30; the second call is usually at 8:30, but as the official report as to the number excused from duty is made at the first the other may be delayed to suit my convenience; for example, this morning I had to go first to Pawnee Landing to attend to drawing rations for the hospital for the next ten days. This afternoon, after Dress Parade, the major and adjutant tried their horses at jumping the ditch we crossed the other day; the adjutant's horse landed in soft mud and turned a summersault, throwing his rider over his head; neither was hurt. Yesterday Lt. Silva[119] of Col. Littlefield's staff reminded me that we had met in the operating room at the Mass. Gen. Hospital. Recently our hospital tents have been made more comfortable by turf fire places and chimneys.

¶ **Tuesday, Dec. 15, 9 P.M.** At brigade headquarters there have been visiting for several days Mrs. Lander,[120] widow of the general of that name; this noon, in the absence of Dr. Brown, I went over the hospital with her and she noted some things that we needed, promising to send them. Learning that she wished to visit the forts on Morris Island then and that Major Sturgis could not accompany her I volunteered. An ambulance was obtained for her and we reached the camp of the 54th between 2 and 3. After an hour there, its colonel, Hallowell entered the ambulance and with her and Capt. Appleton[121] rode on horseback with me. We had a fine

119. Charles Silva would be promoted to captain in the 21st USCT.

120. Jean Margaret Davenport Lander, the widow of Gen. Frederick West Lander, was a renowned British actress before she met and married the explorer Frederick West. After his death in 1862, she joined the nursing corps at Port Royal, South Carolina. Sifakis, *Who Was Who in the Civil War*, 372.

121. John Whittier Messer Appleton joined the 54th Massachusetts as a lieutenant and rose to major before the end of the war. Duncan, *Blue-Eyed Child of Fortune*, 28–9, 33; Yacovone, *A Voice of Thunder*, 309, 315.

ride up the beach and over the scene of the famous attack; Appleton showed us the place in Wagner where Shaw[122] was killed and he was wounded. The fort has been repaired and strengthened by our forces. We had fine views of the blockading fleet, Sumter, Charleston. Between Wagner and Gregg is a patch of low ground where our men are at work; into this were sent several shells from Fort Moultrie across the harbour; I confess to listening somewhat anxiously for the whistle of the shell after noting the discharge of the gun; we were not hit, however. Here is a rough diagram of the location. [**Not with typed diary**]

Of course the forts are too large in proportion. Charleston seems very near, and Sumter appears to be a mass of debris. In front of Wagner I found a skull but lost it on the return. We met Col. Hartwell and all were entertained at dinner at the mess of the Field and Staff of the 54th. During the return ride on Folly Island Col. Hartwell informed me that Dr. Brown had tendered his resignation; he expressed surprise but no regret. It seems that recently a report was made calling attention to the gross defects in the hospital arrangements; Dr. Brown considers the criticisms unjust; I do not for at any time he might have had all the men he wanted for improvements. I did not see the report, but the Council of Administration, Col. Fox[123] and Capt. Nutt, told me it was not intended to censure me at all. I made no special reply to Col. Hartwell, for I do not wish to say anything against Dr. Brown.

¶ **Thursday, 17th, 9 P.M.** This afternoon I went to Morris Island on business and remained to witness the execution of a deserter in the presence of all the troops on the island. He was a ~~conscript~~ **substitute**[124]; the punishment will be a warning to others. The funeral march was "Adeste Fideles" and it will have gruesome associations hereafter.

122. Col. Robert Gould Shaw, son of a prominent abolitionist family in Boston, became immortalized when he was killed leading his 54th Massachusetts on its unsuccessful attack on Fort Wagner. He was buried in a common grave with his black enlisted men. For more on Shaw, see Peter Burchard, *One Gallant Rush: Robert Gould Shaw and His Brave Black Regiment* (New York: St. Martin's Press, 1965); Duncan, *Blue-Eyed Child of Fortune*.

123. Although Fox was a lieutenant colonel, from December 1863 Wilder always refers to him as "Col. Fox" in his diary.

124. Under the Conscription Act of 3 March 1863, a potential conscript could avoid military service by providing a "substitute," generally someone paid to take his place. The exemption claimed in providing a substitute, however, extended only until the next succeeding draft. Men avoiding service in 1863 could also pay a three-hundred-dollar commutation fee. David Herbert Donald, Jean Harvey Baker, and Michael F. Holt, *The Civil War and Reconstruction* (New York: W. W. Norton, 2001), 227–29.

¶ **Saturday, 19th, 9 P.M.** Last night it was so cold that in order to write some business letters I had to intrude upon the tent of the Q.M. Tonight I have a fire of my own and will describe the fireplace. Some of the officers have the little army stoves; they burn "fast and furious" and then go out. Others have ripped up one of the seams of the tent and built a fireplace consisting of an enclosure of palmetto logs lined with turf and surmounted by barrels for a chimney; they are unsightly and liable to crumble. This noon I thought of a modification. I obtained an empty vinegar barrel, made of thick staves and bound with iron hoops; from one side I saw out a portion, leaving about six inches at each end. Then I found a soldier who had served in a tinner's shop and provided him with a lot of empty tin cans; he unsoldered them and then riveted them together so as to make quite long strips; the riveting was done with my cutters and pliers for which, as yet, there has been no special need. By again uniting the margins of the sheets we lined the interior of the barrel at a distance of three inches from it excepting at the edges where the strips are nailed into the wood. The hearth is formed of an old iron pan resting on sand in the bottom of the barrel. The tin interior contracts somewhat at the top and opens into a second barrel set on top of the first; the space between the barrel and the tin is also filled with sand. By ripping up the seams at the sides of one of the strips of which the tent is made a flap was lifted permitting the stove to be set just at and a little within the opening. And the fire promises to be a great comfort.

¶ **Sunday, [December] 20th, 10:15 P.M.** Dr. Brown came in a few moments ago to borrow a book; I have never known him to accord unqualified praise of anything before, but for my new fire place he had only admiration. It is now in full blaze and makes the tent very comfortable. Owing to a change in the hour for reports the Sick Call now comes after breakfast.

¶ **Wednesday, 23rd, 8 P.M.** I understand that Dr. Brown's resignation was based upon his inference from the Report mentioned in a previous letter that he could not please the colonel; the latter had never concealed his dislike of the doctor. The doctor has never spoken to me of the matter, but he has told Dr. Babbitt and the steward, who mentioned it to me. The papers all pass through Brigade headquarters, and this afternoon, happening to call for a blanket at Q.M. Mussey's, the adjutant showed me a document stating to Gen. Vogdes and Gen. Gilmore that the Council of Administration had no right to inspect the hospital, and that if any officer was not fit to perform his duties the regimental commander should prefer charges against him; Dr. Brown's resignation is therefore disapproved and the colonel is indirectly rebuked. The document had not yet reached our regiment so I do not know how Dr. Brown will take it. In the course of conversation Q.M. Mussey said one of our officers had speculated as to Dr. Brown's successor in case he resigned. He replied, "Dr. Wilder, of course." The other said, "No doubt he is an excellent physician, but could he cut off a leg"? He replied, ". . . should have entire confidence in him because surgery has been his speciality." I have no idea what officer it was, and perhaps his opinion is not important; but of course it is unpleasant to know that such things have been said, especially since it is the first time in my life that any doubt of my competence has come to my ears. Of course I realize my deficiencies, and strive daily to fit myself for my duties, for my training has been less complete than usual. So far as I can judge almost every officer has some detractors.

¶ **Monday, 21st, 9:15 P.M.** With a change in the wind my fire smoked today. At first I was in despair but soon I realized that the chimney was not high enough; so I mounted a third and smaller barrel on the top of the second, and a tin can over the hole in the upper one; and now it burns finely again. Yesterday, after the regular inspection, it was inspected by the officer of the day and the entire Field and Staff, and pronounced superior to any other in camp.

¶ **Tuesday, 22nd, 8:30 P.M.** About an hour ago, hearing a loud voice in one of the company streets I went to listen and returned partly amused but more saddened and filled with a desire to help these comparatively ignorant soldiers. They were holding an outdoor debate; it seems to have been in progress for several nights; the question was, which are more attractive, the works of nature or the works of art. What I heard was very extraordinary. Each speaker seemed to wish to say all that he knew upon any subject, and sometimes one had to admit that what he had adduced had no bearing upon the subject. They went back to the creation of man and spoke of all things imaginable. Finally the subject was dropped for this, which is the ruling force, the hope of reward or the fear of punishment? One speaker claimed that the incentive to our armies was the hope of accomplishing some good; but a rascal named Pelett[125] declared that

125. Alfred E. (or C.) Pellett, a 28-year-old sailor from Pittsburgh, Pennsylvania, became "Principal Musician" before he deserted in August 1864. He was subsequently reduced by

he had no hope of anything, but enlisted for fear of being drafted[126]; he further declared his belief that nine-tenths of the regiment were there for the same reason; just then Lt. James[127] came along and called Pellet and told him not to talk in that way. The next speaker was more rational. The great trouble with these men seems to be their tendency to be carried away with large words and high sounding phrases. Would that we had a competent chaplain to advise and instruct them.

¶ **Thursday, 24th, 9:10 P.M.** While I was dressing Capt. Thurber's leg Capt. Grant[128] came in and described his festive trip to Hilton Head. Gen. Gilmore had invited his Division Commanders, and then the Brigade Commanders, and then a certain number of officers from each regiment to attend a ball at Hilton Head: there were many officers' wives and all had a gay time.

¶ **Saturday, 26th, 10:15 P.M.** I have just eaten my dinner; at least it was the second since my breakfast. Yesterday I found that the heat of my fire was threatening to ignite the barrels; so I took them down got some more large tin cans and fixed them so that they seemed to be safe. This morning while I was dressing by the fire I heard a roaring sound then the cry "Fire." The barrels were blazing and the tent in danger. Fortunately the men who sweep up the camp each morning were near; they pulled off the two upper barrels, just in time to prevent the tent itself from taking; as it was the flap that was lifted to admit the stove was consumed. Naturally I was somewhat mortified. So at noon I got the same boy and we took the whole think apart; sawed out one more stave of the barrel and replaced the tin lining, placing turf instead of sand in the intervening space. Then

---

general court-martial in November 1864 but was reappointed in May 1865. Fox, *Record*, 114, 122.

126. Few of the men who enlisted in the 55th Massachusetts would have had to fear the Enrolment Act of March 1863. While free blacks were apparently eligible for the draft under the act, which required the enrollment of every male citizen between the ages of 20 and 45, very few were actually enrolled and drafted. It was not until the February 1864 amendment that legislation specifically included the enrollment of all blacks, slave or free, in the target age group. Eugene C. Murdock, *One Million Men: The Civil War Draft in the North* (Madison: State Historical Society of Wisconsin, 1971), 180; James W. Geary, *We Need Men: The Union Draft in the Civil War* (Dekalb: Northern Illinois University Press, 1991), 67–68.

127. Robertson James, from Albany, New York, was living in Rhodes Island when he accepted his commission in the 55th Massachusetts. He was brevetted captain in May 1865. Fox, *Record*, 105.

128. Charles Edward Grant, from Boston, served as sergeant in the 24th Massachusetts before joining the 55th as captain of Company B. Fox, *Record*, 102.

we narrowed the lining so that the chimney could be composed wholly of large cans; the uppermost one has a hole in one side and is moveable on the next below so as to accommodate it to the wind. The chimney is steadied by three wires attached to the edge of the barrel.

¶ **Sunday, 27th, 9:30 P.M.** Capt. Thurber is not well; his leg does not permit him to walk and I have prescribed the use of my horse, at a slow pace, so that he may get some outdoor air and gentle exercise.

¶ **Monday, Dec. 28th, 8:00 P.M.** I have just written to Col. Hallowell expressing my regret at his resignation. After the review by Gen. Vogdes yesterday afternoon I was invited with ~~Major~~ **Col.** Fox[129] and Major Wales to take a glass of cider with Col. James Beecher, now the brigade commander. Major Appleton was here today for a time. It has rained more or less but is not cold and no fire has been needed.

¶ **Wednesday, 30th, 8:45 P.M.** This has been a very pleasant day; when the sun shines the woods are bright and green, more as in our northern September. This afternoon Capt. Thurber took quite a ride and said it did him good. This evening I sharpened the scalpels knives in my pocket case. Also I reckoned up the cost of my living during the past month and found it to be $22.50, including candles, which are quite an item. I have been having raisins in my bread pudding daily but as they are 50 cents a pound I shall have them only on Sundays. Butter is also 50 cents and canned meats 75 per can, but vegetables and the bread bought off the Q.M. are more reasonable.

¶ **Thursday, 31st, 9 P.M.** Recently the rebels attached one of our gun boats in the Stono River, about two miles off, but were repulsed. It seems so strange for us to be living quietly in the midst of the woods when a determined movement on either side might set us all to fighting. This afternoon the regiment was mustered for pay. One of Capt. Soule's men broke his collar bone today and I set it and bandaged him up. I have been studying books on surgery and medicine considerably lately; it is very important to learn all I can, but I cannot get interested in pure anatomy.

¶ **Friday, [January] 1st, 8:00 P.M.** My little fire is blazing merrily, but the wood is nearly gone so I must retire early. There is a fierce cold wind; I pity

129. Charles Fox had been promoted lieutenant colonel on 1 December 1863.

our poor fellows out on picket along the river. During the day it sometimes blew as if it would carry our tents away. Although the first day of the year I have not been able to do much besides my regular duties; them I do not count as credit, but am not satisfied unless something more has been accomplished in either study or writing or work.

¶ **Saturday, 2nd, 8:30 P.M.** I have a new servant, **Ackers,**[130] today, from another company; older and stronger than the last and less forgetful, I hope.

¶ **Sunday, 3rd, 9:10 P.M.** Col. Hartwell has just been in for half an hour; it is the second visit he has made me; I have never been to any officer's tent except on business. Capt. Thurber reports himself so much better that he will go on duty tomorrow. He considers Billy a wonderful remedy; I hope others will not fall ill in order to receive the same prescription. Thurber says fresh horse outside is much pleasanter to take than "salt horse" inside. I do not like salt beef at all; in fact Col. Fox complains that at the food inspections I am to confine myself to the tea and coffee and leave him the beef and pork; the latter I never touch. My new boy knows little of cooking but the hospital cook, Tilman,[131] is his friend and instructs him. This morning at my usual ride I went to the beach where the returning pickets discharged their rifles, and also fired a revolver over Billy's head; he behaved very well, and will doubtless become used to firearms.

¶ **Tuesday, 5th, 9:00 P.M.** I am glad to have letters from Frank and his mother.

¶ **Sunday, 10th, 8:00 P.M.** At about 9 last night my peaceful tent was invaded by Col. Fox, the Adjutant, Capt. Crane, the officer of the day, and Capt. Soule. I asked them to be seated (fortunately the last brought a chair with him and others sat on the bed). Then I sat before them my stock of raisins and sugar, and said if they wished to brew a stimulating drink there was a bottle of pure alcohol, but they declined. Then, to the tune of Rousseau's dream, they began to sing, very slowly, "Cut my leg off"; after repeating this line three times the fourth line was the single word, "short," shouted so loudly as to astonish me. They explained that they had been

130. George W. Akers had been a plasterer before he left Carthagena, Ohio, to enlist in Company B. He was 19 years old. His name on regimental records is "Akers," but Wilder refers to him as "Ackers." Fox, *Record*, 118.

131. John Tilman, a private in Company A and a bricklayer in civilian life, was also listed as a "Hospital Nurse." Fox, *Record*, 116.

singing in the colonel's tent and would now entertain me if agreeable. They sang for an hour or two, I joining in when I could; Crane has a very sweet voice. I have just returned from the hospital where I drew the worst tooth I have ever seen; but the patient was so glad to be rid of it that he made no complaint. During the week the men have erected a sort of chapel for Sunday worship and evening instruction; it was dedicated this noon, and Col. Beecher delivered a discourse.[132]

¶ **Monday, 11th, 8:30 P.M.** Between five and six Col. Hartwell, Col. Fox, Captains Nutt and Thurber and I amused ourselves with casting a huge hammer with a handle three feet long; Lt. Mowry[133] (whom I omitted above) excelled us all in the throw with both hands, but I was the winner with the swinging throw and the throw over the head.

¶ **Wednesday, 13th, 8:30 P.M.** Yesterday Company F, of which Thurber is the captain, moved to Pawnee Landing in order to learn how to manage a battery of light artillery.

¶ **Thursday, [January] 14th, 9 P.M.** I have just returned from an entertainment little expected on this island. Some time ago was established a Masonic Temple, of canvas, near Gilmore's headquarters.[134] A printed circular invited Colonels Hartwell and Fox to attend a Shakespearean Reading; it was not advisable for both to be absent from the regiment at once, so I accepted Hartwell's for tonight. The course is given by Chaplain (Hudson?) of one of the N.Y. regiments. This was on Henry IV, with several readings from the text. Besides many officers, some high in rank, there was present a lady, quite a handsome one, a very unusual and delightful sight.[135] Folly Island is becoming civilized, but a spark may compel us to relapse into barbarism. The chaplain came in this afternoon to say that he had

132. At the start of the war, Beecher had served as chaplain in the 67th New York Infantry before becoming first lieutenant colonel in the 141st New York Infantry and then colonel in the 1st North Carolina Colored Volunteers. Reid, *Freedom for Themselves*, 25.

133. John Osborne Mowry, a mechanic in Athol before the war, served two years as a corporal in the 27th Massachusetts before being commissioned in the 55th. He became the regimental quartermaster in August 1864.

134. A number of enlisted men in both the 55th Massachusetts and the 1st North Carolina Colored Volunteers were Masons. When Sergeant John Bird died from pneumonia in June 1864, his fellow Masons sent his remains "to his Lodge in Ypsilanti, Michigan, that he might be there interred with Masonic honors." Trudeau, *Voices*, 63; Fox, *Record*, 130.

135. The woman was likely the wife of one of the senior officers, but Wilder offers no further information on her identity.

resigned. It seems that one of the men was impertinent to him and he threatened to blow his brains out and started for his revolver. This coming to the ears of the colonel (the threat, not the pistol) he wrote the chaplain to the effect that a majority of the officers and men desired a change and that he would advise him to resign rather than face a Court of Inquiry.[136] It will be a real relief; would that we might have a new Churchman in his place.

¶ **Sunday, 17th, 8:45 P.M.** I have just returned from the chapel or school house built some time ago of canvas and palmetto leaves. There were present the chaplain, Dr. Brown, the Adjutant, Capt. Crane and Lt. James. After a sort of service, during which the chaplain spoke of his departure, we wrote down the names of the men nearest us, respectively, marking their deficiency in reading and spelling by the numbers from 1 to 5; then the lists were combined and in accordance with the marks the "ninety and nine" who desired instruction were assigned to five classes and books given them accordingly. The school is to be held three evenings a week and I shall not begrudge the time in such a cause.

¶ **Monday, 18th, 8:45 P.M.** I have just come from the school. The line officers and adjutant were busy so Dr. Brown and I were the only teachers. Unfortunately the books are of various kinds, by different writers, but we managed by having them read in turn from the same book; the men were very attentive and interested, especially in little illustrations or anecdotes that we could interject; as the junior officer I took the lower class. In place of my usual morning ride I joined the colonel and adjutant today in a visit to all the picket posts along the western shore of the island. We had a fine ride and I never knew Billy in such spirits; he pranced and kicked up his heels like a boy just out of school; sometimes even it felt as if he were on his front legs only, and the adjutant said he dared not ride too close behind him for fear of his heels. At dinner I began eating with the Field and Staff mess, having been invited. They live better, that is with more variety, than I do alone, but it costs, including the servant, about $7.00 a week. No doubt it is well for all the members of the field and staff to eat together, but I am not sure that I shall continue. I understand that Dr. Brown was also invited but he was not there.

¶ **Tuesday, 19th, 8:30 P.M.** At the school this evening, in place of the usual recitations a very instructive lecture was given by Dr. Brown on

136. Trudeau, *Voices*, 60.

ventilation and other matters connected with the welfare of the men, who seemed to understand and appreciate it. There were present also Capt. Gordon and the two medical officers of the 1st N.C. The chaplain made some further quite needless remarks upon his retirement and then an excellent address was made by Sergeant Iverson[137] of Co. B., the General Superintendent of the school. He is a fine looking man and said to be the natural son of some scion of the well known Georgia family of that name; he and several of the other sergeants are superior in all respects to many white officers that I have seen and I trust they may be promoted.[138] (He deserted later. About this time destroyed an obscene book at cook house)

The next lecture is to be given by me. The colonel has appointed a committee to look after the interests of the school and to raise funds for its support; it consists of Dr. Brown, Captains Bowditch, Crane and Gordon, and myself. Today has been cold and windy.

¶ **Thursday, 22nd, 8:40 P.M.** This has been a long day. I accepted the invitation of Col. Fox to accompany him and two other officers upon the "Grand Rounds." We started soon after 3 A.M., riding up the beach and down the inner shore of the island; the first part was by moonlight. I regret to notice animosities between the field officers and the brigade staff; Major Wales is especially outspoken; his promotion has made him even more conceited and arrogant than before. Since the departure of Col. Hallowell I am less pleased with the state of affairs and as Capt. Bowditch is to be transferred to the 5th Mass. Cavalry, also a colored regiment, and suggested that I should apply for the surgeoncy, I have written Surgeon General Dale that I wish to be considered an applicant.

137. Gabriel P. Iverson, a 31-year-old clerk working in Boston when he enlisted in the regiment, later deserted and moved to Canada. He is described as being a particularly articulate and persuasive voice in the enlisted men's demands for equal treatment. Fox, *Record*, 119; Trudeau, *Voices*, 52, 54.

138. Although black officers were initially commissioned in the Louisiana Native Guard, by the summer of 1863 the War Department opposed the commissioning of African Americans. Gov, Andrew led the way in demanding that qualified blacks receive commissions. Using his power to appoint officers to state volunteer regiments, he commissioned a number of deserving sergeants in the 54th and 55th Massachusetts. The army, however, refused to discharge the sergeants as enlisted men so they could accept their commissions. It would not be until July 1865 that John F. Shorter, James M. Trotter, and William H. Dupree, all senior sergeants in the 55th Massachusetts, became officers. Ira Berlin, *The Black Military Experience*, 305–9; Glatthaar, *Forged in Battle*, 176–77.

¶ **Friday, [January] 22nd, 8:45 P.M.** There has been no snow so far and today is very comfortable; I saw two butterflies. Gen. Gordon[139] is now in command of the island, Gilmore being at Hilton Head and Vogdes having gone north. Day before yesterday Gordon held a review of all the troops on the island, but the Q.M. and I were excused after a few moments. There is no evidence that anything is contemplated beyond holding these islands, but as the colonel and adjutant are having frames made for their tents perhaps we shall move just because we are prepared to remain comfortable here.

¶ **Sunday, 24th, 8:30 P.M.** Bible classes were held this evening, preceded by singing in the chapel. It is very pleasant to teach these simple minded soldiers, and to see their faces light up when they gain a new fact or comprehend a new idea. The Committee has decided to spend a part of the $31.00 already contributed by the officers for writing materials, chalk, etc., and I am authorized to send to Boston for them. Lt. Gannett,[140] who has already offended several times in the same way, came from Long Island, where he is now stationed in a state of intoxication; he was so noisy that the colonel rode off for authority to arrest and confine him; he has served at sea and we are told that he wished to re-enter the navy.

¶ **Monday, [January] 25th, 8:45 P.M.** There are rumours that Dr. Brown has again tendered his resignation. While walking to supper tonight the adjutant put his hand on my shoulder and said, "How would a major's (surgeon's) strap look there?"

¶ **Tuesday, 26th, 10:00 P.M.** For two days I have suffered with a boil on my cheek, quite painful, and rendering it difficult to think; nevertheless I have my promised lecture and was assured it was enjoyed.

¶ **Thursday, 28th, 9:15 P.M.** This evening I was again invited to hear Chaplain Hudson of the N.Y. Engineers on "Richard III"; the next and last is to be on "Hamlet."

139. George Henry Gordon (1823–1886) attended West Point and served in the Mexican War before practicing law in his home state of Massachusetts. A colonel in 1861, he commanded a brigade in 1862 and a division by 1863. He served briefly as the commander of the forces operating against Charleston. Sifakis, *Who Was Who in the Civil War*, 254.

140. Lt. Wyllys Gannett lived in St. Louis, Missouri, before joining the 24th Massachusetts as a sergeant. He was commissioned in the 55th in July 1863. He resigned his commission in June 1864 but was recommissioned the following year and was brevetted captain by the time the regiment was mustered out. Fox, *Record*, 104.

¶ **Friday, 29th, 10:15 P.M.** I have had an usual series of callers on business today, Major Wales, Capt. Gordon,[141] Lt. James, Adjutant Perry,[142] Capt. Hodges, and Q.M. Mussey.

¶ **Saturday, 30th, 8:45 P.M.** This has been a really warm day. I have made a blackboard for the school and ridden up to Pawnee Landing with Q.M. Mussey, who has gone to Hilton Head on business.

¶ **Sunday, 31st, 7 P.M.** Just before supper Q.M. Garrison and I rode to the "White House," the center of the old plantation and apparently the only house on the island; we went to the top in order to get a better view of a considerable fire on James Island.

¶ **Tuesday, [February] 2nd, 8:30 P.M.** While listening to Dr. Marcy's[143] lecture at the school we were interrupted by a message from the colonel, and at his tent found all the other officers, they having been summoned by the "Officers Call," which does not include the staff. The colonel said there was a rumor that the 54th had refused to obey orders and had stacked their arms; that ours would be very likely to follow their example. So he cautioned us to be firm but to be particularly careful to avoid unnecessary harshness; he had a letter today from one of our men asking what was to be done about their pay and threatening to lay down their arms if the money was not forthcoming by the first of the March. He asked our opinions as to addressing the men on the subject. It was agreed to act as if we suspected nothing, but to watch carefully and to avoid anything that might occasion mutiny.

¶ **Wednesday, 3rd, 9:30 P.M.** The officers were paid today for November and December. I received $204.00 of which I shall send $100.00 to Wm. Philbrick, and $15.00 for the reprints of my thesis. Among other things I

141. Capt. John Gordon, born in Exeter, New Hampshire, was a student in Chelsea, Massachusetts, when he enlisted in the 24th, reaching the rank of corporal. He was commissioned captain in the 55th but was forced to resign in July 1864. Fox, *Record*, 102.

142. Leonard Battelle Perry had been a mining engineer in South Natick before being appointed lieutenant in the 55th Massachusetts. He made captain and was assistant adjutant-general by April 1865. Fox, *Record*, 100–101.

143. Henry Orlando Marcy, a physician from Boston, was appointed surgeon in the 35th USCT after serving as assistant surgeon in the 43rd Massachusetts. He was appointed medical director of Florida and later served with Maj. Gen. William Tecumseh Sherman in the Carolinas campaign. Reid, *Freedom for Themselves*, 76, Henry Orlando Marcy Papers, South Carolina Historical Papers.

have been writing out the records of the proceedings of our school committee, of which I was chosen secretary (Where?). Capt. Gordon and I were authorized to arrange for a concert, vocal and instrumental, to be given a week from next Tuesday. A dozen pairs of mittens have been given me, with the thumb and one finger separate. I turned them over to the officer of the guard with the understanding that each should turn his pair over to his successor at the close of his two hours period duty. Q.M. Mussey has returned from Hilton Head and says the 54th was there on the way to Florida;[144] that he mingled with them and heard nothing of insubordination; so probably the rumor was not well founded.

¶ **Thursday, 4th, 8:30 P.M.** Billy misbehaved last night; you see the halter is not the nice one I bought in Boston but an inferior one that someone exchanged it for in Newbern after I left; so Billy slipped it over his head and cantered about the camp and tore his new blanket to shreds. When I saw him this morning he had returned to his stable and was demurely munching his oats. To whip him would have done no good, for he would not have known the reason. I rode up to Pawnee Landing and got the halter repaired. There I met a white soldier, McPhail, who had been one of my patients at Judiciary Square; he recognized me just as I was about to say I had seen him before.

¶ **Friday, 5th, 9 P.M.** Four of our officers are now under my care for various complaints. There is visiting Col. Beecher Mr. Severance, collector of the port of Hilton Head; he is from Boston and knows my father and my brother David. Dr. Mann of the 1st N.C. expresses great surprise that I can bring myself to read and study so much; seems to think I must be very peculiar, etc., I showed him Swedenborg's "Divine Love and Wisdom" and he said he was a spiritualist, but would like to read some of Swedenborg's books.

¶ **Sunday, 7th, 9 P.M.** In accordance with the omen of the frames for the tents of the colonel and others and some improvements we have been making upon the school house, it is said that soon we are to leave for an

144. The 54th Massachusetts formed part of the expeditionary force led by Gen. Truman B. Seymour directed to seize control of northern Florida, to cut off Confederate supplies from that state, open a new area for black recruitment and, as a secondary objective, to restore Florida to the Union. The 55th Massachusetts was soon included. William H. Nulty, *Confederate Florida: The Road to Olustee* (Tuscaloosa: University of Alabama Press, 1990), viii–ix, 72–74.

expedition, and I have been arranging my papers with that in view. At the request of Capt. Soule I have given some instruction to the sergeants and some of the more intelligent men as to the ways of checking bleeding by pressure with the fingers or by a simple tourniquet; I used a soldier for demonstration of the location of the main arteries.

¶ **Monday, [January] 8th, 8:45 P.M.** This evening, at the request of the colonel, in the school house I instructed as to bleeding all the sergeants and corporals in the regiment excepting, of course, those out on picket; the nurses and the band (who will act as stretcher bearers). This afternoon I have been selecting the things that I should ~~carry~~ **take** with me in case some must be abandoned either for the time or permanently. There are some apprehensions of an attack by the ~~rebels~~ **enemy** at the White House, half a mile away; but they must wait for high water in order to use the creeks and that does not occur just now till near daylight, so we may have a fair night's rest.

¶ **Wednesday, 10th, 8 P.M.** This evening I have played whist, the first time since leaving home. The colonel and Lt. Col. were opposed to the major and me. Orders have come for our brigade to go to Jacksonville but there are no transports at hand so we may not leave for several days. In the 1st N.C. are several cases of small pox, and we shall have to be careful not let it ~~attack~~ **infect** our men, the camps are so near each other. I vaccinated 15 men today and more tomorrow.

¶ **Friday, 12th, 10 P.M.** I have just completed the medical papers of 20 men whom we shall leave here. The 1st N.C. has already left and we expect to go soon. I have been busy today vaccinating, etc. The firing was heavy last night.

On board Steamer "Peconic,"
Sunday, 13th, 2:30 P.M. We embarked last night and are nearly at Hilton Head.[145]

Jacksonville, Florida,
Thursday, 18th, 9:00 P.M. Saturday and Sunday nights I was on the transport; Monday in bivouac at a camp near this city, with no cover but

145. The *Peconic* carried Companies A, C, and I along with Fox and Wilder. The remaining companies, plus the colonel and Brown were on the *Collins*. Fox, *Record*, 21.

a rubber blanket to keep off the rain; Tuesday the same, Col. Fox under the same cover; it was so cold that I hardly slept after midnight; last night no sleep till 4 A.M. During the days since disembarking I have been almost constantly in the saddle attending to my various duties. This day closed with the execution of a soldier by hanging,[146] and I was called upon to say the last words to him and decide when he was dead.

¶ **Friday, 19th, 9:30 P.M.** For the first time since leaving Folly Island are we at all comfortable; Col. Fox and I have a small tent in a new camp near that which the 54th formerly occupied and about ¼ of a mile north of our first camp; about six companies left this morning for Baldwin, about 15 miles toward the front; the other four, under command of Col. Fox, are to remain on picket and work on the fortifications. The picket line is about three miles long; this morning, for the 6th time I rode the whole length with Col. Fox; it encircles the three sides of the city not bounded by the St. Johns. The ride is over fields, through woods, across brooks, and is just dangerous enough to be interesting. It requires a daily detail of a captain, two lieutenants six sergeants, twelve corporals and 100 privates; they are at posts in numbers from three to twenty, according to the importance of the localities; on the two main roads leading out of the city are also mounted patrols. As soon as I returned from the picket line I had to overtake the other companies already an hour on the march, in order to get something from the adjutant; returning I enticed and forcibly captured his little dog, "Fanny," that had followed him against orders with a line made of five saddle straps I got her to follow till she was so tired that she tried to climb Billy's legs; so I carried her the rest of the way. After dinner I had to go into the city, and in all have probably added more that 15 miles. We are very tired not merely from continual work but from exposure to all sorts of weather; it is now very cold; indeed, at the north I never suffered so much from cold as since arriving here.

(Sheets 50 & 51 are missing)

146. On 17 February four soldiers committed a rape near Camp Finegan. Three were captured and proved to be men from the 55th Massachusetts. Two soldiers, John W. Cork and Spencer Lloyd from Company B were executed at Camp Finegan. John M. Smith, a 21 year old in Company A, was the man Wilder witnessed hung in Jacksonville's public square. Gen. Seymour, who was present, declared loudly, "Served them right, now let any other man try it if he dares." Dr. Esther Hill Hawks bitterly recorded, "If the same measure had been meted out to white officers and men who had been guilty of the same offense towards black women, Gen. S might have grown hoarse repeating his remarks." Schwartz, *A Woman Doctor's Civil War*, 61.

¶ **Tuesday, 23rd, 11:30 P.M.** . . . night the wounded from Olustee arrived;[147] with my nurse I dressed wounds at the hospital in the city till midnight, and began at 5 next morning. Yesterday I was busy all day; in the evening I went again to do for 60 wounded just received and did not leave till 2 A.M. Today I reported for orders to the Post Surgeon and was put in entire charge of the hospital, a brick building of several stories; not only medicines and surgical appliances had to be provided but food as well; and as I had only colored nurses there was much for me to attend to. Last night I cut a ball from a man's thigh and a piece of shell from the side of another; today I took a ball and pieces of bone from a man shot through the lower jaw and tongue. This evening I shipped 15 of the worst cases on a steamer to the general hospital in Hilton Head and feel pretty tired.

(Sheet 53 missing)

¶ **Thursday, 25th, 8:30 P.M.** After sick call I rode past the picket line with Col. Fox; I jumped Billy over all the felled trees that I could find and he made some prodigious leaps, to the admiration of all. He has become perfectly trained, and I ride with the reins on my little finger guiding him by merely the lightest pressure upon the opposite side of the neck; a cavalry man has sometimes to hold the rein in his teeth and the civilian way of pulling would be impossible. Although the other companies have returned Col. Fox still has direct charge of the picket line and as he wished me to remain with him the consent of Dr. Brown, Col. Hartwell, and Col. Osborn[148] was successively obtained. The hospital in the city I have turned over to another surgeon. Since the battle there have arrived two entire brigades from Hilton Head and Folly Island, and there are said to be 12000 men here the whole plain is dotted with camp fires; many earth works have been put up. There came into my tent a very pretty little dog, supposedly having been brought in by some soldier. I have named her "Miff."

(Sheets 56, 57, and 58 are missing)

147. On 20 February 1864, Union forces under Gen. Truman Seymour, including the 54th Massachusetts and 1st North Carolina Colored Volunteers, encountered Confederate troops led by Gen. Joseph Finegan near Olustee. Seymour lost effective control of the battle, throwing units forward piecemeal, and by late afternoon, Federal forces were in full retreat. The Union expedition of 5,500 men suffered 1,861 casualties and there was widespread fear that Confederate soldiers had killed wounded and captured black troops. Nulty, *Confederate Florida*, 122–69; Reid, *Freedom for Themselves*, 79–88, 93–94.

148. Col. Francis A. Osborn, in command of the 24th Massachusetts, had arrived in Jacksonville just before the battle at Olustee but, like the 55th, his regiment was not utilized by Gen. Seymour. Fox, *Record*, 23.

Yellow Bluff, Florida

Sunday, Feb. 28, 7:45 P.M. We left Jacksonville at noon and an hour's pleasant sail brought us to the place where we landed unmolested.[149] It is a small summer resort, comprising three houses on a bluff at the north side of the St. John; the woods run back towards the country and there are marshes on either side, as in the subjoined diagram. At this point the river is quite narrow so that sharpshooters could easily pick off men on a transport. It is proposed to build a stockade of logs on the highest point of the ridge and to erect an abatis of trees with the branches outward; also to dig a ditch. Still further out is the picket line. With this arrangement a small force can hold the place unless the enemy brings artillery, which seems unlikely. It has been a splendid day. Col. Fox and I went with the officer in command of the pickets beyond the line and were relieved to encounter no rattlesnakes. We found the skeleton of an alligator ten feet long and the den of a small one that whisked into it as we approached. We did not bring our horses, but I did bring Miff; she is very lively and interesting and made friends with all on the boat, while the colonel was bathing she disrespectfully attacked his toes. She was transported to the dock in one of my large saddlebags; Billy was surprised and turned his head to stare at her, whereupon she nibbled his nose. One morning she hid both my socks under the bed and attacked my toes as I searched for them.

¶ **Tuesday, [March] 1st, A.M.** Yesterday was undisturbed. The soldiers worked hard on the stockade and abatis and felled timber for some distance out so as to afford a clear view of the advancing foe. The abatis extends into the marsh at either side and an enemy would find it hard to crawl through in the face of our fire. I had a shelter tent pitched for me near the men in case any were cut while working; I studied Guthrie's "Surgery"[150] as well as I could, but was interrupted by a huge brown spider that crawled up my sleeve. Later in the day a gunboat came down the river and anchored opposite; Col. Fox went aboard and returned with the captain and two other officers; they examined the locality so as to determine how best to cooperate with us in case of attack. Still later came a small

149. Lt. Col. Fox, with Companies B and I plus a detachment of New York engineers, had been ordered to Yellow Bluff, a place about halfway between Jacksonville and the mouth of the St Johns River. Companies K and C joined them in March. Fox, *Record*, 24.

150. Wilder was studying G. J. Guthrie, *Commentary on the Surgery of War* (Philadelphia: J. B. Lippincott, 1862).

steamer with Gen. Seymour[151] and Lt. Michie,[152] the Engineer officer who planned the defences, and an officer of the Signal Corps; it is planned to establish here a signal station intermediate between the city and the mouth of the river which is visible from here; a signal sergeant put on his spikes and ascended a tall pine to see if the city is visible; it is not, so some trees must be cut away. Some rockets were left with us and it was arranged that at 7:30 three were to be fired at intervals of 15 minutes unless answered from the city. The third was answered by one and now they are to be fired only in case of attack. The gunboat has moved down the river so as to fire right across the marsh at the east side of the road by which must approach any large force or artillery. At dusk it fired three shells; two stuck in the road and the third failed to explode and continued to a hill beyond. The explosions scared Miff greatly. So long as the gunboat is here we feel comparatively secure. It is really a delightful locality, and if my horse were here I should feel quite content; however, he needs rest after the strenuous work of the past fortnight. There is little regular work for me here; it is healthy and the men are occupied but not overworked as they were on the fortifications at Morris Island. One of the three houses first mentioned issued as a hospital for the few that need such shelter and care. There are three smaller houses. Col. Fox and I occupy the largest room in the largest house, but our meals are served at the hospital. The company officers occupy another room, and the engineers occupy one of the smaller houses. The soldiers have shelter tents out because in case of attack it would take too long for them to leave the houses. The signals comprise red and white flags for the day and red and white lanterns for night; also red lights to burn in case we are forced to leave and wish the gunboat to send boats for us.

P.M. I was interrupted by firing from the gunboat; there was a man on the shrouds, but we could not see what was aimed at. After dinner, our gunboat was relieved by another that came up the river, and the new captain is now with the colonel reconnoitring the ground. Lt Gannett, in command

151. Brig.-Gen. Truman Seymour, a Vermont West Pointer who had served in the Mexican War, had overall command of the Union army that was defeated at Olustee in February 1864. He was justly criticized in the press, but he went on to lead a division in the Petersburg campaign. Sifakis, *Who Was Who in the Civil War*, 582.

152. Lt. Peter Smith Michie, a Scottish-born graduate of West Point in command of three companies of engineers, had constructed a number of defensive positions in Florida. He became the chief engineer in the Department of the South and then the Army of the James. He later taught natural and experimental philosophy at West Point. Sifakis, *Who Was Who in the Civil War*, 447.

of the picket, brought me the feet of a young eagle that was taken in a tree felled during the absence of the old ones; it measured five feet from tip to tip; the old ones were still larger. Lt Gannett has just caught two catfish, and we welcome the fresh food. At intervals heavy but not continuous firing is heard from the city and we long for a boat bringing news. We bathe in the river, but do not venture far from the shore; partly because it deepens rapidly and partly because the region is called "Little Alligator Swamp" from the abundance of those animals. The woods are delightful and it is not easy to imagine that deadly foes may emerge from them at any time.

8:00 P.M. We are just established in our new quarters in the upper house hitherto used as a hospital and as our eating place. After dark a steamer from J. brought rations, a cook for the hospital, and some utensils; Co. K came. There was a review this morning and this afternoon an attack by rebel cavalry. Miff had an encounter with a lizard about 4 inches long which, after being worried, seized her nose and made her yelp; then it escaped through a crack. My coat and trousers are being repaired by my servant, so that, being short of clothing here, I am housed for a time. It seems odd to be in a house, but there are hardly any closets.

¶ **Saturday, 5th,** I have made a barrel chair and the colonel and I take turns using it for writing or reading. I have also made a rude bed and as the colonel has to work much harder, I think he should use it; sometimes he will rest in the daytime but insists upon sleeping on the floor. With a soldier's assistance I have constructed a flight of steps about ten feet long to enable us to descend the bluff in front of the house to bathe. We are tormented, especially mornings and evenings, by swarms of small midges; their bite is very painful, like the prick of a red hot needle, but there seems to be no venom as with the mosquito.

¶ **Sunday, [March] 6th, 2 P.M.** The rebels have notified our commander to remove women and children since they will begin to shell the town in 24 hours; but as there is no sign of an attack perhaps that was a bluff to cover their departure from our front. During the forenoon at least 12 vessels went up the river and 6 down, but we do not know why. A new enemy is reported; before breakfast this morning, while the cook was at the door, he says a panther (lynx?) came from the woods but on seeing him trotted off again; a sergeant and some men tracked it through the jungle across a sandy patch into another woods, but could not get sight of it.

¶ **Monday, 7th, 9:00 P.M.** My sickest patient has broken out with Small Pox; so he and a special nurse have been placed in a small house and we have moved from this to the one we had first.

¶ **Wednesday, 9th, 7:30 P.M.** The soldiers killed two cattle that came near our lines, so we have some fresh beef. This afternoon, with my boy and a man of Co. B I made an expedition of about two miles out to what is said to be the haunt of alligators. It was a creek in the midst of the swamp west of us: we saw several young ones run into the water but could not secure any; we caught a young racoon that is now in room upstairs with a piece of beef; also a black pig which the soldiers hope to fatten enough to be eatable. It is windy tonight and the house has been so perforated with shells that I must stop the holes lest the candle be extinguished.

¶ **Thursday, 10th, 8:00 P.M.** The gale increased during the night and was accompanied by rain in torrents, thunder, and lightning; as severe a storm as I ever knew; but now it did not cease till noon. The little coon died in the night; probably was not well when we caught it or it would not have been so easy. Just before breakfast the nurse reported that the small pox patient, with whom he had watched till near morning and then fell asleep, had escaped through the window, since the doors were still locked. There was no sign that he had gone down the bluff to the river, so set the nurse and another soldier to beating the thicket between the hospital and the marsh to the east; just as I finished breakfast they got a glimpse of his head far out in the marsh; he had disappeared, but we tracked him through the grass, which was waist-high, and found him too exhausted to move; evidently he had been delirious in the night. The nurse and I wrapped him in a rubber blanket and carried him in our arms to the hospital; it was then raining furiously and our progress was not easy through the mud and tall grass. He seems none the worse this evening. I had forgotten to record that, just as we left Folly Island, a letter from Surgeon General Dale said that he would be very glad to promote me and would bear it in mind; but that no desirable position was then open. Poor Prof. Wyman; I am very sorry for him.[153] I miss my daily rides upon Billy greatly.

153. Wyman had sent news, initially through Col. Hartwell and then by letter to Wilder, of the illness and death of his wife shortly after the death of their infant at childbirth. J. Wyman to B. G. Wilder, 20 March 1864, Wilder Papers, CU.

Friday, 11th, 8:35 P.M. We are back in our old quarters, the third removal. Co. C came today and it was best to let all the line officers be in the same building. I have made a very commodious wash stand from a box, the corners cut off so as to stand in a corner. We have been disappointed as to our mail twice today. At noon a steamer went up and our adjutant Perry on the wheel house with a package ready to throw; but we had no boat in which to go out and catch it. We expected it to be sent down with Co. C this afternoon, but its boat left one wharf just before the other arrived at another. We learned that the rest of our regiment and several others have gone to Palatka, farther up the river.[154] Our last pet is a bat, already quite reasonable. We have had quite a varied assortment of creatures, including flying squirrels, lizards and a scorpion. After supper I extracted a splinter from under the nail of a soldier, having to slit the nail in order to reach it. The afternoon an alligator about two feet long was shot in the head so that its brain was destroyed, but when I dissected it, the heart was beating and the muscles quite active. The man that killed it guided me this morning to a nest in the swamp where on a pile of soft earth 2 feet high and three or four wide were about 50 eggs and about 20 little alligators, all dead, perhaps from cold.

Sunday, [March] 13th, 4:30 P.M. A Sunday school was held this afternoon in Capt. Gordon's quarters. A psalm was read and a hymn was sung, and then he and Lt. Ellsworth,[155] and I and two or three of the sergeants took each a small class for Bible reading and discussion. There was killed today a rattlesnake 5 ft. long and 3 inches thick, and with 5 rattles. I have ~~dissected it and~~ removed the fangs; doubtless there are more of them. Tomorrow I shall dissect it more fully. During the past week I have had a new servant, Andrew Smith[156] of Co. B. When the small pox case developed, as I had no nurse who had had it, my servant, Ackers, who had had it, was detailed as nurse for him and "Andy" had been Q.M. Mussey's servant but was returned to his company when we ceased to be in Littlefield's brigade; he is

154. On 11 March, companies of the 55th Massachusetts, along with the 47th and 48th New York regiments with some artillery and cavalry, all under the command of Col. Barton, occupied Palatka. Fox, *Record*, 25.

155. Thomas Foldes Ellsworth was living in his birth place, Ipswich, when he enlisted as a private in the 2nd Massachusetts but had been promoted to corporal before accepting a commission in the 55th. He was promoted to captain for bravery at Honey Hill. Fox, *Record*, 103.

156. Pvt. Andrew Smith was an 18 year old from Clinton, Illinois, when he enlisted. He would be promoted to corporal, then sergeant, and finally color-sergeant. Fox, *Record*, 119.

very bright, quick and clean, really too good a soldier to be a servant; probably Frank will return before long and then Smith can go to his company.

¶ **Monday, [March] 14th, 8:00 P.M.** An uninjured black snake, 4 feet long, was brought to me today, and to the mingled admiration and horror of the beholders, in order to show that it is comparatively harmless, I seized it by the neck and allowed it to coil about my arm and then my neck.

¶ **Tuesday, 15th, 9:30 P.M.** We have just buried the small pox patient; he died this evening after surprising me by living so long after his terrible exposure. The grave was dug in the woods between us and the marsh; then Ackers and I carried him to it. I read the 23rd psalm and repeated the Lord's Prayer, and then he filled it in so that the men who dug it should not be exposed. This is the first death from the disease. I never saw a grave used before. Gen. Seymour and some officers came this afternoon and left with us two signal men with apparatus; two horses were brought, and there is to be provision for mounting two guns at the large stockade, indicating that we may be here some days yet; so I shall send for Billy.

¶ **Wednesday, 16th, 8:45 P.M.** This afternoon I took Smith and Ackers (the latter fumigated and provided with new clothes) armed with their guns and went where none has been before, viz., around the marsh west of us to another bluff where stands a house, said to have been occupied by a Union man and his daughter, driven away by the rebels. It is a nice house and the garden is tastefully laid out, from it I gathered a fleur de lis. The men fired at some ducks, but hit none. We heard the deep bellow of a large alligator but could not see it. The firing and the presence of men at the point were reported to the colonel, who did not know we were going so far, and at first he thought of sending a company to see what was going on.

¶ **Thursday, 17th, 8:30 P.M.** This afternoon, accompanied by Capt. Gordon and Lt. Ellsworth and Andy, I went again in search of the big alligator; not finding it we kept on along the bank of the river by a path between it and the woods. Suddenly we found fresh footprints of men, and presently reached a house; no one was in it, but on looking over the bank Ellsworth saw Lt. Jones[157] and one of the signal officers sitting on a log; we

157. Dennis Hartwell Jones was a 16-year-old student when his parents allowed him to enlist in the 44th Massachusetts in July 1862. He was appointed to the 55th only to be accidentally shot and killed by a fellow officer while in Florida. Fox, *Record*, 93–94.

separated so as to be on either flank and then Ellsworth fired his pistol over their heads. On looking over the bank again we saw our friends crouched under the edge, their pistols cocked as if intending to sell their lives dearly; it was a rather dangerous practical joke for if either of us had worn a gray hat he might have been shot before the error was discovered. On the return a large eagle flew far overhead. With no expectation of hitting him I fired and a white feather came down; from this I gained the credit for being an unusual marksman, and thereafter refrained from firing at anything. It is cold tonight, but we have warmed the room somewhat by means of a lot of coals on the door of an old stove.

¶ **Saturday, 19th, 8:15 P.M.** This afternoon Capt. Gordon, Andy and I have had another alligator hunt. We secured a "dug-out" and paddled up the creek that winds through the east marsh. We were all well armed in case the alligators should attack our boat. We came upon two sunning themselves on the bank; but they slid off before we came within accurate shooting distance; after waiting in vain for them to reappear about half an hour, we rowed further up the creek and saw a third, but he also escaped.

¶ **Monday, 21st, 8:00 P.M.** Billy arrived on a steamer today; he was as unconcerned as possible, munching from a bundle of hay. Our pier is in process of reconstruction and is now a metre frame with no floor; but in anticipation of his advent I have been keeping at hand three thick hard pine doors; by means of them and two gang planks of the steamer was made a rather narrow path over which Billy walked as steadily as if it had been three yards wide instead of three feet. I regret to say that he accepted me and Miff as matters of course and seemed more interested in the frog grass. Behind our house is a small building that will serve nicely as a stable; I have made a feed box and he is comfortably fixed. On the same boat came Major Wales and Capt. Pope[158] of the 54th; the latter is said to be a very fine officer. Billy just neighed; I suppose he misses the colonel's horse. There is a large dog here and Miff vents her superabundant spirits on him; she attacks him furiously and he endures it without retaliating, although evidently astonished at her audacity. She always accompanies me to Sick Call; two of the companies are half a mile off so I visit them. I walk in front; then comes Miff, generally with a stick in her mouth; the

158. George Pope had served previously in the 44th Massachusetts before being offered a commission in the 54th by Col. Shaw. Duncan, *Blue-Eyed Child of Fortune*, 29.

Wilder's sketch of the assistant surgeon and Miff going to Sick Call.

nurses with the hospital knapsacks. During the call she frolics with the men, who make much of her. On the return trip, she goes first, with the stick, looking back frequently to see if I am following; if I hide behind a tree she places the stick at the side of the path, hunts me up, and then regains it.

¶ **Tuesday, 22nd, 8:00 P.M.** I hardly dare to retire tonight lest I be visited, like the hard hearted butcher, by a Spectre Pig; for today I actually killed a little pig, under the following circumstances. After visiting the hospital and the two companies near headquarters I mounted Billy (unwonted and most delightful luxury) and cantered out to the other two companies; for a time Miff rode in front of me on the saddle but soon fell off and followed Carlo, the big dog. Then I joined Capt. Gordon, the officer of the day, who had borrowed a horse and we slowly made our way through the abatis and among the felled trees beyond until we reached and passed the picket line. About half a mile beyond we came upon three young pigs, white, yellow and brown, seeking their food among the leaves. Although I do not like pork (excepting as lean ham) it is a great desideratum in a camp supplied regularly with only salt meat. So I borrowed Capt. Gordon's pistol and pursued them; Billy seemed to enter into the spirit of the chase and turned on his tracks in great style; at about ten feet the first shot broke a hind leg; the second pierced its neck and I dismounted to kill it. While doing so Billy cantered off but was caught by the captain. I slung the pig, about a foot and a half long, from my saddle and took it to our cook, who was delighted. (These two diagrams are in the sheet [**missing**]; on the back of the smaller is the following: - This is the second story; under our sleeping room is that of Capt. Gordon and the signal officers; under the adjutant's is their sitting and dining room; under ours the room of Capt. Torrey[159] and Lt. Marsh[160]; the common kitchen is under the servant's room.)

Accidental death of Lt. Jones. Y[ellow] B[luff]

Thursday, Mar. 24, '64, 9:00 P.M. Yesterday afternoon three parties went in as many directions, a scouting party, a small party consisting of Capt. Soule, Lt. Jones and two soldiers, and some white engineers and signal men; this third party was unknown to the others. Soule's party had found a boat at a house on the river at the east side of the marsh believed to have been recently occupied by rebel pickets; they were dragging it to the water when they heard the firing of the engineers, close by, at pigs, as was afterwards learned; in their renewed efforts to drag the boat and so escape the supposed enemy, both officers fell and Soule's pistol, being cocked in anticipation of the attack, exploded and the ball pierced Jones' heart. The two soldiers supposing the shot to have come from the enemy, leaped into the river and by swimming and wading over the marsh reached camp; there they met the scouting party, and it was naturally concluded that the rebels had killed Jones and taken Soule prisoner; all was excitement and expectation of attack. But closer questioning of the two elicited discrepancies, and when the engineers came in a party went in a boat and found Soule and the body. A court of inquiry was held and all of the facts brought out. There is no evidence of the enemy at that time and place. The body has been sent to Jacksonville. Jones was an excellent officer and all mourn his loss. I made an examination last night and found the heart pierced by the ball. (The specimen is in the Army Medical Museum, and the case was described by me in the Boston Medical and Surgical Journal for [**blank**],

159. William Haviland Torrey, a machinist from Baltimore living in Foxboro, enlisted in the 24th Massachusetts at the start of the war. He traded his sergeant's stripes for a lieutenant's commission in the 55th in July 1863. Promoted to captain in 1864, he was breveted major by 1865. Fox, *Record*, 103.

160. Alphonzo Marsh was working as a painter in Fitchburg when he enlisted in the 21st Massachusetts at the start of the war. He was commissioned in the 55th in July 1863 and resigned his commission in September 1864. Fox, *Record*, 105.

but with no mention of the name of the officer whose pistol was the cause of the fatality.)[161]

Friday, Mar. 25, 8:30 P.M. This evening we have been changing and improving the arrangements or our room; for beds we now have the stretchers that, in case of need, would carry the wounded. In the steamer this afternoon came most of the regimental property because it all had to be moved from the storehouse in J. Among other things the box containing the cooking utensils of the mess. Unfortunately, in haste and without adequate supervision, the cook had packed them in a box marked with my name; so, awaiting transportation to this place, they were missed both by us and by the officers at Palatka; we blamed them for taking them all and they us; now we can live luxuriously so far as dishes are concerned. A few days ago a man from the other side of the river came in a boat with five barrels of oysters $20.00 per bbl., and 2 ½ doz. Oyster eggs at 4 cents per dozen. Our mess took all the eggs and one barrel of the oysters, making a very acceptable change from the regular diet. The steamer brought a cannon yesterday and the men worked by moonlight so as to mount it at an exposed corner of the stockade; it looks quite formidable. When the alarm occasioned by the death of Lt. Jones occurred Andy Smith begged permission to join his company in case of action; afterward I learned from his captain that he is trying to perfect himself with a view to promotion as a corporal, and so I have in his place David Lee[162] of Co. C. (Smith was promoted[163] and Lee became the best servant I ever had).

Saturday, March 26, 7:30 P.M. I rise at 6 and ride up to inspect the company breakfasts; then we have our own , and after attending to various matters at our quarters and the hospital I visit the latter and attend to the sick of Cos. C and I. Then the nurse and I go up to the other two companies. Then I inspect the entire camp, which really consists of eight separate portions, as to all matters connected with the health of the men. Then, with or without the officer of the day, I go out along the picket line and return in time to inspect the dinners. A party went under Capt. Soule today to the scene of the recent accident and brought back a lot of pine

161. *The above is from my letter of the date. It differs in some details from that on p. 24 of the "Record." Did Soule's party go in the boat or find it at the house; was the firing at cattle or pigs? Could the engineering party have gone without the knowledge of Fox? Did I accompany the party for the body and him? B.G.W.*

162. Pvt. David Lee was a 21-year-old farmer from Xenia, Ohio. Fox, *Record*, 122.

163. By the end of the war, Smith was color-sergeant. Fox, *Record*, 119.

tables and chairs and wash stands; we had our share and the room looks quite civilized. The diagram shows us and dog awake and in repose.

¶ **Sunday, 27th, 8:45 P.M.** For various reasons not existing till now the colonel decided today that we better be out of the hospital building and in the same room with the other officers. So we have moved again. We have the whole second floor of the house. So many windows were broken or missing, and there were so many shell holes in the walls that it has taken ourselves, our servants, and four soldiers, good carpenters, to do it. We have put in six windows and one skylight, and repaired the walls and floors.

¶ **Tuesday, 29th, 8:00 P.M.** Today has been largely occupied in arranging our belongings in the new and quite commodious quarters; indeed we are so comfortable to anticipate speedy orders to move from this lovely spot. A second small pox case has developed; to avoid the destruction of another suite of clothes by a soldier I have had a small tent placed in the woods near by and am taking care of the man myself. He is not very ill and needs little more than his food brought to him. Billy had quite an adventure this morning. I had ridden to the rifle pit at the east side and while there saw Capt. Soule and some of his men bailing out an old scow in the creek some way off at a point they had reached by boat from the river. The marsh looked fairly firm and I started to ride out to him; but in went Billy's legs till his body nearly touched the ground. Off I jumped, but it was impossible for him to find firm foothold. So I stood by his head moving frequently to avoid sinking too deeply myself, and the men at the rifle pit, at my request, ran for quantities of the large and thick leaves of the palmetto, and made a heavy mat under and about him. For a few moments he rested, then with great efforts got first one and then the other front foot out and upon the mat, and gradually freed the others and was safe. On more of the same leaves he walked rather solemnly back to firm ground where the men rubbed the mud off with moss. I forgot to say that I removed his saddle as soon as I alighted. I did a rash thing today, and am almost ashamed to tell it. Under a big stone a soldier found a rattlesnake about three feet long. He put the head of his axe on its head but without crushing it, and bravely took it by the neck. It was brought to me and I got my bone forceps. ~~took the snake from the man by grasping the neck just below his fingers and pulled out the wicked looking fangs that were erected ready to strike. Then I took the snake from the man by grasping its neck just below his fingers.~~ After showing it to the other officers I threw it into the river and one of the officers killed it with a shot gun.

While holding it and realizing the consequences of a sudden faintness or a false step I felt somewhat as when controlling the great artery of the thigh during an amputation of the leg in Washington.

Wednesday, Mar. 30, 10:30 P.M. Q.M. Mussey came down and dined with us. He is no longer brigade Q.M.; has reported to Col. Hartwell, and also asked for leave to arrange his accounts, since some of his papers must be signed by Col. Hallowell.

Thursday, 31st, 9:30 P.M. Yesterday and today I have been at work on the medical reports which must be sent to Dr. Brown. Yesterday the colonel's servant broke out in small pox, so ~~today~~ with vaccine matter brought by a steamer at 6, I have just vaccinated all at headquarters, the hospital, the engineers and signal men, and Companies C and I.

Friday, April 1st, 9:10 P.M. The government tea is so poor just now that Col. Fox and I had made some tea from Sassafras roots today and found it quite palatable.

Saturday, April 2, 8:00 P.M. In an expedition this afternoon I hunted pelicans and caught only ducks, as will presently appear. After dinner I saw two large birds on a sandy flat left by the low tide and near the opposite bank of the river. The glass showed them to be pelicans, so I organized an expedition composed of Capt. Gordon, Lt. Webber of the signal corps, and two soldiers. We took one of the two wide and flat bottomed boats and rowed directly across the river from the pier, as in the accompanying diagram, or rather to the nearer shore of a wide island; we let the boat drift slowly down with the current; but just as the birds came in sight upon the sandy island they flew down stream about a fourth of a mile and settle in the water. The two other officers jumped out and waded to the small sandy island, and I and the two men in the boat took a circuitous course down the river in the hope of getting below them and causing them to fly back within reach of the guns; but when we neared them they flew off and out of sight. On attempting to return we were confronted by ~~not only the current~~ but a furious wind in the same direction so that with all our efforts we drifted further down stream. Moreover we now saw our voluntarily marooned companions frantically waving their hands and handkerchiefs because with the incoming tide their little refuge was rapidly invaded by the water. After half an hour's hard work in vain and seeing that a boat had put off from the dock to their relief we made for the northern shore, but the wind had carried us another quarter mile down stream. What we reached was really another island covered by tall grass. One of the men got out and waded, pulling the rope of the boat while we pushed and paddled as well as we could. Then I took his place in the water, the grass nearly up to my shoulders; I confess a little apprehension of alligators too. When we reached the side of the island nearer the mainland the wind again blew us down stream. But now our hearts were cheered by the sight of the other boat on the way to rescue us, after taking off the two officers. We reached camp at last, tired and soaked, but really none the worse for our experience.

¶ **Sunday, April 3, 7:30 P.M.** This afternoon we were on our feet from 2 till 5 at the monthly inspection of arms etc., in addition to the Sunday inspection of quarters. Afterward I laid down for an hour, the first time since coming here. Three nights ago the transport, "Maple Leaf" was blown up by a torpedo between J. and Palatka[164]; that trip of 70 miles has to be made by night because the river is so narrow that the rebels can get near the boats. Fortunately there were only 70 on board, five of whom were killed. During the last fortnight we have been sending out a sergeant and 3 or 4 men as scouts for 15–20 miles for 24 or 48 hours. They have gained considerable information, and have been at houses where rebel scouts were sometimes located. Recently one of these came in, with another man having crossed the river higher up; he said it would be easy to capture the rest, but before acting on this information Col. Fox thought best to send him to headquarters at J.

¶ **Monday, 3rd, 8 P.M.** Frank returned today and is very well and welcome, especially as the colonel's boy is ill. He brought me a most acceptable gift, a folding camp-chair from Dr. Wm. Nichols[165]; I had given my

164. The *Maple Leaf*, originally a passenger ship serving on Lake Ontario, had been chartered as a transport ship by the U.S. government in 1862. On the night of 1 April 1864, while returning to Jacksonville after dropping off a cavalry detachment at Palatka, the paddle wheeler struck a "torpedo," or mine, and sank off Mandarin Point on the St. Johns River. Four black crewmen were killed in the blast, but the remaining 58 passengers and crew managed to reach Jacksonville. Despite attempts by the army to sweep the river for torpedoes, the transport *General Hunter* was sunk near the wreck of the *Maple Leaf* on 17 April 1864. The *Maple Leaf* is now a National Historic Landmark.

165. This was likely Dr. William Nichols, assistant surgeon in the 3rd Massachusetts Heavy Artillery, Boston, and a graduate of the Harvard Medical School in 1861. The 3rd Massachusetts Heavy Artillery was doing garrison duty in Washington.

barrel chair to the small pox patient and am very glad to have this; it can be carried on my horse. He brought also a flute from father on which I have just played "Home, Sweet Home," Capt. Gordon's transcription of an entire chapter from Owen's "Com. Anatomy,"[166] in response to my request for a single paragraph bearing upon that author's use of a certain term; it was the more kind in him because he is at work on his own thesis. I have been writing out an account of Lt. Jones' case to accompany the heart and the ball to the Army Medical Museum. Frank is in high glee to be back and is as smart and active as ever and more steady. He has a nice suit of clothes. On the way down he had three offers of desirable places. He also earned his passage and $5.00 in addition. He has been studying while at his home and has brought his arithmetic. Now I hear him reading aloud to the other boys.

¶ **Tuesday, [April] 5th, 8:15 P.M.** Billy is developing great powers as a jumper; when we return from the outposts we have to cross a considerable space where the trees have been felled and lie so as to be quite high; he takes them on the run, one after the other or even two or three at once; tonight he jumped a brook five feet wide.

¶ **Thursday, 7th, 8:00 P.M.** I am trying to imitate the Indians and cowboys in stooping from my horse and picking up a hat or stick; so far the horse must be walking and I doubt if I will ever learn to do it at full speed.

¶ **Friday, 8th, 8:30 P.M.** Capt. Hodges came from J. for a short visit. We took him out to the pickets and then in a boat seeking the body of a large alligator that the soldiers killed but been unable to secure; it had floated off.

¶ **Saturday, 9th, 8:10 P.M.** Unless something special prevents I always play the flute for a time after dinner and supper. While about 20 men were pulling upon a rope attached to a scow sunken in the river near the shore the rope broke and they went down like a row of bricks. The scow has been broken up and will be used in completing the pier.

166. The author, Richard Owen, was a noted but controversial British scientist and a specialist in comparative anatomy. By 1863 he was in an increasingly acrimonious dispute with Charles Darwin. Wilder was reading from *Lectures on the Comparative Anatomy and Physiology of the Vertebrate Animals*, first published in 1846. Nicolaas A. Rupke, *Richard Owen: Victorian Naturalist* (New Haven: Yale University Press, 1994), xiv, 97–99, 240.

¶ **Sunday, 10th, 8:10 P.M.** Sergeant Mathes[167] and two men went on a scout yesterday and brought in two men whose examination has just been concluded. They are uncle and nephew and say they escaped from the rebel army 18 months ago and have been living in the woods, concealed except from their relatives. They told straightforward stories and corroborated some of the information we had already gained.

¶ **Monday, April 11, 8:15 P.M.** Gen. Hatch[168] came today and went to the stockade with Col. Fox. He expressed great satisfaction with what had been done and said we had worked so hard that now we were entitled to remain and enjoy it, but that Col. Hartwell had been urging our return to the regiment. He said at any rate the men should be more comfortable and authorized drawing "A" tents for the men. Capt. Gordon and I have also been planning the resumption of the school for the men.

¶ **Tuesday, 12th, 8:25 P.M.** Yesterday morning an officer shot an alligator about 4 ft. long and brought it to me. The ball had crushed his brain. On opening him the heart was found beating and an hour later the rate was 25 per minute. I cut off the tail, and sent it up to the cook to be prepared for our dinner. When he began to skin it, it squirmed so that he was scared and said the debbil was in it; it had to be nailed to the bench. When cooked we all found it delicious and superior to ordinary fish.

¶ **Wednesday, 14th 8:15 P.M.** After supper the colonel and I visited the camps and found the "A" tents of companies B and K all up, a great improvement in comfort and looks.

¶ **Thursday, 14th, 8:15 P.M.** Last night [word missing] said that he and Lts. Ellsworth and Knight were planning to hold prayer meetings and invited me to join them. It was difficult for me to make him understand that I respected the sentiments of those who found help from such exercises, but that they did not appeal to me and he must excuse me. I found that Col. Fox said much the same; he is a Unitarian. Yesterday was brought to me a "King Snake" 5 ½ ft. long. This afternoon I skinned it and had portions fried; the flesh was even more delicate than that of the

167. James Mathes was sergeant in Company I. Thirty-nine years old, he had been a "truckman" in Stapleton, New York, before he enlisted. Fox, *Record*, 140.

168. Gen. John Porter Hatch, a West Point graduate, served in the Mexican War. After recuperating from wounds suffered at South Mountain, he took over command of the District of Florida. Sifakis, *Who Was Who in the Civil War*, 292–93.

alligator, and some of the other officers admired it. I have been doing more or less vaccinating since I began. About a week ago I scraped the skin from one of my knuckles and it has been acting like the result of vaccination; so I suppose some of the virus accidentally got in it. To test it I regularly vaccinated my arm with some of the matter from the knuckle and it "took" in regular form. It is reported that the whole 10th corps is to go to Virginia, that there will be changes in this department.[169] Signal Lt. Weihle had been ordered elsewhere, but he has left his big dog here; so Miff still has a playmate. She is perfectly happy in the saddle in front of me; when it is not convenient to take her I shut her in the upper story of the house; if she hears my voice or Billy's tread she dashes from a window to the veranda roof and runs to and fro crying bitterly.

¶ **Saturday, 16th, 8:10 P.M.** During the last fortnight detachments of our men have been going up the river and felling trees so as to permit signals between our tower and J. Today it was completed and signals have been exchanged. The first was to the effect that another transport, the "Gen. Hunter" had been destroyed by torpedoes near the "Maple Leaf"; one man was killed. In this Florida expedition two transports have been blown up and two lost on the bar; Olustee was a defeat and there have been lost much time, labor and money. In return we have captured two little rebel steamers; one, the "Sumter," passed today; she looks like a mud scow with a shanty on top. Gen Hatch has ordered that the river be patrolled tonight lest the rebels plant torpedoes in the path of our now frequent boats. Lt. Gannet goes in charge of the patrol and one of the men is my former servant, "Andy" Smith; he is a splendid man and soldier. He is also one of nine men selected to manage the cannon in Redoubt Jones. This morning I made out in duplicate five certificates to cover the destruction of the clothing and shelter tents of the small pox patients and their nurse; this will relieve them from paying for the new articles. This afternoon I supervised the carpenters in making tables, desks and seats in the lower rooms of the hospital building. It is said that the 8th U.S. colored also has a school, and if they replace us the furniture will be useful for them.

169. Indeed, most of Gillmore's men were being transferred to Virginia, and the 10th Corps became part of Gen. Benjamin Butler's Army of the James, operating up the James River against Richmond and Petersburg. The 55th Massachusetts returned to Folly Island and was brigaded with the 103rd New York Regiment under Col. William Heine. Trudeau, *Voices of the 55th*, 19.

On the transport "Neptune"

Monday, April 18, 10:30 P.M. We are in sight of Folly Island. I could not write last night for some of the officers were smoking in the very small cabin; I slept outside on the bulkhead and woke at 5. Our departure from Y.B. yesterday was quite sudden, although we had anticipated it enough to be fairly ready. At 9 A.M. the 8th U.S. arrived to replace us; later this steamer with Co. F which has been garrisoning a fort at J.; then came a propeller bearing the rest of the regiment, and finally another boat with the 54th. We got on board this boat about noon. The 54th is ahead of us but the rest of the 55th is still behind. Miff is gay and frisky and Bill is all right, as is the colonel's horse that was brought down from J. yesterday. Notwithstanding all our efforts we had to leave Y.B. without a large alligator. The captain of this boat says the water on the bar will not permit it to enter as yet.

¶ **Tuesday, 19th, 8:45 P.M.** Yesterday it rained more or less all day and the hardest just as we were disembarking and trying to find or make shelter. Hardly had the men reached the camp before 200 of them were detailed to go out and relieve the picket of the regiment that was to go by our steamer to Hilton Head, and whose camp we took. Dark, cold and wet the prospect was far from attractive; but the frames of the tents remained and our men soon set their own tents upon them. The officers in most cases, had taken or given their frames away, so we were in this respect less well off than the men. However, after much trotting to and fro in the mud and water we were all housed after a fashion; in two wall tents, placed end to end were temporarily quartered Col. Fox, Captains Gordon and Soule, Lt. Gannett and myself; also the colonel's boy George. We had some coffee and hard tack and went to bed on the floor. Frank and David and Davis, the man who now takes care of our horses, slept on the hay in the shelter where the horses are and had comfortable beds. All my blankets were wet and I could change only my socks; there was a fine chance for rheumatism but as I never have had any I hope to escape now. After as dismal as were the conditions they were not so bad as often befall marching and fighting regiments, those on the Potomac for example. Occasionally I was roused by large rats running too close or too heavily over the floor. Miff nestled up to me under my blanket. Once, while half awake, I took her for a huge and not too familiar rat and dug my elbow into her ribs; she roused us all with piteous protestations, but we soon dozed off again. At 6 the colonel and I rose and prospected for a permanent location, but could not decide then; so I ordered Billy and found plenty of occupy me till 9 when I went to the Sutler's establishment for some breakfast.

Several camps nearby had been vacated and over the hospital premises of one I set a guard because, in addition to the flooring, etc., there was a nice garden with vegetables just sprung up. **The** Col. ~~[Hartwell?]~~ finally decided to leave companies B, C and K at Pawnee Landing and with Co. I moved a fourth of a mile farther north to the camp of the Conn. Battery which leaves this noon. The rest of the day was spent in putting up tents, arranging the hospital etc. We found the flooring of two wall tents and the frame of one still standing, and a fine fireplace and chimney. So, although pretty tired, we are comparatively comfortable. I have been helping Col. Fox make out Reports and Returns.

Wednesday, 20th, 9:15 P.M. We have become so migratory as to be unable to sleep in the same place two successive nights. Saturday, Yellow Bluff, Sunday, the Steamer, Monday, Capt. Grant's tent near the Pawnee Landing, Tuesday, at the old camp of N.Y., 89th and now we are just settled in two wall tents, placed end for end, with nice frames and a door; we got them at what was formerly the headquarters of Gen. Vogdes, and had them brought here on a team. I hate moving but it could not be helped. The rest of the regiment arrived just as I had got through my work; I had ridden to the other end of the island with Col. Fox. Col. Hartwell has left companies B, C and K where they were; Col. Fox and A and F are at the north end; the sick in quarters of those five I shall care for and Dr. Brown the other and those in hospital. He and the new chaplain[170] occupy the tents we had yesterday; we shall miss the fine fireplace and must get a stove. I had to arrange for dinner for all the field and staff and draw rations for the hospital; this afternoon has been occupied with putting up our own tents and getting into order.

Thursday, 21st, 8:30 P.M. The regimental band came to serenade Col. Fox and well enjoyed the music; he gave them some cigars; the soldiers are very desirous of tobacco (most of them) and under the conditions in the field I think it a proper comfort; I have given away at least ten dollars worth in the last three months. I have asked father to tell Mr. Kingsley[171]

170. John R. Bowles, born in Lynchburg, Virginia, was the pastor of the First Baptist Church in Chillicothe, Ohio, before he took over as chaplain in the 55th Massachusetts in March 1864. Fox, *Record*, 101; Trudeau, *Voices*, 223, 225.

171. Edward Wilkerson Kinsley, a Boston merchant and abolitionist, assisted in the formation of the 55th Massachusetts. He remained very supportive of both black regiments during the war. Yacovone, *A Voice of Thunder*, 62, 70–71; Edward W. Kinsley Papers, Duke University Special Collections.

that some would be very acceptable here. We now have a wall tent for cooking and a stove. I hope we remain here for a time. The camp is very pretty; it is surrounded by a hedge and there are some patches of oats in flourishing condition. There are little grass plots in front of the company tents. The slates and other school things have been divided equally between the two groups of companies, and are in charge, respectively, of Chaplain Bowles and myself. Capt. Soule is the provost marshal and our regiment provides the provost guard for this end of the island, including the landings.

¶ **Friday, 22nd, 7:30 P.M.** Just before supper Col. Hartwell sent for our detachment to come to his camp in order that we might hear him speak concerning the pay of the men and their duty as to obeying orders. It seems that in his detachment, on the return from Florida, a man snapped a pistol at an officer and barely escaped being run through with his sword.[172] That no such trouble occurred in our detachment is due, I think to Col. Fox. He is always solicitous for the welfare of the men, sparing neither trouble nor expense in their behalf. For example, the day after our arrival, he thought our picket detail was needlessly large and walked the whole line on foot and succeeded in reducing the number by 100. I did not go to hear the address. Miff is as popular as ever and is admired even by Dr. Brown.

¶ **Saturday, 23rd, 8:30 P.M.** Col. Fox has been reading me a letter written to his father, Rev. Thomas B. Fox, a close friend of Gov. Andrew, and writer of an article in the Transcript signed with a star. It describes the conditions here and apprehends the impossibility of our continuing in the service if Congress adjourns without making due provision for the payment of the men; the families of some are in actual want. Earlier in the evening was held a meeting of the school committee; the chaplain was made General Superintendent. Major Wales arrived today from Jacksonville where he has been on the staff of Gen. Ames[173]. Notwithstanding his promotion there is some trouble between him and Col. Hartwell and it is rumoured that he may soon resign.

172. The enlisted man, Sampson Goliah, claimed in his trial that his behavior was, in part, due to the government's failure to pay the black soldiers equal wages. His sentence, hard labor rather than execution, was a partial recognition by the court of their unfair treatment. Samito, "The Intersection between Military Justice and Equal Rights," 187–90.

173. Gen. Adelbert Ames, a native of Maine and a graduate of West Point, distinguished himself at Bull Run and Gettysburg. He commanded briefly in Florida. Sifakis, *Who Was Who in the Civil War*, 8.

¶ **Sunday, 24th, 7:30 P.M.** On my return from visiting Fort Green at 10:30 I ~~went in to hear~~ stopped to hear the chaplain preach; he spoke very well and seems likely to be helpful to the men. On reaching our camp no tent was visible. Presently I met the colonel who said they had moved to a ridge a fourth of a mile nearer the ocean, near Vogdes's old headquarters and one of the prettiest and healthiest spots on the island. Meantime it had begun to rain very hard and I went into the tent where most of our belongings had been placed to await the team to transport them. During the transfer they and we got pretty wet. At dinner the colonel explained. It seems that Col. Hartwell came and said the post command wished Fox to be Provost Marshall, with Co. I as provost guard; this pleased us because he and I both like Gordon and Ellsworth of that company. But after dinner Fox went out for an hour and returned with the information that Gen. Schimmelpfennig,[174] commanding the whole island, had countermanded the order and had recalled to the guard some soldiers and an officer from Long Island and we are to remain where we are for the present. It is a pretty spot and commands fine view of the Landing and of the ocean; the latter is just now grand as the result of the easterly storm. At this point I am summoned to a sick man in quarters. It was very dark and there is a road cut through a nearby ridge; one of the two men who came for me tumbled down the bank. Then we had to cross a wide swamp on a narrow bridge of slippery logs, and I was in constant fear of slipping off. Our surroundings are highly respectable. The next tent is occupied by the agent of the Christian Commission[175]; directly opposite is the Q.M., Capt. Cushing, acquainted with old Dr. Wild and with Miss Cushing. Now again come Col. Hartwell to tell Fox that he is going to Hilton Head and the latter must take charge of the entire regiment; in his place will come the senior captain, Nutt. And finally Fox is summoned by Col. Heine,[176] post commander.

174. Gen. Alexander Schimmelfennig, a former Prussian engineering officer, was a brigade commander in charge of the south end of Folly Island. He was perhaps best known for having to hide in a pigsty during the Battle of Gettysburg. Wilder consistently misspells his name. Sifakis, *Who Was Who in the Civil War*, 572.

175. The United States Christian Association was established in the fall of 1861 by the Young Men's Christian Association to provide spiritual and physical assistance to the Union soldiers. By the end of the war, thousands of volunteers had distributed millions of dollars in goods and supplies working in collaboration with the Sanitary Commission.

176. Col. William Heine commanded the 103rd New York Volunteers. Wise, *Gate of Hell*, 239.

¶ **Monday, 25th, 7:45 P.M.** Among the heritages of this location was a noble fireplace of brick and turf erected by Major Morrison; the opening is 3 × 4 feet. In Col. Fox's absence I am enjoying it all alone, but I called the boys in a short time ago and read them something that interested them.

¶ **Tuesday, 26th, 7:45 P.M.** The school was to have begun last night but the roofed space to be used has not yet had the sides attached and the wind was so strong that no candle could have burned there. This morning after sick call at Fort Green I went to Morris Island for some black paint to make blackboards with and some blackberry wine for Mr. Round the Christian Association agent, who had not been well for a few days. Our first camp near the beach is now occupied only by crows. Capt. Soule has done a fine thing. One of his men is a good carpenter and he secured an old hospital tent and had it floored and tables and benches made so that it can be used as a reading room for the men.

¶ **Wed., 27th, 7:30 P.M.** I like living here by myself. My forenoons are pretty much alike as follows. I rise at 6 and have breakfast before 7. Then I walk to the nearer detachment and attend to the sick there and to any civilians that may need attention. By that time David has brought Billy from his stable near the other part of the regiment and I ride off heeding not the cries and struggles of Miff whom David holds and takes back to my tent. On the beach I ride two miles up to Fort Green to attend sick call there. Today I took Billy to the blacksmith at the landing to have his hoofs pared; I let him go unshod because no one else rides him and so he is not in danger of breaking them on stumps.

¶ **Thursday, 28th, 8:00 P.M.** The dreaded removal has taken place. Col. Fox came in this morning with the information that Col. Hartwell had returned and that we both were expected to rejoin the regiment. I packed up my property ready for moving and then attended to my regular duties. When I returned at 11 Col. Fox's tent, etc. were on the team and was to return for mine. He got his horse and we rode down the island by the wood roads to the headquarters of the commander of the island, Gen. Schimmelpfennig, the successor of Gordon. From Pawnee Landing the road was more and more familiar and the horse recognized our former winter camp among the pines. The place was desolate, but the parade ground had been transformed into a pretty garden. After dinner I had just selected a good spot for my tent when up came a terrific gale, filling the air with sand and compelling us to hold fast lest we be blown over.

Just as it blew hardest the ten men undertook to carry my tent, frame, floor, and all. It had been moved so often that the frame collapsed; so the tent was taken off and the frame repaired and by 5:30 it was pitched under considerable difficulties. Then the boys' wall tent was pitched and all made secure. The sand was fine and penetrating. It got into all the exposed food and the proverbial peck of dirt will be forced upon us.

10:00 P.M. Col. Fox invited me to dine with him to the tent of Capt. Crane who had just received a set of Song Books, the Arion, for male voices; the songs were good and sounded well; I sang first bass.

¶ **Friday, 29th, 9:30 P.M.** From 6:30 till the eight o'clock breakfast I worked on my thesis; from 8:30 till one I was occupied with sick calls and camp inspections, for now I have to attend the sick in quarters of the whole regiment. This afternoon I have made a sort of cupboard from a large box which fits into the space in the frame formerly corresponding with the fireplace; in the upper part is a sliding shelf with the toilet apparatus which may thus be out of sight except when in use. After supper the rest of the choir in my tent and we sang again.

¶ **Saturday, 30th, 9:00 P.M.** Q.M. Garrison and I have just returned from Stono Inlet, six miles each way; the deserted camps along the beach were gloomy places. Our regiment was mustered for pay this afternoon, but I was excused because I could attend to one company while another was mustered. I have also made a book shelf and the tent is quite comfortable.

¶ **Sunday, May 1st, 9:15 P.M.** This is the third evening when I have been interfered with by Mr. Hurd, the State Aid Commissioner of Pa. While at Yellow Bluff I had a letter from him respecting one of Capt. Gordon's men who had overstayed his furlough and was in danger of treatment of a deserter. Gordon and I looked into the case and found that the error was through ignorance rather than evil intent. Well, this Mr. Hurd is sixty years old and very large. After our business was transacted he showed that he desired to remain over night and I invited him to do so. Then Col. Hartwell sent word for us to come and get our suppers before the mess tent blew down. During the hour from 6 to 7 the wind was fearful and the tent flapped and the ridge pole bent, so that before we quite finished the colonel advised us to retreat to his tent. After his experience with the tent Mr. Hurd hesitated to accept a seat on a camp bed, but was finally convinced of its security. He is a rather boisterous old gentleman and once laughed so loud that Miff rose and stood in front of him and said "bow-wow" very emphatically. By the way, Miff is very fond of raisins and has a few for dessert.

¶ **Monday, May 2nd, 8:00 P.M.** Today Col. Hartwell put Major Wales under arrest for what he regarded as improper endorsement of an order from the former. Wales has been in hot water since his promotion.

¶ **Wednesday, May 4th, 8:30 P.M.** Just before supper there was a general discharge of shells from several batteries so that several shells at once burst over Sumter; the same thing was done a few days ago; it is said the rebels are trying to mount more guns there. This afternoon I sat in the lookout for half an hour. It is 120 feet high and affords a fine view of Charleston and the James Island works. I am revising my thesis in such time as can be found and am not sorry for the delay since it enables me to improve it in my details.

¶ **Friday, 6th, 10:00 P.M.** "Pride must have a fall." Q.M. Garrison told that he overheard one of the soldiers say, as I rode by, "There goes the best rider in the regiment." Tonight he and I escorted Col. Fox to Fort Green. As we trotted back, Billy stumbled over a small stump in the sand and went down to his knees; I was so taken by surprise that I rolled off. Billy very inconsiderately trotted off and returned to his stable, leaving me to walk. Capt. Hamilton[177] of the regular artillery was wounded in the arm at Olustee; his wife is here to care for him; this evening they and a surgeon and lieutenant of the same regiment took tea with us.

¶ **Saturday, 7th, 9:30 P.M.** For a week the bandmaster of the 24th Mass. has been instructing our musicians, and he says the instruments should be replaced; they were second hand when we got them and have been in use nearly a year. So the colonel appointed a Committee of which I was a member to consider the plans for getting a new set to cost $625.00.

¶ **Sunday, 8th, 4:30 P.M.** The other members of the Band Committee are Fox and Crane; we have drawn up a Circular asking for subscriptions toward the new instruments. Companies A and F returned from Fort Green

177. Capt. John Hamilton, commanding Light Battery E, U.S. Artillery, was Gen. Seymour's chief artillery officer at Olustee. During the battle, his battery was under intense fire and Hamilton was severely wounded.

today; they are relieved by a detachment of the 54th under [Something left out in transcribed copy].

9 P.M. I was called by the colonel to attend to the various needs of five men who had small pox when we went to Florida and who have had a rather trying experience since. They had to be fed and their old clothing destroyed before mingling with the others. Dr. Mann came to say that he had charge of them but they had **not** been troublesome.

¶ **Monday, 9th, 5:00 P.M.** We breakfasted at 6 this morning and I got to work at 6:30. The earlier hour is due to a visitation from the medical director of the island, Dr. Brilliantomski (or something like that) who said he was surprised to find that I had to go to Fort Green, etc. and that Dr. Brown does not attend to any of the detachments. So now Dr. Brown is to attend to companies B and C, and all the calls are to be held earlier. Yesterday morning Capt. Crane and I were at Fort Green when, in response to some shots from Secessionville, on James Island, permission was obtained to fire the 30 pound Parrott gun in the fort. The men have been learning to use it and were delighted at the opportunity to fire it in earnest. The loading was a solemn function and when one rammed in the charge so vigorously that his hat fell off not a smile was seen. The gun had to be elevated 22 degrees in order to cover the 5 3½ miles to Secessionville; we have learned since that the shell was seen from Long Island to fall plump into the rebel works there. On Billy I was within 20 feet of the gun and he seemed little disturbed by it. Col. Fox has just been in to have his finger dressed; he has had a hard time with it, but it is improving; he wants me to attend dress parade with him, and as I have not since leaving the island before I have consented.

8:00 P.M. After the parade the agent of the Christian Commission and the chief clerk of the Q.M. department came for medical attention.

¶ **Tuesday, 10th, 9:00 P.M.** In view of the condition of the men and their families our committee has decided not to proceed further with the plan of getting a new set. Some of our men brought from Palatka several volumes of the Pacific Railroad Reports and I have purchased five at $1.00 each.

¶ **Thursday, 12th, 11:00 A.M.** Last night, about midnight, we were aroused by a tremendous clap of thunder. The previous night Col. Heine sent word that an attack might be expected. So we naturally interpreted the explosion as the bursting of a rebel shell over our camp. It rained till morning.

Recently our troops on Long Island put some shells into barrels with short time fuses and set them adrift; they floated down and exploded near the rebel works.

9:00 P.M. The mail brought news of the passage of a bill to provide for the full payment of the men and for the muster of colored officers. At roll call the men cheered for ten minutes.[178]

¶ **Saturday, 14th, 9:30 P.M.** For several days I have had a boil on one cheek; today it was so painful that although not quite ripe, I lanced it and am much easier. This afternoon there was much firing from both sides and Col. Fox and I watched it from the Lookout.

¶ **Sunday, [May] 15th, 7:15 P.M.** A Hilton Head paper contains reports from deserters and rebel papers of a victory in Virginia and the capture of an entire corps.[179] May it prove true. So often have we been disappointed when the actual truth was known that sometimes we feel as if the war would never end. David Lee takes care of Fox's horse as well as mine. He is very gentle yet capable, and Billy is much attached to him. This morning, instead of setting Miff in front of me on the saddle I put her on Billy's broad back behind me, using one hand to prevent her falling off. To steady herself she dug her claws into his skin and he seemed to think it was a big fly; first he lashed his tail, then kicked with one hind leg and then with the other and finally with both, nearly standing on his head. Notwithstanding his friskiness he obeys well. Two days ago, in order to bring some supplies from Stono, six miles away, I hitched him in the sutler's light wagon and drove both ways without trouble.

¶ **Monday, 16th, 8:00 P.M.** The regiment is to move to Stono, probably tomorrow. Frank has just related an unfortunate affair. Co. Hartwell's boy, "Joe," is a little rascal and Fox and I have seriously contemplated leaving the mess on his account. Frank says that today Joe made a quarrel with

178. The report was wrong. A bill for equal pay did not pass Congress until 15 June 1864, and even that law specified retroactive pay, and bounty payments, only to men who were free in 1861. It was not until 2 March 1865 that the law was expanded to include all black soldiers who had been promised equal pay when they were enlisted.

179. The report probably refers to the bloody fighting at Spotsylvania, where, on 12 May, Gen. Hancock's II Corps broke through Southern lines at the Mule Shoe and captured almost all of the Stonewall division. Southern counterattacks and bitter, bloody fighting, however, resulted in a stalemate. James M. McPherson, *Battle Cry of Freedom: The Civil War Era* (New York: Oxford University Press, 1988), 728–31.

him and threatened to "break his head." Frank collared and shook him and then very properly reported to me. I told him next time to report the trouble first, for we cannot have our boys fighting.

¶ **Wednesday, 18th, __ P.M.** I write in the midst of a thunder storm so terrific that I confess apprehension as to our being struck; thanks, however, to Col. Fox, who preceded me and got a tent up, I am sheltered from the rain. But really the storm and the discomforts of moving are trivial in comparison with the glorious news of the victory at the north (what?),[180] at 6 A.M. the "Ironsides" fired a heavy salute and all the flags were seen to be flying. We left camp at about ten and marched down the broad beach, reaching this end of the island at noon. The tents of Q.M. Garrison and myself had to be left because each, with its frame, requires a team. So I am in Fox's tent and when mine comes it will be set a little way from it and facing, with a "fly" between as a common shade.

¶ **Thursday, 19th, 9:15 P.M.** We rose at 5 and had a fine bath in the ocean, which is more accessible than at the last camp; ~~I~~ **we** inspected the company breakfast and had our own at 6:45. Then I attended sick-call. We are waiting northern papers with accounts of the battles in Virginia. We feel almost shamed to be comfortable here, and in no immediate danger, so far as appears, while our comrades elsewhere are doing and suffering so much. Of course it is in obedience to orders, and if this island were not adequately garrisoned the blockade of Charleston could not be maintained.

The subjoined diagrams show the arrangement of the camp; it is a delightful and healthy location. The companies and hospital are on a sandy plain beginning a little way from the high water mark; only 7 companies are shown but there are ten. The company officers are on low hillocks and the staff on a plateau ten or 15 feet higher, with a fine view of the ocean and the adjoining part of the island the river and islands toward Charleston and the south. Fox and I spent the afternoon arranging things and christened our new habitation by singing half an hour this evening. The headquarters of Gen. Schimmelpfennig are not far off. The grassy plain behind us is a delightful feature.

180. It is not clear to what battle Wilder was referring in his letter. At both Spotsylvania, 5 May to 12 May, and Yellow Tavern, 11 May, Union attacks were repulsed although the Union advance continued. In early May, Butler had led the Army of the James to the outer defenses of Richmond and Petersburg before becoming bottled up. Donald, *The Civil War and Reconstructions*, 377–81.

¶ **Friday, [May] 20th, 8:45 P.M.** I have just had a moonlight walk to and from Gen. S's headquarters to attend to a man who had broken the outer bone of one leg. The day has been very full of duty in connection with the hospital. As shown on the diagram, it is to be near the water, and might be reached by a high tide; so it is to be set on a foundation of large posts etc. four feet high. It was, I think, Dr. Brown's duty to attend to it, but he went off on "business" leaving word for the Chaplain to take charge. Col. Hartwell disapproved and directed me to. All day I have had the aid of a Lieutenant, Sergeant, Corporal and six men with teams; the lumber had to be brought from adjoining deserted camps and in the selection of it I was on horseback more than 4 hours. I feel that some misunderstanding with Dr. Brown might be avoided if he were in our mess, so they have been invited.

¶ **Saturday, 21st, P.M.** By riding about 20 miles to and fro, and by dint of efforts that of course I would not make for my our comfort, I have obtained 20 mosquito nettings for the patients; a bale of hay for beds; 4 pounds of nails, and a new Hospital tent. This and the better of the two old ones have been erected with frames on the foundation; my part is now done, and the interior arrangements are left to Dr. Brown. It was very important to complete the hospital in view of possible casualties from an expedition now on the way to James Island.

¶ **Sunday, 22nd, 5:00 P.M.** The expedition has just returned and we have been hearing Col. Hartwell's account of it.[181] He says that all did not get over until daylight, and then advanced through a marsh in which some sank to their waists; his own trousers were muddy to his hips. They drove in the outposts and after some skirmishing came down towards the left and crossed by a bridge to Cole's Island; here, at the side nearer us, they found a regiment of our troops that supplied them with coffee; that was at noon. The original plan was changed and our men all went over instead of remaining on Long Island as a reserve. One of our men was wounded, but the 103rd N.Y. lost a dozen killed or wounded. Col. H. says our men did splendidly and, so far from showing any signs of fear, they murmured when the advance was halted. One little fellow was dared to come on by a

181. On 21 May, Companies D, E, G, and H, with ten men from both Company B and I, plus the 103rd New York Volunteers crossed over to James Island and drove the Confederate pickets down the island in what amounted to a reconnaissance in force. Phineas Cost of Company E who was shot in the leg was the only regimental casualty. Fox, *Record*, 27.

big rebel. He replied, "I am coming," and levelled his gun, whereupon the other fled. Major Morrison of the 103rd expressed his admiration of the conduct of our men, but for failing to advance he drew his pistol on members of the 103rd and even on an officer. Per contra, when our detail was made, a corporal of Co. I said he did not wish to go because we had not been paid. By the colonel's order I shall issue two ounces of whiskey to each member of the expedition.

¶ **Monday, May 23rd, P.M.** Col. H. directed me to complete the hospital arrangements, so I went to Col. von Gilsa[182] and left the requisitions for the things already obtained, and then, with a team, kept on to the old headquarters of Gen. Gilmore in order to get the fine set of steps that I had seen there. They were so heavy as to take six men to lift them upon the team. We also got some planks and other timber and palmetto leaves for the stable. By dinner time the steps were set up at the hospital. Meantime I had to go again to both Von Gilsa and Schmmelpfennig on business. I forgot to say that the band went to the pier to meet our returning men.

¶ **Tuesday, 24th, 4:00 P.M.** There has been a second expedition; which I accompanied. It seems that, unaware of the expedition of Sunday, Gen. Hatch,[183] at Hilton Head, sent orders to Col. von Gilsa to make a demonstration at the lower end of James Island with all the men we could raise. I took two nurses and a stretcher, and the hospital knapsack; Frank had a thirst for adventure and was allowed to come. Two gunboats went ahead ~~and shelled the rebel batteries~~; one steamer took Col Hartwell and about 400 men; a second, and an hour later, took Col. Fox and three other companies. The troops were on deck so as to make a show. We ascended the Stono as far as Legarville, a pretty place with two churches, a hotel and several pleasant looking houses; it is a sort of neutral ground, occupied first by one side and then by another. The gunboats anchored about ¼ mile further up and shelled the woods of James Island. We kept on to

182. Col. Leopold von Gilsa, a former Prussian officer who served in the Schleswig-Holstein War of 1848–50, was a popular officer with his men but in his first two major battles, his brigade was routed three times. He reverted to command of his first regiment, the 41st New York, and remained a colonel throughout the war. Sifakis, *Who Was Who in the Civil War*, 678.

183. John Porter Hatch was a West Point graduate who earned two brevets during the Mexican War. A cavalry commander, he was wounded at South Mountain. Following his recovery, he was posted to the Department of the South. Sifakis, *Who Was Who in the Civil War*, 292–93.

Battery Island, connected with the James by a causeway. Here we landed one company in small boats. The shells made a great noise, but we saw no rebels. Our men were joined by a company of the 41st N.Y. that had come across Cole's Island. Together they advanced about ½ mile, but found only the deserted picket stations of the rebels, and the places where several torpedoes had been dug up the previous day. A battery on James Island now began to fire on us; one shell exploded uncomfortably near, but most of them struck the ground or fell into the river. An hour before dark the gunboats moved back to Legareville and sent some shells through the houses. At dark we took our men on board; only one was wounded and he by falling on some oyster shells. We stayed in the vicinity till midnight without succeeding in drawing any rebels within reach, and reached the pier at 1 A.M. There had been what, under some circumstances, would be merely a pleasant moonlight excursion. Col. Hartwell suggested that a ration of whiskey be served to each officer as well as a soldier, but I objected on the grounds that there had been no hard service or exposure excepting in the case of Capt. Crane, who while aiding in pushing a boat was himself pushed into the river.

9:00 P.M. One of the sergeants has brought me a skate's egg containing a partly developed young as may be seen when it is held up to the light. He was so desirous to have it that he paid the man who found it $1.00, and I have given him $2.00; I am keeping it in sea water and hope it may live; here is a diagram of it.

¶ **Wednesday, 25th, 5:00 P.M.** This morning I etherized a man and removed his great toe nail by splitting it and tearing out the separate halves; before the invention of ether it must have been a terribly painful operation. The surgeon[184] of the 54th N.Y. was present at our sick call this morning with Dr. Brown; our steward says that he attended the same German university with him and was a great duelist. We learned that Foster is to take command of the department and Hatch of this district. Capt. Gordon has brought me a great magnolia flower with petals four inches long and smelling very sweetly; it grows on the island but as yet I have not come across it.

¶ **Sunday, 29th, 5:30 P.M.** Frank has had some calamities recently. One day while he was holding Billy in order that I might write a note on horseback Billy wanted to get at some grass and after pushing Frank gen-

184. The surgeon of the 54th New York in the summer of 1864 was William H. Briggs.

tly two or three times butted him right over on his back. Yesterday, while Frank was sitting on a stool near the adjutant's horse, the latter, while stamping to drive away flies, actually kicked the boy out of the stables. Today the horse of Col. Fox pawed Miff over and lamed a front leg, and of course Frank sympathizes with her.

¶ **Monday, May 30th, 8:30 P.M.** We begin to tremble for the future of this regiment. In various ways the men manifest distrust as to their ever getting their just pay and suspect the officers in charge of complicity in the deception. Every day's delay increases the difficulty, and we apprehend some outbreak that will ruin themselves and injure their race when, perhaps, justice is about to be done. Their previous experience and their education are not such, in many cases, as to enable them to realize that redress cannot be gained otherwise than by the faithful performance of their military duties, and that any act of insubordination would lead to the taking of the colors and confining them at the Dry Tortugas[185] for the rest of their term of service. Today has occurred an unfortunate incident. Capt. Hamilton[186] had a written order this morning to report with 100 men at the White House for work upon the fort. He found only a sergeant in charge instead of Capt. McHarmar, named in the order. He very properly returned to camp. At noon came an order for him and his men to return. Our men interpreted it as a punishment and showed their feelings in various ways. This afternoon Col. Fox, the chaplain and I rode up there and it was obvious that not more than one-third of them were really working. Of course, from their standpoint, the case is clear. They were enlisted upon the same terms as white soldiers. When offered only $7.00 per month they properly refused it. But when Massachusetts guaranteed to make up the deficiency they again declined, saying they would wait three years, if necessary, till Congress should do them justice. Now they must do so, but it is very hard for them and for us.

After stopping at the fort we rode up to Pawnee Landing. It was quite a ride. This morning, at Dr. Brown's request, I drew up a report as to the prevailing diseases, their nature, violence and duration, and the remedies; it

185. During and after the Civil War, Fort Jefferson, a six-sided brick fort on the remote Dry Tortugas, sixty-eight nautical west of Key West, acted as a prison for deserters and other military criminals. It was used to hold prisoners of war in late 1864. Lonnie R. Speer, *Portals to Hell: Military Prisons in the Civil War* (Mechanicsburg, Pa.: Stackpole Books, 1997), 201–4.

186. Robert James Hamilton, a native of Springfield, served in the 34th Massachusetts before joining the black regiment. Fox, *Record*, 101.

was called for by the Medical Director. A barrel of whiskey has been drawn for the regiment. Since I abhor it, it is appropriately kept in my tent.

¶ **Wednesday, June 1, 11 A.M.** It was impossible to write last night by the reason of the swarms of mosquitoes, and I ignominiously retreated to bed and my netting. Yesterday Dr. Brown was on duty with the Examining Board so I inspected the camp with Capt. Soule, the officer of the day. After dinner I heard Col. Hartwell direct the new Q.M., Mowery, to go to Morris Island on business. I knew that he had not ridden for many years, so I offered to go in his place. Billy went the sixteen miles in good style; when nearly back I overtook Capt. Soule and Billy began to gallop as if perfectly fresh; this infected the captain's horse and we had a fine "finish." On the beach I met Gen. Foster and staff who had arrived after I left camp; I presume they were on the way to inspect the works on Morris Island. Hereafter, for the present, Fox and I will mess together; most of the other officers board at the sutler's. Their breakfast hour is 7, but I must have mine at 6:30 and Fox prefers that hour. Our boys, Frank and George, will take turns cooking and waiting. The cost will be about the same but we like plain food. Today for dinner we shall have canned roast beef, canned tomatoes, boiled potatoes and cream toast.

¶ **Thursday, June 2, 5:15 P.M.** At Col. Hartwell's request Dr. Brown attended sick call this morning so that I might attend to the pickets on Cole's and James Island and take some letters for them. I took a nurse and we were rowed from the pier up Folly Island to a creek as on the accompanying diagram. Along the shore is camped the 74th Pa.

I found a member of the 55th to guide me. I expected to use a horse but the Officer of the Day of the 74th Pa. said the bridges over the creeks were so narrow that he walked, so I started on foot. The rebel picket posts are numbered 1–8 and the other numbers represent ours. There are 150 men under command of Capt. Grant and Lt. Bean[187] and Ladd[188]. Usually the posts are nearly opposite one another; at the extreme right they are at the opposite ends of a bridge 400 yards long. We could see the sentry pacing to and fro and a reserve further off. Our men saluted them and they re-

187. Josiah A. Bean was married and living in South Natick when he was commissioned in the 55th Massachusetts. Fox, *Record*, 106.

188. Nathaniel Eustace Ladd was a shoemaker in Groveland when he enlisted in the 33rd Massachusetts. He was commissioned in the 55th in September 1863, and he breveted major before the end of the war. Fox, *Record*, 104.

sponded politely. The men were very glad to see me, especially such as I had letters. The whiskey was welcomed by all but Andy Smith who never uses it. The whole line is about ten miles long and the day was quite warm although the sea breeze tempered the heat. It was quite the longest walk I ever took and I was gratified to find no aching of my legs or blistering of my feet. I got back to our camp at 2 and after dining **and visiting** some patients, took a siesta. Lt. Boynton[189] has bronchitis but is a good patient, quiet and sensible; Lt Bradish[190] has a boil; Adjutant Perry is somewhat run down. Fox's finger no longer troubles him. David and Amos have improved.

¶ **Friday, [June] 3rd, 7:30 P.M.** I do not think that Brown is liked by many of the officers and I suspect that recently the colonel tried to get him to resign but the matter got so unpleasant that I tried not to think of it, and discouraged reference to it in my presence. Today I secured a great prize. After inspection Fox said the Post Commissary had a big turtle. I found it in the Commissary tent, building, hung up by the legs and his head touching the floor; they said it weighs 280 pounds. Several men, Germans and negroes, were trying to cut it up, having orders to remove the flesh and keep the shell for the Commissary Capt. Leitz. For a time I looked on, but after the lower shell was off a mistake as to the gall-bladder which I corrected led them to resign the knife; so I took off my jacket, rolled up my sleeves, and went at it as of old in Boylston Hall.[191] After getting off most of the flesh, I found Capt. Leitz and offered to purchase the shell; he had intended to send it to Ohio, but finding that I had been a pupil of Wyman and Agassiz he gave me the whole skeleton. I got some men and had it taken to my tent. The flesh is said to be excellent, and Leitz sent some to the commanders of the neighboring regiments. It was a female that had come ashore to lay her eggs; a pailful were taken from her and they are said to be fine eating. I shall prepare the skeleton and send it to Prof.

189. Winthrop Perkins Boynton was a close friend of William Crane, with whom he attended Harvard. He joined the 55th Massachusetts just after Crane and served for a while in the same company. In the attack on Honey Hill, the two friends were killed at almost the same moment during the battle. Fox, *Record*, 92–93.

190. Albert Henry Bradish, born and raised in Boston, was a private in the 44th Massachusetts before joining the 55th. Fox, *Record*, 107.

191. Boylston Hall, Harvard, was built in 1857 as an anatomical museum (primarily for specimens collected by Jeffries Wyman) and a chemistry laboratory. Wilder was one of Wyman's special students who worked with him in his laboratory. Boylston Hall avoided demolition in the 1950s because a stipulation in the Boylston will provide that Harvard would receive income from the bequest only as long as the walls of Boylston Hall stood.

Wyman. This morning noon the Post Q.M. asked me to visit the wife of one of his negro laborers, "contrabands" from the vicinity. She had high fever and much pain in the back, and the eruptions on her baby led me to suspect small pox; I made her comfortable as I could, had her cupped in the back,[192] etc. She and her husband are young, clean and decent.

¶ **Saturday, [June] 4, 8:00 P.M.** This morning I got some of our men who had had small pox to move the sick woman's tent; she had slept in the night and was more comfortable during the day, but died at 5. The chaplain will hold a service.

¶ **Sunday, 5th, 7:30 P.M.** I went again to Cole's Island this morning, but got back at noon for half of the line was picketed by men of another regiment; I had been able to start a little earlier, and by going further up the river (creek?) I saved a mile of sand. This afternoon I vaccinated all of the "contraband"[193] and gave Singleton, whose wife died, a can of condensed milk for his youngest child. Col. Hartwell has gone to Hilton Head on business and Col. Fox is in command; as he is also president of the court martial now sitting, he is very busy.

¶ **Monday, 6th, 7:30 P.M.** Capt. Soule has been detailed to command, with some subordinates, several hundred conscripts at the camp of the 54th N.Y. Col. Heine has ordered sick call to be at 6:30, so I must breakfast at 6. Last night I dreamt that I sawed off both my own legs.

¶ **Tuesday, 7th, 8:00 P.M.** Ten minutes ago a staff officer from Col. Heine galloped up with orders for our regiment to prepare for an attack. A rebel ram is said to be coming down the river.[194] In accordance with orders I

192. In the 1860s, cupping, or bleeding, fell into a class of therapeutics designated as depletive. Cupping (or what is now called wet cupping) was a common treatment. Flannery, *Civil War Pharmacy*, 37.

193. By 1863 regulations required all men joining the U.S. Army to be vaccinated against smallpox unless they could show proof of prior vaccination. Unfortunately, many of the vaccinations did not prevent smallpox, either because the officially supplied vaccine matter was inert or because of improper vaccinations. Before the war, smallpox was uncommon in the Southern states. Humphreys, *Intensely Human*, 95–98.

194. There were three ironclad rams, the CSS *Palmetto State*, the CSS *Charleston*, and the CSS *Chicora*, operating out of the Charleston harbor in 1864. Their presence was a critical part of the successful Confederate defensive operations around the city. The threatened attack did not materialize. Wise, *Gate of Hell*, 83–84; Burton, *The Siege of Charleston*, 125–26.

visited all the detachments, engineers, employees, provost guards, etc. One of our men had his great toe mashed by a cannon rolling upon it. One of our officers at Pawnee Landing sent us half a dozen crooked necked squashes and some string beans, very acceptable.

¶ **Wednesday, 8th, 9:00 P.M.** Soon after tea Capt. Gordon came with his flute to play with me; then the Glee Club of Co. F sang in front of our tent, and then we played some more. Just before supper I cut up a second big turtle for Mr. Johnson, the sutler, who gave me the shell and skeleton for so doing; the operation was witnesses by several officers and about 20 men, and assistants were always ready. Now I can keep one myself and send the other to Prof. Wyman. I read his paper on the Development of the Skate this afternoon.

¶ **Thursday, [June] 9th, 8:00 P.M.** Yesterday I had a letter from Lt. Knight, who had been the Commissary at Yellow Bluff; he says the duty there has been very hard, for they had to picket the river above and below to prevent the planting of torpedoes. This afternoon we were visited by Surg. Pineo, Medical Inspector of the Department; he was formerly in charge of a Washington hospital and remembered me. I happened to be reading the report of the Army Medical Society at which he read a paper on the excision of a piece of nerve to prevent pain in the hand; he had just written on the subject and was glad to see the report; so we had a very pleasant interview. Col. Hartwell returned today, much to the relief of Fox. For dinner we had turtle soup, very good.

¶ **Friday, June 10, 8:00 P.M.** Besides four of our own officers, I visited today Capt. Walton at the headquarters of Gen. Schimmelpfennig. The latter part of the afternoon brought the severest rainstorm I have ever known; it came right through our tents and blew over our cook tent, but it has been set up again.

¶ **Saturday, 11th, 8:00 P.M.** This morning Major Wales brought his large dog for the relief of a dislocated right shoulder; it happened ten days ago but was supposed to be a sprain. He was chloroformed by putting his head in a pillow case and dropping the liquid on it opposite his nose till he went to sleep; the shoulder was then set, but I fear it will always be weak. Col. Fox and I have decided to join the general mess at the sutler's, mainly because Col. urges it on the grounds that the present arrangement gives color to an idea on the part of the men that the two colonels are not agreed respecting the pay question. Hartwell says he has received anonymous letters to the effect that the writers believe if Fox were in command the men would no longer be compelled to obey and serve an unfaithful government. In all this the officers are wholly in accord, but so long as the doubt exists among the men Hartwell desires Fox to express his opinion publicly, and I understand that he has consented. As to the change in the mess arrangements, any private consideration should give way to the public good. It seems that now, as the days are longer, breakfast may be had earlier and I shall be glad to be relieved of the bother of providing in my turn.

¶ **Sunday, [June] 12th, 8:00 P.M.** We find the sutler's mess good. At the two ends of the staff table sit the two colonels; at either side of Hartwell are the adjutant and the Q.M., and at either side of Fox, Soule and myself; the others are Gordon, Crane, Thurber, Goodwin and the Post Q.M. Capt. Cushing, Dr. Brown and the chaplain may join later.

¶ **Tuesday, 14th, 11:45 A.M.** I am writing before dinner, quite unusual; yesterday I did not write at all. I packed up the heart of Lt. Jones and the fatal ball and entrusted it to Lt. Gannett who has resigned and will visit Washington. He and Lt. Stimpson,[195] who has also resigned, have been most frequently in trouble for intoxication and other misbehavior, and it is a great relief to see them leave. But the feeling towards the men is very different. The former is brave and has many good qualities, with an appreciation of the beautiful in nature and art. He seems to err commonly through bad example.[196] Stimpson is a villain; smooth-tongued, loquacious, shrewd enough to keep out of trouble himself but delighting in making trouble for others. While at Yellow Bluff, out of the reach of temptation, Gannett conducted himself well. Yesterday there was a regular northeaster, and again the rain penetrated the tent. Of course, there is always something to do, and I wrote up the prescription book; but, for the first time since I can remember, I actually stuck my hands in my pockets and walked up and down the tents, sometimes singing with Fox.

195. Edward Stearns Stimpson was a clerk from Danvers when he enlisted as sergeant in the 48th Massachusetts before being transferred to the 16th. After being commissioned in the 55th, he served briefly as acting adjutant of the regiment and was favorably mentioned in general orders for conduct during a reconnaissance on James Island in May 1864. Fox, *Record*, 28, 105.

196. Gannett would be recommissioned in the regiment, 1 February 1865, and breveted captain before mustering out of the regiment on 29 August 1865. Fox, *Record*, 28, 104.

8:30 P.M. The paymaster is at the 103rd, and at the suggestion of Col. Hartwell, the officers went there in groups for their pay. Mine was for four months, Jan. to April inclusive, and I received $398.00, and have been settling various accounts. According to a previous agreement Frank now gets $7.00 per month, with his board and clothing.

¶ **Wednesday, 15th, 11:20 A.M.** Again I am writing before dinner, and of a very serious matter connected with the pay. In the first place I feel that Hartwell has not managed the matter well; he has vacillated when consistent firmness was most required. For example, after constant urging by him for a week, Fox reluctantly consented to write out his own views, which Hartwell proposed to have copied and read to the men by the company commanders. Yet after it had been read to the detachment on guard at the headquarters of Gen Schimmelpfennig, and its commander had reported its effect as good, Hartwell says that "perhaps it is not best" and at supper displayed what seems to me a lack of decision and self-reliance. Yesterday he did not let the pay-master come over here, but of course the fact of the payment of the officers became known and the feeling was bitter. At 9 this morning when the picket detail was made the detail of an entire company refused to fall in, but Capt. Grant, the officer of the day, convinced all but two that it was their duty. Some men of Co. G also refused, among them a sergeant; Grant ripped off his chevrons and had him tied up. One claimed to be ill, it proved that he had so declared to me at sick call, but I did not excuse him; I was sent for to decide again and as I declared him able to do duty he went. In my judgment, the two who refused should be tried by drum head court martial and shot; better two than risk using artillery on the entire regiment if their pernicious example spreads. Of course, these things must not be made public till they can no longer be concealed.

8:00 P.M. After supper the band played for us, and Col. Hartwell and Fox and I sat talking; among other things of the refusal yesterday of a rebel officer in charge of a flag of truce to treat with Capt. Torrey because the latter was in a negro regiment; on previous occasions they have treated with our officers.[197] This afternoon Capt. Gordon and I rode to Pawnee

197. The incident triggered anger among the enlisted men of the 55th Massachusetts. Torrey notified the officer commanding the island, Lt. Col. Meitzel of the 74th Pennsylvania Volunteers, who then sent an officer of white troops to treat with the Confederates. The black soldiers felt demeaned by Meitzel and complained in a letter to the *Weekly Anglo-African*. Trudeau, *Voices of the 55th*, 114.

Landing to look at a melodeon belonging to a sutler; he wishes to sell it, but says if he does not we may use it while he is at Jacksonville a few weeks. It is an excellent instrument. We had a delightful ride on the inside or forest road. One of the charms of our location is that we may choose either the wide firm beach or the road through the woods, which is wholly out of sight and even hearing of the ocean, and presents grass and flowers in abundance. Frank has conformed to the fashion in having a boil which I lanced today; hardly a day passes when this sort of "comforter" has not to be opened for somebody.

¶ **Thursday, [June] 16th, 7:46 P.M.** I have sent $100.00 to brother Edward. This morning, passing through the post wagon yard I heard a violin, and found the owner willing to loan it to Col. Fox occasionally. Unfortunately it is a full tone lower than our flutes, but the three instruments sound very well together. Tomorrow five of our officers and 150 men are going to garrison Long Island. I do not think colored troops should be placed in such a location; for if attacked by a much superior force, they could not possibly escape over the creeks and marshes.

¶ **Friday, 17th, 7:45 P.M.** We had another musicale this afternoon. For an hour last evening the rebels kept up a furious cannonade from apparently all their available batteries, but we have not learned either the occasion or the result.

¶ **Saturday, 18th, 7:45 P.M.** I am writing by a new kind of lamp, filled with kerosene; it is arranged to shine from one side only, and water may be heated on it. From a man of Co. I, I bought a pair of long drab colored blinds; one of them I have fitted into the door of the tent, replacing the canvas, and now it looks quite civilized and enables me to ventilate better without exposure. Part of the other blind I have given to the chaplain for whom a carpenter is making a door. Col. Fox and I are rather proud of being able to do little things of that sort ourselves, although of course the regiment contains artisans of several assorts and any heavy work is always provided for. With my new lamp I have just made some hot lemonade, but shall not indulge in it often with lemons at 8 cents each.

As an illustration of the slight impression made in the army by incidents that would be very impressive at home, I have written so far without mentioning the sad spectacle at which I officiated this morning. At the other camp a soldier struck Lt. Ellsworth and was tried for mutiny and condemned to be shot[198]. The sentence was carried out today in the presence of all of the troops on the island, and was probably a salutary warning to the ill-disposed; but think of the non-payment and of the little previous education of many.

[Wilder added the following page to his 1910 transcription.]

A Military execution by shooting

Account by Corporal L. L. Flowers, 103rd N.Y., "History," p.126.

The scene is vividly remembered; the victim sitting on his rough box of a coffin, his eyes bandaged and his hands bound behind him; the open grave, the firing squad drawn up in line; the signal of the officer in charge, the simultaneous volley, and all was over. Four bullets passed through his head and one through his body. Then came the quiet command, "Right face, forward march," given by the different commands and we returned to our camp, there to speculate on the difference between justice and mercy and the penalty inflicted for the disregard of military authority.

¶ **Sunday, [June] 19th, 2:30 P.M.** As the weather grows warmer I feel less inclination to study; there is no longer the pressure of completing my thesis, as there was last summer; then, you see, no one else tries to study and one is liable to so many interruptions; it is rather ungracious to decline to join others who wish to sing. Yet I cannot help feeling that if I improve my time here, it may be possible to take the medical degree in a shorter period; whether or not I ever practice at home I should be an M.D.

¶ **Tuesday, 21st, 5:15 P.M.** Some of Col. Heine's men got another big turtle, said to be larger than the others; I went up to see it and finding the bungling removal of the limbs I took the knife and did it quickly; they thanked me heartily and said I must have cut off lots of men's legs. Some of the bones were lost from the second turtle, and Col. Heine will let me have this in place of it, since he wants it only for curiosity.

198. The enlisted man, Pvt. Wallace Baker of Company I from Hopkinsville, Kentucky, was late and without his equipment falling in for a company inspection on 1 May 1864. He was insubordinate to the officers, and when Ellsworth shoved him, he struck the lieutenant and yelled "do you think that you can strike me, and I not strike you back again?" The situation may have been more difficult because Ellsworth had just recently transferred from the 2nd Massachusetts. Baker was 20 years old when he was shot by a detail from his own regiment. Yacovone, *A Voice of Thunder*, 74–75; Fox, *Record of the Service of the 55th Massachusetts*, 29; Trudeau, *Voices from the 55th*, 113, 223–25.

¶ **Friday, 24th, 4:45 P.M.** Yesterday Col. Hartwell asked me to accompany him to Long Island to look after the 150 men stationed there; I have not been over at all, and the conditions are such that ~~any~~ **the** sick cannot well be sent here and get back the same day. We rode up the beach to Pawnee Landing, left our horses with the picket there and took a boat; the tide was so low that it grounded four times before we reached the end of the long pier at Long Island, and we climbed up at some risk to a mud bath. I should have mentioned that the colonel was "General Officer of the Day." Opposite the pier is a large stockade made of logs, with bastions and loopholes and great gates; into it the forces on the island could retreat in case of an attack in force and hold the enemy at bay for a time. At this point the island is quite narrow and I went to the other side and looked across the creek and marsh to Secessionville where the rebels have several batteries and a tall lookout. Then we walked 2 ½ miles to the south end of the island; there is a battery with several thirty pound Parrott guns; while we were there three shots were fired at the lookout, and with his glass the colonel could see the man descending very quickly. Col. H. was not very well and we were offered the use of some quadrupeds called horses by courtesy on which to ride back to the stockade. On one, a tall gaunt gray, was a dilapidated saddle. The other was smaller and bore not even a blanket, and the rein reached only to its shoulders. The colonel insisted on our drawing lots for the saddled beast, and very properly it went to him. Upon the other I climbed by the aid of Lt. Woodward's hand under my foot, there being nothing to grasp or step from; his spine was like the edge of a board and to avoid bisection I sat far back on his hips. But there I could not reach the rein. Ordinarily it simply followed the Colonel and the path, but when I wished to direct him I had to move forward and pull at the rein since it had no notion of "guiding." The mosquitoes swarmed upon it and the blood they had sucked from him stained my glove when I crushed them. To save myself from his sharp spine I partly supported myself by placing one hand in front and the other behind. But occasionally my spurs would accidentally strike him and then he would break into the most horrible trot. When half way the colonel proposed to exchange, but I replied that it was bad enough for me but would be worse for him. Naturally he reached the stockade first and watched my approach, as did the soldiers. While approaching I ceased to steady myself with my hands and sat as erect and dignified as I could. But disaster awaited me. From the pier the road continued directly to the stockade, raised nearly a foot above the general level and thus higher than the path I was on. On reaching it I prepared to dismount and had my mind on the pier at the right; but the horse saw the gate open and made a sudden bolt **to the left** for the stockade leaving me in the air to fall half sitting to the earth; adding injury to insult he kicked my foot as he left me. Fortunately the blow was light and did no permanent damage though I still feel the effects. On regaining Folly Island I mounted Billy with delight and we had a fine ride back to camp. On the way the colonel's hat fell off and I rode back and picked it from the ground without dismounting; but the cord still remained I picked that up also, and these feats and the ride consoled me for my downfall. Day before yesterday a naval officer came to ask me to visit the wife of the captain of one of the ordnance brigs lying in the river. Fearing the case might involve more than I knew I suggested Dr. Brown, but he begged me to go and I did rather reluctantly. The captain's name was Devereux, a very pleasant man and his wife proved to be a refined lady, about 35 I think. She was attacked with diarrhea ten days ago and the surgeon of the gun boats prescribed some powder which made her very sick and unable to keep anything on her stomach. I relieved the nausea with creosote and am now using opium and camphor.[199] I have taken her a Harper's Magazine, the pictures of which occupy her, but she cannot now sit up to read. They came from Bangor, Me. She wishes to go home and I shall do my best to help her to regain her strength, but if she does not improve soon I shall ask permission to call in Dr Brown or the surgeon of the 54th N. Y. Miff was abducted by one of our soldiers and nearly taken to the next regiment in response, he claimed, to a nioti [sic] reward offered for a dog with white tail. The very tip of her tail is white, but no more and I supposed every member of the regiment was acquainted with her as my dog. The officer of the day took that view and sent the man to the guard house; I went there and talked with him and was sufficiently convinced of his ignorance to secure his release, but the other officers do not share my charitable view. I must get a collar for the little beast.

¶ **Sunday, [June] 26th, 2:15 P.M.** I have just had to do a very disagreeable thing, decline to excuse an officer from duty. Just now several of our officers are under arrest for neglect of duty or other offence, and that renders the work of the others more severe; in consequence some are really ill and

199. Small amounts of creasotum were part of the U.S. Army standard supply table. It was used internally as an antiemetic and in some bronchial conditions. Opium, often considered the most important drug in the whole Materia Medica, was used with camphor to treat bronchitis. The best study of the drugs used during the Civil War is Michael A. Flannery's *Civil War Pharmacy: A History of Drugs, Drug Supply and Provision, and Therapeutics for the Union and Confederacy* (Binghamton, N.Y.: Pharmaceutical Products Press, 2004), 120, 242, 290.

I have excused Capt. Nutt and Lts. Bean, Ellsworth and Marsh.[200] Another has just applied to me and I told him I could not conscientiously excuse him, and suggested his applying to Dr. Brown; as a result he has reported for duty. Of course either of us may properly prescribe for an officer but I shall ask Dr. B., as surgeon, to take the responsibility of excusing them from duty hereafter. Yesterday, in order to be more at liberty today, I visited the patients outside the regiment. Capt. Walton was at breakfast and said he was better; I gave him a bottle of light wine with which to take his Citrate of Iron and Quinine.[201] The engineer patient was better. Then, as the steward was ill, I dressed the stump of the amputated thigh of a rebel who was captured on Johns Island in Feb., and whose wounded leg had to be amputated. Then Capt. Devereux came for me and we took Miff along, to the great delight of his wife. She was feeling somewhat better. Another New England captain was calling and we had a pleasant chat. She is only 26 and they seem much attached. They had been unable to buy ice this morning; there are 10 tons here for issue to the hospitals, and I asked Dr. Brown, now post surgeon, to give me an order for a few extra pounds for her; he declined but finally gave me a piece of what had been drawn for our hospital. This morning as the sutler had not returned with the expected supply I went to Surgeon Hagen, chief medical officer of the district, and he gave me an order for 25 pounds which may last till the sutler comes. Mrs. Devereux felt as if she might take some milk, but on inquiry of the post commissary I learned that the only possible source of fresh milk here is his goat, and as yet no one has been able to extract a drop from her. In the afternoon Sergeant Letts [Lett][202] came and shampooed the heads of Fox and myself with bay rum (which, by the way, some men have become intoxicated upon), in return the colonel gave him some cigars and I a glass of light wine. The sutler has a cat with a kitten. Miff chanced, with no evil intent, to approach the latter too nearly this morning and its mother flew at the intruder furiously and scratched her nose, making her cry piteously. Frank has just brought in a crow with one wing clipped, evidently it has been in captivity for it shows little fear of us and walks about picking up the crumbs we throw to it.

200. Alonzo Marsh, a painter in Fitchburg enlisted as a private in the 21st Massachusetts in July 1861. He served as lieutenant in the 55th from August 1863 until he resigned in September 1864. Fox, *Record*, 105.

201. This was a specific tonic that supposedly combined the virtues of iron (to treat chronic diarrhea) and quinine. Flannery, *Civil War Pharmacy*, 121.

202. Sgt. Levi Lett, a 28-year-old barber from Buffalo, New York, became the regiment's principal musician in November 1864. Fox, *Record*, 114.

Assistant Surgeon Burt Green Wilder.
Wilder was a prolific writer throughout his entire life. The time that he spent in the 55th Massachusetts would have a major impact on his subsequent career. (All photographs are from the Burt Green Wilder Collection, Cornell University.)

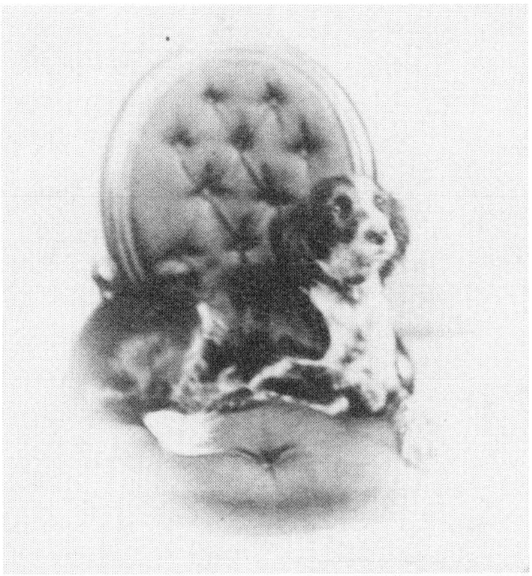

Miff.
Miff was the dog adopted by Wilder while the regiment was in Jacksonville. Until she was sent north in the summer of 1864, Miff was Wilder's constant companion.

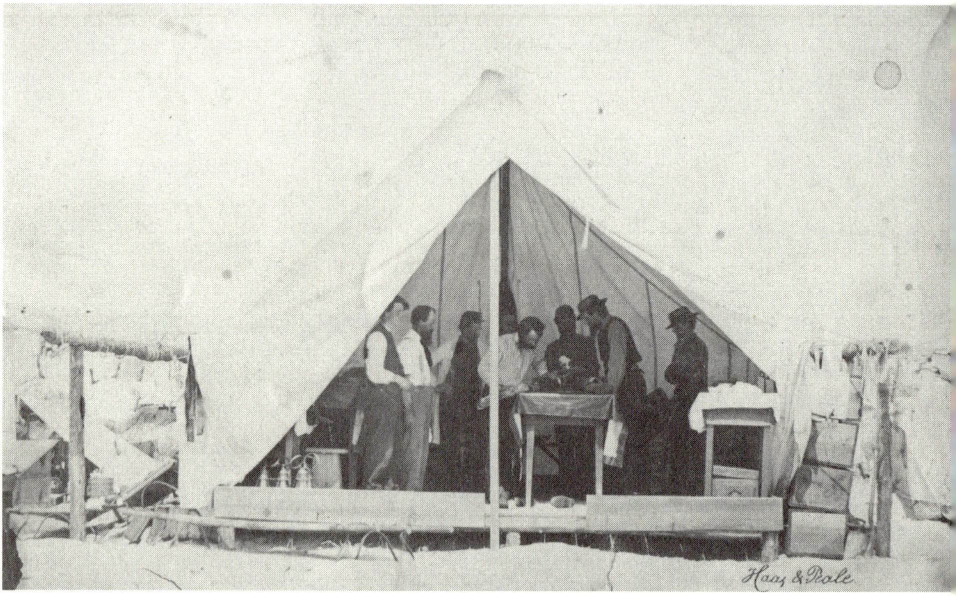

A wounded soldier being examined by doctors on Morris Island.
Wilder is one of the surgeons standing in the tent.

Lieutenant Colonel Charles Barnard Fox.
Fox was Wilder's closest friend in the regiment and the officer with whom he spent the most time.

Lieutenant James M. Trotter.

Trotter was born in Mississippi and resided in Cincinnati, Ohio, at the start of the war. A first sergeant in Company K, he received his commission in April 1864, but, like Sergeants Shorter and Dupree, he was not mustered in as such until July 1865.

Lieutenant John Freeman Shorter.

Shorter was first sergeant in Company D and one of the enlisted men commissioned by Governor John A. Andrew. He was mustered in as an officer only after a long delay by the War Department.

Lieutenant William H. Dupree.

Dupree was first sergeant in Company H prior to being commissioned by Andrew. He worked for the Boston post office after the war.

Captain Charles Carroll Soule.
Soule, a graduate of Harvard in 1862, served in the 44th Massachusetts Volunteer Militia before joining the 55th Massachusetts.

Surgeon William Symmington Brown.
Brown was a Scottish doctor who had served in the 33rd Massachusetts Regiment before joining the 55th Massachusetts. His resignation on 1 July 1865 allowed Wilder to be appointed surgeon on 11 July 1865.

Sergeant Charles L. Mitchell.
Mitchell was a sergeant in Company F. Although commissioned by Governor Andrew, he lost his right foot as the result of a wound at Honey Hill and was never mustered in as an officer because of his disability. He represented Boston's Ward Six in the state legislature of 1866–67.

Reverend John R. Bowles.

Bowles was born in Virginia but lived in Ohio in 1864. He joined the 55th Massachusetts as its chaplain on 27 March 1864, replacing the less popular Reverend William Jackson.

Sergeant Major Abram W. Shadd.

Shadd, a sergeant in Company B, became the regimental sergeant major on 1 July 1865. He was commissioned second lieutenant but was never mustered in because of the mustering-out of the regiment.

¶ **Monday, 27th, 8:00 P.M.** This morning Col. Fox's servant, George, was shot in the leg by Col. Hartwell's boy while carelessly handling a revolver. I reached him very soon and finding the wound to be at the knee sent him to the hospital because injuries of that joint are always serious. Notwithstanding, Col. Fox's wish that a thorough examination be made to determine whether the joint was opened, Dr. Brown made no examination; I trust it will not involve the loss of the limb.

¶ **Tuesday, 28th, 1:30 P.M.** Lt. Ellsworth is having a sad experience. He is far from well himself and the mail today brought word that his two year old child had the croup and had been given up by the doctor and his wife was sick herself.

Dr. Turner, the surgeon of the 103rd [N.Y.] wants me to train his horse as to guiding, etc., and I may try it, letting Capt. Gordon ride mine at the time.

[Wilder indicates in his 1910 transcription that the record for 2 July to 7 July was not based on his original letters but on copies of the letters that had been placed in another portfolio. He suggests that the original copies were destroyed "when the copy was made." He also indicated that "the bracketed portions have been interpolated."]

Rivers Causeway, July 2, 1864

Monday, July 4, 9:00 A.M. Last Thursday, June 30, we (companies and commanders?) marched to Pawnee Landing and after dark took boats to Long Island.[203] There we sat down near the stockade opposite the landing waiting for the 33rd U.S. and the 103rd N.Y., making in all about 1000 men. (Did those regiments join us there or not till next day?) About midnight we were ordered to return to Folly Id., the expedition being deferred 24 hours. Already half devoured by mosquitoes, we (officers or men?) lay

203. Maj. Gen. John G. Foster, who assumed command of the Department of the South on 24 May 1864, hoped to be the man who captured Charleston. After considering and rejecting several plans, he decided on near simultaneous attacks at five separate points. The 55th Massachusetts was part of the assault on the southern tip of James Island while Fort Johnson, on Charleston Harbor, would be attacked by water after dark. Another attack led by Gen. Hatch would strike across Johns Island while Federal ships on the Stono River would shell Battery Pringle. A Union raid commanded by Gen. Birney up the North Edisto River was designed to cut the Charleston and Savannah Railroad and destroy the bridge at Jacksonboro. Despite numerical superiority, none of the Union attacks were any more successful that the action at Rivers Causeway. E. Milby Burton, *The Siege of Charleston, 1861–1865* (Columbia: University of South Carolina Press, 1970), 284–95; Fox, *Record*, 29–32.

upon the ground near Pawnee Landing and were nearly finished by the pests. So after day break we went to a spot nearer the beach where a ridge concealed us from the rebels in their tall lookout at Secessionville. (Did they see us or have any idea of the expedition?) The horses of Fox and myself soon arrived and we rode to camp at Stono, leaving David Lee and Frank at the landing, the former to fetch back the horses at night. We (Col. Fox and I) took a sea bath. Then I attended sick-call and did various little things, and tried to sleep, but in vain. At four, I got a boat and visited Mrs. Devereux (wife of the captain of a vessel who had been under my care) and found her doing well. After supper we went to ~~the~~ **Pawnee** Landing. ~~After dark the 33rd and 103rd began to cross and~~ It was midnight (Friday, July 1) before we reached Long Id. We marched silently down to the fort [Battery No. 3] near which Dr. Brown, the hospital steward and some nurses remained to establish the field-hospital. I kept on with the stretchers-corps, nurse James Henry[204] of Co. H. and Frank, who would not be left. (Dr. W. S. Brown was the surgeon. Henry was one of the best hospital attendants, and carried a surgical dressing-case. Frank E. Thayer, a white boy of eleven years, had accompanied me from Boston as my "orderly" and begged in vain to be in the "storming party." The stretcher-corps comprised musicians and drummers.) The sky was just beginning to lighten when the last boat, containing us, landed on Tiger Id. The margins of this [island] are marshy, and when the tide was low, as was the case earlier in the morning, some (we hear) sank to their waists **and had to be pulled out**; the higher tide permitted our boat to get nearer dry land, yet once I sank to my knees. At the point of crossing, on Long Id., I left one stretcher and eight men to receive the wounded from the boats and carry them to Dr. Brown. At the landing on Tiger Id., I left ~~four~~ **eight** men to take the wounded from the stretchers when brought from the front and put them in the boats (who rowed?). All the others (presumably eight?) and two stretchers I took with me. ~~Following the trail of our troops~~ We found our force formed in column just ready to start. The 103rd in front (at the right), the 33rd next (at the left) and ours last (between the two). Emerging from the trees that concealed them, they entered a marsh where each step was in mud and water. Fortunately Col. Fox, who commanded our regiment (Hartwell being in command of the brigade) guided us (55th)where the water stood, indicating that the soil below was firmer. Frank was left on Tiger Id. As the head of the column reached a

204. James Henry was 27 when he left Middletown, Pennsylvania, to volunteer. Fox, *Record*, 137.

line of bushes at the further side of the marsh shots were fired by the picket behind them; they were driven in and a second line was encountered, which retreated after firing. Capt. Nutt and ~~Co. D~~ **his company (D)** turned to the left, under orders to go down the island in the same direction as on a former occasion (May 21) and communicate with our forces advancing from Coles Id. This he did in fine style, losing no men and taking several prisoners and horses. The main body had now reached a thicket, partly natural and partly artificial, thru which an advance was difficult. The 103rd was now in line (column?) on the right; the 33rd on the left of a sort of dike or raised road (Rivers Causeway); our regiment was **in line** in nearly equal parts on the two sides of the road. (I recall seeing Col. Hartwell or Captain Grant on this road on horseback.) Just as the advance got out of the thicket there were added to the whistling of musket balls the reports of two small cannon, ~~followed~~ **attended** by a horrible screeching over our heads made by the missiles, iron balls (Mather says slugs.) enclosed in a tin can (Were any canisters found with the guns?). Here men began to fall. One of the 33rd, near me, received a ball through his chest; (I recall the great size of the hole.) nothing could be done for him. Here the advance fell back, disordered by the unexpected canister, and our men took their places and rushed up with loud cheers. Finding several wounded near me, among them Capt. Goodwin, I stopped to send them to the rear. (Did I then advance and afterwards return to Capt. Goodwin; or was all done for him then? The former I think.) The bushes prevented me seeing what happened in front, but the cheering continued, and on going forward I saw our men on top of the earthworks where the two guns were, waving their caps and dancing about. The canister shot **had** mostly passed over our heads and although they made a horrible noise I really felt more apprehension from the musket balls that came lower. (I recall my anxiety lest I be hit in the knee). The cannon firing now recommenced but with a deadened sound. Hurrying up I found that the two guns had actually been turned against the enemy; at least three shots were fired upon them.[205] (Has any one else recorded the number?) ~~Every one~~ Our **officers** say our men did magnificently. Altho sick and almost disabled by the boil on his leg and by the toilsome struggle thru the marsh, Col. Fox led the charge, but such was the impetuosity of the men

205. The first black sergeant to reach the guns reported that he turned the one gun that was loaded and fired it at the retreating Confederate, then reloaded it and fired one more time. Edwin S. Redkey, ed., *A Grand Army of Black Men* (New York: Cambridge University Press, 1992), 67–68.

that they outstripped him, rushed thru the thicket and captured the earthwork. In shameful contrast with the valor of the fighting men was the cowardice of the stretcher corps, composed of musicians and drummers. Such was my indignation that I swore at them as I had never before and hope never to again. Had I my pistol I would have shot one of them as an example. Perhaps I had taken them too far to the front, but they were bound to keep with me. Really during the action it was safer there than farther back, for the guns were aimed high and most of the **fatal** wound were in the head. However, at last Capt. Goodwin and Sergeant Evan[206] of Co. A were got upon the stretchers. Even then they were not out of danger. A piece of shell struck the cross-bar of the stretcher just as Capt. Goodwin raised his head to look after the bearers, who had dropped him at the explosion. The enemy shelled the whole line of our communication with Long Id. (What other wounded were sent back or assisted back?) After the stretchers had left I went forward and found our men resting in the field and congratulating each other. Soon however they moved forward **a distance** to a hedge behind which they dug a trench 3 or 4 feet deep. The enemy evidently supposed them still at the ~~redoubt~~ **lunet**[207] for the shells mostly struck there. Behind the ~~redoubt~~ **lunet** I had put ~~my~~ nurse Henry and a few exhausted men till the stretchers returned. For a time Col. Fox remained there. The signal ~~officer~~ sergeant stood on it and probably drew the enemy's fire. Evidently they had the range of it accurately. The heavy shells ~~estimated at 64 pounds by Col. Fox~~ struck and exploded all around it and two struck in it at our backs but fortunately did not explode; the pieces of some came into the ditch **of the lunet**. Now I took the nurse and the drummers and went out over the field to attend to the wounded and look for the dead. Seven **of our regiment** were killed, all but one shot in the head by the canister (crushing the skulls so as not to be entire when found?). Twenty were wounded, of whom two died soon. (How soon and does this refer to our regiment only?) While we were attending to the wounded, the shells came at intervals. There was no protection there and twice I just escaped being struck by fragments of shells that exploded just before reaching us. The wounded were placed on the south side of the raised road and sent or assisted to the rear. In the ditch at the side of the road I found a great fellow of the 33rd crouching as I had seen him during the advance. I asked where he was hurt and he was uncertain and could

206. Sergeant William H. Evans was a 23-year-old farmer from Wayne County, Indiana. He would be discharged in July 1865 for disability caused by his wounds. Fox, *Record*, 115.

207. A lunette was a small fieldwork with its rear open to interior lines.

not show me the wound. I ordered him to go forward and join his company and on his refusing I picked up his gun and threatened to stick the bayonet in him; then he went. I am happy to say that during the advance not one of our men held back but afterwards a few seemed **needlessly** to regard themselves as exhausted. (The narrative of the 2nd was here interrupted to state the occurrences of the 5th.)

To our surprise Battery Lamar[208] has just sent a shell into this field and if the gun ~~were~~ **had been** deflected a little I might ~~be~~ **have been** hit. I would not have ~~stopped~~ **located** here in the first place but Dr. Hagen, the chief medical officer, selected it as shaded, convenient to water, and near the passage to Coles Id. by which the wounded would be taken; after consultation we moved back an eighth of a mile (real distance?) to a great tree ~~near~~ **not far to the rear of** General Schinnelpfennig's headquarters, and have thrown up a semicircular breastwork of earth as high as a man's head. Our first position was just at the end of the line of rifle pits and ~~a battery was~~ **two guns were** stationed in front of us at which the enemy might fire.

¶ [**July**] **6th At noon of the 2nd, Col.** Fox (who was in command of the regiment during the forenoon?), the nurse, Henry, and I ~~went forward to the rifle pits of the~~ **rejoined our** troops. A long trench had been dug in the rear of a dense hedge which evidently concealed them from the enemy since the fire was directed almost exclusively at the lunet; but just as Col. Fox and I decided that that was too hot for us they seemed to discover the location of the troops and commenced to shell that line. We got down into the trench like the rest, and were partly sheltered by some branches. But the sun was very hot and several men were sunstruck ; in some of the white regiments ~~lower down on the island~~ it is said that men dropped dead. I forgot to say that Frank arrived during the forenoon; the path was shelled and he had many narrow escapes. We lay in the trench all day and by good luck had no men killed, although one of the pickets, in the front, lost a finger from a fragment of shell. In the 33rd, however, a man declared that he would as soon be shot outright as slowly baked to death, and got out of the trench and sat on a log on the crest of the bank; a shell struck the log and blew him up; all his bones seemed to be broken; he was alive when I reached him and got him on a stretcher, but I heard that he

208. Battery Lamar was a large earthwork fort anchoring the left of the Confederate lines on James Island. Fox, *Record*, 29; Burton, *The Siege of Charleston*, 109.

died within an hour. (Where were the medical officers of that and the 103rd?)

As night came on, we became anxious for orders from the rear, for there seemed to be no reason why the enemy should not bring artillery down on our left flank and rake our whole line.[209] At one time, indeed, our pickets reported troops massing on the left, but there was no attack, and I dozed off occasionally. **Towards** ~~at~~ midnight, however, came orders to retire. The road led almost straight back. The stretcher bearers and I brought up the rear. (Was there no rear guard?) We were very quiet and the enemy had no notion of the movement. An hour's march (actual time?) brought us into a wide field where were the troops under General Schimmelpfennig. We laid down and slept the few hours before dawn, although there was some firing on the left (Was this on James Id. or Johns, as mentioned by Emilio, p. 208?). At four I rose and went over the ground to select the best place for a field hospital, and finally crossed to Coles Id., where I found Dr. Hagen establishing a field hospital. Here I got a cup of coffee, the first since leaving Folly Id. The troops dug a rifle pit during the day. It was noon before the enemy discovered our retreat; from our lookout, they could be seen to be advancing over the ground cautiously.

6th cont. We were hoping that this new ~~position~~ **location** could not be reached by Lamar, but yesterday some shells came quite close and a fragment struck not three feet from Capt. Gordon's head. Today the~~y~~ **enemy** have not fired much. Our light artillery has started out several times to drive back skirmishers, and the infantry support has had some killed and ~~several~~ wounded. Night before last the pickets were alarmed and there was considerable popping all along the front. Birney's troops have thrown up entrenchments in our rear and, if in need, we can retire to them.[210] The hospital is so well fixed that I rather hate to move.

I am very well, and never tired, although ~~lying~~ **sleeping** on the ground with only a rubber blanket **under me**. When we started a boil was forming on the back of my neck and the exposure has caused it to enlarge and

209. In actual fact, the Confederate forces were stretched almost to the breaking point as they attempted to defend Charleston from the series of Union attacks. Gen. William B. Taliaferro, defending James Island, was so desperate for troops that he requested that the cadets of the Citadel Academy be sent to him. Burton, *The Siege of Charleston*, 286, 288.

210. Following Gen. William Birney's failed attack up the North Edisto River on 3 July, Foster transferred his 1,200 soldiers to James Island to support Schimmelfennig's men. Burton, *The Siege of Charleston*, 289–90.

make my neck very stiff; I cannot see it, but Dr. Hagen says it is a regular carbuncle. (The scar is still visible.)

Col. Fox is now in command of the regiment again. The day after the ~~battle~~ fight he was worse and I advised him to go to camp **on Folly Id.** Two other nights he slept at the hospital with me, but last night ~~out on the field~~ **he was out on the field with the regiment.**

(On my three days visit to James Id. in 1895 I think I recognized the stump of the large tree shown in the sketch; the tree died and was cut down by Nelson Left, who bought the place 13 years before; the diameter of the stump was 7–8 of my left spans. From it to the road leading to the Causeway was 150 of my steps.)

Field Hospital, James Island, July '64
Thursday, [July] 7th, 3 P.M. All day so far I have been superintending improvements to the hospital arrangements. ~~There has been no alarm since yesterday~~. Having at my ~~command~~ **disposal** about 20 men and boys who seem desirous to atone by hard work for the disgrace of the 2nd, I have been able to get ~~things~~ **the hospital** into very fair shape. As shown in the accompanying Diagram it encircles a very large tree, and smaller trees have been set in the ground **at the west** to keep off the afternoon sun. The cooks and utensils for the officers' mess arrived this morning and all dined together. The officers admire ~~it~~ **the establishment** and it is certainly the coolest and safest place on our part of the island now. We only fear that Gen. Schimmelpfennig may regard it as too luxurious and order a move.

7:30 P.M. Half an hour ago Dr. Hawks[211] loaned me his horse and I rode down the island and crossed to Battery Island where the demonstration was made some time ago; I wish Billy were here, but the mosquitoes are most ferocious, and he would be less easy to protect than I.

¶ **8th 6:00 P.M.** Col. Fox and I have supped and now the other officers are eating. Since I do not have to be exposed in the open field like them the least I can do is to provide for their comfort so far as possible, and I think they appreciate the effort. Among other things today I had the stretcher corps cut a path thro the strip of woods at our right and connect it with

211. Dr. John Milton Hawks, an ardent abolitionist, was assistant surgeon in the 33rd USCT and then surgeon in the 21st USCT. After the war he helped found the settlement of Freemanville (later Port Orange). George Schwartz, *A Woman Doctor's Civil War: Esther Hill Hawks' Diary* (Columbia: University of South Carolina Press, 1984), 56.

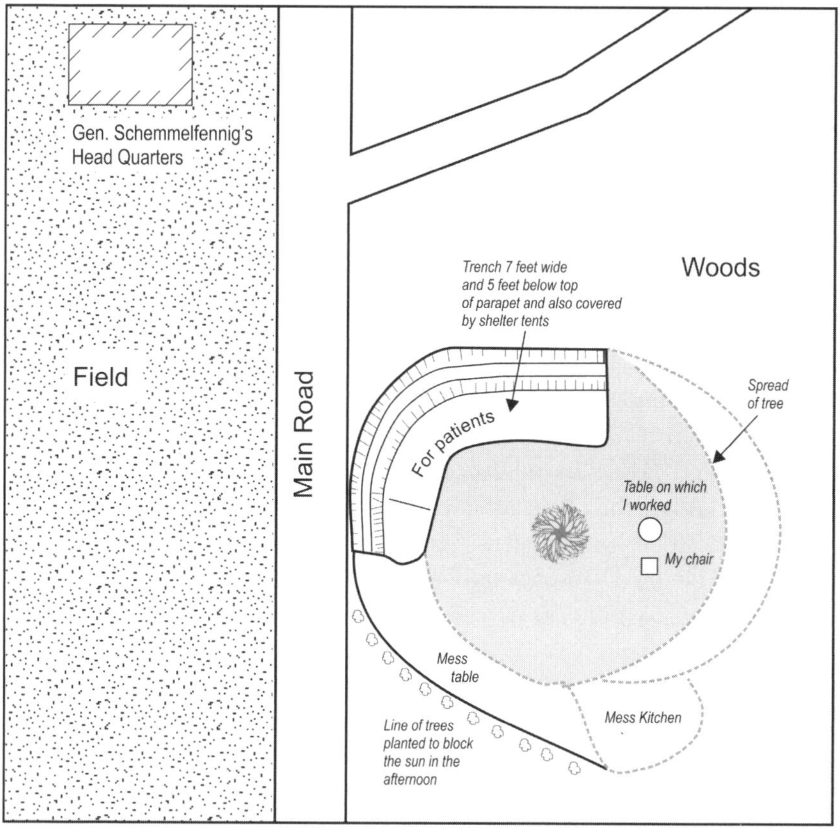

Sketch of the field hospital established by Wilder on James Island after the Rivers Causeway engagement, 2 July 1864.

the path beyond that leads to the Coles Island bridge; in case of need the sick can be taken away by it more safely than as things were before. We have not been disturbed today, but on Johns Island it is reported that Gen. Hatch's forces need help and Birney's brigade has been sent over.[212] I let Capt. Soule and Q.M. of the 54th read Edw. Carter's letter describing the funeral of Carl Shurtleff; they also knew him. Yesterday my mosquito netting was brought and for the first time last night I slept thro. Frank

212. The intense heat slowed the advance of Gen. Hatch's 4,000 men, who could cover only a few miles each day. His tentative attempts to cross the Stono River were pushed back by hastily gathered Confederate troops, and on 9 July, Foster pulled back his forces. Burton, *The Siege of Charleston*, 292–95.

brought Miff today but as Gen. Schimmelpfennig had ordered all dogs to be shot lest they disturb our men or give a sign of our position, I sent her back. One of our men was shot accidentally in the foot; I may not have mentioned that on the 4th, while on picket, a man was shot in the head.

¶ **Sat. 9th, 9:00 A.M.** At 4:15 we were roused by musketry on Johns Island, the other side of the Stono, and it was followed by artillery; after ceasing for a time it recommenced further up, when we inferred that the rebels were retreating; later it seemed to be nearer and the gunboats joined in the firing; now the musketry has ceased and the boats only fire occasionally.[213] Half an hour ago Gen. Schimmelpfennig rode down the road and has just returned.

On the 3rd, the day after the action at Rivers Causeway, a reporter for the Heralds of Boston, New York and the "palmetto Herald" applied to Gen. Hartwell for a list the killed and wounded; having none he referred him to me and I gave him the names and wounds without dreaming that there was any objection. Yesterday, however, I received **a note** from Dr. Brown stating that he was directed by Col Heine, commanding the Post, to ascertain whether I furnished the list, as stated in the paper (which?) of the 7th, and that, if so, a written apology would be necessary; that he only refrained from formal measures (arrest, I suppose) because I probably did not realize the impropriety of the act. I do not now, and my sentiment is shared by colonels Hartwell and Fox and others acquainted with the affair. So I wrote a note, "Respectfully referred to Lt. Col. C. B. Fox, commanding the regiment." He endorsed it with a comment upon the impropriety of the method of communication, and transmitted it to Hartwell who, I believe, means to forward it to Gen. Schimmelpfennig. At any rate I have not been disturbed so far. Heine's regiment did not distinguish itself at Rivers Causeway and the impression prevails that he is sore and wishes to vent his spleen upon somebody. My carbuncle no longer troubles me. Excepting a tremendous shower on the afternoon of the third the weather has been delightful, and the sun may be screened by trees when one is near them; but there are no tents and a rain would be inconvenient. At the present our brigade includes also the 103rd N.Y. and the 33rd U.S., formerly the 1st S.C. The surgeon of the latter is Dr. Hawks, he is from

213. Hatch's initial advance was stopped by a brigade of Georgian troops that had just arrived and gradually pushed back. The heavy guns that Wilder heard were from Battery Pringle.

New Hampshire and a very pleasant man; his wife[214] had a colored school in Jacksonville, but I have not met her. The commissary department of his regiment is fixing a place for the officers' mess at the next tree from ours. The chaplain of that regiment was the Rev. J. H. Fowler[215] whom I met in Cambridge where he was studying both Divinity and under Agassiz. For a time he was a civilian nurse at Judiciary Square. Dr. Hawks say he was captured while trying to cut the telegraph on the Charleston and Savannah R.R., and was captured and imprisoned. There has been shown me a letter dated in the jail at Columbia, speaking of utilizing his quiet confinement in reflection and in the study of human nature. He is an unusual and interesting character. The express brought me a great package of blanks from the Sanitary Commission for sociological and physiological reports of our men when a more convenient time arrives.[216]

¶ **Tuesday, [July] 12th, 8:00 P.M.** As guests at supper were several field officers of other colored regiments awaiting transportation to Hilton Head; afterward the band played to us. Dr. Hagen got a watermelon which was sliced and handed around by Frank; it was very refreshing. In the afternoon I constructed a rude refrigerator by setting a vinegar barrel inside a larger whiskey barrel, filing the intervening space with shav-

214. Dr. Esther Hill Hawks graduated from the New England Medical College for Women in 1857 and practiced in several locations with her husband. During the Civil War, she followed him south and worked as a contract physician in General Hospital Number 10 in Beaufort, South Carolina, as well as establishing schools for the freedmen in several places throughout the South. She published an account of her work in *A Woman Doctor's Civil War.*

215. Fowler's commanding officer, Thomas W. Higginson, described him as "simple, reverential, and impressive" and believed that he was the only chaplain to be held as a prisoner of war. Thomas Wentworth Higginson, *Army Life in a Black Regiment* (Michigan State University Press, 1960), 30, 180–81.

216. President Lincoln authorized the establishment of the United States Sanitary Commission in June 1861 to supplement the inadequate services of the Army Medical Bureau. Because life insurance companies underwrote a large portion of the commission's expenses, they were happy to subsidize any program that could provide data on the statistical averages of the physical condition of the population. The commission, initially under the direction of Frederick Law Olmsted, began an anthropometric survey of Union soldiers, collecting physical and social information on 8,000 white soldiers by early 1863. Following the inclusion of black soldiers in the Union Army, the program, now under the direction of Benjamin A. Gould, was expanded to include black soldiers. What Wilder received were questionnaires, extensively modified, with specific instructions for the collection of information on black soldiers. Lundy Braun, "Spirometry, Measurement, and Race in the Nineteenth Century," *Journal of the History of Medicine and Allied Sciences* 60, no. 2 (2005): 145–46: Haller, *Outcasts from Evolution*, 20, 22.

ings; the spigot runs thro both so that the water from the melting ice may be drawn off. I found Mrs. Devereux much better, indeed no longer in need of treatment, although she must be very careful of her diet. As I was leaving the vessel Capt. D. asked me for my bill. I told him there was none, and that I did not suppose a government officer would charge much in any case. It has been a great satisfaction to relieve her and I have enjoyed my acquaintance with them both. I shall try to send her north under escort of one of our officers. Capt. Gordon thinks of resigning, at the advice of his home physician, because he has chronic diarrhea; Capt. Goodwin and Lts. Ellsworth and Marsh left for the Head today, and Capt. Nutt is about to ask for a furlough. The few officers left will have to work harder. Congress has adjourned. Col. Hallowell did not succeed in reaching Washington, and our men are very restless.[217] The next few weeks will be a trying period unless the authorities do the next best thing, ~~and~~ **viz.,** muster our two regiments out of the service. What a pity to lose such fine soldiers for a few thousands of dollars.[218] The conduct of our men in the action of ten days ago is praised on all sides, and Col. Fox says it is a very great compliment to assign the two captured guns to the front of our headquarters tent as trophies. All our wounded have been sent to Hilton Head; our hospital was needed for the sick resulting from exposure during the recent operations.

¶ **Wed., 13th, 11:00 A.M.** The sea bathing is more delightful than ever and our entire camp, desolate as it might appear to civilians, has a really home-like aspect after the James Island experience. Dr. F. H. Brown writes that he is establishing a large hospital at Readville, and if we are mustered out perhaps I could find a place there or at the Surgeon General's in Washington; I should prefer to be in the service while the war lasts.

8:00 P.M. On visiting Capt. Walton at Gen. Schimmelpfennig's headquarters I learned that Col. Hartwell is now in command of the Post because Col. Heine is under arrest for various offences, one being his threat to arrest me while in the presence of the enemy and not under his immediate command; so I am not much disturbed at the threat itself. Gen. Foster

217. On 13 July, Hartwell was assigned to command of the Post of Folly Island. He would not rejoin the regiment until it was about to be mustered out, serving as either post or brigade commander during the intervening time. Fox, *Record*, 32.

218. On 16 July 1864 members of Company D had addressed a petition to President Lincoln that outlined their service and their demand for equal pay. It also demanded their "immediate discharge, having been enlisted under false pretence." Trudeau, *Voices*, 116–17.

came up from the Head this afternoon; he was accompanied by Medical Director Glym and a Medical Inspector; they occupied Dr. Brown and me with inspection of the camp and hospital until 7:30. The barrel ice-chest works well; ten pounds has lasted all day and tomorrow I shall put in 25 pounds with the expectation of its lasting 4 days.

¶ **Thursday, [July] 14th, 8:30 P.M.** While passing the camp of the 26th U.S. colored today (it waiting for a steamer for the Head) there accosted me a young mulatto whom I recalled as having been in Judiciary Square Hospital; he was at first the servant of Cadet Laschelles, and afterward of Adams and myself; he was an excellent servant and looks like a fine soldier.

Last night and this morning we feared the long dreaded explosion among the soldiers was at hand.[219] After we had retired the Sergeant Major informed Col. Fox that the men had resolved to do no duty today. This morning the sergeant of the guard ordered the reveille not be sounded, and a number of the men assembled on the beach with the expectation that Fox would address them. He went quietly down and told them that, under the circumstances there was only one thing for him to say, viz., All who do not return at once to their quarters will subject themselves to the charge of mutiny and be dealt with accordingly. He left them and they presently returned to their quarters and quietly attended the roll-call. Later, when the picket details were made out, some refused to excuse these and they went. Only three still held out and when they were summoned before Col. Fox and told plainly what would be their fate if they persisted in disobedience they acknowledged their mistake. Fox is very cool and quiet about it, and seems to be to deal with the question more effectively than Hartwell.[220]

¶ **Friday, [July] 15th, 8:00 P.M.** Just as I returned from a ride to Pawnee Landing with Col. Hartwell to look for lumber the mate of one of the vessels brought me a seaman with a badly cut hand; it seems that he and oth-

219. Fox reported two "partial combinations among the enlisted men to refuse duty," but the prompt action of company officers and the arrest of a few dissenters ended the protest. Fox passed off the illegal assembly on the beach as not a deliberate mutinous act. Adding to the bitterness of the men was the news that the discharge of Trotter, Shorter, and Dupree had been disapproved because "no law existed for their muster as commissioned officers." Fox, *Record*, 33.

220. Fox, in his *Record*, played down the seriousness of this event. "It was doubtful, however," he wrote, 'if the men as a body realized the mutinous tendency of their action at first, for a few plain words caused them at once to disperse." Fox, *Record*, 33.

ers had mutinied in respect to their food and he was wounded with an axe; the cut was from the middle of the little finger side of the hand half a way across, and it had bled a good deal; I washed it off, sewed it up, put on a plaster and a bandage, and if he keeps the arm in a sling it may heal.

¶ **Saturday, 16th, 8:00 P.M.** From 7 A.M. till now, excepting rather hasty meals dinner and supper, I have been constantly occupied with no chance of study, flute, or horseback. After sick-call of about 80 men I visited in turn and at various places some men at the guard house, and men from detachments, a clerk of the post Q.M., the sick of three different vessels, several engineer ol [sic] soldiers and their captain (with whom I arranged fro some lumber for the Post Hospital), and two of our own officers. Being Saturday I made out the weekly return of sick in the various detachments. Then I made out a certificate for the engineer captain on which he may obtain furlough. After dinner, Lt. Bean occupied an hour with his examination for discharge on account of disability.[221] After making out quadruplicate receipts for the lumber I spent the rest of the afternoon upon the regular prescription book which had got in arrears during the expedition. To cap the climax, while the band was playing for us after tea the captain of the steamer came to ask me to visit his mate; on reaching the pier I found that he was the one whom I had visited this morning but by some blunder the captain was not informed. I tried not to lose my temper. I have sent $40.00 to Dr. N. and $100.00 to brother Edward.

¶ **Monday, [July] 18th, 8:00 P.M.** Today my duties kept me on horseback most of the time after sick-call. Among other things I went to the White House with a team and men to get the lumber for the post hospital; I saw every piece selected and loaded.

¶ **Thursday, 21st,** It is just a year since we left Boston for the war. I am sure it has been of use to me in all respects; excepting, of course, it is not directly in the line of my chosen line of science. I feel more power to resist temptation, and even my bodily health, of which I have never had reason to complain, has improved, contrary to my expectations.

¶ **Saturday, [July] 23rd, 7:30 P.M.** In accordance with the wishes of his parents, Frank will go North tomorrow so as to continue his schooling.

221. Bean was not discharged for disability. He was brevetted captain in March 1865 and mustered out with his regiment on 29 August 1865. Fox, *Record*, 106.

Like all boys he is careless, and like some, he thinks a good deal about money; that may enable him to prosper in business but it is more important to be solicitous as to service. He will take Miff because the sand is not good for her and the knowing ones here say that she is too valuable to be left to the chance of loss or injury. (She was adopted by Miss Nichols and Dr. N. became much attached to her; she had various adventures and a litter of puppies, and was stolen in Washington where Dr. N. the younger had taken her. There is an excellent photograph. One of our officers said she was part spaniel and part setter.)

Night before last there was a terrific thunderstorm and one bolt was very near. Yesterday, when I went to see a patient on one of the vessels I found that the foremast had been struck and most of it ripped off in great pieces; but no one was injured. Today died a civilian employee at the wagon yard; he had the jaundice and obtained a bottle of poor blackberry wine and foolishly drank nearly the whole of it and died in a sort of convulsion before I could reach him.[222] In order to assure myself that his complaint was not Yellow Fever I made a post mortem in one of the new post hospital tents and got Dr. Hagen to inspect the viscera; we decided that it was merely jaundice.

¶ **Sunday, [July] 24th, 7:45 P.M.** This has been an unusually restful Sunday. It rained all the forenoon and my patients on the vessels are all improving and probably will not think it worth while to send for me; so, besides the regular sick-call I had only to ride in various directions to visit Capt. McKenna of the engineers, Lt Crocker of the battery, one patient at post headquarters and one at the pier; so I was through at 10:30 and till dinner studied and played flute. After dinner we sent for Capt. Gordon to help dispose of a watermelon that he gave us yesterday; having been kept in our ice-barrel; it was most refreshing; then he and I played flute and Col. Fox joined in as bass. There has adopted me a bobtailed kitten that is very amusing. The latter part of the afternoon Fox and I cantered up the beach about four miles and returned by the wood road; the rain had ceased and it was delightful. Frank and Miff left this morning. David Lee takes Frank's place, and the horses are cared for by Waldron who used to care for those of Col. Hartwell. George whose leg was shot is getting about on crutches and can do certain things, i.e., clean the brasses, the candlesticks, spurs, sword and pistols. For the first time

222. A number of blackberry-based preparations, generally involving the root, were popularly believed to be effective against diarrhea. Flannery, *Civil War Pharmacy*, 127–29.

in several weeks Miff came and got into bed with me as if realizing that it was her last chance.

A clerk at headquarters upon whom I performed an operation the other day tried to pay me and when I refused he gave me a useful little military manual, with blank forms, etc. We expect Dr. Brown to return from the Head today. I do not think he ought to go home till Dr. Babbitt returns; my own duties occupy me about twice as long as his do and I would be glad of time for inspecting the several detachments under my medical care. Day before yesterday Col. Hartwell asked me to accompany one of his staff to select a common graveyard for all at the post; we chose a ridge half way between the sea and the river and about half a mile from this end of the island; it is to be leveled and enclosed. The new post hospital will be the finest on the island; it is built by the engineers on a small high plateau the sides of which have been turfed so that at a distance it looks like a small fort; without the turf the sand might wash or blow away undesirably. All day yesterday it blew a furious gale and while half a dozen of our men were coming from Long Island in a sailboat it shipped so much water as to sink and one was drowned; the rest were rescued by another boat.[223] That reminds me that, on the 2nd, a boat load of men from another colored regiment in tow of a steamer was capsized and 20 were drowned. This summer deaths from sickness have been fewer than last; the weaker men died then and the others have become acclimated and learned how to take care of themselves better; probably, also, we have become better able to recognize the beginnings of a severe case and so put him in the hospital at once. Our band has gone up to serenade Gen. S. It is the only band at the post and affords much pleasure to others besides our own regiment. Capt. Crane's Company H has been placed as garrison at Fort Delafield, near the pier, and they fire the guns at sunrise and sunset; they are the very guns used by Gilmore against Fort Pulaski. We are informed that the order for the proper payment of our men has been issued but it will require some weeks to straighten out the accounts of so many for so long a time.

¶ **Monday, 25th, 7:30 P.M.** The surgeon of the 33rd U.S. colored called and described the forlorn condition of his hospital for lack of lumber and bunks; not every surgeon is so fortunate as to have as patients an engineer captain and a boss carpenter; so I loaned him a few of the bunks not

223. The man drowned was Pvt. Beverley Bell from Quincy, Illinois. His pre-war occupation was "sailor." Fox, *Record*, 33–34, 118.

yet needed. This afternoon Col. Hartwell held a grand brigade drill of the four regiments, 54th N.Y., 103rd N.Y., 33rd U.S., & our own; the tide was low so the beach was wide.

¶ **Tuesday, [July] 26th, 7:30 P.M.** After supper I loaned Billy to Capt. Gordon and rode Dr. Turner's horse, and Col. Fox joined us; on the beach we were joined by Major Wales, Adjutant McKay,[224] Captain Quentin and Walton and a lieutenant; eight abreast we presented quite an imposing cavalcade on the beach.

¶ **Wednesday, 27th, 8:30 P.M.** Before supper we were called upon by a sergeant and three men of the engineers who were at Yellow Bluff. Afterwards, just as Col. Fox and Capt. Gordon and I had reached the pier a man came running up to me to say that another soldier was hurt. It proved to be one of the engineers who had plunged into water thinking it was deep and struck his head on a shall [sic] and broke his neck; he was paralyzed below the neck. As quickly as possible he was taken to the new hospital; his father is in the same company and is attending him; his case is desperate, I fear. Including this new patient there are now six in the hospital.

¶ **Tuesday, 28th, 9:00 P.M.** As apprehended the injured man is worse. It has been a busy and trying day in many ways.

¶ **Friday, 29th,** Tice, the injured man is better, at any rate more comfortable. I am very fortunate in my staff, especially the cook, whose ministrations are probably sometimes of more value than my own. Q.M. Ritchie[225] of the 54th and sister dined with us today. It is now right after dinner. Tice is not probably suffering much if any for he seems unconscious much of the time and occasionally delirious. It is very hard for his father; he wishes to write to his wife but I advised him to wait, and give him no encouragement of the boy's recovery. This morning ~~just as I had left~~ after bathing and dressing at the beach and half way to my tent I heard cries for help; turning I saw some way out the head of a man apparently struggling; some others nearer the water had already gone to his aid and were likewise shouting for help. I occurred to me that a shark might be in the case so I

224. George Frederick McKay, a bookkeeper from Boston, served as a private in the 13th Massachusetts before his commission in the 55th. He rose to brevet major before being mustered out in August 1865. Fox, *Record*, 104.

225. Lt. John Ritchie, a member of the Harvard class of 1861, was the regimental quartermaster for the 54th Massachusetts. Duncan, *Blue-Eyed Child of Fortune*, 32, 296.

caught up a branch with which to engage his teeth and went into the water up to my waist[226]; but Col. Kozlay[227] of the 54th N.Y., who was already in the water was nearer him and had reached him; so I cast away my stick and helped bring him out. It seems that a captain who could not swim went out too far; the waves were quite high, and upset Col. Fox this morning; two or three in succession overcame the captain and but for Col. Kozlay's assistance he might have been drowned. During the forenoon I met Col. K at the tent of his surgeon, Dr. Hagen, and was astonished to be thanked for my assistance, which was really only secondary to his. This evening, at our own regiment, the story was that a drowning man was saved by me, but I promptly disclaimed anything more than good intentions.

¶ **Saturday, 30th, 8:30 P.M.** At midnight I was called to Tice. He had sunk during the day. I got Dr. Hagen to visit him with me today and said that all that was possible had been done; that the most was to make him comfortable. He died at 3 and I examined the injury, finding the spinal cord had been partially crushed by the breaking of a vertebra and that it was inflamed still further. Dr. Hagen came to look at it too. I have saved the piece of the cord, about six inches long and shall send it to the Army Medical Museum. (It and Jones case are described in the B.M.& Surg. Journal, LXXI, 292–294, and on pp. 427 & 533 of Part I of the "Med. And Surgical History of the War.")

¶ **Sunday, 31st, 11:00 A.M.** There visited us yesterday Mr. Tomlinson,[228] General Superintendent of the Freedman's Bureau on St. Helena Island where Capt. Soule's father is.[229] He brought 3000 water melons for the

226. There had been previous shark attacks. James W. Hagy, *To Take Charleston: The Civil War on Folly Island* (Charleston, W.Va.: Pictorial Histories Publishing, 1993), 72.

227. Eugene Arthur Kozlay, a Hungarian who had immigrated to America in 1850 following the unsuccessful war for Hungarian independence, helped organize the 54th New York Infantry Regiment and served as its colonel. He was brevetted brigadier general in March 1865. Mark M. Boatner, *The Civil War Dictionary* (New York: Dave McKay, 1959), 468.

228. Reuben Tomlinson, an officer of the Pennsylvania branch of the American Freedmen's Union Commission, was one of the first agents sent south by the Port Royal Relief Association of Philadelphia. He became superintendent of the Freedman's Bureau's education division in South Carolina during the early summer of 1865. Willie Lee Rose, *Rehearsal for Reconstruction: The Port Royal Experiment* (New York: Vintage Books, 1964), 78, 316.

229. Richard Soule was superintendent at Frogmore, St. Helena, and he would become frustrated that he did not have enough power over his black workers. Lee, *Rehearsal for Reconstruction*, 69.

54th and 55th Mass., and the 33rd U.S. Col. Fox and I each received one, but one was enough and I gave mine to my patients.

¶ **Monday, [August] 1st, 7:30 P.M.** Col. Fox says there a number of white hairs among my black ones; I suppose they are where they do not show in the glass for I did not know it; never mind, I was never better in my life, and feel younger each day; the chaplain asked my age and was told to guess; he said 25.

¶ **Tuesday, 2nd, 7:45 P.M.** Q.M. Mussey came in today, looking like a ghost; less well than when he left, and I think it wise for him to resign.[230]

¶ **Wednesday, 3rd, 7:30 P.M.** Some great improvements have been made about our quarters; the sand has been turfed and the walks bricked, and rows of the Spanish dagger planted; the green is a great relief from the glare of the sand. I have prepared the specimen from Tice and written a history of the case. So far I have seen or heard ours are the most attractive quarters on the island; the only objection to such improvements is that they are commonly precursors to a move. In that case perhaps they will be enjoyed by others. Capt. Gordon bequeathed me his bedstead, somewhat more substantial than mine, and to it have been attached posts to support the very essential mosquito netting. This diagram shows the present arrangement; the only entrance is at the post of the sentry.

¶ **Saturday, 6th, 8:15** After dinner there were several of what are called "minor operations," viz., a sergeant to have a tooth drawn, a man with a boil to lance, another to be blistered over the eyes preparatory to an application of strychnine in the hope of enabling him to see at night[231]; lastly a man who had run a great fish-hook into his finger; it had to be filed off close to the finger and then I cut down on the point which is barbed and extracted it with forceps. There was an expedition today to the adjoining Island, Kiawah, in the hope of meeting the 60 officers said

230. Mussey resigned his commission on 19 August 1864. Fox, *Record*, 100.

231. Although strychnine is a very toxic alkaloid, doctors in the mid-nineteenth century recommended it in diluted form, frequently with iron, for a series of illnesses. The army issued strychnia among its standard supply. Flannery, *Civil War Pharmacy*, 122, 248; W. Braithwaite, ed., *The Retrospect of Practical Medicine and Surgery* (New York: Stringer & Townsend, 1858), 49–50.

to have escaped Macon, Ga., who would probably try to reach our lines between here and the Head; but none were found.[232]

¶ **[Friday], 7th, 11:15 A.M.** A gunboat has just towed a Monitor to the mouth of the Stono; we wonder why, having heard nothing lately as to a rebel ram descending the river.

7:15 P.M. A patient from the Battery entered a week ago with fever, and last Tuesday declared that he was "gone up;" but yesterday and today he has been about and has walked a mile or more; he will go home on furlough by the next steamer. I believe his rapid recovery has been largely due to the excellent food prepared by my most capable cook; my medication consists mainly of tonics, with stimulants when needed. As yet I have lost no fever cases. At supper Q.M. Cushing told me that my medical supplies for the post hospital had arrived excepting the liquor, which were stolen and drunk up by the civilian employees of his department while unloading them; but that if I would state the value he would deduct it from their pay.[233] The sutler outdid himself for our dinner today; here is the menu: - Boiled Ham, Roast Beef, Chicken pie, corn, mashed potatoes and tomatoes, both fresh and canned; for desert bread pudding, mince pie, cake and ice cream; the last had a slightly salty flavor but was not bad and was highly appreciated. This unwonted luxury contrasts strongly with most of the past and probably with most of the future.

¶ **Monday, [August] 8th, 8:20 P.M.** I have been told that requisitions are commonly cut by the authorities; nevertheless I asked for only what I really believed we needed for the post hospital; to my delight not only were all the specified articles sent but a few that I had not thought of and am very glad of; while waiting for them I have had to borrow from other surgeons, and it was a real pleasure to unpack and arrange our own supplies and feel independent; the cook is also a fine carpenter and has made shelves and tables for the drugs and instruments.

232. Although there were numerous attempts to tunnel out of Camp Oglethorpe (Macon), most were unsuccessful. The number of successful attempts is unknown, and by July 1864 Confederate authorities had begun shipping Union prisoners out of Macon with the approach of George Stoneman's troops. Lonnie R. Speer, *Portals to Hell: Military Prisons in the Civil War* (Mechanicsburg, Pa.: Stackpole Books, 1997), 266–68.

233. Alcohol was a part of the army's standard supply table. Flannery, *Civil War Pharmacy*, 239.

¶ **Wednesday, 10th, 2:30, P.M.** After I had retired last night Q.M. Mowry brought me a shovel-nosed shark, three feet long that had been taken in a net; I removed the brain in the presence of several officers; it is an interesting form; unfortunately I have never been able to study the brains of sharks.

¶ **Thursday, 11th, 8:30 P.M.** Capt. Devereux came in this afternoon and said he had lost a $500.00 bill and had some reason to suspect Corp. Purcell[234] who is acting as his steward; I sent for the Orderly Sergeant of Co. I, and as he is very shrewd he may be able to discover the culprit. The captain will take my turtle skeletons. (No mention of it being my birthday.)

¶ **Saturday, 13th, 8:30 P.M.** After my morning work I accompanied Col. Fox and Major Wales by invitation, to the Monitor, "Montauk," [235] which has been moved from the mouth of the Stono up the Folly River. It is not so large as I anticipated; the dents made by the rebel shots are distinct upon the turret. Commander Johnson was very courteous and showed us all parts of the curious vessel. She carries two guns, of 11 and 15 inch bores respectively. The turret sides are 6 or 8 in. thick yet in several places the entire thickness is bent inward by the rebel missiles. There is a surgeon on board. It must be a hot and restricted place at the best. The latter part of the afternoon David Lee and I dug up the shell and bones of the largest turtle and took it to the beach in a tub and washed it as clean as we could by throwing pails of water on it. As I might have foreseen the shell has come apart but of course Prof. Wyman can wire the segments together. The bones did not smell very well and David occasionally intimated that if it depended upon him alone they would be left to the bugs.

¶ **Sunday, 14th, 3:30 P.M.** The usual Sunday inspection was hot enough between 11 & 12, but under the tent, sheltered from the sun and exposed to the sea breeze, it is very comfortable. An officer loaned me "Aurora Leigh" and I tried to read it in the spare hour before dinner but failed to find it interesting or instructive; I fear I must be very defective. Yesterday my aver-

234. Armstead Percell, a 23-year-old barber from Uniontown, Pennsylvania, became corporal in September 1863. He was demoted in September 1864. Fox, *Record*, 140.

235. The *Montauk*, a single-turreted monitor commissioned in December 1862, had seen service against Fort McAllister, in Georgia before joining the Union fleet attacking the Charleston harbor fortifications. It stayed at Stono until early the next year. Burton, *Siege of Charleston*, 133, 163,291; Wise, *Gate of Hell*, 252, 253.

sion to whiskey got me into discredit comparable with that in Washington where it was proposed to expel me from the Natural History Society for a like reason. While we waited [for] a boat to take us to the Monitor the captain of the steamer, "Golder Cate," then at the pier, invited us to look at his boat; took us to his cabin and hospitably asked what each would drink. Major Wales took whiskey, Col. Fox ale, and I water (fortunately it was iced.) The captain was greatly astonished and said that [it] was not a liquid in which I could drink to their healths, but they all would drink to mine. (He was older than any of us, but Fox and Wales are or were about my age and are both dead whereas I propose to last at least another ten years.)

I am more and more disgusted with the general habit of using liquor upon the slightest occasion; it is dangerously common among officers, as far as I can learn.[236] In this regiment I believe the proportion of abstainers is unusually large. Nutt and Crane are, I believe, total abstainers; Gordon, Soule, Boynton, Bean, Garrison, Ellsworth, like myself, are simply "temperate," taking wine or malt liquors if we wish or think them necessary.

¶ **Monday, 15th, 7:15 P.M.** We resurrected and cleaned the other turtle this afternoon, and I hope the bones of both will be dry to send by Capt. Devereux.

¶ **Thursday, [August] 18th, 8:45 P.M.** I have just completed the postmortem of the man who had been ill for several days, and who, I think, might have been saved had he been taken to the hospital earlier; the hospital was full but I notified Col. Fox that an additional tent, frame and all, was to be had; he notified Dr. Brown, but nothing was done, and now it has been set up just in time to receive his dead body. The examination was made in the presence of Drs. Brown, Hagen and Crandall[237] of the 33rd U.S.

¶ **Friday, 19th, 8:30 P.M.** By direction of Col. Fox hereafter "Reveille" and "Tattoo" are to be played by several of the band upon their respective instruments instead of, as hitherto, only upon bugles.

236. Wilder believed, and would later write, that without the abuse of alcohol in the army, the war would have ended a year earlier. Burt G. Wilder, *The Fifty-fifth Regiment of the Massachusetts Volunteer Infantry, Colord* (Brookline: Riverdale Press, 1919), 8.

237. Surgeon William B. Crandall had prior service in the 16th New York and died four years after the war ended. Higginson, *Army Life in a Black Regiment*, 207.

Among the things I shall send by Capt. Devereux is a canister shot that I cut from a man's leg after the James River Causeway fight.

¶ **Saturday, 20th, 8:15 P.M.** Dr. Brown says that, for a time, he will relieve me of the morning sick-calls; I am glad both because I have plenty to do, and because it is well for him, as surgeon, to know the sort of cases that arise day by day.

¶ **Sunday, 21st, 8:00 P.M.** Col. Fox has called together the orderly sergeants of the several companies to explain to them and through them to the regiment the latest announcement of the government as to the pay. I do not envy him his task or the much abused men the position in which they are placed: it will be particularly hard of those who were actually in slavery at the time of enlistment.[238]

¶ **Monday, 22nd, 8:15 P.M.** Today has been passed a crisis, the last, I trust, connected with the matter of pay, viz., taking the oath that they were free on or before April 19, 1861.[239] The companies were called up separately and the matter was stated to them; such as could not conscientiously take the oath stepped out, and the others held up their hands and were sworn by the colonel. Some were disposed to hold back and one whole company was sent back to quarters because several of them were under the delusion that, by declining, they might leave the service; they will come to their senses.

¶ **Tuesday, 23rd, P.M.** This morning I was summoned to appear as a witness at the court of inquiry now in session at Fort Green upon the case of Major Wales; he was advised by me to take a rest of a day or two and thereby incurred the displeasure of Gen. Schimmelpfennig and asked for a court of inquiry. Capt. Cushing was going to Morris Island in his

238. When Congress finally equalized pay for white and black soldiers, they added a restriction. Soldiers who were slaves at the start of the war received retroactive pay only to 1 January 1864. All others would receive the full retroactive pay after they swore an oath that they were free on or before 21 April 1861. It would not be until 3 March 1865 that Congress would give full retroactive pay to all black soldiers who were promised equal pay when they enlisted.

239. Although Wilder would later state that 247 of the enlisted men had been slaves, the instruction to the men was that anyone who was not actually held as a slave on 21 April could call himself a freeman. Only two or three acknowledged having been slaves, although others were so held, Fox believed. Wilder, "The Brain of the American Negro," 49; Fox, *Record*, 34–36.

ambulance and invited me to ride in it. My testimony was soon given and I then went to Morris Island and obtained from the Sanitary Commission a dozen pair of carpet slippers and also a bundle of old magazines for my patients. My orderly, David Lee is, all agree, the best of the officers' servants. He is very neat, and quiet, always cheerful, and almost too ready to sacrifice his own comfort for that of others. He is very handsome, and so really good that it is a pleasure to have him about. Just then I was called to a patient who was in a spasm, foaming and grinding his teeth; he had to be held to prevent injury to himself and others; I administered chloroform and, "post hoc, non ergo propter hoc," he came out of his spasms.

¶ **Wednesday, 24th, 8:00 P.M.** One of my marine patients brought me a basket of fine peaches.

¶ **Friday, 26th, 8:20 P.M.** Yesterday arrived from friends at the North five large shoe boxes filled with books, magazines, **slates**, comfort bags, etc.

¶ **Saturday, 27th, 8:20 P.M.** I have at last completed the re-revision of my thesis and shall send it to be printed when the society recommends publication; I wish it off my mind so as to begin the (measurement) statistics of the regiment, so long contemplated.

¶ **Sunday, 28th, 8:00 P.M.** Capt. Devereux came to say good bye and to ask for my picture; having none Col. Fox gave him his copy and I will replace it later. The two guns captured on James Island have been taken away by the artillery detachment; we miss them, but of course they are more likely to be useful elsewhere.

¶ **Monday, [August] 29th, 7:30 P.M.** Capt. Soule perpetrated a fine bon mot at supper. On firing drill this afternoon, some of the men of Co. I discharged their guns prematurely; so when, at the table, Lt. James, in command of that company, said that he had been unable to account for four guns since the action at Rivers Causeway, Soule said "It would be very easy for you to declare that they went off by accident and failed to come back."

¶ **Tuesday, 30th, 7:45 P.M.** I have had an "A" tent set on a stockade 4 feet high so that it is nearly as commodious as a wall tent; in it my "washerwoman," McGrath, will take up his quarters, and if a patient dies the body can be kept there over night. I have been rather dreading the severe sickness of a negro under my care as post surgeon on account of the general prejudice against the race among certain classes of the whites. This afternoon I admitted a negro with dysentery and was much gratified to note that he was treated by the staff, cook, steward and nurses, with no discrimination. The past year has done wonders towards convincing the ~~public~~ **soldiers** that the negro in entitled to be treated as a man.

¶ **Sunday, Sept. 4th, 8:00 P.M.** I had a rather funny time this afternoon working over a man's lower tooth. It was decayed yet so firmly fixed that at last it broke off well near the tips of the roots, and perhaps will not trouble him. The steward was holding the man's head and the instrument slipped and struck him on the nose; the next time they slipped and hit me on the nose; the patient was in pain already and for a few moments we all sympathized heartily.

¶ **Tuesday, [September] 6th, 8:00 P.M.** For half an hour I have been listening to the band which has been making a special effort for the entertainment of Chaplain Humphreys[240] of the 2nd Mass. Cavalry, an old friend of Fox and Thurber; he was captured by Mosby[241] in Virginia and has been confined at Macon and Charleston, and was exchanged recently. He says he was pursued by Mosby himself but his horse was better and he escaped; later he returned to our wounded and was taken.

¶ **Wednesday, 7th, 8:00 P.M.** Dr Brown's leave has come and we have been arranging for the work while he is away, about three weeks. The detachment and Post hospital will be under the care of Assistant Surgeon Budd of the 54th New York and I shall have our hospital as well as the men in quarters; I do not like such changes but it seems best. Col. Fox and Chaplain Humphreys were discussing the Rivers Causeway action and the former was commenting upon the fact that the rebels fired high and most of our wounds were in the head, down came the staff of the regimental colors and the eagle struck Mr. Humphries on the head; he declared that his first impression was distinct that he had been struck by a canister shot. Later he joined us in singing and displayed a fine bass voice.

240. Chaplain Charles A. Humphreys wrote an account of his experiences, *Field, Camp, Hospital and Prison in the Civil War, 1863–1865*, that was published in 1918.

241. John Singleton Mosby, a Virginian lawyer before the war, won greatest fame, or notoriety, as a partisan ranger in northern Virginia. Sifakis, *Who Was Who in the Civil War*, 460.

Sunday, 11th, 5:00 P.M. Col. Fox attends the service every Sunday, when his duties permit; he does not always agree with the chaplain but considers that he should set an example; I am not always through my morning work, and there is always plenty to do, and in fact I do not relish any other New Church preaching and finally cannot regard my example as very important.

Monday, 12th, 8:45 P.M. Today I have had a lot of men at work about the regimental hospital, filling in between the posts where the sand had blown away, overlaying it with turf to protect it, and planting the Spanish Dagger Palm in front for a green relief to the eyes of the patients. This afternoon I drew a tooth for Lt. Davis of the Cavalry and we were both pleased at the readiness with which it came.

Tuesday, 13th, 7:30 P.M. While visiting the picket, line this afternoon Col Fox was accompanied by not only a squad of cavalry but by the adjutant, chaplain and myself, and it was quite a cavalcade. The tide was higher than ever before, and part of the way the water reached the bodies of our horses. Suddenly Billy began to jump as if stung by a hornet; on dismounting I found on his leg a cactus with long and very sharp spines, and did not wonder at his capers. Dr. Budd has received the acceptance of his resignation and will leave at once; he says Dr Hagen is in a great "hubbub" (German for quandary?) because he and I will then be the only Medical officers on the island. I told Dr. Budd, that of course I would again take the post hospital.

Thursday, [September] 15th, 11:15 A.M. This morning Col. Fox received a letter from one of three sergeants who had stopped at the Head on the way north on furlough; he said they had been paid in full from enlistment the same as whites of the same rank; the good paymaster borrowed the money to pay them, his own not having arrived. There is general relief at this important news; the delay in the actual payment can be put up with since the principle is settled. The new steward of the post hospital, Sclitz, has a flute and plays better than I, so I invited him to take the upper part as Capt. Gordon formerly did. While awaiting the detail of this steward, and not to have the patients lack proper food, I persuaded his colonel, to let him remain although the regiment was ordered away. Now comes a formidable official document from the War Department through the several channels inquiring as to his whereabouts; he has fortunately left me and is awaiting transportation at the

Head, and I do not anticipate serious trouble from the irregularity, since it was connived in by his colonel.

8:15 P.M. A box came for Dr. Brown and I opened it and found that the jars of preserved fruits had leaked onto his books, so I wiped the latter off and repacked the box. This afternoon the regiment was inspected by Capt. Danielson [Danilson][242] of the 33rd U.S. In leaving one of our hospital tents the step gave way and let him through, but he was not hurt and was very good natured about it. Just as I sat down to supper I was summoned to attend to a man who had chopped off two of his fingers with a hatchet; fortunately the instrument was sharp and the cuts were clean.

¶ **Friday, 16th, 11:30 A.M.** I am having a somewhat unpleasant experience with our regimental hospital steward.[243] Sometime ago Dr. Brown made out charges against him of incompetence and drunkenness, but did not send them and left them as a warning to him. Since then he has improved somewhat but is unfit for the place; a fortnight ago Col. Fox sent an application for his discharge to Gen. Foster, inclosing letters from Dr. Brown and Col. Hartwell. The application has come back with the endorsement that only a court martial can discharge him. But Dr. Brown did not leave the charges with me and it would not be easy for me to prove all the things I believe him to have been guilty of; nor have I the desire to injure him so much. So I have told him, showing him the document, that he might choose between awaiting the return of Dr. Brown and the pressing of the original charges and pleading "guilty" to the milder charge of incompetence before a court martial now sitting. He agrees to the latter.

¶ **Sunday, 18th, 8:00 P.M.** Night before last, notwithstanding my wish expressed to Col. Fox that no one would hurt himself, for I did not want to get up, "bang" went a gun and soon after a man was brought to the tent. His gun had gone off while his hand was over the muzzle and the ball had shattered his middle finger and one of the next was hurt. I did not stop to dress, but got out my pocket case, sat in one chair, placed the man in another with a basin on his knees and presently the finger was off. He grunted a little but behaved very well and both his hand and the hatchet

242. Capt. William H. Danilson subsequently became a major in the 128th USCT. Higginson, *Army Life in a Black Regiment*, 208.

243. Richard Hecker, a chemist from New York City, was discharged by the General Court-Martial. Wilder makes few mentions of his hospital stewards. Fox, *Record*, 114.

case are doing nicely. Having only my nightshirt on the mosquitoes drove me almost crazy; I suspect I made more fuss than the patient.

¶ **Monday, 19th, 9:00 P.M.** At midnight died my first loss from fever; this afternoon I made a post mortem and found that it was typhoid.

¶ **Tuesday, 20th, 7.30 P.M.** For some days six men, three from Co. F and the three from H, have been declaring themselves unable to do duty by reason of swollen abdomens; the condition was obvious but I suspected them of purposely inducing, it by improper food or drink. This forenoon, after the other patients were disposed of, I gathered these six together and told them what I suspected. They maintained that they were really ill. Still I doubted and actually chloroformed one of them as if preparatory to opening his abdomen to let out the water; still he did not yield and I shall have to wait for further evidence.

In the afternoon I rode to Pawnee Landing and crossed as before to Long Island. Major Wales loaned me a horse (not the one that threw me) and we rode along the west shore of the island in good view of the rebel camps and the line of forts across the island; excepting by a complete surprise no small force could hope to capture them. The Long Island woods abound with large spiders like the one from which I wound the silk last summer; they occupy large webs between the trees and in one of them my straw hat was caught and held. Col. Hartwell wrote to Col. Fox today that advising him to resign soon, and saying that he had decided not to because he heard that if he did most of the captains would also.

¶ **Friday [September] 23rd, 8:00 P.M.** I am pleased to learn that some of the misunderstandings between Colonels Hartwell and Fox have been removed, and that there is more likelihood that the latter will remain with the regiment.

¶ **Saturday, 24th, 7:45 P.M.** Lt. Woodward has been mustered in as captain and returned from the Head yesterday. At dinner today Capt Soule made a comical presentation speech and bestowed upon him a monstrous pair of shoulder-straps, more than a foot long.

¶ **Wednesday, 28th, 8:15 P.M.** About 2 last night I awoke hearing the most dreadful screams and howls; I jumped out of bed, got into my greatcoat and ran out; the sound led me to my own hospital and there, just outside the door, my nurse was struggling with a burly civilian who had entered the hospital about a week ago, apparently sick, and soon dangerously so, very weak, hiccupping and vomiting blood, and with a yellow tinge suggesting yellow fever. About this time, however, I began to be suspicious of him and he, perceiving it, pretended last night to be crazy; got out of the tent, yelled that a man was going to kill him. I spoke very sternly to him and soon he ceased to yell; we got him in bed and then my suspicions were confirmed by his saying that he was crazy and wanted to go home. A really crazy man might say that he wanted to go home but they usually think all other folk are insane. I then ascertained that he had been for eight years a soldier in the regular army; then I ordered him to keep quiet or suffer the penalty of disobedience. He admitted that the blood that he pretended to vomit came from biting his cheeks. Such a man knows too many tricks, and I wish I could get rid of him. An army doctor should have a lawyer at his elbow. That attitude towards the apparently sick is very irksome to me.

¶ **Thursday, 29th, 8:00 P.M.** With half a dozen soldier mechanics I have been making needed improvements of the hospital; they complimented me highly upon what they regard as my "engineering." This afternoon I went to Long Island as before. There is some apprehension there as to an attack by the rebels for two corporals of the 54th N.Y., stationed there on picket, deserted last night and would be able to give important information as to our numbers and location.

Major Wales has been collecting butterflies for me and has sent a box containing about 20 finely mounted and handsome specimens; I imagine not every entomologist has majors and brigadiers to collect for him; probably the poor insects themselves care not a pin who impales them.

¶ **Friday, 30th,** Our Company B was actually paid today. The officers were also paid and I am settling accounts. I shall send a check of $100 to Dr. Nichols and one to my father. A member of Co. B expended some of his unfamiliar wealth for a pair of elegant boots that may last him a week.

¶ **Sunday, Oct. 2nd, 4:00 P.M.** The congregation was quite large today, Col. Fox tells me, attracted partly by the presence of a melodeon.

¶ **Tuesday, [October] 4th, 7:30 P.M.** Dr. Brown arrived today. The steamer from New York was overcrowded and several had been refused. He declared he would "sit on the bowsprit" and the clerk let him on. If Dr. Babbitt were here I might get a furlough myself, but no one seems to know where he is. The members of the Field and Staff do not play cards on account of the example; except myself, they all play chess or dominoes.

¶ **Wednesday, 5th, 7:30 P.M.** Three soldiers have asked me to take care of about $300, and I have reluctantly consented with the proviso, as stated in the receipt, that I will not be responsible for its loss. They are doubtless influenced by the fact that two sergeants of Co. H had all their money stolen last night. Today I pulled a monstrous back tooth. The patient said a doctor in Annapolis tried to pull it and failed and he paid him $5.00 to cease his efforts. It took all my strength as well as skill; fortunately the man's jaw was stout and his head firmly attached to his shoulders.

¶ **Thursday, 6th, 8:30 P M.** I have completed the histories of the two surgical specimens, Jones and Tice, and shall send them to Dr. F. H. Brown for publication if thought worthy.

¶ **Friday, Oct. 7th, 7:15 P.M.** I have been lying down for half an hour, listening to the Glee Club; they sing very finely but not long enough. My enjoyment was somewhat marred by three interruptions for sick persons; Lt. Roberts[244] is about the same, better than yesterday. I hope I shall not be called up in the night as I was night before last to ride up the island and see him. First I had to get the "countersign" from the colonel and at three different points was made to dismount and give it to as many sentries; they knew and performed their duties with an obstinate firmness that was commendable but troublesome. At Mr. Roberts' tent I found the post-adjutant, Lt. Dewhurst, and his wife, a very pretty and refined lady.

This afternoon a brigade review was held on the beach; we thought it very creditable and so said General Scammon[245] at the close; the 33rd came over from Coles Island and returned afterwards. At inspection I wear only

244. There were two Roberts in the regiment, both from Weston, Massachusetts, and both lieutenants in September 1864. William C. Roberts, 29, was the older, and Charles L. Roberts, 21, the younger. After the war, both became provision dealers in Boston. Fox, *Record*, 106–7.

245. Eliakim Parker Scammon, a West Point graduate, was dismissed from the army in 1856 for disobeying orders but he re-entered when war started and rose to divisional commander. He was twice captured by the Confederates. After the war he served as diplomat, government engineer, and college professor. Sifakis, *Who Was Who in the Civil War*, 571.

my sash, but at a review, the sword is necessary in order to salute; so I borrowed the chaplain's.

All the men are now paid off and great is the custom at the sutler shop. The general feeling among the men is vastly improved and now it is possible to insist upon some points as to dress and appearance which had to be overlooked before. The men are gratifyingly scrupulous in repaying little sums loaned them by the officers long ago, usually without even a memorandum of the transaction. One man handed me 25 cents which he says I lent him in Newbern. Several officers have spoken of the matter, and I have yet to learn of any failure.

Col. Fox has had Col. Hartwell's two tents rearranged for himself, so if Dr. Babbitt comes he can occupy the other end of my establishment. The new General Scammon seems a very quiet and pleasant man. He was one of those confined under fire in Charleston and probably has personal reasons for the capture of the city.

¶ **Saturday, 8th, 7:45 P.M.** Col. Fox and I went to Pawnee Land this morning by boat because his horse is ill. We had the boat that Gen. Gilmore formerly used and four fine boatmen. They rowed part of the way and then hoisted a sail and passed a pontoon loaded with soldiers. After transacting our business we ascended the old lookout; the air was clear and Sumter was in plain sight, a mass of ruins in one sense but in another stronger than ever. Returning the men hoisted two sails but the wind was so strong that one was blown to pieces. In the afternoon I rode over the low land back of our camp and saw the first turkey buzzard; it flies rather heavily and has to prepare to get ready to ascend in a comic way.

¶ **Sunday, 9th, 4:30 P.M.** It is quite cool, rather too cool for sitting within but bracing without, especially while riding. Billy was so exhilarated that I could hardly persuade him to keep his feet on the earth; his antics amuse me so that I laughed till both feet escaped from the stirrups. At 10, just as the call sounded for inspection a captain of a vessel begged me to visit a fellow captain with him; I was glad to be excused; he offered to pay me but I only permitted him to give me some Epsom Salts, a drug often needed, of which our supply is just exhausted.[246] The chaplain has a furlough, and left for the Head with his son. In his place I have been stamp-

246. Epsom salts, or magnesia sulphas, was a water-soluble bitter-tasting compound often given with senna as a cathartic laxative. Flannery, *Civil War Pharmacy*, 121

ing and indorsing a lot of letters for the men. In the afternoon I got a requisition for two stoves for the hospital and selected them at the post quartermaster's.

¶ **Monday, Oct. 10, 7:45 P.M.** About midnight I was summoned to the hospital to settle a dispute between the cook and the [**blank**]; the former accused the latter of stealing his watch; he was evidently intoxicated, so this morning, when he declined to tell me where he got the liquor I told him he would be returned to his company, and have already made out the application; I may not get so good a cook, but he is also passionate and overbearing.

At about two P.M., in accordance with previous arrangements, the enlisted men, without arms, formed a procession and, while the band played, marched to the front of headquarters; there they formed a semicircle, the band, the committee of sergeant and the president and secretaries of the meeting in the center; seats were placed for the officers but the latter were merely spectators. The ceremony was a celebration of the victory of the colored race as represented by the payment of our men. The colonel declined an invitation to speak and it was all in the hands of the men. After music and prayer there were excellent addresses by the sergeants. The major of the 54th New York came over and there was quite an audience from that regiment.[247]

Afterward David and I went out behind the camp and practiced shooting at bottles; David made the best record. Lt. Roberts is much better and all the other patients are improving.

¶ **Tuesday, 11th, 8:15 P.M.** Several of the officers have just been inspecting a very pretty sight, viz., my cat with four kittens born this morning.

¶ **Wednesday, 12th, 7:00 P.M.** In a Boston Journal of recent date I have just read the narrative of Chaplain Fowler, lately released from captivity of a year. On the way to Pawnee Landing this afternoon I overtook Major Cofax of the 54th N.Y., and had a pleasant chat with him. He was one who escaped from Libby Prison.

10 P.M. Col. Fox and I have been entertained with other officers at the quarters of Capt. Soule. A series of amusing tableaux was given ably by

247. A detailed description of the celebrations was published in both the *Christian Recorder* and the *Weekly Anglo-African*. Trudeau, *Voices*, 150–54.

him and Capt. Thurber; some of them were good hits at the peculiarities of some of us, and afterwards there were nice refreshments. (T. forgets; see slip under "memory")

¶ **Thursday, 13th, 8:00 P.M.** At midnight the camp was aroused by two cannon shots followed by musketry. All made ready for an attack but the firing did not continue and the adjutant went to the gunboat on the river, whence the shots evidently came and found that, in accordance with an admirable plan, the alarm was given as a practice drill for the crew, but we agreed it would have been considerate to inform us in advance. The accompanying diagram shows the new arrangements of the four tents of the adjutant and Q.M. My two tents are opposite; one was formerly occupied [**part is missing**] of Col. Hartwell at present.

¶ **Friday, 14th, 8:45 P.M.** I studied till dinner. Then I mounted Billy and went with the men and a team to get trees to plant in front of the hospital to keep off the wind. They are 15–20 feet high, and will be inserted firmly in a trench and serve as a windbreak. Last night a rather terrifying dream may have been occasioned by the alarm. With many others I seemed to be on bluffs at the west side of this island (there really are none) when suddenly from James Island came flashes like lightning followed by thunder claps like light artillery the earth itself was seen to be thrown up as if by the explosion of mines; gradually the same conditions appeared on Long Island and Coles Island and had just reached Folly River. Then we tried to escape but I got stuck in a bog and my frantic struggles awoke me.

¶ **Sat., 15th, 8.30 P.M.** At ten Col. Fox and I rode to Pawnee Landing; it was a warm and beautiful morning, and the road through the woods was delightful; flowers, birds and butterflies abounded, and war seemed far off. After attending to some sick I obtained from Lt. Elliott in charge of the bakery the promise of half a dozen iron bake-ovens that had ceased to be useful for their original purpose but would make fine open fireplaces such as I mean to have at the hospital. Lt. Elliott rode back to camp with me on the beach. To show how strong and well Billy is, after the four mile ride up through the woods he cantered all the way back on the beach, and was then ready for another ride, while the other horse was weary. I found the "grove" already planted and very acceptable in looks as well as in usefulness. After lancing a "gum-boil" for an officer I began to make some further improvements in my domicile with the help of David, Corporal

Wood,[248] who is a good carpenter, and another soldier. My door and its frame are now in the middle of the space between the two tents covered by the fly; the spaces at the sides of the door are now closed in by canvas. In my own tent, where the door used to be is now a diamond shaped window with a sliding cover, so that from it I can summon David. Under it the shelves at either side are now connected.

¶ **Sunday, 16th, 8:00 P.M.** Breakfast is now at 8 and sick-call at 7:15 and I commonly get through in time. Naturally, and for two reasons, the number desiring excuse from duty is less since pay day. Besides the few who might pretend to be ill there were doubtless others who were so depressed by the conditions of their families that they really felt unfit for work. All are now cheerful. On pay day, in addition to the greenbacks themselves and checks, the Adams express[249] alone took north $65,000.00 from the men and a few of the officers. I am glad to record a pleasant item respecting Dr. Brown. This afternoon he came and asked if I would not like to apply for a leave. I replied that I had been thinking of it but hesitated till the return of Dr. Babbitt. "Oh," said he, "he evidently does not intend to return, and the sooner you apply the better." On my still hesitating he said he could get along. Of course he can, for it is just what I have been doing and the hospitals are in better condition than before he left. Col. Hartwell has twice asked me if I did not mean to apply, and other officers have spoken of it. Evidently the idea is approved.

¶ **Tuesday, 18th, P.M.** Army life is not favorable to elegance of expression or handwriting, and I must try to avoid the haste that interferes with improvement in those respects. I fear my writing will never be very good, but if I ever practise my writing should be so clear as not to cause misinterpretations of prescriptions. Col. Fox has just been in to say goodnight to the little family, as he does every night. The mother cat is the gentlest and kindest we ever have known.

248. This was probably John Wood in Company K, who was promoted to corporal in July 1863 but reduced to the ranks in July 1865. Fox, *Record*, 144.

249. The Adams Express Company was founded in 1854 by Alvin Adams to facilitate the transfer of securities and parcels between Boston and New York. The company expanded rapidly and during the war played a role as paymaster for both the Union and Confederate armies until it was forced to create a separate company, the Southern Express, to handle payments to Southern troops. Adams Express money envelopes allowed soldiers a relatively secure way of sending money home.

This morning Col. Hartwell left for the North. My already low opinion of him is now even lower. He has deliberately broken three promises to Fox. 1. that the latter, being married and having been longest in service, should have the first opportunity to go north. 2. that Fox should be allowed to read Hartwell's account of the action at Rivers Causeway which differs in some essential points, so Fox has been told, from that accepted by the officers generally. 3. that Hartwell should take measures to correct in the minds of our officers the impression he himself created that Fox's friends were influencing Gov. Andrew against him with the knowledge and approval of Fox himself. When Fox learned of this impression he wrote at once to his father who wrote to him and Hartwell disclaiming all knowledge of such a thing, and convincingly even for Hartwell, who then promised to set it right with the officers; yet now he has gone away and left the act of justice undone. He has treated me with uniform courtesy and even consideration; nevertheless I regard him as a crafty and unscrupulous man. I am glad to say that our officers no longer credit the false impression, if indeed they ever did. Soule was officer of the day and Fox and I accompanied him over the picket line, and I visited several outlying patients. Returning on the beach we saw a dozen newly hatched turtles scrambling down from the bank toward the water; I captured several.

¶ **Thursday, 20th, 7:15 P.M.** Capt. Walton says that a rebel paper states that Sherman has abandoned and burned Atlanta and vanished. Perhaps W. who is with him will suddenly turn up on the coast. This forenoon I studied. Yesterday I dissected the finger that the man chopped off the other day and found it very interesting. There is no news of Dr. Babbitt, and he is reported "absent without leave."

¶ **Friday, 21st, 8:15 P.M.** I have just taken the first official step toward obtaining a leave of absence by sending a paper for the endorsement of Surgeons Brown and Hagen as to the propriety of asking for it now. I was in a dismal mood, feeling that it would not be right to go now, when Dr. Brown came in and said there was some prospect that Hagen, whose time has expired, might remain in the service, and that a new assistant surgeon might be appointed for his regiment; at present, while Hagen is acting as chief medical officer and on the staff of Gen. Scammon on Morris Island, it is under the care of an assistant surgeon of the 33rd U.S. It is an old and seasoned regiment and quite small so that the sick are comparatively few.

¶ **Sunday, 23rd, 6:00 P.M.** A very kind letter from Prof. Wyman outlining a plan for my employment at the north in case the service does not attract me to remain longer in it. It is a fair question whether it is best to remain in official relations with one whom I cannot respect more than I do Dr. Brown. He cannot accuse me of hesitating to do whatever he suggests; the trouble is that he leaves to me both the plans and the execution of all improvements. A recent event has aroused me deeply. It has become really cold and he got a requisition for the hospital and dispensary. Behold, the first stove is put up in his own tent at once, and none in the hospital. Col. Fox sent him a note about it and now one of the others has been put in the dispensary and the other in one hospital tent, the other being left unwarmed; Col. Fox says he is tempted to put him under arrest. While trotting rapidly on the wood road yesterday Billy stumbled over a concealed root and we fell, he on my leg, which is consequently lame, and I on my shoulder which likewise feels pretty sore today; it is the first time we have had such a mishap. Just before daylight this morning there was heavy firing toward the harbor, and we have since learned that a blockade runner was destroyed by our guns.

¶ **Monday, 24th, 8:15 P. M.** Most of today has been spent in getting and utilizing men, teams, lumber and tools for the fireplace at the post hospital and for frames at the regimental; lime is needed for mortar with which to lay bricks, and I rode to Pawnee Landing to arrange for a supply; one of the artillery men is a regular mason and will do that part of the work.

¶ **Tuesday, 25th,** Bricks are needed for the bakery at Pawnee Landing. To send north for them would take considerable time. So yesterday an expedition under Major Wales was sent to Legareville for some from the ruins of the houses. There were obtained about 500 the cost of which is estimated by Q. M. Cushing at about $1.75 each; still such expeditions interest and occupy the men and give then desirable experience. Capt. Soule accompanied it and after breakfast this morning he read to us an account of it purporting to be taken from the "Daily Folly Islander." It was irresistibly comic and amused us all immensely; it reminded me of his editorial attacks upon me as a rival editor at the High School.

¶ **Wednesday, 26th, 7:30 P.M.** I have just received my communication as to the "Leave" with Dr. Hagen's endorsement that he will approve it as soon as he returns from the Head about Nov. 1. Recently we have been playing whist and for one I see no reason why not; I have never known any playing for even the smallest stakes. Great deeds were done at the post hospital today, and by all concerned. In addition to the four men detailed for the work and two men with a team to bring another load of sod, five of the seven patients have done what they could. The iron and brick fireplace with turf backing has been completed and a merry fire is comforting all. Recently the cat has been restless perhaps recognizing the approach of cold weather and the absence of a stove in my tent. Last night she carried three of the kittens under the floor of the adjutants tent, just where the stove stands, and where it was probably warm. The fourth kitten woke me with its mewing and I took it into bed where it miraculously escaped crushing during my sleep. Now the whole family has been moved to a warm corner of the colonel's tent until my stove is put up.

¶ **Thursday, 27th, 7:30 P.M.** Dr. Brown has decided to lower the hospital tents, which were set needlessly high, as it appears, from apprehension of the surf at high tide. I went to Coles Island for a big cross-cut saw but on my return found that the posts had been chopped off sufficiently. This afternoon David and I have set up my stove.

¶ **Friday, 28th, 7:30 P.M.** I have been working for some time at intervals upon a ring of hard rubber upon which is wound silk from the spider so abundant on Long Island.

¶ **Saturday, 29th, 8:00 P.M** At the celebration of "pay-day" it was thought best for the men to manage it all, so the officers only showed their sympathy and interest by sitting a little back. In civil life of course there would have been references to the misconduct of the government; but the Army Regulations expressly forbid public criticism of any higher authority, so nothing of that sort was said.

¶ **Sunday, [October] 30th, 3:00 P.M.** The wife of Capt. Dewhurst has gone to the Head, and the only lady on the Island now is the wife of a captain commanding one of the forts. I cannot refrain occasionally from reflecting upon my commodious establishment. The two wall-tents, framed, with the intervening fly-covered space, make a room 25 ft. long, 9 ft. high and wide, substantial doors, a window and a stove; there are shelves for my books, instruments, writing material and toilet apparatus.

Rings of Spider Silk

Saturday, Oct. 29th, 7:30 P.M. About a year ago I wound off many yards of silk from a spider on a bit of lead pencil. I told Major Wales of it and while on Long Id., where the spiders abound, he wound some silk upon a ring cut from a hard rubber ruler. He then made one each for the colonel, adjutant and Q.M. and, he says, was intending to make one for me – but I had already planned to make one. He got a lot of spiders and made a little machine by which silk could be wound off as on a reel by turning a crank, the spider being secured (how?) a few inches. Out of the ruler I cut a ring with a double groove and a signet where the grooves cross. On this I wound yesterday and this afternoon. By means of a couple of pins at one end of a swivel moved by the thumb I guided the thread in the grooves and at the crossing turning the crank with my right hand. Some of the time I wound from 4 or 5 spiders at once, their threads all passing between the pins so as to be under my control. The hardest part is to keep the eye constantly on the thread for an instant's carelessness would have made trouble. On account of the crossing my ring had to be wound much more slowly than the others. Here is a calculation of the length. [**Most of the handwritten notes attached are illegible except for the final entry – 24,300 inches on this ring**]

¶ **Monday, [October] 31st, 8:10 P.M.** The new steward writes very well so for the first time I am able to delegate some of the actual writing of the monthly reports.[250] I have been making a cedar wood case for the ring; the latter is finished but I may make another. The major talks of making for Miss B— a ring, a breast-pin, earrings, and perhaps bracelets. Col. Fox has commenced a cross for his wife. He has suggested replacing our wooden wheels by the armorer's "gear drill stock," and it is a great improvement. I shall probably use it in making a large plain ring to show to the Natural History Society when I come north. So far as I know spider's silk have never been obtained in this way before. The fates seem to obstruct my leave. The 54th N.Y. has been moved to another part of the Island, leaving Dr. Brown and me the only medical officers at this end. He has to visit Morris Island once a week and one of us has to visit Long Island once or twice. Even if others approved my going I cannot conscientiously under present conditions. If I knew how to reach Dr. Babbitt I would state the case to him and even offer to pay him to remain here during the month of my absence.

¶ **Saturday, Nov. 5th, 8:00 P.M.** Since Dr. Brown asked for only 20 days (he was really away less) I have hesitated about asking for the usual 30; but he

250. The new hospital steward was John Sutfen. Fox, *Record*, 114.

tells me it was because he had reason at that time to think the longer time would not be approved by Dr, Hagen and advises me to ask for 30. So I have written my formal application to the adjutant general of the dep't, and Dr. Brown has approved it. In behalf of Col. Fox our adjutant has added a very complimentary endorsement, and it will then go to post and district headquarters. I have also sent a note to the Medical Director of the dep't in case it is referred to him by Gen. Foster.

¶ **Sunday, 6th, 7:00 P.M.** ~~Yesterday~~ **This AM** several of us visited the new camp of the 54th N.Y. near our former winter camp. Prof. Wyman writes that the turtles have reached him.

¶ **Monday, 7th, 7:15 P.M.** During the hour before supper several of us engaged in a hearty game of baseball that recalled the High School days, when Mr. Horr[251] used to come out and play with us.

¶ **Thursday, 10th, 8:00 P.M.** I have just witnessed part of a religious service at the chapel tent. One of the men became so excited that he was hysterical and screamed rather than spoke; that aspect of religion does not appeal to me at all.

¶ **Friday, 11th, 8:30 P.M.** I have just come from what reminded me of certain conditions at Judiciary Square. In the post hospital is a soldier shot through the abdomen, probably fatally. So far it has required three men to attend to him, so frequent are his wishes for a change of position, not withstanding the opiate given to induce sleep and lessen the danger from the inevitable inflammation. He is Wm. Barden [Bardin][252] of Co. B and had been confined to the provost guard house for some time. He is said to have advanced to strike the guard and the latter shot him. This was at 4:30 P.M., and he was brought to my hospital at once. He evidently does not expect to live and has requested that his watch be sent to his mother and his dice-box burned; he declares that all his troubles have come from card playing.

¶ **Saturday, 12th, 7:45 P.M.** The wounded man died at ten last night and this morning I examined him in the presence of Dr. Brown. The wound

251. John E. Horr was principle of the Brookline High School. Wilder Papers, CU.

252. William Bardin was a twenty-two-year-old sailor from Memphis, Tennessee, when he joined the 55th Massachusetts. Fox, *Record*, 118.

was a fearful one; the ball perforated the bowel in two places, then passed through the spine, struck the pelvis and fell back into the abdomen. I have preserved the ball and the piece of the spine.

¶ **Sunday, 13th, 8:00 P.M.** Major Wales and the Q. M. have been at Long Island this afternoon catching spiders, and we all will be able to continue our silk manufactures.

¶ **Wednesday, 16th, 7:45 P.M.** This afternoon I have wound off on a ring that Major Wales gave me nearly 900 yards of silk from the spiders. Using the large machine, the cog wheel of which turns 40 time per minute and the ring itself 4½ as fast; so, by ascertaining the diameter of the ring and noting the number of minutes actually employed one may calculate the length of the silk wound out. I must have a showy specimen for the natural History Society and shall utilize this one cut out by Major Wales. The periphery is grooved and there are notches at four opposite sides, so that the silk may be wound across as well as in the groove and it will present all possible aspects.

¶ **Thursday, 17th, 9:15 P.M.** All day I have been winding silk upon the exhibition ring which has now, by moderate computation, 2500 yards.

¶ **Saturday, 19th, 10:15 P.M.** Yesterday I finished the ring which now carries 3400 yards of silk, more than two miles. The calculations involve large numbers and troublesome fractions, and occupied me all last evening.

¶ **Sunday, 20th, 2:15 P.M.** Friday forenoon the hospital was inspected by the District Inspector; it has never before [been inspected] and I requested it. He expressed himself gratified at the condition of every part, particularly the kitchen, which he pronounced "unexceptionable," and at the various devices, fire-places, doors, etc.; said he wished all were in as good order. I really have never seen a camp hospital so complete. Great credit is due my cook and nurses, most excellent men selected by me for their positions. Saturday afternoon I got together the various specimens to take north, including a dozen of the spiders that have been so thoroughly "silked."

¶ **Tuesday, [November] 22nd, 7:30 P.M.** Today, after the rain of last night, it is really cold, and the wind renders it almost impossible to keep warm. Dr. Babbitt has returned and occupied the other half of my habitation, as Fox did formerly. He is well and says he was in a hospital and could not be spared at the time the order to rejoin the regiment was received; so the order was revoked but we were never told. I understand that a Commission will inquire so as to clear him of the charge of absent without leave. The mysterious and vexatious delay in granting my application for leave, sent in on the — of—, is at last explained. My application, duly endorsed by the authorities of the post and district and by the district medical director, has been returned disapproved by the medical director of the department on the ground that I had failed to comply with an order which, it seems, was written October 22nd but not received by me till Nov. 17th. The case is as follows. During August and September, for various reasons, the post hospital did not save any rations, and therefore had no "hospital fund" with which to purchase delicacies, stimulants or extra diet for the patients. But in my hands was a sum of money found on the body of a man who died and whose friends could not be located. This I used for the purchase of extras. Afterwards I admitted to the hospital two men who were very ill, indeed likely to die. Not being employees of the government their employers paid 30 cents a day for their board; one of them handed me $4.00, but both sums were expended for extras. Then the post council of administration voted $16.00 for wine for the hospital, and it was so expended; so, finally, was the $9.00, the value of the brandy that was stolen by the Q.M. employees and returned to me by the Q.M. But as all these items were strictly unofficial my Monthly Report of the Hospital Fund would not indicate that the patients had anything besides the regular rations. Therefore, and to avert misapprehension, I made out a separate statement of all of the above names items, stating the source of each and the articles obtained with it, and sent the statement with the Report, never imagining that any fault would be found with it. It seems, however, that the medical director wished to know my authority for making the expenditures and asked for an explanation which I sent him on the 18th [of November]. Col. Fox did not think the matter sufficiently important to delay granting my leave, but apparently it was; so today, when the application disproved reached me I sent them back at once stating that my full account of the matter had already been sent, although evidently not received when the leave was returned. This matter is very unpleasant, aside from the delay in getting away; the fact is if I had said nothing about it no one would have been the wiser; nevertheless I did what was right and should do the same again.

¶ **Wednesday, 23rd, 10:30 P.M.** Just before supper Col. Fox received a telegraphic summons to report at once to the General on Morris Island. I wished to see the medical director of the district and explain my affairs to him, so I offered to accompany him. He had already ridden six miles today and I ten. After a hasty meal we started for the Inlet but there found that the information had been communicated to the post commander and that Fox need not cross. Not even the adjutant is to be told, but I suspect that it has something to do with the expected arrival of Sherman at the coast. Col. Fox's application for a leave has been returned disapproved, and he thinks mine may have been on the same grounds of anticipated movements; in that case, although disappointed I shall feel happier. We returned when I began to write.

¶ **Thursday, [November] 24th, 7:00 P.M.** In accordance with the proclamation of the president and orders from dep't headquarters the usual drills were omitted. At nearly half past ten nearly all the men attended the sermon by the chaplain, which was excellent. Major Wales is to leave at once and permitted me to pack the jars containing my specimens in the pigeon holes of his desk. He has given me a piece of thread made from the spider's silk; I had made one but lost it yesterday; I am glad to have a bit to show for the practical value of the discovery depends largely upon the strength of the thread. Dr. Brown has assigned me the duties as follows, it being unusual for all three of us to be together in the regiment; he will take the regimental hospital, Dr. Babbitt the sick in quarters and I am to continue in charge of the post hospital. I submitted my recent difficulties to him and he says my only mistake was in saying anything about it, for otherwise nothing would have been thought of it; nevertheless I think I did what was right. This afternoon was a grand parade and then a review by Col. Kozlay; then we played ball till dark.

¶ **Friday, 25th, 7:15 P.M.** Last night we had whist as a sort of farewell to the major; he and I won most of the games as against the colonel and adjutant. There are various and unmistakable indications of an approaching movement, and of course that will prevent my renewing my application. This afternoon I have cleaned and sharpened the surgical instruments.

¶ **Saturday, 26th, 8:15 P.M.** Orders to be ready to embark have been received and all have been very busy; I have given up the post hospital and Dr. Brown has asked me to take charge of the stretcher corps, so I have been instructing them on their duties and exhorting them not allow bursting shells to affect them as at Rivers Causeway. I have completed my Monthly Report and copied the account of the recent shooting case for Dr. Brinton. It is splendid weather for marching or fighting.

¶ **Sunday, [November] 27th, 5:30 P.M.** We are on the steamer, **"Mary Boardman,"** and are to start ~~in an hour~~ **soon**, taking five days rations.

¶ **Monday, 28th,** Noon, on steamer in Broad River, S.C. This ~~is a~~ large ~~and safe~~ propeller soon ~~which~~ took us out of Stono Inlet and turned southward. After crossing the bar Col. Fox opened his sealed orders and found that we were going to Hilton Head. The night was foggy but neither cold or windy. The quarters of the officers were unusually commodious. Most of us retired at 9. At 2 we anchored in Port Royal Harbor and Col. Fox went to the steamer "Cosmopolitan" expecting to report to Gen. Hatch; but the latter had already gone on shore. The regiment is ~~somewhat dismembered so far~~ **divided**. Most of the companies are on this boat under Col. Fox, and with us are the adjutant, the chaplain, and Dr. Brown; but Dr. Babbitt is with Captain Nutt in command of two companies that embarked upon ~~a small~~ **another** steamer. ~~Finally, since~~ The horses could not be accommodated on the boat **so** they and our boys were sent to Lighthouse Inlet and put on the "Golden Gate;" it has arrived but we have not yet communicated with her. Col. Hartwell returned from the north and came on board this morning. The steamer on which he came brought a large mail and the officers and men are very happy in consequence. A jollier set of soldier never started on an expedition from which some of them may never return. **At Folly Island**, when some of them were told that they were not well enough to accompany us they fairly cried and begged to be taken. I have not seen a ~~dismal~~ **gloomy** face or heard a ~~dubious~~ **dismal** word. We had a good breakfast at 9 o'clock, and the steamer then started up the river for five days coal from the wharf at Parry Island where we are now. Our precise destination is not yet announced, but as Sherman is reported within 30 miles of Savannah, and we are escorted by gunboats, we infer that the expedition is of some importance.[253] Most of the 54th Mass. are here and a N.Y. regiment (56th?).

¶ **Thursday, 29th, 11:00 A.M.** On same steamer. Our boat finished coaling at midnight and then, when ready to start, was so enveloped in fog that it was unsafe to move. Soon after daybreak we ~~started~~ **moved** down the River to report at the Head for orders; on the way we met a tug with

253. The expedition was the result of a request from Gen. Sherman to Gen. Halleck. Sherman expected to reach the coast by December, and he wanted the Charleston and Savannah Railroad cut to delay Confederate troops trying to reinforce Savannah.

Major Nutt on board; he succeeds Wales.[254] He said that the rest of the expedition started some hours ago, and that our destination was Boyd's Neck; so we started up stream again but when abreast of Parry Island, on the opposite side, we saw two steamers stuck in the mud, the water on the flats being shallow at low tide. Col. Fox went on one of them, returned and set off again with our row boats, probably to aid in landing the troops. We hope our men can soon disembark for they are much crowded here. So far our ~~grand~~ expedition has been checked by perhaps unavoidable conditions, the fog and low tide. Last night I had the most comfortable bed since leaving home; it was made up for Col. Fox, but as he had to be up and down he would not occupy it and said it should not go to waste, so I accepted it. The larger brigade is commanded by Gen. Potter[255]; the smaller, consisting of four colored regiments, by Col. Hartwell.[256] Our adjutant, McKay, has been taken by him as his adjutant, and is replaced by Lt. Hall.[257] Capt. Goodwin has returned but was sent to Folly Island in place of Capt. Crane who, being at the Head, was taken on his staff by Col. Hartwell.

Broad River, Boyd's Neck

Friday, [December] 2nd, 2:00 P.M. For three days it has been impossible to write, so occupied have we been, some of the time in the most tragic way. We landed **at Boyd's Neck** Tuesday afternoon and bivouacked near the

254. William Nutt was promoted to major on 28 November 1864. Gen. Hatch, who led the 6,000-man expedition, was slowed by a heavy fog, incompetent guides, and little sense of urgency. A rapid Union advance early on the morning of November 30 would have seized the Honey Hill fortifications before significant Confederate forces could arrive, but Hatch delayed. His attempt to throw a series of uncoordinated small units along a narrow causeway against strongly fortified position was a recipe for failure. Union casualties were over 850 men. Leonne M. Hudson, "A Confederate Victory at Grahamville: Fighting at Honey Hill," *South Carolina Historical Magazine* 94, no. 1 (January 1993): 19–33.

255. Gen. Edward Elmer Potter saw most of his wartime service off the Southern coast. A New York lawyer before the war, as brigadier general he served in the operations against Charleston and then in the Carolinas Campaign. His brigade included the 56th and 127th New York, the 25th Ohio, and the 35th USCT, plus a battery of the 3rd Rhode Island Artillery. Sifakis, *Who Was Who in the Civil War*, 518; Fox, *Record*, 41.

256. Hartwell commanded the 54th and 55th Massachusetts, plus the 26th and 102nd USCT. The last two regiments were sent in the wrong direction and only rejoined the brigade in the late afternoon. Fox, *Record*, 41–42.

257. Josiah C. Hall left his teaching job in Cincinnati to join the 75th Ohio and was promoted to sergeant before moving to the 55th Massachusetts. After being severely wounded at Honey Hill he was promoted to captain "for bravery and gallantry in the battle-field." Fox, *Record*, 103.

water. Wednesday we arose an hour before daylight and at dawn started inland toward the railroad. Gen. Hatch was with Potter's brigade in advance; our regiment was the first of the four comprising Hartwell's brigade. There was some firing nearly all the way, for the ~~rebels~~ **confederates** kept a brass field piece in the narrow road along which we had to move in a narrow column; much of the way there were thick woods on both sides. About the middle of the forenoon our regiment halted in the midst of a field for about an hour, and then, firing having commenced in front, we advanced in that direction where the other brigade was already engaged. The spot selected for the first reception of the wounded was about an eighth of a mile from the fighting line and so I can describe only what was told me of the fight itself. It seems that when the head of the column reached a sharp turn in the road it was confronted by a rebel earthwork mounting several guns. No serious effort to take this was made till Hartwell volunteered to lead a charge.[258] The order to advance seems to have reached only four of our companies. The way was further blocked by a slough with logs in it. The woods at the side of the road were filled with rebels. In a very short time we lost 120 killed and wounded. Co. B alone lost 30. Hartwell was shot in the hand but kept on till his horse was killed and fell on him. Lt. Ellsworth dragged him from beneath the animal at the risk of his own life, for the colonel was wounded twice more, tho not dangerously. Capt. Crane and Lt. Boynton were killed; Capt. Woodward and Lt. Jewett[259] were wounded, and Capt. Soule slightly, but he is on duty. The charge was unsuccessful, but the artillery and most of the infantry remained in action till dark when they were gradually withdrawn.[260] There was a dense fog after dark. During the charge and immediately after the wounded came ~~back faster than I could attend to them, but I was able to send all to the rear~~ **or were brought to me in great numbers**. The more severe cases were sent back to Dr. Brown after being temporarily dressed, but I ~~took~~ **cut** out some balls, ~~cut off~~ **amputated** wounded fingers, etc. The stretcher corps did finely and some nearly injured themselves. The chaplain and Q.M. helped. Dr. Brown had the hospital in a small church. Our regiment did not begin to retire till ten, and then we

258. Wilder is mistaken. Two previous assaults on the fortifications had already been driven back. Hudson, "A Confederate Victory at Grahamville," 25–26.

259. E. Harris Jewett served as a private in the 6th New York Cavalry before accepting a commission in the 55th Massachusetts. Fox, *Record*, 106.

260. In his after-action report, Hartwell stressed the destructive fire from the Confederate artillery and praised the courage of the 55th Massachusetts. *Official Records*, ser. 1, vol. 44, 430–32.

had to stop at the church for 20 wounded left behind by the other regiments. They were carried in shelter tents for we had only 6 stretchers. Col. Fox and the four companies not in the charge held the road bravely. I did not reach the Landing until after midnight, and getting the wounded on the hospital boat kept me up till two. Saturday morning we advanced again to some woods about three miles from the Landing; we were near a road and behind a hedge and ditch. We were occupied in various ways all day and slept there on the ground. We were roused several times by picket firing, but there was no real attack. Today we have strengthened the position materially. I am well but tired. Billy has been on the go too but is well.

¶ **Saturday, 3rd, 11:14 A.M.** This is a great change from the almost too luxurious life recently on Folly Island; there has been hard marching, hard fighting, hard lying and "hard tack," for till yesterday we had only that and not much of it. Fortunately on the steamer we were able to obtain good meals and therefore save what we had put up for the expedition; out of those, Col. Fox and I selected some salt beef; a jar of mustard for him, a can of condensed milk for me, and for us both a can of peaches. [**Part of a line is illegible**] Fortunately the weather is favorable, bright and warm during the day although cool at night and really frosty in the morning. We had no shelter till last night when our boys, David and George, put up a piece of canvas big enough to cover Col. Fox, Major Nutt and myself, and them. Our clothing is an overcoat and rubber piece.[261] That is all the men have, and some lost **even** those either in the fight or while carrying off the wounded. I fear the exposure will cause illness. Just a dawn yesterday the rebels open fired on our center from one or two field pieces at the edge of a wood and killed several men of a battery; but the latter replied and soon silenced them. Last night we got little sleep, for besides the straggling picket firing at midnight there was a regular volley fired at our right, causing our regiment to get under arms with great alacrity; it was learned this morning that it was cause by a small body of rebels coming out at the edge of the wood and giving orders as if a brigade were about to advance; we think it was "impertinent and inconsiderate." This morning our lines are extended further to the right, and **are** therefore less strong than at first, but we have the advantage of position and there is reason to believe that the enemy comprises comparatively undisciplined troops ~~and have~~

261. Wilder appears to be referring to a rubber blanket often used as a poncho by infantrymen and first issued during the Civil War. *Arms and Equipment of the Union* (Alexandria: Time-Life Books, 1996) 196, 215.

armed with inferior weapons; the three balls cut out by me were of as many **different** patterns, and round balls are common.[262]

¶ **Sunday, 4th, 4:00 P.M.** We retired early **last night** but had little rest for at four separate times mounted troops came down the road and fired at our pickets and were answered. All night we heard at intervals the cars of the railroad and infer that troops are being rushed to Savannah which we understand is threatened by Sherman. After breakfast I rode out some way with Surgeon Mowrey of the 35th U.S., accompanying a reconnaissance towards the right. So far there has been no sickness; Dr. Babbitt held the first sick-call but none asked to be excused from duty. Then I rode to the Landing for some cheese and condensed milk. Then Dr. Brown and I compared the lists of the killed and wounded made by me day before yesterday with the one made by him at the church hospital; after adjusting the discrepancies I dictated a third list to the sergeant major to be sent to Brigade Headquarters.

¶ **Monday, 5th, 4:30 P.M.** This forenoon, after going to the Landing I accompanied the regiment on a reconnaissance as far as the church; we advanced slowly, flanked by a strong line of skirmishers under Capt. Soule; all behaved splendidly and drove back the rebel pickets; one of our men was wounded and sent back on a stretcher. The battery shelled the rebel line for half an hour and we then withdrew; the object was to distract attention from the more serious demonstration made by five regiments on another road; it is reported that they had quite a fight.

¶ **Thursday, 6th, 3:00 P.M.** There was no firing last night but we did not feel very safe because, in order to send a large force on an expedition up the river, the Naval Brigade on our left was replaced by the 102nd U.S., and other troops were withdrawn from our right leaving our brigade of two regiments to hold the entire line. Our regiment now ~~holds~~ **extends half a mile from the road at** the edge of the woods ~~and half a mile more~~ so that the men are six feet or more apart; if the ~~rebels~~ **confederates** know our weakness and are not themselves too much occupied with Sherman they may make trouble for us. Last evening we had a call from Lt. Perry, now Hartwell's adjutant; he reported that the expedition up the Coosawhatchie road had a skirmish with the rebels and that suddenly from

262. A round ball would indicate that it was not fired from a rifled musket, which took a minié ball, but rather from the less accurate smooth-bore musket.

their ranks, at the risk of destruction by the opposing fires, ran a man who declared himself a Union man known to Perry and Hall. He proved to be a former member of a Union battery who, having been captured, enlisted in order to escape. He said that yesterday morning the rebels heard that Sherman was crossing the Savannah River at Hudson Ford and were in great consternation; that on the day of the fight they had 2400 men about here, but half of them had gone to Savannah; the remainder are twice our force. This forenoon I went to the Landing on business and found that Dr. Brown was about to perform an **important** operation; so I remained to assist; ~~there were~~ other surgeons ~~there~~ **were present**.

¶ **Thursday, 8th, 2:45 P.M.** ~~Soon after dark on Tuesday orders came to make another move to the right~~ Tuesday, at midnight Col. Fox and I moved back to Brigade Headquarters at the cross-roads; said headquarters consists of a shelter of boughs. The other two regiments came in and went to the Landing; it began to rain and was pretty uncomfortable. Then the section of artillery came and stopped at the edge of the woods in our rear. It was now 3 A.M. and Col. Fox anxiously awaited orders for our much attenuated regiments to come, for the favorite time to attack is just before day. Suddenly a portion came in supposing that the order must have missed them; to our regret and their disgust they had to return. The brigade adjutant then went to the General's headquarters for information and was told that orders would be sent when it was time to move. After waiting an hour Col. Silliman[263] rode back himself and found the General and all his staff gone. So he took the responsibility ~~to~~ **of** order**ing** the withdrawal of our men. Col. Fox rode out to the left wing, the adjutant to the right, and Lt. Hall, aid-de-camp, to the center. Within the hour half the companies came in but the rest were delayed. ~~Their position and ours~~ **The situation** was ~~dangerous~~ **perilous** for if the ~~rebel~~ **confederate** pickets advanced and found ours gone they might make a sudden attack and find us comparatively scattered **and unprepared**. Col. Fox and I rode out some distance and listened attentively but could hear no movement on the ~~rebel~~ **confederate** front. Finally the missing companies came in and we formed in line and marched to the Landing. Lt. Roberts was ill and I ~~gave~~ **loaned** him my horse. On reaching the Landing at daybreak we found that we were to hold the position, all other forces having gone to a point higher up the river. A breastwork across the neck was at once thrown up and

263. Col. William Silliman commanded the 26th USCT, a regiment raised at Riker's Island, New York, on 27 February 1864. Fox, *Record*, 44, 46.

headquarters was established at the only house, that of Col. Boyd. Col. Fox occupies a tent outside; a room is given up to the hospital and another to the nurses. I have charge of the sick, about 30 left from the other regiments; Dr. Brown went with the brigade commander; Dr. Babbitt has charge of our regiment.

¶ **Friday, 9th, 4:00 P.M.** During last night heavy firing could be heard towards Savannah but we were undisturbed here. It ~~grew~~ **is** cold and damp and our situation is somewhat dismal; the land is between two small creeks running up from the river; but right opposite is an island so that, unless coming to this landing, the steamers keep to the main channel on the other side of the island and we do not even see them clearly. I have sent 8 of my sick to their respective regiments, and am providing for the remainder as well as I can with no cooking utensils of our own. Yesterday and today I borrowed a kettle from the artillery and made excellent soup from fresh beef, onions and potatoes; but the latter are now gone and we must depend upon hard tack; fortunately cattle were driven in before we fell back and there is plenty of beef. Col. Fox and I rode along the line of defense; we have five field pieces; he set one in the center and the others at the flanks; the position is naturally strong. Yesterday the gunboat in the creek at the right practiced firing across our front[264]; it also sent a hundred pound shell so that, as seen from our lookout, it burst over one of the rebel picket posts and men were seen dragging away wounded or killed and horses. The line is about one eighth of a mile from the house; there are only a few cavalry. The location is shown on the diagram.

¶ **Saturday, 10th, 4:00 P.M.** Dr. Babbitt was summoned to care for another regiment. Major Nutt commands this regiment, and he and the company officers are with it. This room therefore contains only the three officers of this post, Col. Fox, commander, Capt. Soule, Q.M., and myself, surgeon. There is also a post adjutant. Yesterday at 5 Gen. Foster came here on his steamer, the "Cosmopolitan;" he was confined to it by an old wound, so his assistant medical director, Dr. Buchanan, came ashore and Col. Fox then went to the steamer. He learned that up the river our advance had got within 50 yards of the railroad, but was then exposed to an enfilading fire from a battery. Larger cannon were then taken with the intention of cutting away the woods and silencing that battery before

264. The wooden side-wheel gunboat, *Pontiac*, commanded by Capt. Luce, remained at the Landing to provide artillery support. Fox, *Record*, 45.

another advance is made. At night a welcome boat brought us rations and took two of our pieces to the front. However that leaves us four and our defenses are strengthened daily. We learned that Col. Silliman had his leg shot off and that Lt. Hill[265] was killed. Our mess now includes the Lt. of Artillery and three cavalry officers.

¶ **Sunday, 11th, 3:30 P.M.** After breakfast the "Cosmopolitan" came and took away all the invalids; a relief as we have no cooking utensils and quinine is running short; most of them had malaria. The naval officers came on shore today and were so inconsiderate as to accept an invitation to dinner; we could offer them only beef soup, hard tack and some butter obtained from the steamer. I miss the white sugar badly. Likewise the opportunity for extended rides; we are like a circus and must go round and round within a small area.

¶ **Monday, 12th, 6:30 P.M.** This has been a pleasant day. The uncomfortable period of the twenty-four hours is from 2 till daybreak; it is then cold and commonly foggy. These southern houses are not calculated for cold weather; this one stands quite high from the ground and the wind has full sweep beneath. The door of this room is gone and all the windows **are** broken; we have covered two of them, but at night it becomes so cold that one of us has to keep the fire going in the fireplace. The beds are laid each night, bundles of straw, and we lie with our feet to the fire. The men have constructed "wigwams" of the long grass and branches of the trees; some of them have been covered lightly with earth. In front of each hut is a semicircular wall about 2 feet high for a fireplace. In return for some fresh beef the gunboat has sent us half a dozen candles, much needed. Just now I am writing on a box by one candle; Capt. Soule on another box by a second candle, and Col. Fox is sitting on the floor reading by the same. Lt. Chickering is a cousin of Alleyne Adams. Col. Fox prefers to sleep in a tent because most of the regiment must, but **he** is not feeling very well and we have persuaded him to stay in the house tonight. His bed of state is to be the dining table, consisting of two boxes covered with straw. A cavalry man was just brought in whose horse had reared and fallen on him so as to cut his head; he became excited and was determined to go out on picket so that his comrades could hardly bring him

265. Lt. Edwin Ruthven Hill, who served both in the Mexican War and in the 2nd Massachusetts and the 4th Massachusetts Cavalry before joining the 55th, was killed while riding on the skirmish line at Deveaux's Neck. Fox, *Record*, 46, 94–95.

in; I calmed him somewhat by discussing other topics with him, and **finally** persuaded him to let his hair be cut off and his wound dressed; at last I got him to sit by the fire and read a paper and hope he will consent to keep quiet. After tea Fox and Soule and I sang for a time. It is moonlight and very pleasant, warmer than during the forenoon when water froze in the dipper. I borrowed a few books from the surgeon of the gunboat today.

¶ **Wednesday, 14th, 4:00 P.M.** There joined us last night the chaplain, Lt. Carter[266] and **[blank]** (recently commissioned and on the way to the Head for muster), and Capt. Grant; the latter says a monstrous mail for Sherman's army arrived on the Fulton, that he conversed with a scout from Sherman's army who reached the Head within a day or two, and that Sherman had communicated with the fleet off Savannah.

¶ **Thursday, 15th, 4:00 P.M.** We hear that Fort McAllister has fallen and that Sherman dined with Foster on the latter's steamer in the Savannah River. There was heavy distant firing during the forenoon but not now. Yet there are still ~~rebel~~ **confederates** not far from us yesterday. An officer of the gunboat went up a creek to a point about two miles from here and incautiously approached a house from which he was fired upon and wounded in the shoulder; the men with him ran away and they ~~rebels~~ evidently supposed that he went off or was carried; perhaps there were only a few and they feared capture themselves. A larger party went out and found ~~him~~ **the officer**; he had fainted from loss of blood, but they got him here at 7. The commander of the gunboat sent for me to consult with his surgeon.[267] Of course I went and found that he had not even examined the wound. The pulse could not be then felt in the arm and the nerves had evidently been injured though not destroyed; the bone was uninjured. The surgeon asked if I advised amputation and I relied at once in the negative as to any operation except tying the arteries in case bleeding recommenced. It gave me an unpleasant ~~sensation~~ **impression** to find amputation even suggested in such a case by a man twice my age, and a regular graduate of a medical school, and I realized how much had been gained by me from the hospital experience in Washington and subsequent study. In view of the danger

266. George H. Carter worked as a clerk in Boston when the war started. He served in the 44th Massachusetts before his appointment to the 55th. He was brevetted captain in early 1865. Fox, *Record*, 107.

267. The acting assistant surgeon of the *Pontiac* was J. W. Sherfy.

from sudden hemorrhage under circumstances when assistance might not be at hand as on an isolated gunboat, we decided to send the patient to the Naval Hospital at the Head; so a rowboat went up to Gregory's Point last night and this morning a tug came down and took him away.

I am trying to improve the sanitary conditions here. The grounds around the house have been thoroughly policed and today a new well has been dug. For an eighth of a mile on all sides of the house the soil is dry and hard, but beyond it is soft and almost boggy, water being reached at about 2 feet from the surface. In the selected spot we dug about six feet through sand and then encountered gravel with small pebbles, the first we had seen; it was very hard, like conglomerate and had to be cut out with an axe for about 2 feet; then, as if a shell had been broken, the water was plentiful and of good quality. It is irksome to be so ~~limited~~ **circumscribed** in riding; the outside limit is a mile and even there a soldier's horse was shot recently. Two days ago David recommenced the care of Billy and the latter has improved 50 percent in appearance. I shall be very sorry to lose David; he does more for us all in the house than any other.

¶ **Friday, [December] 16th, 3:30 P.M.** Following the cold snap it is really warm today, almost uncomfortable in the shade and in the summer clothes, all we have, except greatcoats.

¶ **Sunday, 18th, 3:45 P.M.** I have made an exchange of trousers with Capt. Soule. He bought a pair of dark blue on the gunboat, and the ones I had were light blue; the opposite color was appropriate for each so I gave him $2.00 in addition. **Lt. Chickering and** I dined on the gunboat by invitation of the surgeon. We had pea soup, boiled tongue, macaroni, and baked Indian pudding, all very good. The captain eats alone. The surgeon is very well informed on matters in general; he was once captured by the rebels and is emphatic in declaring that retaliation in kind is the only way to check their barbarity to our prisoners. After dinner we sat on deck for a time and read papers and books, and then we, the guests, were put on shore in great style, an eight oared boat with a coxswain. The navy would not suit me, mainly for lack of horse exercise. A cavalry man came just now to have his finger examined; he had it nearly chopped off with an axe. Now I shall ride the picket line with Col. Fox.

¶ **Monday, 17th, 7:00 P.M.** Capt. Soule came today with rations for 5 days. He reports that up the river, our guns demolished an engine and prevented the passage of trains since yesterday morning. This afternoon I accompanied Col, Fox to the old cotton press beyond all the pickets, where in the day time a man is kept as a lookout. About half a mile off we could see the ~~rebels~~ **enemy** mounting a field piece in the small work constructed by the naval brigade at our left before we came back. By means of signals arranged with the gunboat the latter was able to make one of eight shells burst right over the works.

¶ **Tuesday, 20th, 3:30 P.M.** Firing in the direction of Savannah has been heavy all day so far.[268] This morning I accompanied the Colonel to the lookout when we saw a mounted ~~rebel~~ riding through their works. On our return I found the cavalry men trying to corral eight cattle; I joined and think I was of as much service as any one of them, for Billy seemed to enter into anything unusual like that; but at last the animals, more active than **those** ~~we see~~ at the north, broke right through us and escaped to the woods. By the aid of further reinforcements **on foot** they were at last turned back and secured. Today Col. Fox had a new line of rifle pits dug about one third the way to the first, and on the left of the road; tomorrow the same will be done on the right; this inner line would be used in case we were compelled to abandon the first. There is no possibility of retreat from this place and the men would undoubtedly fight hard to hold it. We are reduced to hard tack and fresh beef, good but rather monotonous.

¶ **Wednesday, 21st, 4:30 P.M.** This morning half a dozen infantry and as many cavalry from the rebels came down the road to within rifle shot of the lookout and fired at us while the colonel and I were there; we were not hit and a few shells from the gunboat sent them back. The colonel and I both cut some wood today for warmth and exercise. David remarked that it was evidently harder for me than cutting off legs.

¶ **Thursday, 22nd, 11:00 A.M.** A steamer is unloading rations for 5000 of Sherman's troops that are expected here.

¶ **Friday, 23rd, 1:00 P.M.** At 7 a steamer brought Lt. Elliott with two field pieces which were landed; but reloaded again two hours later on account

268. Sherman's forces had captured Fort McAllister below the city a week before. Although Sherman moved his forces against the city, he left one escape route for Gen. Hardee, and on 21 December, Hardee abandoned Savannah. John F. Marszalek, *Sherman: A Soldier's Passion for Order* (New York: Free Press, 1993), 306–8.

of some change of plan by Gen. Hatch. We learned that Savannah is in Sherman's hands, and that Hood[269] was beaten in Tennessee. Capt. Soule ~~has~~ returned last night with sweet potatoes, butter, condensed milk and books, so for a day or two we shall live luxuriously.

¶ **Sunday, [December] 25th, 3:30 P.M.** I have just returned from a ride with Col. Fox to the lookout. The sergeant who went out a little earlier with a scouting party reported that in the woods at the right he came upon a picket post of three men about **one fourth of** a mile from our lines; they exchanged shots but without effect on either side; he also said that the "long roll," the signal of general alarm, was beaten further off; our mounted videts heard the firing; we could see nothing unusual. Yesterday the surgeon of the gunboat came to me to look at wounds caused by the accidental discharge of a gun on their picket boat. The ball passed through the arm of one man, smashing the bone midway between the shoulder and the elbow; then grazed the hand of a second man and buried itself two inches into the back of a third. The ball had been cut our, but he wished to consult **me** as to the arm. We cut down upon the bone and found that the damage extended about two inches; so we cut off the splintered ends and hoped the sound ends may unite and the limb be saved. We sent Capt. Luce[270] of the gunboat a can of milk and some other things, and their cook made us a nice pudding; he also sent us a piece of Washington pie which we cut very accurately into five pieces and eat with great deliberation and satisfaction at the close of a Christmas dinner of roast beef, sweet potatoes, bread and coffee. Capt. Soule has decorated these rather ~~dismal~~ **forlorn** rooms with moss and evergreens, and they really look quite cheerful. (Now is something very serious respecting Col. Fox.)

Alleged cowardice of Col. Fox at Honey Hill: extracted from a private letter from B. G. Wilder dated Boyd's Neck, Broad River, S.C., Dec. 25,"64.

"When the regiment formed in line Col. Fox and Major Nutt were both on the right and at the other end from Col. Hartwell when he called for the

269. Gen. John Bell Hood, a soldier at his worst in command of the Confederate Army of Tennessee, achieved a Pyrrhic victory at Franklin before having his army virtually destroyed by the Union general George H. Thomas at Nashville. Sifakis, *Who Was Who in the Civil War*, 316–17.

270. Lieutenant commander Stephen Bleeker Luce joined the United States Navy in 1841 and served as the head of the Department of Seamanship at the U.S. Naval Academy. He took commander of the *Pontiac* on 1 September 1864. Luce helped found the Naval War College after the war and served as its first president.

charge in which he was wounded, and in which, I hear, he has written that he thanks God the rest of the regiment did not engage. Not hearing the orders to advance Col. Fox left Major Nutt in command of the four companies and rode back to the road for orders. Here he was met by the aid-de-camp of Gen. Hatch who told him about it and informed him that he was now in command of the brigade; so he remained there or thereabouts for an hour or more, unable in the confusion to ascertain the truth of his seniority; as a matter of fact there were two or three his seniors. He also collected and reorganized the remnants of the companies so cut up in the charge. No thought entered his mind or mine that his being away from the regiment at the time could be misconstrued, especially by those familiar with his previous record. But it was easy to see how his enemies might misinterpret it to his disadvantage. The first I heard of it was from the chaplain the day before yesterday; he asked me if I had heard any unfavorable criticism of Col. Fox. I was astonished and appealed to Soule thinking that my known intimacy with Fox might have led to its concealment from me. Soule said that Major Nutt had received a letter from Lt. Perry, who is Gen. Hatch's adjutant, speaking as if the general was displeased and suggesting that a court of inquiry be asked to settle the matter; adding some expressions which (for I was permitted to read it yesterday morning) greatly lowered my opinion of both the writer and the receiver of the letter. Soule told Nutt that he should inform Fox and did so night before last. Fox at once called the officers together and declared that if they indorsed the view of the letter he should resign as soon as the present expedition was over. Nutt said he did; the others said nothing. Soule thinks it absurd to question the colonel's courage, but for his sake and that of the regiment, thinks it would be well to have the charges passed upon by a Military Commission. Fox says he has been in too many fights to condescend to sustain his reputation before a court of inquiry in this department, and especially when the only direct charge comes from one of our own officers who was never before under fire. Nutt is very ambitious and would probably be glad to see the colonel go, as did Major Wales; Hartwell and Perry, his cousin, are aiders if not originators of the calumny. I am more surprised and outraged than Fox seems to be, but we say little about it. I cannot bring myself to really admire Hartwell's taking the responsibility, if he did. Of leading the men against a work impossible for so small a number to take by direct assault."

¶ **Monday, 26th, 6:15 P.M.** This forenoon I was at the gunboat on business and was invited to remain and see the regular practice. For the first time I stood near a large gun and could watch the nine-inch shell as it

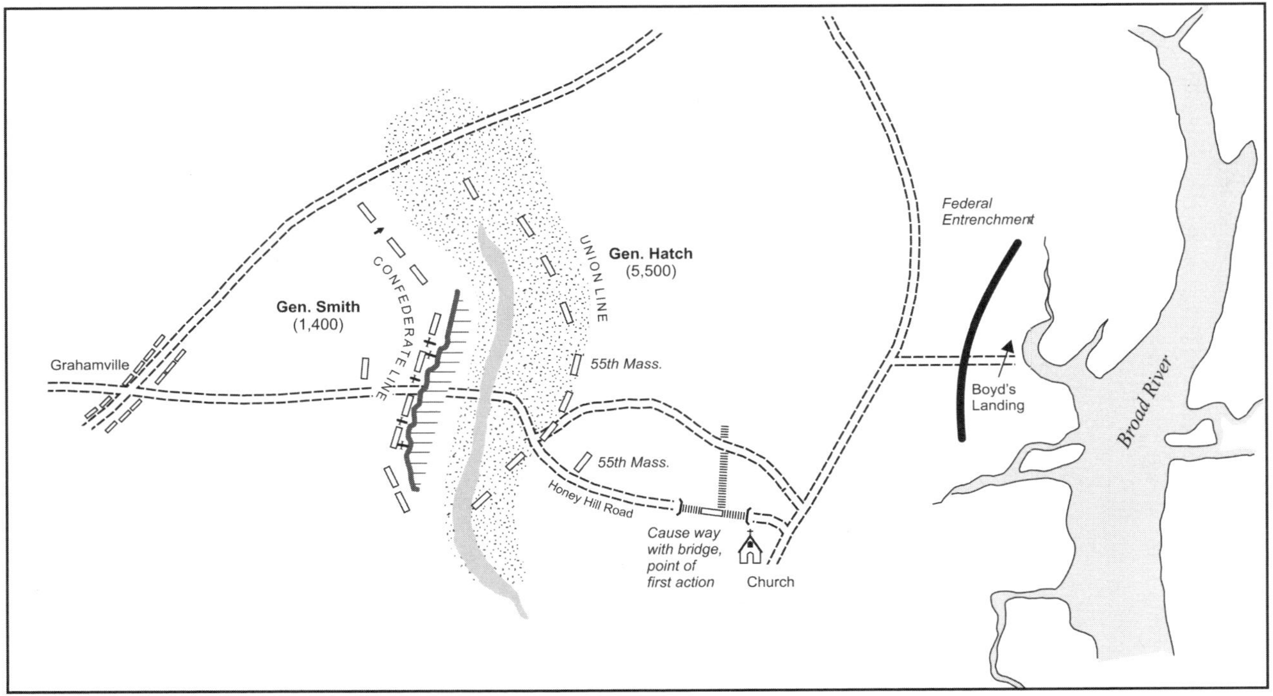

The Battle of Honey Hill, S.C., 30 November 1864. The detachment of the 55th in the middle of the Union line was the three companies commanded by Major Nutt.

suddenly appeared high in the air and then burst either in the air or near the earth. Capt. Joseph Green, my uncle, was expected today; he ranks as a colonel in the army and is second in command to Admiral Dahlgren.[271] I hear that he is much liked, and the captain of the gunboat said, "You have a price for an uncle."

¶ **Tuesday, 27th, 7:45 P.M.** Col. Fox and I have just returned from a call at the gunboat where I found Capt. Green. He was very cordial and he was so surprised that I had had no leave that he urged me to pack right up and go north with him; but this is certainly not the time to go. This forenoon I accompanied a reconnaissance in the direction of the naval battery work now occupied by the rebels. Half a dozen spare horses were mounted by some of our soldiers, so that there were about 20 "cavalry" headed by Col. Fox, Captains Soule and Thurber, Lt. Chickering and myself; about 40 infantry followed as a reserve, remaining at the cotton press. With a line of mounted skirmishers in front we rode to the top of a slight elevation about half way to the battery where a brass gun was mounted the other day; nothing could be seen now of it, but two musket shots were fired at us; one went close to Chickering. A few shots were fired in return and we then fell back slowly, hoping to draw out any force that might be stationed there; but we saw only the pickets and probably there was no considerable force this side of the church.

¶ **Wednesday, 28th, 11:20 P.M.** All regret profoundly the impossibility of recovering the bodies of Crane and Boynton; under the circumstances it is remarkable that even the wounded were brought off. Both were very highly esteemed as men and soldiers. This morning we went out again with a field piece and fired a few shots, but there was no special result. Our little demonstration may serve to distract the enemy somewhat and draw men from other points.

¶ **Friday, 30th, P.M.** At 5 A.M. Capt. Soule ~~with~~ **and** 20 men went into the edge of the woods at the right. An officer of the gunboat, with an equal number, went up the creek in boats to a point still further to the right; at 8:30, at a signal from the boat, they were to advance towards the left while

271. John Adolphus Bernard Dahlgren, an ordnance officer before the war credited with the invention of the 11-inch Dahlgren gun, commanded the South Atlantic Blockading Squadron. When Sherman reached Savannah, it was Dahlgren who opened communications between the general and Washington. Sifakis, *Who Was Who in the Civil War*, 165–66.

we went out on the road with a field piece. We saw mounted men at the naval battery; on our retiring a little, half a dozen rode to the left and three came slowly towards us; they had apparently not seen our gun for when it was fired and the shell whizzed over their heads they rode back very quickly. Soule soon joined us and the presence of those who had gone to the left was manifested by a shot that barely missed him. The boat party returned a little later saying that they had found a cavalry picket in the wounds and exchanged shots with them. At my return I found that the surgeon of the "Pontiac" had come for me to look at the arm he operated on the other day; the man had **a** chill; the wound seemed to me to be doing well, but I agreed with the surgeon as to the advisability of sending him to the hospital at the Head. (We learned today that the patient that was sent there some time ago began to bleed again and that the arm was removed; I take for granted that it was found impossible to control the hemorrhage.)

¶ **Saturday, 31st, 8:40 P.M.** Our pickets do not remain at the cotton press at night; last night a rebel picket was heard to come from there and his horse's tracks were seen this morning; tonight an effort will be made to capture him.

¶ **Sunday, Jan[uary] 1st, 10:45 A.M.** I was up three times in the night to see to our fire, for it was very cold. While doing so I always think of the poor fellows out on picket; we should be thankful for our quarters, rough as they are. It is still cold and I am writing on the steps where the sun shines. This house is surrounded by trees, and one, an oak, is twenty-one feet in circumference; its branches, **draped with moss**, would shelter half the regiment. ~~; it is draped with moss~~ About the dooryard are many laurels with abundant evergreen leaves; the branches are so thick as to shelter the horses even when it rains. For three meals we have had no bread, only potatoes and onions. We have been singing for an hour; had I anticipated the length of our stay, I would have brought my flute. For the first time in my life there are minutes and even hours when there is nothing particular to do; my books and papers are all in the Folly Island camp, so I cannot study. This afternoon a steamer brought rations for us and forage for the animals. Gen Hatch and the medical director also came; the former went out to the cotton press with Col. Fox; the latter got my reports for Dr. Brown. His name is Burton; he looks as if he drank and his manners do not suit me, but he was very courteous.

¶ **Monday, 2nd, 6:45 P.M.** A party from the gunboat went up the creek and, according to instructions from Gen. Hatch, set fire to the houses there and a big blaze and smoke they made.[272] Another party from the boat went up the road (Coosawhatchie?) and came upon a rebel picket so near his reserve they dare not try to capture him and shot him dead. Shortly after a man came riding down our road from the naval battery waving a shirt (once white) on a stick; he was received by our picket and brought to Col. Fox, a good specimen, he says, of the "poor white trash." His horse looked like oats were an unknown article. He said he had been conscripted and had served two years, but had never been in a fight; he and another had been ~~set~~ put on ~~the~~ picket ~~post~~ this morning; he sent his companion for water and had ~~come in~~ deserted; he had been for some time trying to come in but his family are in or near Savannah; **he said** that others were ready to desert and that, for one, he was tired of fighting a "rich man's war;" that at Grahamville is a brigade of 1500 men, and three lines of picket posts between them and us. For safe keeping he was ~~sent~~ put on board the "Pontiac" until he can be sent to Gen. Hatch. This afternoon Capt. Luce and Dr. Sherfy of the "Pontiac," and Fox, Soule, and Chickering and myself rode out in all directions as far as is permitted and so got quite a ride. Last night the fire was so hot as to ignite the floor beneath the hearth and the floor had to be ripped up and much water used for its extinguishment.

¶ **Tuesday, 3rd, 7:15 P.M.** The "Pontiac" ~~is~~ was ordered off to assist with Sherman's troops and left at ten o'clock; a little later her place was taken by a tug, looking like her baby, and carrying only two guns instead of fourteen. Her commander came on shore after dinner and we all rode the lines in order that he might be familiar with the situation; he loaned us some books. Later a steamer came to our landing with Dr. Burton and some wounded on board; he invited us to his cabin and offered us whiskey, which, to his amazement, we both declined. Later we rode the lines again.

¶ **Thursday, 5th, 6:30 P.M.** Just after dinner a man was brought to me who had stumbled and fallen on his elbow with such force as to dislocate the arm at the shoulder; the head of the bone ~~was plainly~~ **could be** felt in front under the clavicle. I tool him upstairs and with the aid of the steward and two nurses tried to get the bone into place, but in vain. Then, to relieve his pain and relax the muscles I gave him chloroform and tried again without

272. Gen. Hatch believed that Confederate lookouts were using the houses of the Fripp's plantation. Fox, *Record*, 47

success; I was quite discouraged and unhappy and announced that he would have to be sent to a hospital where there might be more assistance and special appliances. While wandering about disconsolately my eye fell upon a monstrous crowbar left here by former occupants; twice as heavy as the ordinary bar. It suggested to me a possibility. The patient, now revived from the chloroform, was placed in a box chair. The wrist of the dislocated arm was slung to his neck by a bandage; a great pad was put in his armpit; then a loop of broad stuff was placed at his elbow and the arm of the bar was put into it; gradually for half an hour the bar was ~~carried~~ **moved** further and further through the loop, and thus more and more weight **was** brought to bear upon the muscles that resisted the reduction; then we laid him on the floor; the two nurses pulled arm **away** from the body and the steward and I manipulated the parts; after four unsuccessful efforts a snap indicated the return of the bone to its place and there was immediate relief to all concerned; I really doubt whether the patient's physical pain equaled my dread of failing.

¶ **Friday, 6th, 7:45 P.M.** Early this morning a dozen colored people came in, eight men and four women; they said they came from a plantation beyond Grahamville, that more were trying to come in and begged that a gun might be fired as a signal to them, which was done. They said they had been in the woods and swamps for ten days, and their condition may be imagined. On being given the opportunity of a room upstairs they promptly bathed and cleaned their clothing and now present a very decent appearance; the women have been singing and their voices are pleasant. David and Corporal Smith went out beyond the picket line today and dug some sassafras roots with which tea was made for supper; it was not ~~at all bad~~ **"half-bad."** (When we were at Dr. Burton's cabin the other day something was said about "Honey Hill" that led Col. Fox to refer to the animadversions upon his conduct; the doctor said he need not trouble himself as long as the general was satisfied.)

¶ **Saturday, 7th, 7:45 P.M.** On picket today a man shot himself accidentally in the foot, but the ball fortunately passed between the bones.

¶ **Sunday, 8th, 11:00 A.M.** Again last night the beams under the fireplace caught fire and things had to be ripped up and water used. It was and is quite cold and we had a rather uncomfortable breakfast. Yesterday, Lts. Ellsworth and Bean took forty men and went after cattle; they drove back the pickets at the naval battery and burned the shelters there; then went up the Coosawhatchie road and drove off a picket reserve of six mounted men who ~~shot~~ **fired** as they retreated but hit none of our men. They shot three cattle and butchered them and came in with the meat at about 4. After dinner the colonel and I rode to the cotton press; we heard the shots at the cattle and from their number apprehended that a fight was in progress; so the cavalry and a company of infantry were ordered out, but presently our men appeared at the edge of the woods.

¶ **Tuesday, [January] 10th, 8:00 P.M.** Yesterday morning Gen. Hatch came in a steamer to arrange for removing our wharf and leaving a couple of scows by which we may embark when the time comes; while he was on shore his revolver and dressing-case were stolen; we did not learn of it till this morning and by close searching and questioning the case was found but the revolver has not turned up; three suspects have been sent to the General for inquiry.

¶ **Tuesday, 10th, P.M.** Three more negroes came in this morning; they report that the rebels are taking up the railroad at some point between Savannah and Charleston. This noon six mounted rebels rode quite near our picket at the cotton press but when our men rode out to meet them and answer their shots they retreated. All day the picket at the naval battery has been larger than usual, but no serious attack is expected. (Col. Fox's father writes advising him to simply live down the allegation against him; the adverse feeling seems to me already diminishing.)

¶ **Wednesday, 11th, 6:45 P.M.** A staff officer has brought orders for us to leave tonight and to proceed to Fort Thunderbolt near Savannah; we all rejoice at the prospect of leaving this place. At noon, while one of our corporals was getting wood just beyond the picket line a rebel suddenly appeared and asked if he would like a prisoner. "To be sure," replied the corporal, "Are there any more of you?" The man said there were not, and was brought in; he is a Kentuckian and by far the smartest and most intelligent we have seen; he was one of Wheeler's cavalry[273] and was to have been tried at Grahamville by courtmartial this morning for uttering treasonable sentiments; but being a favorite of a high officer he was permit-

273. Joseph Wheeler, a Georgian-born West Pointer, commanded all of the mounted troops in the Army of Tennessee, and after the fall of Atlanta, his corps was left to deal with Sherman while Hood moved into Tennessee. Wheeler, because of his later service in the Spanish-American War, was one of the few Confederate veterans buried in Arlington National Cemetery. Sifakis, *Who Was Who in the Civil War*, 708.

ted to escape. We are all packed and ready to go as soon as the steamer comes. It is quiet and moonlight.

Steamer "Fountain," off Hilton Head wharf

Thursday, 12th, 9:45 A.M. We all got away safely and quietly last night, most of us on this steamer, which awaited **the coming of** Col. Fox and the pickets in two small boats. The ~~rebels~~ have probably discovered our absence long ago; doubtless also they have appropriated my rubber overcoat which I was so careless as to leave on a chair. We reached the Head at 1 A.M. Col. Fox went ashore soon after daylight and has not returned. The horses came on a scow with the cavalry men; it is towed behind us; I can see Billy and David. It is a new and clean boat but so "cranky" that six men on the upper deck will tip it one way or another and the officer of the day has to be very strict.

Steamer "Wyoming," Skull Creek

Friday, 13th, 1:00 P.M. We started at about 2 P.M. yesterday. The two scows were first towed towards the shore. The larger one grounded about a hundred yards from the beach and all of the horses had to be pushed overboard and made to swim ashore; some resisted stoutly, but all were safely landed and then put in a stable; our Q.M. will remain with them till proper transportation arrives. Last night and till eight this morning we remained in the creek and Col. Fox spent the night in vain efforts to have a safer steamer sent us. We then hauled up to the pier. The men were not permitted to leave the pier, but the colonel, Capt. [**blank**] and I walked up to a little restaurant kept by a nice colored woman who, after insisting that she could do nothing for us, ended by getting us a fine breakfast of eggs, bread, flapjacks, coffee, butter, and molasses. I found a terrier, two cats, a hen and some chickens to occupy myself with. Before noon this steamer came to our relief. Dr. Brown was at Seabrook and spent the night at the house of a doctor there. He and Dr. Babbitt are ordered to rejoin the regiment and he advises me to apply at once for a leave. I am concerned for the property at the post hospital on Folly Island, for which I am responsible.

Camp near Savannah

Sunday, 15th, 10:30 A.M. I left off writing on the steamer and went on deck to observe the country that we were passing through. We passed Fort Pulaski which guards the Savannah entrance and entered a creek connecting the latter with Warsaw Sound, passing ~~behind~~ **inside** Tybee Island. After entering the sound the shores became gradually higher, with occasional bluffs 20 feet high. We passed a rebel battery just completed and deserted, the five cannon remaining in the embrasures. Two miles further up and about 6 miles below the city is Fort Thunderbolt, an old earthwork, partly dismantles, commanding the river. We landed at sunset amid a throng of Sherman's troops who were amazed at the apparition of colored soldiers. They offered us no violence, but during the evening a few were hustled or struck with sticks.[274] We marched out to a field at the edge of a wood and bivouacked for the night, building fires and lying on the ground; it was quite cold and we of the field and staff had left our blankets with our horses. Next morning Col. Fox and I walked out to look up a better camping ground and found one in a field surrounded by woods, with some old houses. To this spot we removed after getting our breakfast. As soon as the word was given the men rushed for the houses like tigers upon their prey, and in an hour they were down and most of the lumber removed. I had to attend to the burial of some horses. About the middle of the forenoon Sherman's men began to pass towards the landing on the way to Beaufort and one brigade settled right around us; its commander said he had orders to occupy this spot and as our own orders were indefinite we moved again, taking most of the lumber with us and finding another home from which to get more. At dress parade it is interesting to see the countenance of ~~the troops of~~ Sherman**'s men** and ~~see~~ **hear** their comments upon the **proficiency of the** colored soldiers. They "came to scoff" and remained to "admire." W.N. is here. In the afternoon we shall visit the wonderful cemetery, "Bonaventura."

Fort Barlow

Saturday, 6:30 P.M. Yesterday and the day before it rained. The fire in front of my tent smoked so that I could not sit but had to lie down. The colonel and adjutant had a sort of shelter but it leaked so bad that they had to dodge the drops. The rations of the men are out and the officers have little money; yesterday we got some oysters and cooked them with farina.

8 P.M. Dr. Babbitt's brother, an officer in Sherman's army, came after him, so this morning I went to visit the sick at the other fort, Jackson, manned by us. The way is along the dikes through the rice fields and they are very slippery after the rain and the fog is dense.

274. Historians have argued that Sherman's hostility to black soldiers disseminated throughout his army. Many shared his attitude that it was "an insult to our Race to count them as part of the [draft] quota." Glatthaar, *Forged in Battle*, 197; Marszalek, *Sherman*, 271.

¶ **Monday, 23rd, 8:30 P.M.** Yesterday afternoon I started for Savannah without my overcoat because it looked like clearing, but before I had gone half a mile it began to sprinkle and increased steadily; I supped at the Pulaski House and saw not only many officers but some northerners and some ladies. At 7:30 when I started for camp it was still raining and so dark that I left Billy to make his own way, which he did with his nose to the ground, often through water, at times up to his body. I missed my rubber coat badly. Occasionally it lightened, only to be blacker afterwards. Once, however, the lightening helped me out of a dilemma; Billy suddenly stopped and would not budge. While wondering why a flash revealed a telegraph wire between his legs and we had to back off it. We reached camp thoroughly drenched, and the poor huts looked like palatial mansions. After seeing Billy made comfortable I hung myself up to dry and am glad to say that neither of us is the worse for it today. In my absence they had callers, four gentlemen who came on the "Greyhound" with supplies from Boston[275]. Among them was Charles Carleton Coffin,[276] "Carleton" of the Journal, Mr. Briggs,[277] a ship builder, and Mr. Glidden[278] of Glidden and Williams; the **name of the** fourth I forget. It seems that their steamer got aground in the river and they came ashore. The fourth went to town last night; Mr. Glidden slept with Lt. Harmon; the others went to Mr. Archbold's for the night but all three came to breakfast with me. I liked Mr. Coffin very much. This morning horses were found for them and we rode into town together.

¶ **Wednesday, 25th, 7:00 P.M.** For a wonder I have not been in town today, or to ride excepting to visit Mr. Archbold's wife; she is much better. I had to give Billy a good switching this morning; neither he nor the colonel's horse would cross a certain narrow spot on the causeway leading over the marsh just below the fort and as our spurs were so dull as to make no

275. A meeting in Savannah called by the mayor in late December 1865 agreed to submit "to the national authority under the Constitution" and to bury "bygones in the grave of the past." When the mayor suggested exchanging rice for needed Northern supplies, Boston politicians and businessmen, and hundreds of small contributors who gave from $5 to $500, raised over $34,000 to send provisions to Savannah with no obligations.

276. Coffin began writing for the Boston *Journal* and the New York *Tribune* in 1850, at the age of 27. During the war, he was an official correspondent for the *Journal* and was present during many of the actual battles.

277. Harrison O. Briggs, who ran a shipbuilding operation in Boston with Edwin Briggs, offered his services to accompany the shipment to Savannah.

278. William T. Glidden, co-owner of the *Greyhound*, had offered to transport the supplies free of charge.

impression they danced and backed around until I feared they would both go over the edge; so I dismounted and found a switch and persuaded Billy with it and the colonel's horse followed. The Archbolds are very grateful for my attention and medicine and are disposed to give me whatever they can spare **in the way of food.**

On Steamer "Louisa"

Thursday, 26th, 9:30 P.M. My leave has come; it was given to Col. Fox this morning at post headquarters. It is for 30 days, but I shall try to go to Folly Island first. Billy will be safe in David's care. It is the first time since leaving Boston that I have been off duty.

"Norfolk," Port Royal

Friday, 27th, 7:00 P.M. I slept on the "Louisa" and took breakfast, and then found that she was not likely to touch at Beaufort; found this, a propeller, but her loading progress is very slow. 11:00 P.M. We reached Beaufort at 9.

Port Royal House, Hilton Head

Saturday, 28th, 7:30 P.M. On a boat I was glad to meet Rev. Mr. Fowler, chaplain of the 33rd U.S. Also Col. Hartwell, who told me he was promoted to be Brig. Gen, on recommendation of Gen. Foster; a reward for rashness and sacrifice of the lives of others. (Letters illegible)

Folly Island

Tuesday, 31st, 8:00 P.M. We left the Head yesterday having to tow a brig; both were so heavily loaded, that our progress was very slow. At ten we reached the dock at Morris Island and waited an hour for a boat to take us to Folly Island; then another hour for a wagon to take us and the mail to Stono Inlet. The load was so heavy and the horses so tired that I walked for a mile or two. At post headquarters I reported to Adjutant Dewhurst, and to his wife, and found a black kitten. With Col. Kozlay I walked to camp and delivered the mail. I visited the post hospital and began to open my trunk and boxes. The colonel's tent and mine had been taken down and I am in one of the Q.M.'s. I saw Capt. Goodwin at tea; he said I looked as brown and rough as one of Sherman's soldiers.

¶ **Wednesday, Feb[ruary] 1st, 8:00 P.M.** All day I have been working at my papers. There are two monthly returns of Q.M.'s property; and the invoices and receipts for turning them over to my successor, Dr. Grosvenor; certificates as to articles lost or destroyed; a yearly return of medical stores with invoices and receipts, all in triplicate. The post hospital has been very useful, serving as a temporary home for the sick of the 54th N.Y. and for those of our own men who were too ill to accompany us. The cat and kittens were living in the mess room, happy and playful.

¶ **Thursday, Feb[ruary]. 2nd, 8:00 P.M.** Capt. Goodwin and Lt. Ladd played whist after tea with Lt. Sprague and me, and Dr. Brown sat by and looked on. All my papers are finished and I am not responsible for any property.

¶ **Friday, 3rd, 8:30 P.M.** We are waiting for the steamer to take us.

¶ **Saturday, 4th, 7:00 P.M.** We still await the steamer, as she is in the river, I suppose we shall get off some time. Our Q.M. who should be on hand all the time and ready to look after things is intoxicated all the time; so are most of the officers on the island. The amount of whiskey drinking, especially among the Germans, is terrible. They say it is only while they are off duty, but in my opinion there is never a time when one is not liable to be called upon. I wish the use of whiskey were prohibited excepting under medical advice, but too many of the doctors use too much. I borrowed Lt. Dewhurst's horse this afternoon, but had rather an uncomfortable experience. It was half blind and evidently had not been used for some time. The excitement of riding with other horses made him uncontrollable; once I had to stop him by running into a thicket, and again by heading him for the sand bank at the side of the narrow road leading out to sea, or he might have carried me into the ocean.

¶ **Sunday, 5th, 4:00 P.M.** We left Folly Island at 3 and arrived here [**Hilton Head**] at noon. To our surprise the regiment has left, we know not for what place.[279] Again I hesitate as to leaving, but Dr. Brown urges me to take the opportunity. Dr. Babbitt, who is with the regiment, has been commissioned surgeon in one of the colored regiments and after he leaves it will not be so easy. There is no food at the hotel and Capt. Goodwin and I camped out last night under a blanket on the dock; the slope of the dock cause me to roll away from him carrying the blanket with me; after discovering it he held on more tightly.

279. At the end of January 1865, the regiment had been ordered to Morris Island but stopped at Hilton Head. Gen. Foster reassigned the regiment to take part in an expedition led by Gen. Potter up the North Edisto River. The regiment was back on Folly Island by 7 February. Fox, *Record*, 51–52.

U.S. Navy Receiving ship "New Hampshire"

Monday, 6th, 8:30 P.M. I got a room last night at the Port Royal House through the kind offices of Capt. Hodges, but it contained two other men and no table. I am on this ship for tonight in order to reach the "Massachusetts" in the morning; the officers are all going to bed.

Steamer "Massachusetts": off Charleston

Wednesday, 8th, 11:15 A. M. We are waiting for the mail from the fleet. After breakfast I went in a small boat to the Flag ship to ask Admiral Dahlgren for permission to go on the "Massachusetts;" he was very polite and at once wrote a note to the captain of this boat, I was assigned to a room with three berths but no bedding; Navy officers always carry their bedding with them; I would rather have fewer berths and at least one blanket. They will take no pay, even for board. Had I known this I should have hesitated before asking for passage; but I get home much earlier than if I waited for the regular boat. While at the Head Gen Littlefield,[280] superintendent of recruiting, offered me the surgeoncy of the 104 U.S. Colored Troops.

8:45 P.M. We started at 2 and have a strong wind astern; the ship rolls heavily. The officers are very pleasant.

¶ **Thursday, 9th, 7:00 P.M.** We passed Cape Hatteras at noon and the water is smoother.

French Hotel, New York

Saturday, 10th, 10:15 P.M. We were delayed by the ice and did not reach Philad'elphia and did not land till 11:30, just too late to catch the 11:15 train for New York, which would have enabled me to catch a train for Boston tonight.

Young's Hotel, Boston

Monday 13th, 4:30 A.M. I have just arrived from New York and will get a little sleep.

[Wilder did not write his daily letters while at home.]

280. Brig. Gen. Milton Smith Littlefield practiced law in Illinois and supported Abraham Lincoln before entering the war as a captain in the 14th Illinois. He became colonel of the 21st USCT before taking over a brigade on Folly Island. A man of contradictions, his postwar activities won him the dubious title "Prince of Carpetbaggers." Boatner, *Civil War Dictionary*, 485; Richard Nelson Current, *Those Terrible Carpetbaggers* (New York: Oxford University Press, 1988), 236–38, 240–41.

On the way South, French's Hotel [New York]
Monday, [March] 6th, 11:30 A.M. The chief Q.M., Gen Van Vliet,[281] expects to send a vessel south in a day or two.

On transport, "New York"
Thursday, 9th, 10:00 A.M. (There was an unexpected delay and I went back to Boston) The berths are not selected till the steamer sails. I found Capts. Woodward and Thayer on board. There is a heavy fog; the mate has just announced that the captain will not come on till tomorrow morning.

¶ **Friday, 10th, 1:00 P.M.** Dr. Guler has just come on board; I remembered him from Washington and he was polite enough to say that he remembered me.

7 P.M. We started at 3 P.M. having taken on board only about 300 soldiers. It is too cold to write.

¶ **Sunday, 12th, 3:45 P.M.** Mr. H. F. Durant is on board and the only civilian whom I like. He is a Boston lawyer who some years ago was counsel for the so-called rioters in the case of Sims, the fugitive slave.[282] He is a very fine looking, grey haired, very refined and pleasant, though some what sad, having recently lost his only son. With him I enjoy talking very much. There is a New York merchant going to Savannah as an agent for the refugee's union commission and in part for his health, finally there is a rebel Brigadier named Harrison whose grand plantation near Savannah was destroyed by Sherman's troops, but he has shown that what he did was under compulsion; he returns ruined as to property.

¶ **Monday, 13th, 4:00 P.M.** This morning I talked to Mr. Durant as to the Spider project and he was much interested. We arrived this forenoon and a boat will go to Charleston this evening. Capt. Hodges said he has seen

281. Gen. Stewart Van Vliet, a graduate of West Point who served in Mexico in the supply service, was Gen. McClellan's supply chief before his clashes with the navy caused him to be relieved. He spent the balance of the conflict organizing supplies in New York and forwarding them to the field armies. Sifakis, *Who Was Who in the Civil War*, 673–74.

282. Thomas Sims was an escaped Georgia slave who had reached Boston before being arrested under the federal Fugitive Slave Law in April 1851. His trial and return to his slave owner, the "Sims tragedy," became a cause célèbre among Massachusetts abolitionists. Albert J. Von Frank, *The Trials of Anthony Burns* (Cambridge: Harvard University Press, 1998), 27–29, 90–91; Leonard Levy, "Sims' Case: The Fugitive Slave Law in Boston in 1851," *Journal of Negro History* 35 (January 1950): 39–74.

Gen. Littlefield this morning and he said the 103rd was to be filled to its maximum first[283]; later I saw Gen. Littlefield himself and he was very complimentary; said he had forwarded my application to Gen. Saxton offering to furnish certificates. I signed the name of McGrath to the bills I spoke of, but the Q.M. said as it was only his mark there should be a witness; so I have sent them to Col. N. P. N. Hallowell in New York, telling him all about it. An officer of our regiment was here today and says all is well and that it is near the city.

Camp at Rickersville, near Charleston

Tuesday, [March] 14th, 9:45 P.M. Our steamer left the Head at midnight. I awoke just in time to pass Morris Island and see from the inside the forts that we had been so long looking and firing at from the outside. The city presents a most melancholy appearance, the lower part deserted by the inhabitants, the only sign of life being the guard on the wharf and a few idlers. Capt. Woodward and myself got our things to the wharf and then waited for the sergeant of the guard to pass us through. We got some breakfast at a restaurant and came to District Headquarters, where we found Lt. Perry, Gen. Hatch's adjutant. Capt. Woodward got a horse and rode out to send mine in with a team for our things. The headquarters are in the house of Major Pringle of the C.S.A. It is an elegant mansion. There is a garden and stables.

9 P.M. I had the opportunity to take a shower-bath in Lt. Perry's room, and to play on a fine melodeon. At last Col. Fox and David and the horses arrived, and we rode out Meeting Street to the camp which is just outside the old rebel line of rifle pits. Brigade Headquarters are in one house and ours in another, with the hospital in a wing of the latter. Col. Fox surprised me by saying that Dr. Brown had told Gen Hartwell that he should soon go home, having been out three years, and hoped I would stay on and succeed him. I learned that on James Island Col. Fox behaved very bravely, on that and other accounts Col. Hartwell has said that he is quite satisfied and has told the Major [Nutt] that he is; and that if the latter does not withdraw his remarks he should ask for a prefer charges against Fox.

¶ **Wednesday, 15th, 9:45 P.M.** The officers have just left. They came to adopt resolutions as to the deaths of Crane, Boynton and Hill and to ar-

283. It is not clear if Wilder was referring to two regiments or put down the wrong numbers once. The 103rd USCT was organized at Hilton Head, 10 March 1865; the 104th USCT was organized at Beauport, S.C., 28 April–25 June 1865.

range for paying for the casket in which the body of Hill was sent home. Later two of the band played some dance music on the violin and guitar and they were called in and we danced; Col. Fox and I were partners and in the last Hartwell joined. On separating, we all sang "Auld Lang Syne." I rode in the woods alone this morning and with Fox this afternoon

¶ **Thursday, 16th, 11:30 A.M.** This morning I talked to Fox about the silk project and he says if he were to be interested in it he could bring $50,000 to it. I rode out afterwards and jumped Billy over some logs so high that David said, "Good Gracious, Doctor."

8:30 P.M. Orders have come for our transfer to James Island. While in the city this morning a boy ran after me and asked if I was a doctor; and if so would I go and see a sick lady; I went with him and found a young girl ill with the cold and fever; her mother is in the country and a colored woman is caring for her. She has a small white curly dog ~~which perhaps I can get~~ **with whom I made friends.**

James Island

Saturday, Mar[ch] 18th, 7:45 P.M. The regiment was taken across to James Id. yesterday afternoon, but the tide was too low to permit horses to come so Dr. Brown and David remained with our horses. The colonel wished me to accompany him. We halted for the night at a building that had been a rebel ordnance depot; the men stacked their arms in the field about the house; the officers entered the house and lit a match to see the way, when some loose powder exploded and they rushed out thinking a mine might explode; they fell over each other and knocked a small boy heels over head down the steps; most of them slept there but I preferred to place a stretcher in a small wood house. In the morning I held the first sick-call since my return and then we came to this place. Like yesterday the weather was beautiful. James Island is much larger than I supposed, with **several** creeks and **some slight** elevations. Our quarters were the Headquarters of Gen. Elliott who commanded the island; there is a large house of three stories, surrounded by trees and plantation houses of various kinds; five companies are to be here; three at Fort Pemberton and two at Fort Pringle. The hospital is to be in some small houses on a rising ground and Dr. Brown is to be there. Just now the officers of the 54th N.Y. which is to be relieved by us but is not yet gone occupy the larger part of this house, but when they go the line officers of the five companies will also be in the house. (Who?) The colonel, adjutant and I are in a large front upper room. Yesterday at Charleston I called upon my young lady patient and found her much improved; I ~~got~~ **took** her some tomatoes (canned) and some soda crackers and advised her to look up some other doctor rather than wait for me. The band received the new instruments just after dark night before last and sat up half the night so as to appear to a good advantage on the march yesterday. While the regiment marched in from camp, I went to have my two horses shod. The new one has improved his appearance, and the ball has come out of his leg; he is very easy going and sedate and looks upon Billy's pranks in a paternal way.

¶ **Sunday, 19th, 9:00 P.M.** I have had exercise enough this afternoon. We started right after dinner, the Colonel, Adjutant **Mutelle** [Mutell][284] and Capt. Goodwin, the latter on my spare horse. We rode along the entire line of earth works from Fort Pringle at the ~~right~~ **west** to Lamar at the ~~left~~ **east**. Their strength is extraordinary. **Between the two forts above named** there are ~~half a dozen separate~~ **smaller** works connected by a parapet and with traverses to protect the guns and men; ~~there~~ **outside** is a broad wet ditch; outside **that**, and beyond a series of lunettes for ~~skirmishers~~ **outposts**. Thirty or forty guns could have been brought to bear upon our ~~attacking~~ columns ~~moving~~ **advancing** over a level plain obstructed by felled timbers. We passed through Lamar ~~against~~ which ~~our attack was directed~~ **we had hoped to capture** last July and continued down the road to ~~the small battery which we did take and found~~ Rivers Causeway passing the ditch and bank that protected us from the shell that whizzed over out head. ~~A little further on~~ **In front of the lunette** we found, as we feared, the bones of our slain lying (apparently) as they fell but scattered (**presumably**) by the ~~carrion crows~~ **buzzards**; (**apparently**) not a particle of earth had been cast over them; six skeletons were found **but no entire skulls**.[285] ~~The skulls were missing whether used as trophies by the soldiers or as specimens by the doctors.~~ Col. Fox is to have the bones gathered and buried. Capt. Thurber joined us before reaching this place and he and I returned to Fort Pringle while the others went by Lamar to Fort Johnson. I held sick-call at Pringle and then at Pemberton, where Co. C, I and G are stationed, and then reported to Dr. Brown, returning to supper after dark. It was a delightful ride and Billy enjoyed it too; at least 15 miles.

284. Charles W. Mutell, a bookkeeper in Springfield before the war, served as a sergeant in the 42nd Massachusetts before accepting a lieutenant's commission in the black regiment in December 1864. He was brevetted captain in March 1865. Fox, *Record*, 101.

285. The entry for 4 July 1864 reported that all but one of the fatalities in the 55th Massachusetts suffered canister shots to the head. Crushed and partial skulls on the battlefield would be consistent with such wounds.

¶ **Monday, 20st, 8:15 P.M.** This morning Capt. Goodwin and Soule took a party of men and gathered all the bones of twelve skeletons, including not only our own but the other regiments, and were met by the entire regiment; they will be buried soon with appropriate ceremonies.[286] This morning I arranged a supply of medicines in the hospital panniers and in the two knapsacks[287]; the first to be kept here, the other two in the two forts respectively. After dinner Col. Fox and I walked out to select a place for the cemetery, where our first dead man was buried this evening. A man of Capt. Goodwin's company was taken with bleeding at the lungs and was sent to hospital where he will probably die. There is a case of varioloid.[288]

¶ **Wednesday, 22nd, 8:45 P.M.** This morning I rode back the way we came to the long bridge over a creek which was partly burned by the rebels when they retired and imperfectly repaired by our forces. Col. Fox had given an order that our team should not cross it. Yesterday, however, a teamster did attempt to cross it and when over the deepest part the bridge gave way and only the driver and one horse was spared. I found yesterday, and still more today, several cocoons of a large specimen suspended from the bushes. On opening one I found it filled with live spiders about the size of pinheads. I cannot imagine what they live on. Unlike our protégés they have no brush on the legs. On some cocoons were small holes which led me to think at first that the inmates had escaped; but on opening them, in addition to the proper inhabitants were other cocoons, smaller and oblong, containing numerous black bodies, the chrysalides of a small ichneumon fly, a few of which had just come out with their wings. I also found a few fragments of what appear to be the remains of the chrysalis skin of caterpillars. Putting all these things together I infer that the caterpillars were enclosed with the spider's eggs for the purpose of furnishing food for the young spiders when hatched, and that the little ichneumons having ascertained the fact pierced the cocoon and deposited the eggs in the caterpillar; these eggs had hatched and produced the small black

286. Wilder's account of the way in which the soldiers were killed, the collection of their bodies, and their subsequent burial perhaps explains the "mystery" of the headless bodies discovered in 1987 on Folly Island, a "mystery" that has been incorporated into their tourism literature. See www.FollyBeach.com/ghosts.php.

287. By 1863 many other Union regiments had replaced the cumbersome medical knapsacks with a new supply kit, the surgeon's field medical case. *Arms and Equipment of the Union*, 226.

288. Varioloid is a mild form of smallpox occurring in people who have already had the disease or who have been vaccinated.

cocoons and in a few cases they had transformed to the fly; so the little spiders were defrauded of the food so carefully provided by the parent spider. Nevertheless the latter have grown, so the matter is far from clear. So far the little spiders are quiet and remain within the cocoon even when it is cut open. I am interested to know how and when they make their way out. The brown silk that forms a loose mass within the cocoon is very large and strong, as is also that which suspends the cocoon in the bush but the cocoon itself seems to consist of a thin inside layer of silk smeared with gum which renders it water proof.

¶ **Thursday, March 23rd, 11:00 P.M.** Major Wales arrived at tea time.

¶ **Friday, 24th, 8:45 P.M.** I have written to Capt. Hodges to send the boxes of instruments for measuring from the Head.[289] This morning Major Wales borrowed from Major Nutt the horse he sold him when he left the regiment. We visited Fort Pemberton and Pringle and turned to the left at Secessionville and found some houses that we thought might be the quarters of Gen. Elliott; we were in error as to our present quarters being his; but the larger house had been burned and the smaller one had been used for ordnance. Then we started for Fort Johnson but recollecting an impassable bridge and it being nearly noon, we concluded to return by a new road, on which, however, when less than two miles from camp, we encountered another broken bridge and we had to retrace our steps and did not reach camp till 1:30 P.M. We found several cocoons and a cocoon of the Cecropia.

¶ **Saturday, 25th, 8:45 P.M.** Soon after breakfast, Wales and I started, having first sent a corporal and four men to Fort Johnson with a request to loan them a boat which they were to row down the creeks to Secessionville where we would meet them and go to Long Island. We saw a bird attack a cocoon and tear a piece out of it; it would be strange if that were the way the young spiders escaped. We rode to Pringles and along the line to Lamar. We ascended the tall lookout and gained a fine view of this and adjacent islands. Seeing nothing of the expected boat and it being low tide, and after looking

289. The standard instruments provided by the Sanitary Commission to Wilder for his collection of the required measurements included a large andrometer, spirometer, dynometer, platform balance, facial angle, calipers, and measuring tape. Methodological problems, however, plagued all collectors. There was never an adequate protocol to adequately define the spectrum of racial categories, confusion surrounded the correct use of the facial angle instrument, and measurements with the spirometer could be conducted in several different ways. Haller, *Outcasts from Evolution*, 23–26.

about for a boat in which we might row ourselves we explored the houses and cabins of Secessionville and then set off for Fort Johnson, thinking either to see our men in the boat or to meet them on the road, in case they could not get one. We visited all of the forts on the way and so missed our men who, as we ascertained at Fort Johnson at 1:30, had not been able to get a boat and has started off to tell us but as we might as easily miss them if we tried to overtake them, and having learned that the long bridge was not able to bear our horses we looked over Fort Johnson and returned that way, having ridden all over the part of James Island held by the rebels and about 25 miles, with an excellent appetite for dinner at 3 o'clock. We found that Col. Fox had been to Charleston having been sent for by Col. Hartwell. The latter has ascertained that Major Nutt, not daring to press the charges directly against Fox, had decided to resign for promotion in one of the colored regiments, giving as a reason his inability to get along with his commanding officer. Fox says that if he does this he will disapprove this resignation unless he prefers charges.[290] He will not give him the opportunity to say such things in another regiment. Also that he will ask for a regular court martial. Of course Hartwell feels badly about it. He is coming over tomorrow to attend the burial of the remains of the men killed on the 2nd of July. Fox is very hard at work making our returns and reports; our adjutant is away and Lt. Carter, acting in his place, is inexperienced.

¶ **Sunday, [March 26th, 7:30 P.M.** The ceremonies this day were very impressive yet simple. All the bones were packed in one coffin and carried by men who had themselves been wounded in the same action; and the coffin was draped by the United States flag and those of Mass. and of Ohio, from which state several of the men had enlisted. On it, and buried with it, was a beautiful wreath of roses and jessamine and some other white flowers made by Major Nutt. The entire regiment attended, voluntarily excepting those who could not be spared from the various camps; the detachments from Pemberton and Pringle walked 2 and 5 miles respectively. At the ground the chaplain gave an excellent discourse; it is inside a fort with Charleston in plain view. Hartwell wore his star for the first time and looked very well in it. He and Wales shook hands, but somewhat coolly. Yesterday as Major Wales and I passed the long wharf we saw on it, under guard of our picket, some furniture which they had confiscated from a sergeant of some head quarters

290. Nutt remained with the regiment, and in June 1865, when Fox resigned his commission, he was promoted to lieutenant colonel. Nutt was mustered out with the 55th Massachusetts on 29 August 1865. Fox, *Record*, 99

in town who thought it would be a "good thing to have in the g [sic] house." We told Col. Fox of it and he sent a boat around for it, and this morning our eyes are gladdened by the sight of a white marble topped table, sideboard, a black marble top center table, two hair cloth chairs and two hair cloth sofas; one chair and one sofa we gave to the line officers; and the other chair to Major Nutt; we retained the other things, which give the room a much more agreeable look, besides being very convenient.

¶ **Monday, [March] 27th, 8:00 P.M.** I have ridden at least 30 miles today, and Billy is as frisky the last mile as the first. Major Wales and I went down the Island to the place where we fell back after the attack of July 2, and crossed to Coles Island. Here we found some of the 3rd N.Y. Artillery making a raft on which they proposed to cross to Long Island and carry rations to one of their number who was left there in charge of some property but who is now unsupplied because some members of our Co. C who were here yesterday for their property carried off also the boats by which they had been accustomed to take rations to them. We had expected to use these boats. Finding that the rafts would not be ready for some hours we kept on throu the belt of woods on Coles Island thinking to find some signs of our spider, but we saw none. So we returned by the other side of the island. So far all the bridges had been fair, but after crossing ourselves one long and frail footbridge, less than four feet wide and with no railing; really just planks laid on trestle work, before leading our horses over we found a sort of causeway or low corduroy over a marsh apparently without bottom, for a pole could be thrust down into the mud without touching hard soil; when nearly over this we came upon a dead horse who, trying to cross had stepped between the treacherous logs and, unable to regain his footing, had broken his legs and died miserably after still further damaging the causeway. This looked bad, and so evidently thought our horses, but we disliked to go back, involving a detour of 5 or 6 miles; so, after consultation, I held the horses and the major, pulling some logs from the mud and taking up others behind us, got enough to make a narrow path by the side of the body, which after having looked at we hoped the horses would now pass; but Billy, after carefully stepping over a gap before coming to the repaired place, forgot to take a long step with his hind leg, and it went through and the other followed; for a moment my anxiety was intense; but I let him alone so as not to confuse him, and by getting a firm hold with his front feet and crouching almost flat he gave a spring and extricated himself; then he walked calmly by the dead horse and upon the bridge; the other horse, either from greater experience or observing Billy's accident, or from having longer legs, did not slip; we were greatly relieved when we were safely over. We found the raft nearly completed but promised the men to ask Col. Fox to have one of the boats sent back; and, after arranging to be there and cross on it tomorrow we returned across James Island to camp.

¶ **Wednesday, 29th, 9:00 P.M.** With no great shame I admit to being somewhat tired tonight; having ridden about twelve miles and walked about 15 between breakfast and a 6 o'clock supper, and a part of the walking was due to Billy's only caper. I sent a note to Capt. Hamilton at Pemberton this morning asking him to send the boat he had promised me today round to the creek between Long and Tiger Islands to await the arrival of the major and myself who proposed to ride to the latter island rather than go in the boat all the way. We went first to the hospital and then by a cross road running along between a wood and a swamp into the road we commonly took to Fort Pringle, This was about ten o'clock There is a ditch as usual on each side of the road, and a sort of dike thrown up beyond it; on top of the dike many of the bushes on which we are accustomed to find the cocoons; and indeed we did find them here till I stuffed my pockets full, about a hundred; there were more in the swamp beyond, and it was useless to gather any more of them. On reaching the line of forts we went through by the first road and as this did not lead quite in the direction of which we wished to go we decided to strike across the island, hoping to reach a more direct one. Alas, I was reminded of the lines of Coventry Patmore,[291] "A road's a road," etc. For soon we got among the trees felled by the rebels all along the front of their lines to obstruct our advance; they were so closely piled as to prevent any jumping which would have been easier for the horses than the very high stepping and short turnings and twisting to go around such as we could not get over. At last our wanderings were stopped by a marsh we dared not venture into and now it was out of the question to return the same way and we made for the forts themselves in the hope to strike some cross road. But no. After jumping over ditch and off from the rifle pits outside the main line of forts, we had the choice between a swamp on either side and the ditch and parapet in front. Having found a dry place in the former and a less steep place in the latter we valiantly charged and

291. Coventry Kersey Dighton Patmore was an English poet whose best-known poem, *The Angel in the House*, contained the phrase cited by Wilder. The full passage is:

A road's a road, though worn to ruts;
They speed to travel straight therein;
But he who tacks and tries short cuts
Gets fools' praise and a broken shin—

carried the work. Some distance to the right we found a new road, which none of us had ever before noticed, perfectly straight and evidently unfinished leading through the swamp in the direction we wished to go, so we advanced on it for about a fourth of a mile the horses sometimes sinking pretty deep, till we were stopped by a place six feet wide that we dared not ride through and disliked to walk through leading our horses. After examining the depth of the mud with a stick I proposed to put on it some wood that might bear us and relieve the horses of our weight. The major jumped over the ditch at the side to get some wood, and I, forgetting Billy's bad habit of taking a run on his own account, let go of him for a moment to adjust the wood in the mud when no sooner was my back turned than he started off, followed by the other horse. In vain we shouted "whoa," and entreated them to return; they only went the faster and the last I saw of Billy was a series of contemptuous flings **of his heels** in our direction as he disappeared through the works in the general direction of camp. Here we were, several miles from camp. ~~I fear we both ejaculated a short but expressive word, but it did no good~~. At first, by a sort of instinct we started after the horses, but we reflected that we were already half way to our original destination, so we turned in that direction. After walking a mile or two we met Major Nutt and Capt. Thurber on horseback and requested the latter to see that our horses were attended to if they came his way and that they were sent up to Fort Pringle, where we should stop on our way back. We passed over the battle ground of July 2, and found, about a hundred yards beyond where the other skeletons were found, another, mostly in a ditch; I got the bones together and some one will go for ~~it~~ **them** with a bag. I could find no ~~head~~ **skull** or even parts of ~~heads~~ **one**, although ~~parts of skulls~~ **such fragments** were found among the others on closer examination. Presently we came to the wide marsh between James and Tiger Islands which our forces crossed to the attack; it was deep and sticky enough but not as on that occasion; then we reached Tiger Id. and the spot where we landed from Long Id. Here, to our great disappointment, we found no boat; on the opposite shore was the raft, but it might as well be a hundred miles off. There was no sign of men and shouts and whistles failed to bring them. We concluded that the boat Capt. Hamilton was to send Sunday had been used to take them all away after the raft had been poled up from Coles Island. We were disconsolate and pretty hungry, for now it was one o'clock. To add to our discomfort it began to rain. In the hope to see Coles Id. from the lower end of Tiger we walked the whole length of the latter in the wet grass only to find that another island intervened between Coles and Tiger and we could se nothing of the former. The major smoked a pipe and we started at two, reaching Pringle at 4. Here we found our horses, they having been apprehended by Major Nutt while hesitating between two roads. A good canter brought us to camp, tired and hungry, but I had to attend to some sick, so we waited for supper. It seems as if we were fated to never reach Long Id.

(A sheet is missing here, No. 1 of the 30th)

¶ **Thursday, 30th,** Corp. Andrew Smith has just been summoned by the colonel to tell what he has done today. A few days ago we were informed that one of the greatest rascals in the regiment, Pelette,[292] the former drum-major, reduced for misconduct, and Ditcher,[293] of Co. F, who was once drummed through the camp for stealing from a wounded comrade, had been seen in Charleston in citizen's clothes, evidently intending to desert. This morning Capt. Grant took Smith and Serg. Letts, Pelette's successor, and two men. Capt. Grant went to the house where they were said to be and found them. Pelette at first refused to go and Smith took him aside and explained to him what a crime desertion is. He asked permission to change his cloths and see his wife. Permission was granted, and while in the house he contrived to escape and get into the street. Smith ~~pursued and meeting some of the 54th Massachusetts he~~ learned that Pelette had gone to the square in which some of the regiment were awaiting transportation. Here Smith found him; upbraiding him for his treachery and told him he must go with him; Pelette refused and Smith told him he had his choice, since he himself had none, to follow him or be shot. Pelette evidently did not think Smith would keep his threat, (as he afterwards admitted) and began to move off; Smith fired and the ball entered his left breast; he cocked it for a second shot when Palette said he would go with him, but had gone only a few steps when he fell. Smith left him with the 54th men and got a stretcher and notified Capt. Grant; Pelette was taken to the hospital where his death is expected. Col. Fox told Smith that he could not have acted otherwise; that, hard as it was for him, his prompt action might be the means of saving the lives of others who might be tempted to follow Pelette's example & be shot for disobedience. Smith's story was manly, simple and straightforward, with no sign of boasting or mock regrets; for he knew he had done his duty and obeyed his orders. From this incident our men will recognize the

292. Alfred C. Pelette was reduced on 8 November 1864. He was a 28-year-old sailor when he enlisted in Company C. Fox, *Record*, 114, 122.

293. Benjamin F. B. Ditcher, an 18-year-old barber from Boston, deserted the regiment in July 1865. Fox, *Record*, 130.

authority and power of the non-commissioned officers and on that account, it is well that it was not a commissioned officer. (Pelette recovered, deserted again and is said to be at Chestnut Hill)

¶ **Friday, 31st, 8:30 P.M.** Today was held an inspection of the regiment by Gen. Hartwell; the five companies here this morning and the other five this afternoon. Last night I played almost if not quite the only practical joke of my life. The Q.M. had been in town on business and returned about midnight with a bottle of (or so he said) very fine whiskey. He brought it in and some glasses and asked us to take some. It was politely declined by the colonel, Major Wales and myself. We all retired, leaving the bottle on the table. I thought it would not present a very good appearance to the officer of the day when he came to report at reveille and it occurred to me to exchange the content of the bottle for vinegar of about the same color and quantity. I then told the colonel and the major and we retired. Pretty soon the clink of the glass was heard and an exclamation of disgust and in stalked the Q.M., angry yet amused.

¶ **Sunday, April 2nd, 3:30 P.M.** Soon after breakfast Fox and Wales and I went to Johns Island for the first time. We took a bridge near Fort Pringle and crossed to Battery Trenholm, the largest in the vicinity. It has embrasures for 23 guns & 14 were left in position, but spiked. It commands the only bridge to James Id., and Col. Fox will ask permission to move most of the regiment to it. I have another small pox case; the first has recovered. Yesterday, noting that the little spiders seem more active in the sun, I dropped a cocoon in the bottom of a jar and put in a wire bent as a loop, the convexity towards the mouth of the jar. When it was set in the sun the little ones came out (through the rent I had made) and ran up and down the wire and made a net between the two arms. But as soon as the sun was cut off they became quite and huddled together like bees. After dinner I took David and the two horses and borrowed a pair of high boots from the Adjutant and went to a marshy field not far from the field; here in water about a foot deep were many bushes bearing the cocoons; my boots enabled me to gather them, and David got some, riding one horse and leading the other on dry ground. Capt. Soule says Major Nutt is making out charges against Col. Fox; the latter says that he will very likely admit the facts but deny the alleged motive.

¶ **Tuesday, 4th, 11:30 P.M.** Yesterday Major Wales and I started on our first successful attempt to reach Long Id. Leaving our horses at Pringle

Capt. Thurber furnished us with a boat and crew who rowed us down Stono River to what we supposed to be the right channel; after ascending for a mile we found we were in error and retraced our track and went lower down; this took us between Coles and James to the lower end of Long; here we encountered mosquitoes in great numbers, hungry from long fasting; from them we protected ourselves as well as possible by our handkerchiefs. We soon found one common cocoon and then a second; then half a dozen like the one mentioned as having been found a week ago; it is of loose silk containing yellowish spiders less quiet than those from the common cocoons. These cocoons are not glazed, and are protected from the wet by being made on the underside of an evergreen plant vine. We walked the whole length of the island, 2 ½ miles, but found no others. We saw two big owls and killed a big black snake. On returning to the boat we found that the tide was too low to permit returning in her and we set across to Tiger Id. and walked back over the island to Pringle. The results of the expedition were negative. I counted the cocoons and find about 500, containing at a moderate computation, 250,000 spiders. We have decided to place most of them in a belt of woods on Coles Id. where there is ample protection for them, and where the land is less likely to be taken for agricultural purposes. We have cut small holes for the escape of the young spiders and strung them on cords, about 20 to three feet. This afternoon we got a dispatch from Gen. Hartwell that our regiment and the 54th N.Y. and a section of artillery are to go on an expedition into the country for 8 – 10 days, leaving the baggage here under guard.

Camp at Rickersville

Wednesday, April 5th, 7:30 P.M. I rode to Coles Id. this morning, about 20 miles in 2 ½ hours, and disposed of the cocoons as planned. We left the island at about 3:30 and are to spend the night here.

Goose Creek

Wednesday, 12th, 4:30 P.M. Porcher Mansion.[294] More than a thousand colored people of both sexes and of all ages have followed us.[295] Capt. Soule and I with two companies are left to guard them. Some rebel

294. The house was part of Philip Johnston Porcher's plantation called Otranto. (He renamed the plantation Goslington but the original name was more commonly used.)

295. Fox described in considerable detail the long refugee train of freed people attached to the regiment at this point. Many were terrified because of the belief that Confederate cavalry had murdered "unarmed colored men, and perhaps women, left behind in the swamp." Fox, *Record*, 72–73.

cavalry are on the other side of the river, and have taken some stragglers. We are quartered in and about the house of Mr. Porcher, on a beautiful place, about one-fourth of a mile from the bridge.

¶ **Thursday, 13th, 3:00 P.M.** An officer came up last night with the glorious news of the capture of Richmond and Petersburg with 2500 prisoners and 500 guns. We hardly knew whether to laugh or cry. The joyful news was communicated with the soldiers and through them to the colored refugees; for an hour there was great rejoicing. At noon today a man with his family from Columbia was passed into our lines by the rebel lieutenant on the other side of the creek; he said the rebels had known what had happened five days ago, and we were impressed by their dogged determination to hold out to the last. Gen. Hatch sent an order to send out as many mounted men as could be spared the way we came to convey an order to Col. Chipman[296] who, with his regiment, the 102nd U.S.C.T., started out after us two days ago but by following our rear met us not. By the utmost only 16 horses and mules can be found for the duty, and they are tired and ill fed; the officers, however, had no power to revoke the order, so this morning Lt. B. Roberts started with his little force. In an hour he returned reporting that after driving back the half dozen pickets at the other end of the bridge and emptying two saddles he came upon at least 30 more at a turn in the road and was forced to fall back; the number seems probable, for the man who came thu [sic] yesterday said that at least 25 were together at what seemed to be their headquarters. It was not thought prudent to make a second attempt and a report was sent to Gen. Hatch. This forenoon I made the rounds of the whole camp; among the colored people there were naturally some women and children ill, which embarrassed me somewhat; I was careful not to hurt any of them with too much medicine. There are two cases of measles, and probably will be more. Our ~~expedition~~ **force** numbered more than 1000 men, about 700 being from our regiment and the rest from the 54th N.Y., with ~~a section~~ two pieces of artillery. The furthest point reached was Eutaw Springs, and during the last two days we held the rear; the ~~rebels~~ **enemy** followed close behind, shot one ~~colored man~~ **negro (not a soldier)** as he was climbing a fence and might have made trouble for us; ~~but the colonel ordered the artillery to send~~ a couple of shells ~~after~~ **were fired at** them and then we ~~saw~~ **could see** them riding thru

296. Col. Henry L. Chipman was the son of a Michigan Territorial Supreme Court justice and lived in Detroit before accepting his commission, first in the 2nd Michigan and later in the 102nd USCT. Boatner, *Civil War Dictionary*, 154.

the woods on a parallel track. ~~A few miles from Goose Creek we left the state road and took the road to the right leading to Monks Corners, near Biggins Creek; here we turned again to the left~~ We stopped at Pineville, a small town in the woods. Here, a few days before, the negroes made a stand against the rebel scouts, and after killing some of ~~them~~ **the latter**, they were defeated and sixteen of them killed. In the town we found some outspoken rebels and some pretended unionists. That night we ~~pushed on to the~~ reached the plantation of Marzzck [?] Porcher, whose house was burned next morning by our rear guard; he was sent a prisoner to Charleston and his overseer, a very respectable old man, was left ~~to live on the place and have~~ **in** charge of such negroes as ~~might~~ **chose to** remain ~~with him~~. At noon next day we reached Eutaw Springs, the scene of a battle in the revolution. Here **was seen** the first rock since leaving the coast. The water bubbled in a very interesting way at the bottom of a depression. Here we stopped for 24 hours, sending small parties in different directions for forage and to look for Gen. Potter's command on the other side of the Santee. Just before reaching here Gen. Hartwell and two of his staff rode alone to a house at some distance from the road when they were fired upon by half a dozen rebels, but escaped unhurt to our forces. Capt. Torrey then rode out with a flag of truce and while talking with the lieutenant in command a party from the 54th N.Y. came up and unceremoniously captured him and three of his party and carried them to the general; on the way here they were most improperly robbed of their horses, guns and even blankets; the lieutenant said that he had lain in the bushes that day and had seen our whole force pass; they were naturally enraged at the violation of the flag of truce and still more so when, on being released, their equipment could not be found. The same lieutenant is now in command of ~~those~~ **the force** on the other side of the creek for we have today seen a pass in his writing admitting a man to our lines. We marched about 20 miles a day, starting at 6 or 7, halting at noon for dinner, and keeping on till dark and once till near midnight. From Eutaw Springs we crossed to the state road which we reached at noon of day before yesterday, David rode my other horse, but as they had been pretty hard worked during the previous week we often got off and walked. Both that horse and the big saddle-bags which he carried were very useful; no other officer has one or the other.

[13th, cont.] 6 P.M. A recent order forbids the detail of soldiers as officers servants, and David has been really acting as Headquarters orderly and had time to do what I needed; but the arrangement was irregular and undesirable. Among the refugees is a man named Edward Gailliard, a light mulatto, the son of his master, and unusually well appearing; he has a wife and two children; David has been showing him how to care for Billy.

Camp at Rickersville

Friday, [April] 14th, 9:00 P.M. There has been a great celebration over the glorious news from the north; surely the war must be over soon. Among the children is another little fellow named Robert whom I may try to get.

¶ **Sunday, 16th, 4:15 P.M.** Soon after dinner yesterday Col. Hartwell rode out and said that Hon. Henry Wilson and others of a visiting party would leave Charleston at 2:30 to look at us and the refugees, and he wished all to be present. We waited in vain till 5, and then I went to Charleston on business, meeting the distinguished visitors on the way. This morning vaccinated all of the recruits. I have secured the little boy, Robert; he is too good to be lost; he can help Edward in various ways; if I am promoted he will serve as my second servant; if not there are many who will be glad of him. Gen. Hartwell rode out with Rev. Henry Ward Beecher and others and ladies; he and others spoke in Charleston this afternoon but I had some business letters to write and let David and Edward go to hear them.

St. Andrews Parish

Monday, 17th, 8:30 P.M. We have moved again to a place right across Wappoo Creek from James Island.

¶ **Tuesday, 18th, 7:45 P.M.** This is a fine old house on a triangle of land between the Ashley and the Wappoo Creek[297]; here were the headquarters of a brigade of Sherman's troops; I am writing in a front room on the lower floor, but raise ten feet from the ground. Only two companies have yet come, the others awaiting the arrival of the 102nd U.S. This morning I was busy attending to the transfer of the headquarters property and visiting the hospital on James Id., where there are several small pox cases. This location is preferable to the one on James Id., being higher, more open to the sea, and more accessible from the city.

¶ **Wednesday, 19th,** On the way across the river we met another with the sad and terrible news of the assassination of the president. It has cast a gloom over all. ~~The rebel~~ Sympathizers **with the deed** have the grace **or the prudence** to conceal their feelings. Many houses and stores are draped.

297. The regiment had moved to Crescent Farm, owned by the Steinmeyer family.

Minute guns are fired all day. (It was not I but Wales(?) who thought of drawing silk directly from the worm as from the spider; and on the same day Prof. Wyman suggested it; the patent covers that and drawing it directly from the insect.)

¶ **Thursday, 20th, 8:30 P.M.** The rest of the regiment is here.

¶ **Friday, 21st, 8:45 P.M.** This is named "Camp Hallowell." The subjoined plan gives an idea of the arrangement of this house. At the left of the table is a window looking over the garden and towards the sea; at the other side of the window is a closet with shelves. Under the piazza all around and under our room it is open; the single basement room being under the large office. The space under our room I have had floored today and arranged for a dispensary and for making measurements for the Sanitary Commission; for the present the regimental hospital is dispensed with; the very sick are being sent to the post hospital in the city. Today I have unpacked and set up all the instruments except the andrometer which needs to dry out before running smoothly.

¶ **Sunday, 23rd, 8:40 P.M.** After sick call I gave chloroform to a man on whom Dr. N. Brown operated on account of a wound on the hand caused by the accidental discharge of his gun while on picket last night. The colonel, adjutant, Major Wales and I rode over the picket line; we have to maintain it because the rebel cavalry and scouts, according to the refugees, do not accept the surrender of Lee as the end of the war. The little spiders are fed according to a suggestion of Major Wales, by dipping a string in blood and hanging it in their jar; they take hold very well, especially the new kind that we think may be the young of the Nephila.

¶ **Monday, 24th, 8:10 P.M.** The work has been divided between Dr. Brown and me as follows: - He attends to the sick call of the companies here between 7 and 7:30, while I ride out to the other two companies in the forts.[298] This afternoon I went to see the Major at his work room in the citadel; the officers of the 35th U.S.C.T. give him every facility. I have the advantage of the clerical aid of Nicholas Said,[299] the native African, who is very intelligent and writes an excellent hand.

298. Companies B and F were stationed at two redoubts. Fox, *Record*, 75.

299. Said was captured by Tuarag slavers in his youth and was a slave in parts of Europe and Asia before being manumitted by a Russian nobleman. He traveled to the United

¶ **Tuesday, 25th, 8:30 P.M.** Today I got eight large window shutters with which the Dispensary has been floored nicely, and some curtains have been hung on wires so as to screen off the parts in which the measuring is done. My instruments being ready I began on Said. By the way, he is very philosophical in his mind and interested in unusual things, religious problems, etc. A flag-of-truce from Gen. Lovell[300] says that the regular troops have been disbanded upon orders from Gen. Johnston[301]; nevertheless the refugees are ill treated and sometimes killed, perhaps by men who have taken the oath but who go out at night; if some were hanged the others might cease their depredations.

¶ **Thursday, 27th, 10:00 P.M.** All day I continue to vaccinate, and now all but one company are done.

¶ **Friday, 28th, 8:49 P.M.** The vaccination is complete excepting about six men; Dr. Brown says we are ahead of any other regiment in that respect. This forenoon I measured three men, including David Lee. In order to show the amount of colored blood I have ruled spaces in which are stated the facts regarding the parents and grand-parents.

¶ **Sunday, [April] 30th, 8:00 P.M.** Said has read more than half of the D.L. & W., and expressed his intention to read all of Swedenbordg's [Swedenborg's][302] works. Major Wales and I differ in our measurements in this respect; after the full inspiration measurement he thinks the man should be measured in his ordinary condition, and says Dr. Buckley

---

States with the intention of returning to Africa, but he never left America. He was teaching in Detroit when he enlisted, and after serving as corporal and sergeant, he was reduced at his own request and detailed to the hospital. In 1873 he published *The Autobiography of Nicholas Said, a Native of Bornou, Eastern Soudan, Central Africa.* A new edition of his book, edited by Precious Rasheeda Muhammad, was published in 2002 (Cambridge, Mass.: Journal of Islam in America)..

300. Gen. Mansfield Lovell's unsuccessful defense of New Orleans turned many against him although his forces had been inadequate given what he faced. In March he was directed to join Gen. Johnston's forces in the Carolinas. Sifakis, *Who Was Who in the Civil War*, 396.

301. Gen. Joseph Eggleston Johnston, an effective commander who clashed with President Jefferson Davis, was given the task of stopping Sherman in the Carolinas but not the resources to accomplish it. Sifakis, *Who Was Who in the Civil War*, 346–47

302. Emanuel Swedenborg was an eighteenth-century theologian, scientist, and Christian mystic. After a spiritual awakening in which he believed he was selected by God to reform Christianity, he wrote eighteen theological books. The one being read by Said was *Divine Love and Wisdom*.

used that measure; while I think there should be a complete expiration so as to show the mobility of the chest; the differences should be stated in connection with our results.

¶ **Monday, May 1st, 8:45 P.M.** I have written to Dr. Gould[303] as to the measurements. Gen Hartwell has sent an order for us to be ready to march and scientific work may be interrupted. While riding on the picket line with Col. Fox we saw a rattlesnake about 4 feet long with a splendid set of rattles.

¶ **Tuesday, [May], 2nd, 7:45 P.M.** This morning, and yesterday morning, I gave a lesson of 15 or 20 minutes to Robert; he is very bright and desirous to learn; he has already learned his letters and is beginning to spell short words.

¶ **Wednesday, 3rd, 9:15 P.M.** Among the six men I measured today I found one whose fingers extended ½ inch below his knee, and the spread of the arms is a foot more than his height; rather a monkey.

¶ **Saturday, May 6th, 9:30 P.M.** We are to leave tomorrow at 6:30 and the day had been fully occupied with preparations, for Dr. Brown is on Gen Hartwell's staff and in disregard of an order that says that no detail of a medical officer shall prevent his doing duty with his regiment unless it has three on duty; he is content to stay in town and do nothing.

Summerville

Tuesday, 9th, 5:45 P.M. We left Camp Hallowell before 7 on Sunday morning. During the first mile we followed the main road from Charleston to Savannah but soon turned off to the right on a narrower road, often completely overhung with branches; it was less dusty, but bad enough owing to the long drought. On the way we passed few houses, all deserted, and saw only a few colored people. At sunset we encamped in a field surrounded by woods about 14 miles from Charleston. Here, about 8 o'clock, occurred a terrible tragedy. Our men sometimes quarrel but never before seriously. That evening two of Capt. Soule's men had some words and while one was sitting on the ground the other came up behind him and struck him with a club on the side of the head. I reached him without delay; he was gasping

303. Benjamin Apthorp Gould, the first American to hold a doctorate in astronomy, administered the commission's survey. Haller, *Outcasts from Evolution*, 22–23, 29.

and his heart was beating slowly, so I determined to give him a chance for his life; I cut the scalp and raised the depressed fragments of the skull but he died while I was operating; his brain was deeply bruised. He was buried the next morning and his murderer will be tried by court martial.[304] We started early and marched till noon; the knapsacks bore heavily and it was one of my duties to decide what men should be relieved of them or even ride themselves. Towards noon we crossed the Ashley River and came upon a higher and better country, hilly in places and with many flowers. We passed only one house occupied by whites and they seemed to be Unionists, for they cried at the sight of the flag and at the music.

This is a beautify town, on high land, covered with trees excepting in the center, and very healthy although we miss the sea-breeze. Most of the houses are good and none have been destroyed. It has always been the rendezvous of the rebel cavalry but on a large tree at the outskirts of the town we found a written order from Major Jenkins, dated last Saturday, in which he disbands all his men in accordance with orders from Gen. Lovell commanding; which agrees with the report of their flag-of-truce of Saturday evening. On our march we met a few armed men but no force and had no trouble. The inhabitants seem quiet and well disposed, tho doubtless some feel bitter.

7:45 P.M. The "Harper's Magazine and Weekly" are great treats to the people of this house, a clergyman and his wife, who are very nice and sensible; by the accounts of others and from their present manners and conversation he was never in favor of secession and even warned the planters of his parish of the retribution certain to follow their refusal to educate their slaves. Yet he says a great change has taken place among them in this respect. At a public meeting old Judge Wardlaw who, six years earlier, had framed and introduced the bill which became law prohibiting the instruction of slaves, stated that as the law was still in force he could not allow it legally but that any one who wished was welcome to teach the slaves on his plantation. The major of the town is still here but most of the inhabitants are old men, women and children; some of the houses are protected by the provost guard.

¶ **Wednesday, [May] 10th, 8:40 P.M.** This morning I called upon Dr. Westcott, a fine old gentleman with a long beard; he had asked the clergyman,

304. Regimental records indicate that Pvt. Lewis Dickinson of Parkersburg, Virginia, was murdered by Pvt. John Shaw from Wayne County, North Carolina, and that Shaw deserted after being released from arrest in July 1865. Fox, *Record*, 77, 142, 143.

Mr. Mood, to ask me if I could lend him a certain instrument. At supper time we were visited by three rebel officers in full uniform, mounted but not armed; the highest in rank was a captain; they had been detached from Johnston's army before the surrender and wished to give their parole. They were very quiet and gentlemanly. As a guide for Gen Hartwell, we sent David; the colonel thought he would be a fine specimen of a colored soldier. This afternoon I inspected my spiders and found the young had emerged from the cocoons pierced by the ichneumons but none from the entire ones; yet when opened the young were found in great numbers.

¶ **Thursday, 11th, 8:40 P.M.** Billy stepped into a vacant post hole today and we had a fall resulting in the loss of some skin from the end of his nose and from one of my legs; luckily his leg was not broken, the hole was in the grass and almost invisible. It is reported that some depredations have been committed by our men and Col. Fox has gone out in the rain with an officer and some men to try to catch the disturbers. This noon I was summoned before the military commission which is trying Shaw for killing Dickerson; the accused was present but does not seem specially concerned.

¶ **Saturday, 13th, 12:00 A.M.** We moved yesterday to a place about one-fourth of a mile from the former camp; there is a larger house for headquarters, another for the hospital and a small one for the boys and quartermaster's men. Our baggage arrived before night. The mess arrangements are in my care tho I would rather pay twice as much and be relieved of them. We had plenty of milk, butter, eggs and blackberries, but this morning our hard bread was all gone and I have had to arrange for some meal to make mush for dinner. Last evening a rebel lieutenant and surgeon came in to give their paroles. This house looks as if it had two stories, for the front is raised and there are blinds as if it had two stories, so that at first we hunted for stairs; but it really has but one.

8 P.M. This camp is very pleasantly located on a hillside along the foot of which is a little run in which the men may bathe. The place and our quarters are very pleasant but we do not fancy the conduct of some of the people, especially the women; companies B and F have been acting as provost guard, but many of them would not appear on the streets till this noon when our men were relieved by white troops. Yesterday I was called upon by a Mr. Collins, a New Churchman, formerly of Savannah, who heard of me through Mr. Johnson, with whom Mr. Heyward stopped when in

Charleston and upon whom I called a week ago; Collins is quite strongly secession, but knows enough to accept the inevitable. Service is to be held at one of the churches and the ministers wish a separate place reserved for colored troops; I would prefer that they stay away. It was intimated to us that the general and others would be at the house of the mayor, an unrepentant rebel, and that the presence of the band would be acceptable; but Col. Fox very properly thinks if the inhabitants cannot stand us as guards they should not enjoy our band. A day or two leave of absence was given Nicholas to go to Charleston and marry a young woman who he met in camp at Rickersville.

¶ **Tuesday, 16th, 8:50 P.M.** This morning I met a Confederate doctor, the surgeon of the 3rd S. C. Cavalry, and had a pleasant chat with him; he will let us have some straw for the hospital beds.

¶ **Thursday, 18th, 9 45 P.M.** We have orders to leave for Orangeburg. There has been a change in the attitude of some folks here. The mayor and four others actually went to Charleston to ask that we be retained in place of a white regiment, the 56th N. Y., but in vain. My old horse is ill, like the major's and we shall leave them here lest their complaint infect the other; a Mr. Morse will care for mine and receive $25.00 if he recovers; if not, nothing; he will be put out at pasture

Orangeburg, May '65

Saturday, 20th, 4:10 P.M. We left Summerville at nine yesterday on a strange train of freight cars. The first contained the officers, their baggage and the sacks of oats for the horses; the second, with slats at the sides, the horses themselves and the men to care for them; inside and out; then four cars with the regimental baggage, and then 18, full of soldiers inside and out. Our progress was slow, mainly because of 2 hot boxes[305]; in fact we had to stop at Branchville because the car containing our horses was so defective in that respect. While a better car that we found there was being substituted the horses had to stand on a platform and as the engine was so near I thought best to stand by Billy's head, while Edward stood behind him to prevent his backing off. The others left their horses to their servants and one of them did back off and sprain his leg. Suddenly the platform gave way under us, but fortunately none was seriously

305. Wilder was referring to the overheating of axle bearings housed in a box packed with oil-soaked rags or cotton to reduce friction.

hurt. There were seven horses. We reached this place, or rather its outskirts, at 4 in the afternoon; we had to stop here because for a mile this side of the town and all the way beyond far as Columbia, the rails were torn up and twisted by Sherman's men. The horses were unloaded by piling bales of hay at the sides of the cars. After having some tents pitched for the sick and making arrangements for supper and shelter for ourselves, Col. Fox and I rode up to the town. The Colonel's verbal orders were to guard the town, but we found that, contrary to orders; the Lt. Col.[306] of the 25th Ohio had brought his regiment up to the town instead of remaining at Branchville; on hearing that Col. Fox outranked him by several months he remarked that he would not be commanded by the colonel of a "nigger regiment." Fox's orders were not in writing and did not contemplate the presence of other troops, and Hartwell himself is expected today, so he thought best not to have any trouble and we remained outside the town. Hartwell's three staff officers here, Captains Blaw and Torrey and Lt James, showed their condemnation of Horgton [Haighton] by remaining here last night and today.

¶ **Sunday, 21st, 2:15 P.M.** In the train yesterday came the 54th N. Y. and all of brigade headquarters. After dress parade the general was to go up to the city and Col. Fox said it was good plan to show as full a force as possible, in view of the fact that the acting mayor of the place had tried to secure the retention of the 25th Ohio; so I went with the party, consisting of Gen. Hartwell, Capts. Blaw, Torrey, Nelson, and Holcomb, Lt. James, Col. Fox, Dr. Brown, and myself. Suddenly Billy leaped right up in the air and soon the cause appeared in the form of a man riding a horse without a saddle, with a halter only, dashing by. The horse was evidently running away and it was soon out of sight, I predicted that something would happen, but Dr. Brown said it would not be proper to ride on. About one-fourth of a mile further on we found a detachment of men and two wagons halted; the men were gathered about a civilian lying against the fence, his head bruised and bloody; some whisky was given him and having ascertained that no bones were broken he was left in my care and the rest rode on. It seems, that in spite of the rider's shouts, the runaway horse surprised the party and knocked down this man and a lieutenant; the latter's lip was cut a little but this man was struck by the horse's hoof. He proved to be a Kegler, from Boston, to whom I had been introduced only

306. The lieutenant colonel of the regiment at this time was Nathaniel Haighton, who would open a foundry and machine business at the end of the war.

half an hour before and whose pleasure or business visit was thus marred. Soon the general's coach came along and the injured men were helped into it and we rode up to the town. We had been directed to the hotel and, it being now nearly dark, we took this to be a large white house near the road.

A gentleman came out and said it was not the hotel but if any one was injured we were welcome to bring him in, so he got a rocking chair for the Mr. Kegler and a basin and water, and after I had put a stitch in the officer's lip I washed and dressed Mr. Kegler's head. A rebel captain who was living there assisted and we had a pleasant chat; both he and the old gentleman, who had been chaplain of a regiment, were on James Island in July last; the other was a Presbyterian clergyman; he got a little brandy for Mr. Kegler. We then went on to the real hotel and left Mr. K. there and I reported to Dr. Brown and reached camp about 8:30, hungry and tired. This forenoon I rode up to inquire for Mr. K; he was fairly comfortable but suffered some from both his head and the hand, which had been bruised in the fall. He had brought a load of ice from Charleston and my fee was as much ice water as I could drink.

¶ **Monday, 22nd, 8:10 P.M.** Never, since our first landing at the desolate north end of Folly Id., have we been so without comforts and even the power of presenting a respectable appearance. The war is over and we are in no danger of losing clothing or camp equipage from the enemy yet we were ordered to leave the latter behind although other regiments brought most of theirs; we have had no pay for nearly nine months and are thus without the means of presenting a creditable appearance before those who especially need to be impressed with it. Finally, our brigade commander, who has for months seemed to be losing interest in the regiment of which he is still the nominal commander, now signs his name simply "Brevet Brig. Gen. Vols." Some of the officers feel very badly at the condition of things.

We broke camp soon after seven and marched through the town in fine style, to the wonderment of the inhabitants. I forgot to mention that the dress parade last evening was attended by fully a thousand negroes of both sexes and all ages who were rejoiced to see a regiment of their own color presenting such discipline and skill. We came up to the old revolutionary camping ground selected by Col. Fox and myself last Saturday. A log house had been put up for him and a wall tent each for the adjutant, major, quarter-master and me. In front of mine I have had made a shelter of Pine-boughs covered by canvas for Robert, whom it seems best to keep separated from the other boys; Edward and David sleep near the horses. The camp is in the midst of pine trees and is healthy and pleasant.

¶ **Wednesday, 24th, 9:15 P.M.** This forenoon I rode over the rising ground in the rear of the camp and came upon quite a large place inhabited by an elderly lady, the mistress, her daughter, the husband of the latter, who had been a Confederate surgeon, their children, a younger lady, and a soldier. The mistress promised to share with us the butter they made. I had a pleasant talk with the doctor and the soldier. They declared their intention to treat their former slaves as required by the government, and some of the latter with whom I talked said they were well treated. This afternoon I have been unpacking the measuring instruments; all came in good order excepting the scales which I had not packed well; a corner of the platform is broken but Serg. Jenkins thinks he can repair them. To his great surprise I lifted on the machine over 500 pounds, but he has beaten me by more than 100; he is a large man and has always been very athletic; he is the only one who has blown as much as I on the spirometer. Robert took a fine lesson today, mainly on the effect of the final e on the penultimate vowel; I did not use those terms but he understood.

¶ **Thursday, 25th, 8:40 P.M.** This morning I had a glimpse of the Confederate Major Generals Lovell and Preston with their staffs as they were about to enter a house to confer with Generals Hatch and Hartwell; they were a fine looking couple.

¶ **Friday, 26th, 8:30 P.M.** Tonight came an order from the Sec'y of War to Gen. Gilmore to discharge two sergeants in order to accept commissions, a thing we have long striven for.[307]

¶ **Saturday, 27th, 9:00 P.M.** Most of the day has been spent utilizing an empty tent box given me by the Q.M. Part of it I converted into shelves for

307. The two sergeants were James M. Trotter and William H. Dupree. A special order remustered John Freeman Shorter, who had been severely wounded at Honey Hill, so that he could be commissioned. All three men officially became second lieutenants on 1 July 1865. A fourth sergeant, Charles L. Mitchell, who had been commissioned but was discharged for disabilities following Honey Hill before he could be officially mustered out as an enlisted man, was accepted as an officer by the Association of Officers of the 55th Massachusetts. Fox, *Record*, 96–97, 108; Trudeau, *Voices*, 231, 241; Berlin, *The Black Military Experience*, 308.

my own tent, and the rest into a table for our mess to stand in the colonel's log house and so relieve my own table. I am getting supplies for the mess in an odd way. Having no money we get sugar on credit from the sutler and exchange it with the colored people for butter, berries, plums, peas, and other vegetables, and some times for corn bread; with other articles from the sutler we fare quite well, but wish the paymaster would visit us.

¶ **Sunday, 28th, 8:45 P.M.** Col. Fox and Capt. Hamilton leave tomorrow and will probably not return. I attended the chaplain's service this afternoon. The colored people come in considerable numbers to attend and to see the dress parade; they often ask me for medicine or advice. Billy has exhibited a strange taste, for ground coffee; he likes it almost as much as sugar.

¶ **Monday, [May] 29th, 8:45 P.M.** Robert made a comical mistake today in his lesson. I printed ME and asked him what it spelled; he replied "You" which was natural and logical, tho and polite, but he soon saw the error and laughed at it. He is getting along well; knows all the vowels and their short and long sounds and the effect of a final e. I am teaching him the Lord's prayer, a phrase at a time; he and David are remarkable boys, and I am much impressed at the effect of a word from them when I am annoyed or perplexed by others. This morning a negro brought me a basket of peas, pears, beans and cucumbers and a plate of thimbleberries from Mrs. Gramelin, the mother of the doctor; I wrote her a note of thanks and shall send some coffee and sugar.

¶ **Tuesday, 30th, 8:50 P.M.** I have sent Mrs. Gramelin some sugar, coffee and tea and she has sent a leg of veal, some peas, cucumbers and berries.

¶ **Friday, [June] 2nd, 11:00 P.M.** Major Wales arrived last night. I have been at work on my Monthly Report.

¶ **Sunday, 4th, 9:30 P.M.** Major Wales and I took a long ride today to a village called Jonesville where lived a Mr. Farnham of whom the major wished to inquire respecting a lady friend of Miss Baddish. We started at about half past eight, but twice missed our way, arriving between 1 and 2. We were very hospitably received by Mr. F., his sister and Mrs. F; his sister and their mothers, who, with the children and some boarders, make a family of 15; our horses were stabled and we were invited to a good dinner. We found a good piano there and I played a little and chatted till five, being advised to avoid the heat of the day. Mr. F. had been a wealthy planter and had lost much to Sherman's men, but he was disposed to accept the situation. The lady of whom the major was to make inquiries had gone to Charleston already. Being directed, our return trip was shorter, and we cantered most of the way. Near a house, about a mile and a half from camp, we met two soldiers on a narrow path; they seemed in haste; I called out, "What regiment?" One replied, "102nd." But they had no passes and I made them approach, and give their names and found that they were members of our Co. G. So I ordered them to turn back and walk ahead of me. The path was narrow, with a deep cutting for the railroad on one side and a dense thicket on the other. The major rode behind me. On reaching a bad place where, to avoid falling into the cutting, we had to ride very cautiously, I heard a few suppressed words and then a rustling into the thicket, and on getting across the bad place I found one man had gone. Drawing my revolver I called twice "Come out of there," and as there was no response I fired; the major came up and fired, and I again till five shots had been fired. It did not occurred to us that one might dismount at a time and keep firing till he dared conceal himself no longer; so we rode with the other man to camp. The one who escaped will have several heavy charges to answer for if he ventures to return. Orders have been received for all regimental and company commanders to put their accounts in shape with a view to being mustered out. Examining Boards have been appointed to determine the relative merits of officers and ascertain whether they desire to remain in the service.

¶ **Monday, 5th, 11:00 P.M.** The man who eluded us yesterday was found dead in the thickets[308]; a shot had entered one eye and passed through the brain; the autopsy was made by Dr. Brown and myself and signed by Dr. Brown; the direction of the ball indicated that he was lying down at the time with the intent to escape. A board of officers was appointed by Major Nutt to determine the merits and responsibilities and their report, with that of Dr. Brown and my testimony has been sent to Gen. Hatch. For various reasons I have assumed that the ball was from my pistol. Of course I am sorry, but the lesson was sadly needed; there were twenty men in the guard house for "running guard," and Major Nutt, in indorsing the Report, not only upholds my action but thanks me for putting a stop to

308. Pvt. William Morris, a twenty-one-year-old from Fremont, New York, was the soldier shot "in attempting to avoid arrest." Fox, *Record*, 134.

the increasing evil. The men do not like the idea of the major firing, but have nothing to say against me.

George T. Garrison's account in his Diary of the killing of Private Wm. Morris, Co. G, 55th Mass., June 4, 1865; his entry is the 5th.

"Late yesterday afternoon Dr. Wilder and Major Wales came across two Co. G men who were outside the camp limits without passes. They arrested them and in bringing them towards camp one of them ran into a thicket by the roadside. The Dr. at once called upon him to come out or he would fire into it; but receiving no answer from the man he fired into it. The man, however, did not come out nor could the Dr. hear him moving about. After firing into it a number of times he came to the conclusion that the man had escaped, and left for the camp with the other prisoner. This forenoon the place was searched and the dead body of the man found. He was undoubtedly killed by the first fire of the Dr. The shot took effect right between his eyes. It has caused considerable feeling among the men of the regiment."

So far as I have found in this diary Garrison makes no further reference to the matter. June 10th, with Capt. Woodward and Companies A and I he went to Fort Motte, S.C., and probably remained there till the regiment went North. The foregoing extracts were first seen by me and copied Dec. 22 and 23, 1918, and I have never seen or heard any other comment on the matter.

¶ **Tuesday, 6th, 10:00 P.M.** Edward returned this afternoon. His baby died in Charleston Sunday and being refused transportation on the train he walked all the way to Branchville, fifty miles; there the train admitted him. Robert is doing very well; comes in every night at 8 and washes his feet and sits on his couch waiting for me to hear him say his prayers, which he has now learned.

¶ **Wednesday, [June] 7th, 10:30 P.M.** I have just returned from a call on Mrs. Gramelin and Dr. Sally. I enclose a letter from Gen Hartwell. Having learned from the first sergeants that the men would feel better if a more comprehensive and perhaps less partial body than one composed of our own officers, should pass upon the killing of the man I have requested a Board of Inquiry and forwarded it to Gen. Hatch.

¶ **Thursday, 8th, 9:00 P.M.** This morning, being called to visit a couple of white women a little way from camp I brought back with me a yellow and white kitten; it has devoured a saucerful of milk and has vanquished the largest lizard after a pitched battle.

Friday, 9th, 8:00 P.M. An order has come in to send two companies at day break to Fort Motte on the Congaree; if Dr. Brown were with the regiment I might be sent with them; as it is I shall send my best nurse and a knapsack with ordinary supplies.

Saturday, 10th, 8:00 P.M. Last evening I made a box out of a cartridge box and muslin and glass in which my spiders can be secure and at the same time under observation.

Sunday, 11th, 4:00 P.M. One of the kittens just came running into the tent shaking its foot to free itself from a big beetle that had seized with its jaws the persecuting member. I had to attend to the biggest pet of all, Billy. He was set free after dinner and having trotted about the camp, stolen hay from the place where it is kept and quarreled with the other horses, one by one, suddenly remembered that the lumps of sugar sometimes given him come out of the cook's tent, and put in his nose to ask for some; Andy, the cook, chanced just then to be in conversation with a young woman of his own color at the other end of the tent, and both their backs were turned so Billy was not seen; he was seen by an outsider to intrude his head still farther and finally attempt to enter bodily; the ~~sound startled the pair and their jump startled him and in the endeavor to turn and escape the tent was~~ young lady was surprised. Andy got some sugar and went outside to propitiate the monster; the latter took the sugar and tried to reenter for more; Andy had to show him some and then run off, whereupon Billy followed him till David was found and tied Billy up. The spectators were much amused. Yesterday, soon after supper, we had the pleasure of welcoming 2nd Lt. Trotter, late sergeant major. He and two other sergeants were commissioned by the governor a year ago but for one reason or another their muster in has been delayed by the proper officers; two months ago one of them who was wounded at Honey Hill, was mustered but at once mustered out as unfit for service[309]; the order for his muster stated that it was for peculiar circumstances, his good conduct and his wound, and we could not judge what would be done in the other two cases. Several of our own officers were opposed to it and have threatened to resign if it were done; but now that it has been done we hear nothing of resignation,

309. Wilder is referring to John Shorter.

in that sense.[310] The men cheered the officer's advent and at Headquarters we gave him a hearty welcome. He is a fine man in every way; At Readville he made the address when his company presented Capt. Soule with a sword.

¶ **Monday, 12th, 9:00 P.M.** Among the cocoons I found today two with a small hole gnawed at the side of the pedicle, so perhaps the little ones do make their own way out. The order for the Court of Inquiry has arrived and Gen. Hartwell, who returned from Columbia, has detailed two officers from each of the two regiments.

¶ **Wednesday, 14th, 9:30 P.M.** I have been making observations on the spiders as to the result of letting them remain in water and as to the tendency of the young to seek the light, whether natural or artificial. The Court of Inquiry met this afternoon, but as just then there arrived from Gen. Hatch the endorsement of the first, approving it and exculpating me from blame, The Court adjourned without calling witnesses; I suppose they will make a report.

¶ **Thursday, [June] 15th, 9:00 P.M.** Adjutant Mutell informs me that Major Nutt's first draft of his report on the Honey Hill action contained most shameful aspersions on the conduct and motives of Col. Fox. The spiders were exposed too long to the hot sun today and in some cocoons all were killed and in all some; I must be more careful. Robert has taken some young mocking-birds and their appetite for black berries is impressive.

¶ **Saturday, 17th,** The second Court was relieved on the arrival of Gen. Hatch's approval of the finding of the first.

¶ **Tuesday, 20th, 8:30 P.M.** It rains nearly every afternoon between 4 and 6, and commonly there is lightning. Last Saturday a colored man walked 21 miles for medicine for his wife, and today another came 18 miles for

310. Although officers commissioned in the black Massachusetts regiments had been selected for their reported "firm Anti-Slavery principle" and being "superior to a vulgar contempt of color," serving alongside black officers was a real test of what those terms meant. A fierce opposition to slavery was not the same thing as a belief in black equality. In addition, background and class could trump principle. Samuel Willard, a member of an old Massachusetts family, was commissioned in the first black regiment even though "he was strongly opposed to Negro Regiments until he was offered a Captaincy, and then he suddenly changed." Miller, "Brahmin Janissaries," 226.

his child; hardly a day passes without application from some for medicine or advice, which I am glad to furnish.

¶ **Wednesday, 21st, 8:45 P.M.** Lt. Bean was in this evening and said he had his resignation written and that it would not need many such exhibitions as this morning to make him send it in. There was an open altercation between the provost marshal, the nominal guardian of the public conduct, and an enlisted man whom he suspected of trying to gain the favor of an abandoned woman of his own color. It is said that the general commanding the district of Charleston lives openly with the wife of one of his own officers' staff. Among our own officers those whom I know to be free from such contamination are Captains Soule, Thurber, Goodwin, Ellsworth and Hall, and as many lieutenants, and Col. Fox and Major Nutt and Dr. Brown and the Chaplain. As for our trying to elevate the colored people, too many of the whites need to reform themselves.

¶ **Friday, [June] 23rd, 10:00 P.M.** My last pet is a young sparrow-hawk, handsome and dignified and perfectly tame; I got it for $2.00 from one of the men. It perches on my head or shoulder and is now asleep on a rafter of the tent. It pays no attention to the two cats, and when one of them came too near it leapt upon its head but did not bite it.

¶ **Saturday, 24th, 8:00 P.M.** Edward brings word that my old horse died at Summerville; so did the major's horse, Charley; I am glad Billy was spared.

¶ **Monday, 26th, 9:00 P.M.** Said wishes all of Swedenborg's theological works and I shall order them from Edward Carter for him.

¶ **Wednesday, 28th, 8:40 P.M.** In Charleston yesterday I dinned with Capt. Goodwin who is in the Inspector's department and lives with his superior, a major of the 25th Ohio and Quartermaster Hagen in a magnificent house close to the water and fronting the harbor; it belongs to a member of the wealthy family of Ravenels[311] and the location is the most delightful in the city. I called on Dr. Briggs of the 54th who, like myself, would like to make some measurements but has little time; I should not

311. The Ravenel family was one of the most prominent plantation families in antebellum South Carolina. The house mentioned by Wilder was likely the Italianate mansion built by John Ravenel in 1849 overlooking the harbor. His son, Dr. St. Julian Ravenel, helped design the "David" class semi-submersible spar torpedo boats, the first of which damaged but did not sink the *New Ironsides*. Burton, *The Siege of Charleston*, 219.

blame Dr. Gould if he asked me to turn over my instruments to one who could give more time to the matter.

During the evening I met Major George Pope; he and Dr. Briggs as well as Capt. Goodwin and Adjutant Perry offered me accommodations for the night, but I preferred to go to the hotel. There I saw the advertisement of the theater and ventured to attend. There was only a band of negro minstrels whose performance was rather flat although there were a few good songs and some funny jokes. It has been very warm today, about 100 in the shade at noon.

¶ **Friday, [June] 30th, 7:30 P.M.** I do not wonder at the inactivity of the people of this locality; It was bad enough on the sea islands, but there we had a sea breeze and the refreshing surf. I understand that last evening was to be a sort of farewell party at Dr. Brown's; he was up here yesterday afternoon and asked the major to come; I had thought of making a farewell call but as he said nothing to me I shall not go; my disinclination is increased by the knowledge that Hartwell is to be there; I have never talked of him but I understand that one of our best captains, the adjutant and a lieutenant declined for the same reason. In my mind his worst fault is his behavior in respect to the muster in of the three colored sergeants. Originally he seemed to favor it, but I understand that now he has opposed it and has detached them from the regiment. There are no finer men or better soldiers in the regiment, but they are looked down upon because of a little colored blood. Even Col. Fox seems to be giving way to prejudice in the matter. With all of his faults Major Nutt is sound on that point.

¶ **Saturday, [July] 2nd, 9:30 P.M.** Just after supper a corporal of Co. E was shot through the wrist, accidentally, by a comrade; the bones are splintered and joint opened, but the surgeon of the 102nd U.S. approves my decision to save the hand if possible.

¶ **Thursday, July 20th, 10:40 P.M.** Yesterday I rode 25 miles to see some sick colored people at a plantation more than 12 miles away. The new assistant surgeon, Lathrop,[312] is to have charge of the post hospital; doctors are scarce here; for ten days I have had charge of the 103rd.

312. W. H. Lathrop served as a private in the 44th Massachusetts from August 1862 to July 1863. Following the war he practiced medicine in Chicago. Fox, *Record*, 100.

¶ **Sunday, 23rd, 7:30 P.M.** On the day after he was injured Corp. Young was chloroformed and I enlarged the wound and removed the injured small bones and the injured end of one of the arm bones, leaving the vessels, nerves and tendons; but the case requires frequent attention, dressing twice and sometimes thrice a day. Dr. Lathrop is a Boston boy and a Harvard graduate; he was a cadet in West Philadelphia and a contract surgeon at City Point; he looks young but is my senior by a year or two, and very pleasant and attentive to his duties. Oddly enough, like the other three members of the medical staff of this regiments, he uses neither alcohol or tobacco or profane language. He adapts himself very readily to my riding habits and has ridden with me at various times 5, 10, 25 and even 30 miles to carry medicine to the people hereabouts. I have had to make a special requisition for supplies for the latter. Yesterday morning, having hastened sick call, I went on the cars to Branchville to visit Co. G, which is stationed there; the train does not return till 2 so it rather spoils the day. There is no surgeon either with Co. A at Fort Motte, but as that is 25 miles off and not on a railroad they will have to do without. A sick sergeant of our Co. G, a very nice, quiet and soldierly man, came back with me to enter the Post Hospital; the conductor would not let him ride in the nearly empty first class car, where white privates went to and fro at their pleasure. I have reported the case to Gen. Hatch, with a protest at the discrimination, and Major Nutt has forwarded it with a strong endorsement.

¶ **Monday, 24th, 9:45 P.M.** A letter from General Dale informs me that on the 11th of July I was recommended to the adjutant general of the state for the surgeoncy of this regiment and that my commission would soon follow.

¶ **Tuesday, 25th, 9:15 P.M.** At the beginning of a great storm yesterday was a stroke of lightning that stunned a man in the next regiment; as the surgeon was absent I had to attend to him.

¶ **Thursday, 27th.** Col. Fox has sent me a lovely pair of shoulder-straps appropriate to my higher rank.

¶ **Saturday, 29th, 9:00 P.M.** Yesterday I went to Branchville and visited not only Co. G but other sick in the vicinity. Gen Hartwell tells me that the protest against the treatment of a colored sergeant on the train was forwarded to Gen. Hatch by him with an endorsement; and that today came an answer from the latter to the effect that the matter would be attended to at once; of course it would be foolish and do harm to insist upon the southerners going further than we go at the north, and they may still exclude a civilian because he is colored; but all United States soldiers are alike, white or black, and if a colored soldier is decent and well-behaved he must be allowed the same privileges as a white one.

¶ **Sunday, [July] 30th, 5:40 P.M.** I have just been reading to Robert portions of the 2nd and 3rd chapters of Matthew, explaining as simply as I could, hoping at least to familiarize him with the names of the persons and places and give him some idea of what occurred.

¶ **Wednesday, August 2nd, 8:30 P.M.** I have made some measurements today. Also, drawings and notes upon a curious ear of a man in the 102nd; it is very small and has no opening whatever; the other ear is smaller than usual; he tells me that his father and sister are similarly defective.

¶ **Friday, 4th, 8:40 P.M.** Major Nutt entangled me in a conversation from which I have just escaped, on the war, the country, the regiment and things in general; unfortunately he is aware of possessing an unusual amount of shrewd common sense and likes to talk too much, as if for practice; I am not a good subject for that sort of thing.

¶ **Saturday, 5th, 9:45 P.M.** My commission came today; likewise the major's and he has applied for us to go to Charleston to be mustered. I cut a shot from a negro's leg, one of six that are in it; they and eleven more (which were got out previously) were shot into his leg by his master two years ago; this was hard to find and as the others could not be felt I did not think best to search for them. He says that formerly they were hung and shot and torn by dogs, but when we came, "Ah, there was a heap of dodging then."

¶ **Sunday, [August] 6th, 7:30 P.M.** Before supper I rode over to the little house in the woods to see a baby that had been ailing a few says, and found it better. When we came up here I was apprehensive that my lack of previous attention to the diseases of women and children would prove embarrassing; but so far, of the hundreds attended to by me none, so far as I know, have died and all have improved. But I long for an opportunity to study all sides of the profession. The two kittens are a source of entertainment not only to me but the whole field and staff; they are made welcome at the other tents and play very interestingly together.

Charleston Hotel

Tuesday, 8th, 6:45 A.M. Major Nutt, Lt. Carter and I came to the city yesterday and were mustered out and in by Capt. T. J. Robinson, formerly adjutant general for the brigade on Folly Island.

11:00 P.M. I went to James Island today and got a dozen spiders of the kind that makes the cocoon. With the machine I wound from three at once.

Orangeburg

Friday, 11th, 8:00 P.M. Tuesday forenoon was occupied with various business. Having got some lunch and hired a nice man I went to the foot of Tradd St. where I found the only way to get to James Island was to take an old flat bottomed boat full of colored men, women and children; wind and tide were against us and it was two o'clock before we reached the house on Wappoo Creek where used to be our headquarters. It is now occupied by the agent of the Freedmen's Aid Commission. My man carried in a bag a dozen of the paper boxes we had made and we went through the old familiar fields; we found plenty of the cocoon-making spiders and one freshly made cocoon; the spiders are more active and less manageable that the Long Island species.

¶ **Saturday, 12th, 8:45 P.M.** Wednesday Carter and I rose at 4 o'clock and went to the steamer at the wharf expecting to go to Hilton Head to be paid; But Gen. Hartwell informed us that it was of no use for positive orders had been received to muster us out as soon as our papers could be ready and the paymaster would not pay us. I got an early breakfast and found a man named Henry to accompany me to Long Island. We secured transportation in a dispatch boat bound for Fort Sumter which could land us at Fort Johnson on her return; I was glad to see the famous fort at close quarters. The wind and the tide were against us and it was 9 before we got there. After a time we were set ashore at Fort Johnson and were so fortunate as to meet two non-commissioned officers of the 54th Mass., a company of which is stationed here. They guided us to the place of a colored man, Edward Green, on the shore of the island, half way from Fort Johnson to Secessionville. After a hot toilsome walk we found Green and got a boat and a man who professed to be familiar with all the channels; but it turned out that he supposed we sought Folly Id., and that he had never even heard the name Long Id.; in fact there is no attraction there excepting my spiders. The 54th men said they would go too for fun, so after devouring some water melons we starter; the tide was on the ebb and just high enough to carry us over some ugly oyster beds and mud flats; the "guide" steered and the others and myself took turns at rowing; when we reached a position opposite the head of Long Id. and I found the man still steering towards the east I questioned him and discovered his error; it was then one o'clock, too late to retrace our course or to continue to the regular landing on the Folly Island side; so as the marsh did not look very bad and was only an eighth of a mile wide I left him in the boat; the two soldiers followed me; the marsh proved to be of the "bottomless" variety; clear soft mud, with scattered clumps of coarse grass; by pressing against these clumps with the side of the foot we could gain some support, but with every step we sank over our ankles and in holes occasionally to our knees when two thirds across we were dismayed to encounter one of the small creeks that meander through the marshes; the corporal said he would try it and as it came only to his hips we followed; there were no banks, properly speaking, only slopping muddy sides; we struggled through and up the other side and finally reached dry land. Leaving the soldiers at the shore I skirted the shore next Folly Id. to the old landing, then struck across by the stockade to the other side; there were plenty of spiders, indeed it was difficult to avoid their webs; the mosquitoes also were out in full force and after I put one spider in my hat I had to use a stick with one hand to make a path through their nets and with the other hand protect my face from the mosquitoes; I emerged from the woods at the westerly of two points on the island and had to cross to the other; there I found that my soldiers had captured four spiders, and had put them in the cap of one of them. It was now 2:30; the marsh was bad enough before but now we were tired and at times it seemed as if we would sink beyond recovery; at last we reached the boat and were greeted with the remark that the southerners never would have gone through a marsh like that for anything, and no wonder the Yankees had won. After various delays I reached the city looking as if I had slept in the street; the wonder is that the hotel admitted me.

Hilton Head

Tuesday, 15th, 9:15 P.M. Capt. Hodges very kindly took my account to the chief paymaster and obtained an order to pay me from Mar. 1 to Aug. 4, a great relief on many accounts.

¶ **[Thursday] 17th, 10:00 P.M.** This afternoon I was summoned to the post hospital to consult as to what should be done for a colored youth whose leg was crushed below the knee by a cart falling on him; the limb will probably have to come off.

¶ **Friday, 18th, 10:00 P.M.** This morning another consultation was held over the injured man. There were present Dr. Pillsbury, a contract surgeon in charge of the post hospital, Dr. Lathrop, and Dr. Pffeffer, the assistant surgeon of the 54th N.Y. The surgeon, Dr. Root, being away, I was the senior medical officer. When it was decided that the leg should come off I offered the opportunity to Dr. Pillsbury , but he did not feel very well and preferred that I should do it.

¶ **Sunday, 20th.** The patient is doing well and the stump looks finely.

Mt. Pleasant

Friday, [August] 25th, 8:30 P.M. Yesterday the regiment was brought to Charleston by rail and we are located at this really pleasant place opposite the city. The officers are all together in a large house near the water.

¶ **Saturday, 26th, 8:30 P.M.** With the consent of Col. Nutt I have moved my belongings and the hospital to a nice large house on the bluff, formerly the headquarters of the confederate commander; there is a nice stable for Billy and an attic room for the spiders.

¶ **Sunday, 27th, 7:40 P.M.** This house stands on the highest part of the bluff near the water. I have taken two rides today and am impressed with the resemblance of the two sides of the harbor as shown in the diagram. Paul, my man, says Billy is getting too impudent to take North; today a returning confederate soldier, in rather a shabby uniform, was walking along the edge of the bluff and Billy ran at him so impetuously that he nearly fell over into the water; later he would not allow some harmless goats to feed near him; he ended by nearly running over a cow; but it is all play, and he can be led any where with a lump of sugar; this morning he followed Paul up the steps and through the house and out at the back.

I have been watching the spiders today and have observed things that convince me that a full summer might be spent in observing and recording their habits, especially the different uses of the several pairs of spinners. I had not thought of bringing the kittens along but several officers said they should if I did not; Robert tied them together and they behaved very well on the cars. Here they are quite at home already. Q.M. Mowrey wants to keep one.

¶ **Monday, Aug. 28th, 10:00 P.M.** I went to Charleston today, taking Robert so that he might see his brother, Jacob. Today I had to dismiss the cook, Andy Hill, for an attempt at dishonesty.

¶ **Thursday, 31st, 8:00 P.M.** Dr. Lathrop is to be mustered out and become a contract surgeon and is to be stationed at Fort Moultrie. I like and respect him highly; we have worked well together and he has helped me as much as possible.

The Arachnidan El Dorado

Friday, Sept. 1st, 11:00 P.M. Having been on the go since 9 this morning I have had some supper and will record the day's doing. This has been the most successful and probably is the last trip to the often sought Long Island. The wind was too strong for sailing so we got a large row boat from a man named Billy; as assistants I took a nurse named Birrel, David Lee, two men of his company, and Robert; the man whose wrist was wounded was taken as a passenger, he has been so confined. As freight we took a supply of eatables and one of the wooden boxes with tin trays and small paper boxes. The waves were high and sometimes terrifying, but hard rowing took us to the creek that runs behind Morris Island. Up this we rowed or pushed the boat a mile or two till stopped by the end of the creek. We left the corporal and one man with Billy in the boat and walked over the hot sand of Morris Island to the wharf at Lighthouse Inlet. There we found a boat with oars and a sail, and at 2 reached the landing at Long Id. Here the box was left in the path and the trays of boxes were carried by Birrel. In front of him walked Robert with one or two boxes ready for David; the latter, when I brought down a spider with a stick, dexterously put a box over it and secured it with a rubber band and marked it with a pencil. The recent storm had destroyed some webs but we found about 80 and captured 60 of the largest. They are much larger than the James Id. species and their webs are three and even four feet in diameter; sometimes they were spread so high that we had to throw sticks at them; sometimes they closed their legs when the stick struck the web and dropped to the ground. Rain began while we were taking them, and while we were returning to the boat it came down in torrents and the wind blew so violently that we could hardly row or sail and were soon drenched to the skin; we protected the spiders, however, and regained Morris Id. after dark and retrudged our way across to the boat were we found our allies wondering what had befallen us. The moon came out on our row home and but for our damp cloths and blistered hands it was pleasant enough. The four men came up to my house to eat, dry their cloths, get a ration of whiskey and sleep; I have had some coffee and feel rejoiced over the success of the expedition.

¶ **Sunday, 3rd, 7:00 P.M.** The unexpected delay in our departure is not only irksome for the officers and men but threatens the health of the latter; most of the tents were turned in and none are raised from the ground; there has been a marked increase in fever and today there are two quite serious cases that may have to be left here. Yesterday forenoon David helped me go through the boxes of spiders; not infrequently a male was captured with the female and kept in the same box. I turned some of the females loose in the room and made some interesting notes on their habits. I saw one devour surplus silk, some of it that which is coiled up when returning on a line, and some that of other spiders and other species; perhaps they might be fed on the silk of less valuable spiders or even a substance likely to be useful in that way. I have been reeling from some of them. Last night I carelessly left the door open and the cats jumped and pulled down and devoured three of the James Id. species.

¶ **Monday, 4th, 9:00 P.M.** This afternoon I set free a very large female in the hope that she would make a cocoon; instead of which she invaded the net of another and drove her out and repulsed [unreadable] . . . she belonged there. Another female not only repulsed a male that invaded her net but bit off two of his legs. I am trying to ascertain the limit of the supply of a single individual. Saturday I had supposed I had exhausted the supply of one, but today wound 250 yards from the same. Query, is it possible to get all the silk from one? And do they exhaust their own supply for either the net or the cocoon?

¶ **Wednesday, 13th, A.M.** We are at the dock in order that the colonel may report to the military authorities, and then I suppose we shall return to Galloupe's Id.[313] to be mustered out. Robert and Billy are well; the cats were not brought.

313. Gallup's Island is located in Boston Harbor. The 55th Regiment was mustered out in Mt. Pleasant but it would not be formally discharged until its return to Boston. Wilder traveled with the first six companies on the steamer *Karnac* and arrived 13 September. The remaining four companies on the *Ben Deford* had a rough passage and did not reach Boston until 20 September. Fox, *Record*, 83–84.

A Selected Bibliography of B. G. Wilder

A PARTIAL LIST OF SCIENTIFIC PUBLICATIONS

(This list is far from comprehensive. In May 1911, the *Ithaca Journal* credited B. G. Wilder with 6 books and 220 technical scientific papers, plus another 230 reviews written primarily for the *Nation*. Most of the pre-1886 scientific papers cited here are drawn from the *Wilder Quarter-Century Book*.)

1861 Contributions to the comparative myology of the chimpanzee [1861]. *Boston J. Nat. Hist.*, VII, 1859–1863, 352–84.

1862 Note on the muscles of the hog's snout. *Boston Soc. Nat. Hist. Proc.*, IX, 1862, 1.

1864 Histories of two surgical specimens in the Army Medical Museum. *Boston Med. and Surg. J.*, LXXI, 1864, 200–210; 2 figs. *Medical and Surgical History of the War*, pt. I, 427–533.

On morphology and teleology, especially in the limbs of mammalia [1863]. *Boston Soc. Nat. Hist. Proc., Mem.*, I, 1866–69, 46–80; 3 figs.

A case of imperforate ear in an adult man [1865]. *Boston Soc. Nat. Hist. Proc.*, X, 1866, 222.

Pathological polarity, or what has been called symmetry in disease. *Boston Med. and Surg. J.*, LXXIV, 1866, 189–98.

Termeyer's "Researches and experiments upon silk from spiders: 1810–1820." Translation revised. *Proc. Essex Inst.*, V, 1866, 51–79; 2 figs.

1867 On the morphological value and relations of the human hand. (Abstr. of paper read before the National Academy of Sciences, Aug. 1866). *Amer. J. Sci.*, Series II, XLIV, 1867, 44–48.

The hand as an unruly member. *Amer. Nat.*, 1, 1867, 414–23, 482–91, 631–38; 9 figs.

1868 On the *Nephila plumipes* or silk-spider [1865]. *Proc. Amer. Acad. Arts Sci.*, VII, 1868, 52–57.

On a cat with supernumerary digits [1865]. *Boston Soc. Nat. Hist. Proc.*, XI, 1868, 3–6.

The harmlessness of the bite of *Nephila plumipes* [1866]. *Boston Soc. Nat. Hist. Proc.*, XI, 1868, 7.

On a method of recording and arranging information [1867]. *Boston Soc. Nat. Hist. Proc.*, XI, 1868, 242.

On symmetry and distorted symmetry in the leaves of plants [1867]. *Boston Soc. Nat. Hist. Proc.*, XI, 1868, 313–15; 2 figs.

Extra digits. (Paper read at the annual meeting of the Massachusetts Medical Society, June 1868.) *Mass. Med. Soc. Pub.*, II, 1868, 22; 1 plate.

How spiders begin their webs [1868]. *Amer. Nat.*, II, 1869, 214–15; *Zoologist*, III, 1868, 1301; *Bruxelles Soc. Entom. Belg. Annu.*, XIII, 1869–1870, 2-3.

1870 *Human locomotion. How we stand, walk and run.* 18 pp.; 18 figs. New York.

1871 Intermembral homologies, the correspondence of the anterior and posterior limbs of vertebrates [1871]. *Boston Soc. Nat. Hist. Proc.*, XIV, 1871, 154–88, 309–39, 399–420; 5 figs.

1873 Cyno-phrenology. *Boston Med. and Surg. J.*, LXXXVIII, 1873, 73–78.

The outer cerebral fissures of mammalia (especially of the carnivora), and the limits of their homologies. *Amer. Assoc. Adv. Sci. Proc.*, XXII, 1873, (pt. 2), 214–34; 19 figs.

Cerebral variation in domestic dogs and its bearing upon scientific phrenology. *Amer. Soc. Adv. Sci. Proc.*, XXII, 1873, (pt. 2), 234–49; 6 figs.

Lateral asymmetry in the brains of a double human monster. *Amer. Assoc. Adv. Sci. Proc.*, XXII, 1873, (pt. 2), 250–51; 3 figs.

The papillary representative of two arms in a double human monster, with a note on a mummied double monster from Peru. *Amer. Assoc. Adv. Sci. Proc.*, XXII, 1873, (pt. 2), 251–56; 3 figs.

The habits and parasites of *Epeira* [*Argiope*] *riparia*, with a note on the moulting of *Nephila plumipes*. *Amer.Assoc. Adv. Sci. Proc.*, XXII, 1873, (pt. 2), 257–63; 8 figs.

The nets of *Epeira* [*Argiope*], *Nephila* and *Hyptiotes* [*Mithras*]. *Amer. Assoc. Adv. Sci. Proc.*, XXII, 1873, (pt.2), 264–74; 3 figs.

On the lateral position of the vent in *Amphioxus* [*Branchiostoma*], and in larvae of *Rama pipiens* [*Calesbiana*]. *Amer. Assoc. Adv. Sci. Proc.*, XXII, 1873, (pt. 2), 275–300; 10 figs.

On the composition of the carpus in dogs. *Amer. Assoc. Adv. Sci. Proc.*, XXII, 1873, (pt. 2), 301–2; 3 figs.

Variation in the condition of the sense-organs in foetal pigs of the same litter. *Amer. Assoc. Adv. Sci. Proc.*, XXII, 1873, (pt. 2), 303–4.; 2 figs.

The pectoral muscles of mammalia. *Amer. Assoc. Adv. Sci. Proc.*, XXII, 1873, (pt. 2), 305–7.

Variation of the pectoral muscles of domestic dogs. *Amer. Assoc. Adv. Sci. Proc.*, XXII, 1873, (pt. 2), 308.

The need of a uniform position for anatomical figures with a recommendation that the head be always turned toward the left. *Amer. Assoc. Adv. Sci. Proc.*, XXII, 9, 1873, (pt. 2), 274.

The present aspect of the question of intermembral homologies. *Amer. Assoc. Adv. Sci. Proc.*, XXII, 1873, (pt. 2), 274.

1874 Note on the gestation of the little brown bat, *Vespertilio subulatus. Amer. Soc. Adv. Sci. Proc.*, XXII, 1874, 141–43.

1875 Preliminary medical education. *Boston Med. and Surg. J.*, XCII, 1875, 2.

On a foetal manatee and cetacean, with remarks upon the affinities and ancestry of the Sirenia. (Abstr. of communication before the Boston Society of Natural History, April 7, 1875.) *Amer. J. Sci.*, Series III, LII, 1875, 105–14; 1 plate.

Notes on the American Ganoids. I. On the respiratory actions of *Amia* and *Lepidosteus*. II. On the transformations of the tail of *Lepidosteus*. III. On the transformation of the pectoral fins of *Lepidosteus*. IV. On the brains of *Amia, Lepidosteus, Acipenser* and Polyodon. *Amer.Assoc. Adv. Sci. Proc.*, XXIV, 1875, 151–93; 3 pls. *Boston Soc. Nat. Hist. Proc.*, XIX, 337.

1876 On the brains of fishes. *Phil. Acad. Proc.*, XXXVIII, 1876, 51–53.

Note on the development and homologies of the anterior brain-mass with sharks and skates. *Amer. J. Sci.*, Series III, XII, 1876, 103–5; 1 fig.

A brief account of the development and general structure of the brain. Ithaca, N.Y., 1876; 5 figs.

On the serrated appendages [serrulae] of the throat of *Amia. Amer. Assoc. Adv. Sci. Proc.*, XV, 1876, 259–63; 1 plate.

On the tail of *Amia. Amer. Assoc. Adv. Sci. Proc.*, XXV, 1876, 264–67.

On the brains of some fish-like vertebrates. *Amer. Assoc. Adv. Sci. Proc.*, XXV, 1876, 257–59.

Notes of lectures on physiology and hygiene. Ithaca, N.Y.: Andrus & Church, 1876. 63 pp.

1877 On the brain of the *chimaera monstrosa. Phil. Acad. Proc.*, XXIX, 1877, 219–50; 1 plate.

The external branchiae of the embryo *Pipa. Amer. Nat.*, XI, 1877, 491–92.

Should comparative anatomy be included in a medical course? (Introductory lecture in the Medical School of Maine, 1877.) *N.Y. Med. J.*, XXVI, 1877, 337–69.

On the respiration of *Amia. Amer. Assoc. Adv. Sci. Proc.*, XXVI, 1877, 306–13.

1878 An apparatus to show the action of the diaphragm in respiration. *Boston Soc. Nat. Hist. Proc.*, XIX, 1878, 337.

On a remnant of the spiracle in *Amia* and *Lepidosteus*. (Paper read before the American Association for the Advancement of Science, 1878.) *Amer. Nat.*, XIX, 190.

1879 The anatomical uses of the cat. *N.Y. Med. J.*, XXX, 1879, 347–60.

Frozen sections of the cat preserved in alcohol. (Paper read before the American Association for the Advancement of Science, 1879.) *N.Y. Med. Record*, XV, 1879, 311.

Emergencies. How to avoid them and how to meet them. New York: G. P. Putnam's Sons, 1879.

Health notes for students. Ithaca, N.Y.: Andrus & Church, 1879.

1880 Preliminary laryngoscopy upon the cat. Laryngol. *Arch.*, I, 1880, 50–51.

The cerebral fissures of the domestic cat (*Felis domestica*). *Science*, I, 1880, 49–51; 2 figs.

The two kinds of vivisection, *sentisection* and *callisection*. *N.Y. Med. Record*, XVIII, 1880, 219; *Nature*, XXII, 1880, 517; *Science*, I, 1880, 210.

The foramina of Monro; some questions of anatomical history. *Boston Med. and Surg. J.*, CIII, 1880, 152–54.

The foramina of Monro in man and the domestic cat. (Paper read before the American Association for the Advancement of Science, 1880.) *N.Y. Med. Record*, XVIII, 1880, 328.

Partial revision of the nomenclature of the brain. *Amer. Assoc. Adv. Sci.*, 1880, 328.

Criticism of the accounts of the brains of the lower vertebrates given in Packard's Zoology. *Amer. J. of Sci.*, XIX, 1880, 1–2.

1881 Criticism of Spitzka's "Notes on the anatomy of the encerphalon, etc." *Science*, II, 1881, 48.

A partial revision of anatomical nomenclature, with special reference to that of the brain. *Science*, II, 1881, 122–26, 133–38.

How to obtain the brain of the cat. *Science*, II, 1881, 158–61.

The brain of the cat (*Felis domestica*). A preliminary account of the gross anatomy. *Amer. Phil. Soc. Proc.*, XIX, 1881, 524–62; 4 plates.

On a mesal [mesad] cusp of the deciduous, mandibular canine of the domestic cat (*Felis domestica*). *Amer. Assoc. Adv. Sci. Proc.*, XX, 1881, 242.

1882 Note on the ectal ("apparent") origin of the N. *trigeminus* in the cat. *Amer. J. Neurol. and Psychiatry*, I, 1882, 337–38.

The habits of *Cryptobranchus* [*Megalobatrachus*]. *Amer. Assoc. Adv. Sci. Proc.*, XXXI, 1882, 482. *Amer. Nat.*, XVI, 816.

Anatomical technology as applied to the domestic cat; an introduction to human, veterinary and comparative anatomy. New York: A. S. Barnes, 1882. 2d rev. ed., 1886. Senior author with S. H. Gage.

1883 Some points in the anatomy of the human brain. *Amer. Neurol. Assoc. Trans.*, 1883; *J. Nerv. and Ment. Dis.*, N.S., VIII, 1883, 81–82.

On the removal and preservation of the human brain. (Paper read before the American Neurological Association, 1883.) *J. Nerv. and Ment. Dis.*, N.S., VIII, 1883, 81–82.

On the brain of a cat lacking the callosum. (Paper read before the American Neurological Association, 1883.) *Amer. J. Neurol. amd Psychiatry*, II, 1883, 491–99; 4 figs. *J. Nerv. and Ment. Dis.*, N. S., VIII, 1883, 62 (Abstr.) Neurol. Centralblatt, II, 517 (Abstr.).

On the alleged homology of the carnivoral *Fissura cruciata* with the primatial *F. centralis*. *Amer. Neurol. Assoc. Trans.*, 1883. *J. Nerv. and Ment. Dis.*, N.S., VIII, 1883, 62–63.

Preliminary medical education at Cornell University. *Med. Student*, I, 1883, 3.

On the use of vaseline to prevent the leakage or evaporation of alcohol from specimen jars. *Amer. Assoc. Adv. Sci. Proc.*, XXXII, 1883, 318. *N.Y. Med. J.*, XXXIII, 1883, 244. Also in *Colorado Med. J.*, 1883, and *Internat. Rev. of Med. and Surg. Technics*, 1884. Senior author with S. H. Gage.

1884 Methods of studying the brain. The "Cartwright Lectures" for 1884. *N.Y. Med. J.*, XXXIX, 1884, 141–48, 177–83, 205–9. 233–37, 373–77, 457–61, 513–16, 653–56; XL, 113–16; 64 figs. (Abstr. in *N.Y. Med. Rec.*, XXV, 1884, 141–43, 197–99, 225–27, 365–67, 449–50, 545–46.)

On encaphalic nomenclature. *Amer. Neurol. Assoc. Trans.*, 1884. *J. Nerv. and Ment. Dis.*, 1884, 18, 50.

Do the cerebellum and the oblongata represent two encephalic segments or only one? *Amer. Assoc. Adv. Sci. Proc.*, XXXIII, 1884, 523–25; *Science*, IV, 1884, 341; *N.Y. Med. J.*, XL., 1884, 324.

On some points in anatomical nomenclature. *Amer. Assoc. Adv. Sci. Proc.*, XXXIII, 1884, 528–29.

The existence and dorsal circumscription of the porta ("Foramen Monroi") in the adult human brain. *Amer. Assoc. Adv. Sci. Proc.*, XXXIII, 1884, 526; *N.Y. Med. J.*, XL, 1884, 324.

The relative position of the cerebrum and the cerebellum in the anthropoid apes. *Amer. Assoc. Adv. Sci. Proc.*, XXXIII, 1884, 527.

Exhibition of preparations illustrating (*a*) the existence and circumscription of the *portae* (*foramina Monroi*) in the adult human brain; (*b*) the presence of the *crista fornicis* in the foetal and new-born human brains; (*c*) two additional cases of absence of the callosum in the domestic cat; (*d*) the covering of the cerebellum by the cerebrum in a young chimpanzee whose brain was hardened within the skull. *J. Nerv. and Ment. Dis.*, XI, 1884. *Proc. Amer. Neurological Association*, 1884, 11–13.

The foramen of Magendie in man and the cat. *N.Y. Med. J.*, XXXIX, 1884, 458. *Health Notes for Students*, New York; G. P. Putnam & Sons, 1879, reprinted 1887, 1890.

1885 The use of slips in scientific correspondence. (Paper read before the Society Nat. Eastern United States, 1884.) *Science*, V, 1885, 44.

Encephalic nomenclature. Coelian terminology: the names of the cavities of the brain and myelon. *N.Y. Med. J.*, XLI, 325–28, 354–57, 1885; 8 figs.

Paronymy *versus* heteronymy as neuronymic principles. (Presidential address at the eleventh annual meeting of the American Neurological Association, 1885.) *J. Nerv. and Ment. Dis.*, XII, 21. (Abstr. in *Neurol. Centralblatt*, Dec. 15, 1885.)

Educational museums of vertebrates. (Address [as vice president] before the Section of Biology of the American Association for the Advancement of Science.) *Amer. Assoc. Adv. Sci. Proc.*, XXXIV, 1885, 263–81. (Abstr. in *Science*, VI, 1885, 222–24.)

On two little-known cerebral fissures, with suggestions as to fissural and gyral names. *Amer. Neurol. Assoc. Trans.*, 1885. *J. Nerv. and Ment. Dis.*, XII, 1885, 350–52. (Abstr. in *Neurol. Centralblatt*, Dec. 15, 1885.)

On a seldom-described artery (*A. termatica*), with suggestions as to the names of the principal encephalic arteries. *Amer. Neurol. Assoc. Trans.*, 1885. *J. of Nerv. and Ment. Dis.*, 1885, XII, 2. (Abstr. in *N.Y. Med. J.* and *N.Y. Med. Rec.*, June 27, 1885, and in *Neurol. Centralblatt*, Dec. 15, 1885.)

The names of the encephalic arteries. *N.Y. Med. J.*, Nov. 28, 1885.

Neuronymy. *N.Y. Med. Rec.*, Aug. 1, 1885, 139.

Exhibition of preparations illustrating (*a*) the enlargement, yet complete circumscription of the porta in an alinjected hydrencephal; (*b*) the continuity of the diacoelian endyma from the mesal surface of the thalamus over the habena to the diatele; (*c*) the insula in a dog, monkey, chimpanzee and porpoise. *Amer. Neurol. Assoc. Trans.*, 1885, 49–51. *J. Nerv. and Ment. Dis.*, XII, 1885, 364–65.

Experiment antagonizing the view that the serrulae (serrated appendages) of *Amia* are accessory respiratory organs. *Amer. Assoc. Adv. Sci. Proc.*, XXXIV, 1885, 313–15.

Address. Proceedings at the unveiling of the tablet to the memory of Louis Agassiz. June 17, 1885, 22–27.

1886 The collocation of a suture and a fissure in the human foetus. *J. Nerv. and Ment. Dis.*, XIII, 1886, 463–68; 1 fig. (Abstr. in *N.Y. Med. Record*, July 31, 1886; *Science*, Aug. 6, 1886, and *Medical News*, Aug. 7, 1886.)

Notes on the brain. *J. Nerv. and Ment. Dis.*, XIII., 1886, 464–72.

Exhibition of the medisected, alinjected head of a murderer. *Amer. Neurol. Assoc. Trans.*, 1886. *J. Nerv. and Ment. Dis.*, XIII, 1886, 633.

Remarks upon a living frog which was decerebrized more than seven months ago. *Amer. Neurol. Assoc. Trans.*, 1886. *J. Nerv. and Ment. Dis.*, XIII, 1886, 301–15; 5 figs. (Abstr. in *Neurol. Centralbl*, V, 501.)

The paroccipital, a newly-recognized fissural integer. *J. Nerv. and Ment. Dis.*, XIII., 1886, 301–15; 5 figs. (Abstr. in *Neurol. Centralblatt*, V, 501.)

The paroccipital fissure. Letter to the editor, *N.Y. Medical Record*, Oct. 2, 1886, 389–90.

Human cerebral fissures, their relations and names and the methods of studying them. *Amer. Nat.*, XX, 1886, 901–2; 1 plate.

Notes on the foramen of Magendie in man and the cat. *J. Nerv. and Ment. Dis.*, XIII, 1886, 206–7.

1887 The dipnoan brain. (Abstract of paper on the brain of *Ceratodus*, with remarks upon classification and the general morphology of the vertebrate brain, read by invitation before the National Academy of Sciences, April 22, 1887.) *Amer. Nat.*, XXI, 1887, 54–58; 3 figs.

Remarks on the classification of vertebrates. *Amer. Nat.*, XXI, 1887, 913–17; (Abstr. in *Amer. Assoc. Adv. Sci. Proc.*, XXXVI, 1887, 251). See correction in *Amer. Nat.*, XXI, 1887, 1033.

A sketch of the life of W. S. Barnard. *Amer. Nat.*, XXI, 1887, 1136–37.

1888 The relation of the thalamus to the paracoele (lateral ventricle). *J. Nerv. and Ment. Dis.*, XIV, 1889, 436–43; 2 figs. Also *Amer. Neurol. Assoc. Trans.*, 1888, 313–20.

An illustrated encyclopedic medical dictionary, being a dictionary of the technical terms used by writers on medicine and the collateral sciences in the Latin, English, French and German languages. Coauthor with F. P. Foster. Vol. I, 1888, Vol. II, 1890. Vol. III, 1892, New York. "Professor Wilder furnished lists of the 10 500 terms used by writers on the anatomy of central nervous system, with bibliographical references" for the Preface.

Reports [as chairman] of the committee on anatomical nomenclature with special reference to the brain. *Amer. Assoc. Adv. Sci. Proc.*, 1888, 1889, 1890.

1889 Brain, gross or macroscopic anatomy. *Reference Handbook of the Medical Sciences*, edited by A. H. Buck. Vol. VIII, 1889, 107–64; 104 figs.; also vol. IX, 99–110; 2d ed., vol. II, 136–218.

Brain, malformations of, which morphologically instructive. Ibid., 189–94; 10 figs.

Brain, removal, preservation and dissection of. Ibid., 195–201; 5 figs.

The relation of the thalamus to the paracoele, especially in the apes. *Assoc. Amer. Anat., Rec.*, 1889, 20. (See also note on p. 317 of first paper cited under 1888.)

The heart as the basis of an intrinsic toponymy. *Assoc. Amer. Anat, Rec.*, 1889, 25.

Preliminary reports [as secretary] of the committee on anatomical nomenclature. *Assoc. Amer. Anat., Rec.*, 1889, 515–37; 2 figs. Senior author with S. H. Gage.

Anatomical terminology. *Reference Handbook of the Medical Sciences*. Senior author with S. H. Gage.

1890 Do the Barclayan terms cause obscurity? Letter to editor. *Science*, XV, 189, 224.

The subfrontal gyre in man and apes. Address before the Alumni Association of the Medical Department of the Niagara University, 1890. See *Buffalo Med. and Surg. Journal*, XXIX, 1890, 648.

Remarks on the brain of Chauncey Wright, with commentaries upon fissural diagrams. *Amer. Neurol. Assoc. Trans.*, 1890. *J. Nerv. and Ment. Dis.*, XVII, 1890, 753–54.

On the lack of the distance sense in the prairie dog. *Amer. Assoc. Adv. Sci. Proc.*, XXXIV, 1890, 340; *Science*, Aug. 22, 1890.

Exhibition of diagrams of the brains and medisected heads of man and a chimpanzee. *Amer. Assoc. Adv. Sci. Proc.*, XXXIX, 1890, 375–76. Abstr. in *Amer. Nat.*, XXIV, 1890, 980.

Exhibition of diagrams illustrating the formation of the human Sylvian fissure. *Amer. Assoc. Adv. Sci. Proc.*, XXXIX, 1890, 346–47.

1891 Fundamental principles of anatomical nomenclature. *Med. News*, Dec. 19, 1891, 708–10.

The morphological importance of the membranous or other thin portions of the encephalic cavities. *J. Comp. Neurol.*, I, 1891, 201–3.

1893 Brain, gross or macroscopic anatomy. *Reference Handbook of the Medical Sciences*, Supplement, edited by A. H. Buck, 1893, 99–11; 10 figs.

Brain, methods of removing, preserving, dissecting and drawing. Ibid., 111–21; 2 figs.

Meringes. (The envelopes or membranes of the brain and spinal cord). Ibid., 606–16; 11 figs.

Physiology practicums: directions for examining the cat, and the heart, eye, and brain of the sheep, as an aid in the study of elementary physiology. Ithaca, N.Y.: Press of the Ithaca Journal, 1893. 70 pp.; 27 plates.

1894 Revised interpretation of the central fissure of the educated suicide's brain. *J. of Neur. and Ment. Dis.*, XXII, 1894, 314–19.

Exhibition of a Suicide's Brain, with two pistol ball wounds. *J. of Neur. and Ment. Dis.*, Dec. 1894, 421–23.

Morphology as a factor in disease. *Trans. Congr. Amer. Phys. and Surg.*, XXIII, 1894, 23–26.

1895 The central fissure of two philosophers. *Assoc. of Amer. Anat. Proc.*, XIX, 1895, 71–72.

1896 Neural terms, international and national. *J. Comp. Neurol.*, VI, 239.
The dorsal sack, the aulix, and the diencepholic flexure. *J. of Neurol. and Ment. Dis.*, August 1896, 543.
The ectal relations of the right and left parietal and paroccipital fissure. *Amer. Nuerol. Trans.*, 37.

1898 Some misapprehensions as to the simplified nomenclature of anatomy. (Address of the president of the Association of American Anatomists), *Science*, April 21, 1898, 340.

1900 Revised interpretation of the central fissure. (Paper read before the American Neurological Association.) *J. Neurol. and Ment. Dis.*, Oct. 1900, 579.

1903 *The brain of the sheep.* Ithaca, N.Y.: Press of the Ithaca Journal, 1903.

1904 *Alcohol and narcotics.* Albany: New York State Education Department, 1904.

1906 The brain of rhinochemaera. *Proc. Amer. Phil. Soc.*, XLVII, 37–39.

1907 The educational uses of sharks and rays, especially the Acanth shark. *Proceedings of the twelfth annual meeting of the New York State Science Teachers Association.* Bulletin of the University of the State of New York, no. 431, 1907, 95–96. (This refers to his previous papers on the same subject.)

1911 The methods of a veteran investigator and teacher. *Science*, XXXIV, 1911, 865.

A PARTIAL LIST OF POPULAR PUBLICATIONS

(Wilder gave numerous talks and presentations to general audiences and various veterans groups.)

1866 "How My New Acquaintances Spin." *The Atlantic Monthly*, Aug. 1866.
"Memoirs of a Cripple." *Our Young Folks*, September 1866.

1867 "Two Hundred Thousand Spiders." *Harper's New Monthly Magazine*, Mar. 1867.

1868 "Unwelcome Guests of Insects." *Harper's New Monthly Magazine*, Sept. 1868.

1869 "Beast, Bird, and Fish." *Harper's New Monthly Magazine*, Nov. 1869; Dec. 1869.

"The Practical View of Spider's Silk." *The Galaxy*, July 1869.

1870 "Beast, Bird, and Fish." *Harper's New Monthly Magazine*, Jan. 1870; Feb. 1870.

"Time Works Wonders." *The Atlantic Monthly*, Mar. 1870.

"Right and Left." *The Atlantic Monthly*, Apr. 1870.

"Equal Yet Diverse." *The Atlantic Monthly*, July 1870.

1871 "Aye-Aye!" *Scribner's Monthly*, May 1871.

"Kings of the Air." *Scribner's Monthly*, Jan. 1871.

1872 "As Others See Us." *Scribner's Monthly*, July 1872.

1874 "A Baby Fox." *Popular Science Monthly*, V, 1874.

"Jeffries Wyman." *Old and New*, XI, 1874.

1875 "Sketch of Dr. Jeffries." *Popular Science*, Jan. 1875.

"The Triangle Spider." *Popular Science Monthly*, VI, 1874–75.

"Bats and Their Young." *Popular Science Monthly*, VII, 1875.

What Young People Should Know: The Reproductive Function in Man and the Lower Animals. Boston: Estes & Lauriat, 1875.

1876 "Is Nature Inconsistent?" *The Galaxy*, Apr. 1876.

1877 "Garpike, Old and Young." *Popular Science Monthly*, XI, 1877.

1883 "Vivisection in the State of New York." *Popular Science Monthly*, XXIII, 1883.

1891 "Are Intercollegiate Athletics to Stay at Cornell?" University of the State of New York, *105th Annual Report of the Regents*. 1891. Albany: James B. Lyon, 1893. 360–75.

1905 "Two Examples of the Negro's Courage, Physical and Moral." Address given at the Garrison Centenary, Dec. 10, 1905. *Alexander's Magazine*, Jan.–Feb. 1906. See also *Sunday News*, Charleston, S.C., Dec. 7, 1902.

Agassiz at Penikese. Ithaca, N.Y.: Press of the Ithaca Journal, 1905.

1907 "What We Owe to Agassiz." *Popular Science Monthly*, LXXI, 1907.

1914 *The Fifty-fifth Regiment of Massachusetts Volunteer Infantry*. Brookline, Mass.: Riverdale Press, 1914; reprinted 1917, 1919.

1918 "Should Our Young Soldiers Be Encouraged to Smoke?" *Good Health*, Feb. 1918.

Index